Global Political Transitions

Series Editors
Imtiaz Hussain, Independent University of Bangladesh, Dhaka,
Bangladesh
Finn Laursen, University of Southern Denmark, Odense, Denmark
Leonard Sebastian, Nanyang Technological University, S. Rajaratnam
School of International Studies, Singapore, Singapore

The series publishes books dealing with important political changes within states and in relations between states. The two key questions it seeks to answer are: to what extent are countries becoming more democratic/liberal, and to what extent are inter-state/inter-regional relations creating/demanding new 'governance' arrangements? The series editors encourage submissions which explore local issues (where the local could be a state, society, region) having global consequences (such as regionally, internationally, or multilaterally), or vice versa, global developments (such as terrorism, recession, WTO/IMF rulings, any democratic snowball, like the Third Wave, Fourth Wave, and so forth) triggering local consequences (state responses; fringe group reactions, such as ISIS; and so forth).

More information about this series at
https://link.springer.com/bookseries/15583

Robert G. Patman · Patrick Köllner ·
Balazs Kiglics
Editors

From Asia-Pacific to Indo-Pacific

Diplomacy in a Contested Region

Editors
Robert G. Patman
Programme of Politics
University of Otago
Dunedin, New Zealand

Balazs Kiglics
Programme of Languages
and Cultures
University of Otago
Dunedin, New Zealand

Patrick Köllner
German Institute for Global and Area
Studies (GIGA)
University of Hamburg
Hamburg, Germany

ISSN 2522-8730   ISSN 2522-8749 (electronic)
Global Political Transitions
ISBN 978-981-16-7006-0   ISBN 978-981-16-7007-7 (eBook)
https://doi.org/10.1007/978-981-16-7007-7

This Palgrave Macmillan imprint is published by the registered company Springer Nature Singapore Pte Ltd.
The registered company address is: 152 Beach Road, #21-01/04 Gateway East, Singapore 189721, Singapore

ACKNOWLEDGMENTS

The editors would like to express their gratitude to a large number of people and institutions for their assistance in the making of this book. The idea for this volume evolved from the theme chosen for the 53rd University of Otago Foreign Policy School. As Co-Directors of that School and editors of this book, we wish to fully acknowledge the support that helped make this book project possible.

First, we would like to thank colleagues on the Academic Committee of the 53rd School: Professor Ben Schonthal, Associate Professor Jenny Bryant-Tokalau, Professor Paola Voci, Dr. Heather Devere, Honorary Associate Professor Jacqueline Leckie, Dr. Simon Ryan, Dr. Lena Tan, Dr. Dennis Wesselbaum, Mr. Peter Grace and Associate Professor Marcelle Dawson.

Second, we would like to thank all the contributors to this book. They constitute an outstanding team of international specialists in the Indo-Pacific region. They graciously accepted our editorial advice and took the time and effort to revise their drafts into polished and insightful chapters.

Third, we wish to express our sincere thanks for the encouraging and patient support that was given to the preparation of the book manuscript by the staff at Palgrave Macmillan. Such assistance was invaluable and much appreciated by the editors of this volume.

Fourth, we wish to thank those organisations whose support and generosity helped play a significant role in bringing together our team of contributors. Without this support, it would have been more difficult to bring this book to fruition. We are grateful to: the German Institute for Global and Area Studies (GIGA); the University of Otago; the Konrad Adenauer Stiftung, Canberra; the Australian High Commission, Wellington; the US Embassy, Wellington; the New Zealand Ministry of Foreign Affairs and Trade, Wellington; the National Assessments Bureau, Department of the Prime Minister and Cabinet, Wellington; the Asia New Zealand Foundation, Wellington; and The New Zealand Institute for Pacific Research.

Finally, and most importantly, we would like to thank our families, particularly our partners, Martha, Nina and Pattama. Their support was indispensable throughout the endeavour to produce this book.

August 2021   Robert G. Patman
                                                                     Patrick Köllner
                                                                     Balazs Kiglics

CONTENTS

NOTES ON CONTRIBUTORS

Dr. Alan Bollard is a Professor of Practice at Victoria University of Wellington, and Chair of the NZ Infrastructure Commission. He is also Chair of the NZ Centres for Asia-Pacific Excellence, Chair of the New Zealand Portrait Gallery, NZ Governor for the Economic Research Institute for ASEAN and East Asia, Research Fellow at Hebei Normal University, Advisor to the Asia New Zealand Foundation, Advisor to New Zealand's 2021 APEC hosting and has written widely on the Asia-Pacific. Until recently he was Executive Director of the APEC organisation in Singapore. Previous positions include Governor of the Reserve Bank of New Zealand, Secretary of the NZ Treasury and Chair of the NZ Commerce Commission.

Dr. Kurt M. Campbell is the former Chairman and co-founder of The Asia Group. He previously served in government as the Assistant Secretary of State for East Asian and Pacific Affairs in the Obama administration and as Deputy Assistant Secretary of Defence for Asia and the Pacific in the Clinton Administration. Campbell was formerly the CEO and Co-Founder of the Center for a New American Security, Senior Vice President at the Center for Strategic and International Studies and Associate Professor at Harvard's John F. Kennedy School of Government. In January 2021, Campbell joined the Biden-Harris Administration as Coordinator for Indo-Pacific Affairs.

Evelyn Goh is the Shedden Professor of Strategic Policy Studies at the Australian National University, where she is also Director of Research at the Strategic and Defence Studies Centre. She has published widely on US-China relations, regional order in East Asia, Southeast Asian strategies towards great powers and environmental security. Her recent books include *The Struggle for Order: Hegemony, Hierarchy and Transition in Post-Cold War East Asia* (Oxford University Press, 2013); (with Barry Buzan) *Rethinking Sino-Japanese Alienation: History Problems and Historical Opportunities* (Oxford University Press, 2020); and the edited volume *Rising China's Influence in Developing Asia* (Oxford University Press, 2016).

Ian Hall is a Professor of International Relations and Deputy Director (Research) at the Griffith Asia Institute, Griffith University, Queensland, Australia. He is also an Academic Fellow of the Australia India Institute and the co-editor (with Sara E. Davies) of the *Australian Journal of International Affairs*. He has been awarded several major research grants from the Australian Research Council and the Australian Department of Defence. He has published three single-authored books and more than seventy articles and chapters in various outlets, including *Asian Survey, European Journal of International Relations, International Affairs* and *Third World Quarterly*. His most recent book is *Modi and the Reinvention of Indian Foreign Policy* (Bristol University Press, 2019). He is currently working on a study of how Hindu nationalists want to change the world.

Aurora Javate de Dios is a Senior Project Director of the Women and Gender Institute, a centre for feminist training and research at Miriam College in the Philippines. She is presently Associate Professor at the International Studies Department at the same school teaching UN and global governance; women's human rights; Philippine migration; and women peace and security issues. She served as an Expert in the UN Committee on the Elimination of All Forms of Discrimination Against Women (UN CEDAW) and was the Philippine Representative to the ASEAN Commission on the Promotion and Protection of Women's and Children's Rights.

Raphaëlle Khan is an Associate Research Fellow of the Institute for Strategic Research (IRSEM) and an Associate of the Asia Center, Harvard University. She is also a non-resident Visiting Scholar at the Center for the Advanced Study of India at the University of Pennsylvania. She received her Ph.D. in International Relations and History from King's College London. Among her recent publications is the co-edited volume *Theorizing Indian Foreign Policy* (Routledge, 2017). Currently she works on a book on India's role in the transformation of the international order and global and imperial conceptions of sovereignty between World War I and the 1960s.

Balazs Kiglics is a recent Ph.D. graduate and a Teaching Fellow in the Languages and Cultures Programme at the University of Otago, New Zealand. His thesis explored the role of values in contemporary Japanese elite perceptions of Japan-China relations. He has worked as the coordinator of the annual Otago Foreign Policy School since 2015. Kiglics has co-edited the volume *New Zealand and the World: Past, Present and Future* (World Scientific, 2018). His research interests include Japanese studies, international relations of the Asia-Pacific and intercultural communication.

Patrick Köllner is a vice president of the German Institute for Global and Area Studies (GIGA), director of the GIGA Institute for Asian Studies and professor of political science at the University of Hamburg. His Asia-related and comparative work has been published in journals such as *Democratization, Japanese Journal of Political Science, Journal of East Asian Studies, The Pacific Review, Politische Vierteljahresschrift*. Recent co-edited publications include *Comparative Area Studies: Methodological Rationales and Cross-Regional Applications* (Oxford University Press, 2018) as well as special issues on think tanks in East Asia (*Pacific Affairs*, 2018) and on political transformation in Myanmar (*Journal of Current Southeast Asian Affairs*, 2020).

Mingjiang Li is an Associate Professor at S. Rajaratnam School of International Studies (RSIS), Nanyang Technological University, Singapore. His main research interests include Chinese foreign policy, Chinese economic statecraft, the Belt and Road Initiative, Chinese politics, China-ASEAN relations, Sino-US relations and Asia-Pacific security. He is the author, editor and co-editor of 13 books. His recent books are *China's Economic Statecraft* (World Scientific, 2017) and *New Dynamics in US-China Relations: Contending for the Asia Pacific* (lead editor, Routledge, 2014). He has published in various peer-reviewed outlets.

Robert G. Patman is one of the University of Otago's inaugural Sesquicentennial Distinguished Chairs and his research interests concern international relations, global security, US foreign policy, great powers and the Horn of Africa. Publications include *Strategic Shortfall: The 'Somalia Syndrome' and the March to 9/11* (Praeger, 2010), co-edited books titled *China and the International System: Becoming a World Power* (Routledge, 2013); *Science Diplomacy: New Day or False Dawn?* (World Scientific, 2015) and *New Zealand and the World: Past, Present and Future* (World Scientific, 2018). Robert is currently writing a volume called *Rethinking the Global Impact of 9/11* (Palgrave Macmillan, 2022).

Elaine Tan was appointed Executive Director of the ASEAN Foundation in Jakarta, Indonesia in 2014 and served for two terms, ending her assignment in January 2020. Currently, she is Chief of Party of the USAID ASEAN Policy Implementation project. She has been Senior Officer and Head of the Human Development Unit at the ASEAN Secretariat in Indonesia and Head, Resident Coordinator's Unit of the United Nations in Timor-Leste. Tan served as Programme Director for Yayasan Sejahtera in Malaysia and the United Nations Development Fund for Women in both Timor-Leste and Cambodia. She has a Bachelor's degree from Smith College and a Master in Development Studies from the University of Leeds.

James To is a Senior Adviser (Research and Engagement) at the Asia New Zealand Foundation. One of his roles is to support the delivery of the Foundation's Track II diplomacy programme which seeks to inform New Zealand's thinking around regional and international foreign, defence, economic and trade policy. James has a Ph.D. in International Relations from the University of Canterbury. His publications include *Qiaowu: Extra-Territorial Policies for the Overseas Chinese* (Brill, 2014) and 'Beijing's Policies for Managing Han and Ethnic-Minority Chinese Communities Abroad' (*Journal of Current Chinese Affairs*, 2012).

Vangelis Vitalis is the Deputy Secretary (Trade and Economic) in the New Zealand Ministry of Foreign Affairs and Trade. He was the Chief Negotiator who concluded CPTPP, the ASEAN-Australia New Zealand FTA and the bilateral FTA with Malaysia. He is currently Chief Negotiator for the EU-NZ FTA and the APEC SOM Chair for 2021. A former Ambassador to the EU and subsequently to the WTO, he also chaired the WTO agriculture negotiations, helping to draft the text of the 2015 Nairobi Ministerial Decision to eliminate agricultural export subsidies.

David A. Welch is a University Research Chair and Professor of Political Science at the University of Waterloo and teaches at the Balsillie School of International Affairs. His 2005 book *Painful Choices: A Theory of Foreign Policy Change* (Princeton University Press) was the inaugural winner of the International Studies Association ISSS Book Award, and his 1993 book *Justice and the Genesis of War* was the winner of the 1994 Edgar S. Furniss Award for an Outstanding Contribution to National Security Studies. He is currently co-editor (with Toni Erskine and Stefano Guzzini) of the journal *International Theory*.

ABBREVIATIONS

₹	Rupees
4IR	Fourth Industrial Revolution
5G	Fifth Generation of Wireless Communications Technologies
9/11	Terrorist Attacks of 11 September 2001
AANZFTA	ASEAN–Australia–New Zealand Free Trade Agreement
AB	Appellate Body
ABS–CBN	Alto Broadcasting System—Chronicle Broadcasting Network
ACCTS	Agreement on Climate Change, Trade and Sustainability
ADIZ	Air Defence Identification Zone
ADMM+	ASEAN Defence Ministers' Meeting—Plus
AEC	ASEAN Economic Community
AI	Artificial Intelligence
AIIB	Asian Infrastructure Investment Bank
ANZUS	Australia, New Zealand, United States Security Treaty
AOIP	ASEAN Outlook on the Indo-Pacific
APEC	Asia–Pacific Economic Cooperation
APSC	ASEAN Political-Security Community
ARF	ASEAN Regional Forum
ASCC	ASEAN Socio-Cultural Community
ASEAN	Association of Southeast Asian Nations
BIMSTEC	Bay of Bengal Initiative for Multi-Sectoral Technical and Economic Cooperation
BJP	Bharatiya Janata Party
BRI	Belt and Road Initiative
BRICS	Brazil, Russia, India, China and South Africa
BUILD	Better Utilization of Investments Leading to Development

CAPS	Centre for Air Power Studies
CBM	Confidence-Building Measure
CCCS	Centre of Contemporary China Studies
CEAC	Council on East Asian Community
CENJOWS	Centre for Joint Warfare Studies
CEP	Closer Economic Partnership
CER	Closer Economic Relations
CIA	Central Intelligence Agency
CII	Confederation of Indian Industry
CLAWS	Centre for Land Warfare Studies
Comecon	Council for Mutual Economic Assistance
COP	UN Conference of the Parties
Covid-19	Coronavirus SARS-CoV-2
CPEC	China–Pakistan Economic Corridor
CPR	Centre for Policy Research
CPTPP	Comprehensive and Progressive Agreement for Trans-Pacific Partnership
CSBM	Confidence- and Security-Building Measures
D-10	Proposed Forum of Ten Democracies
DDS	Diehard Duterte Supporters
DEPA	Digital Economy Partnership Agreement
DMZ	Demilitarised Zone
DSD	Democratic Security Diamond
EAC	East Asian Community
EAS	East Asia Summit
EDSA	People Power uprising
EEC	European Economic Community
EEZ	Exclusive Economic Zone
ERIA	Economic Research Institute for ASEAN and East Asia
EU	European Union
FCRA	Foreign Contribution (Regulation) Act
FIRRMA	Foreign Investment Risk Review Modernization Act
FOIP	Free and Open Indo-Pacific
FONOP	Freedom of Navigation Operation
FTA	Free Trade Agreement
G20	Group of Twenty
G7	Group of Seven
GATT	General Agreement on Tariffs and Trade
GDP	Gross Domestic Product
GFC	Global Financial Crisis
GHG	Greenhouse Gas
GIGA	German Institute for Global and Area Studies
ICS	Institute of Chinese Studies

ICWA	Indian Council of World Affairs
IDSA	Manohar Parrikar Institute for Defence Studies and Analyses
IF	India Foundation
IMF	International Monetary Fund
INDOPACOM	Indo-Pacific Command
IPCS	Institute of Peace and Conflict Studies
ISEAS	Institute of Southeast Asian Studies
KNZFTA	Korea–New Zealand Free Trade Agreement
MAGA	Make America Great Again
MEA	Ministry of External Affairs (India)
MFAT	Ministry of Foreign Affairs and Trade (New Zealand)
MNZFTA	Malaysia–New Zealand Free Trade Agreement
MOFA	Ministry of Foreign Affairs (Japan)
MP	Member of Parliament
MPI	Ministry for Primary Industries (New Zealand)
NAM	Non-Aligned Movement
NATO	North Atlantic Treaty Organization
NBN–ZTE	National Broadband Network—Zhongxing Telecommunications Equipment
NDA	National Democratic Alliance
NGO	Nongovernmental Organisation
NITI	National Institution for Transforming India
NMF	National Maritime Foundation
NRG	NRG Energy company
NSA	National Security Advisor
NSG	Nuclear Suppliers Group
OBOR	One Belt One Road
ODA	Overseas Development Assistance
OECD	Organisation for Economic Co-operation and Development
OED	*Oxford English Dictionary*
OFBJP	Overseas Friends of the BJP
OFPS	Otago Foreign Policy School
OPEC	Organization of the Petroleum Exporting Countries
ORF	Observer Research Foundation
₱	Philippines Peso
PACER	Pacific Agreement on Closer Economic Relations
PACOM	Pacific Command
PCA	Permanent Court of Arbitration
PIC	Pacific Island country
PIF	Pacific Islands Forum
PLA	People's Liberation Army
PMO	Prime Minister's Office
PNG	Papua New Guinea

POGO	Philippine Offshore Gaming Operator
PRC	People's Republic of China
QUAD	Quadrilateral Security Dialogue
RAMSI	Regional Assistance Mission to the Solomon Islands
RCEP	Regional Comprehensive Economic Partnership
ROK	Republic of Korea (South Korea)
RSS	Rashtriya Swayamsevak Sangh
SAARC	South Asian Association for Regional Cooperation
SARS	Severe Acute Respiratory Syndrome
SCO	Shanghai Cooperation Organisation
SEM	Single Economic Market
SME	Small and Medium-Sized Enterprises
SPMRF	Dr. Syama Prasad Mookerjee Research Foundation
SSL	State Secrecy Law
SWIFT	Society for Worldwide Interbank Financial Telecommunication
THAAD	Terminal High Altitude Area Defense
TPP	Trans-Pacific Partnership
UN	United Nations
UNCLOS	United Nations Convention on the Law of the Sea
UNCTAD	United Nations Conference on Trade and Development
US	United States
USI	United Service Institute of India
VFA	Visiting Forces Agreement
VIF	Vivekananda International Foundation
VUCA	Volatile, Uncertain, Complex and Ambiguous
W̶	Won
WEOG	Western European and Others Group
WHO	World Health Organization
WTO	World Trade Organization
¥	Yen

LIST OF FIGURES

From Asia–Pacific to Indo-Pacific: Diplomacy in an Emerging Strategic Space

Patrick Köllner, Robert G. Patman, and Balazs Kiglics

The purpose of this book is to analyse how states of different international status as well as regional organisations have been shaping the emerging Indo-Pacific region and how, in turn, they have been affected by regional dynamics and cross-cutting global trends. The authors, a unique combination of international scholars and practitioners from and beyond the region, examine relevant trends and show how the regional diplomacy of the United States and China, Japan and India, Australia and New Zealand has unfolded in the first two decades of the twenty-first century.

P. Köllner
German Institute for Global and Area Studies (GIGA), University of Hamburg, Hamburg, Germany
e-mail: patrick.koellner@giga-hamburg.de

R. G. Patman
Programme of Politics, University of Otago, Dunedin, New Zealand
e-mail: robert.patman@otago.ac.nz

B. Kiglics (✉)
Programme of Languages and Cultures, University of Otago, Dunedin, New Zealand
e-mail: balazs.kiglics@otago.ac.nz

© The Author(s), under exclusive license to Springer Nature Singapore Pte Ltd. 2022
R. Patman et al. (eds.), *From Asia-Pacific to Indo-Pacific*, Global Political Transitions, https://doi.org/10.1007/978-981-16-7007-7_1

1

Going beyond official foreign policies, the authors also focus on organ-isations and institutional processes in the foreign policy realm, such as Track II diplomacy and international affairs think tanks, and they discuss how APEC (Asia–Pacific Economic Cooperation) and ASEAN (Associa-tion of Southeast Asian Nations) have been affected by major global and regional trends and sought to re-energise and reorient themselves. Finally, the contributors to this volume address large issues of peace, prosperity and populism in very specific ways by examining what trust and empathy mean for the resolution of conflicts concerning North Korea and the South China Sea, what the changing dynamics of globalisation mean for New Zealand, a champion of free trade, and how populism Duterte-style has left an imprint on the foreign policy of the Philippines.

This volume emerged from the 2018 Otago Foreign Policy School (OFPS), arguably New Zealand's premier international affairs conference, established in 1966 at the University of Otago. The annual conference differs from other conferences on the academic circuit in that it brings together, under an overarching theme that changes from year to year, speakers drawn from not only academia but also a range of professional realms such as diplomacy and journalism, enabling a fruitful exchange of perspectives. For the 2018 OFPS, the University of Otago teamed up with the German Institute for Global and Area Studies (GIGA), a publicly funded, non-university research institute forming part of Germany's Leibniz Association. GIGA subscribes to a global approach to scholar-ship and seeks to connect academics and practitioners, reflecting Leibniz's motto of 'theoria cum praxi'. Incidentally, the OFPS also epitomises this vision and approach. Imbued with a mission to maximise outreach, the conference not only is open to the interested public but also counts among its participants the most recent cohort of entrants to the New Zealand Ministry of Foreign Affairs and Trade.

By tradition, the OFPS is opened by a speech from New Zealand's foreign minister. In 2018, the then foreign minister and Acting Prime Minister Winston Peters outlined the next steps in his country's foreign policy towards the Asia–Pacific region (Peters, 2018).[1] Since the time of the conference, the New Zealand Government has also come to use

[1] For their support of the 2018 conference, the editors of this volume express their gratitude to the Canberra office of the Konrad Adenauer foundation and its director Beatrice Gorawantschy, to the New Zealand Ministry of Foreign Affairs and Trade, the New Zealand Institute for Pacific Research, the German Institute for Global and Area

the term 'Indo-Pacific' when referring to the wider region (Scott, 2020). New Zealand's recent embrace of this nomenclature, which until some years ago was only known to marine biologists studying the fish and mammals traversing the Pacific and the Indian Oceans, reflects a wider trend towards employing the term 'Indo-Pacific' in official and academic discourse, in some ways supplanting the older 'Asia–Pacific' one.

The term Indo-Pacific had been used by strategic thinkers in India and Australia since around the middle of the first decade of the twenty-first century. It was developed in the early 2010s by governments in Delhi, where the term aligned with Prime Minister Narendra Modi's 'Act East' policy, and in Canberra, where the term was first employed in the 2013 Defence White Paper as a 'framing device' or an 'enabling metaphor' to refer to Australia's two-ocean strategic environment centring on Indonesia (Sargeant, 2020, p. 27; see also Beeson & Lee-Brown, 2021; Heiduk & Wacker, 2020, pp. 24–27). These early adopters were followed by Japan, whose long-serving Prime Minister Shinzō Abe had already spoken, during an official visit to India in 2007 when he first served as premier, about the confluence of the Pacific and Indian Oceans. During his second, much longer stay in office, policy-relevant ideas crystallised around the idea of a 'free and open Indo-Pacific'. There are three important dimensions to this policy vision: balancing—developing a stable, multipolar balance in the region that can accommodate both a rising China and the formerly hegemonic United States; connectivity—building and improving infrastructure in the countries of the region and for better connecting the Indian and Pacific Ocean parts; and order-building—emphasising the importance of maintaining commonly accepted rules and norms of interstate behaviour (Envall, 2020, pp. 69–71; Hatakeyama, 2020).

While there are important differences in terms of how this vast region gets demarcated in Australia, India and Japan (see Heiduk and Wacker [2020] and Dolven and Vaugh [2020] for details), in all three countries the Indo-Pacific denotes an emerging, multipolar mega world region that matters profoundly not only in economic and demographic terms but also against the background of China's rise and regional (as well as extra-regional) responses to this development, in geostrategic terms. Essentially, a 'strategically focused vision of the Indo-Pacific' (Beeson &

Studies (GIGA) and the University of Otago. Responsibility for this volume rests solely with the authors and the editors.

Lee-Brown, 2021) tends to dominate in relevant policy discourses in these three countries. As Mark Beeson and Troy Lee-Brown (2021) suggest, the 'Indo-Pacific was always primarily a strategic initiative and a way of responding to the rise of China and the possible threat it poses'.

The same holds true for the United States, where the Indo-Pacific entered the foreign policy lexicon in 2010, when Secretary of State Hillary Clinton and Assistant Secretary of State Kurt Campbell started using the term in publications and speeches foreshadowing the United States 'pivot' to the Asia–Pacific region. The pivot, in turn, included a strengthening of strategic relations with India and Australia as well as an improvement of relations with secondary regional powers such as Vietnam (Medcalf, 2015). Under the Trump Administration, the United States seemed to follow Japan's lead and mainstreamed the 'free and open Indo-Pacific' as a policy concept during a tour by the president to the region in 2017. The Trump team then adopted early in 2018 a national security strategy for the Indo-Pacific region (ABC, 2021; Medcalf, 2021) and subsequently renamed its former Pacific unified military command 'US Indo-Pacific Command' (USINDOPACOM, see Fig. 1).

As Rory Medcalf (2015), an early proponent of the term, notes, an 'Indo-Pacific definition of Asia lends further legitimacy to India's growing role as a strategic actor in East Asia, including the South China Sea and Western Pacific. It also offers a rationale for a stronger US–India relationship'—both, it should be added, in bilateral terms and in the plurilateral context of the revived Quadrilateral Security Dialogue (Quad). As the 'principal [institutional] expression of the Indo-Pacific idea' (Beeson & Lee-Brown, 2021), the Quad brings together the United States, with two of its allies in region, Australia and Japan, and India, engaging in ministerial dialogues, military exercises, and broader foreign and security policy co-operation. Notably, these four democracies largely share an interest in balancing China and making sure that the Indo-Pacific remains multipolar in structure.

Overall, as Felix Heiduk and Gudrun Wacker (2020, p. 8) emphasise, 'the (different) concepts of the Indo-Pacific as a geographically and strategically understood space are based on specific political intentions and interests. The term 'Indo-Pacific' itself, as well as its use, is therefore never merely descriptive or value-neutral.' Nick Bisley (2020, p. 128) suggests that '[w]here the notion of the Indo-Pacific makes its contribution is as a device to organise policy in a [climate of] geopolitical [contestation].' Medcalf (2015) notes in this context that '[t]he way policymakers define

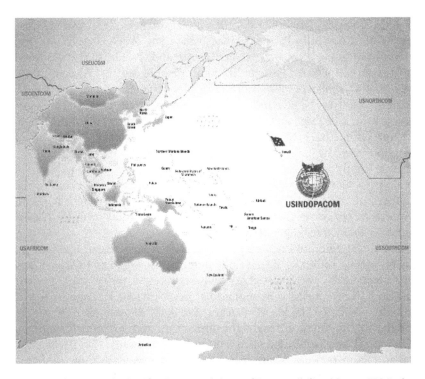

Fig. 1   The US Indo-Pacific Command Area of Responsibility (*Source* US Indo-Pacific Command, 2018)

and imagine regions can affect, among other things, the allocation of resources and high-level attention; the prioritisation of security partners among countries; and the membership and agendas of regional diplomatic institutions'.

In fact, other states and regional entities, beyond Australia, India, Japan and the United States, have also embraced the 'Indo-Pacific' term in recent years, adding yet more 'quite subtle but different shades of meaning depending on national or policy perspectives' (Sargeant, 2020, p. 26). Led by Indonesia, whose government under President Joko Widodo developed a policy framework for maritime affairs, the initially reticent ASEAN adopted the term in 2019 with a view to safeguarding its claim to centrality in regional affairs (ASEAN, 2019; Medcalf, 2020, pp. 161–165; Nabbs-Keller, 2020). Meanwhile, some European states published strategy papers and other policy documents outlining their approach to the Indo-Pacific. France, which has overseas territories and administrative departments in the Indian and Pacific Oceans, started the process in 2018 (Fisher, 2020, p. 37; Heiduk & Wacker 2020, pp. 38–40; Ministère des l'Europe & des Affaires étrangères, 2019). Germany and the Netherlands followed suit in 2020, possibly foreshadowing a joint European Union (EU) approach to the region (Federal Foreign Office, 2020; Strangio, 2020). Finally, policy circles in the United Kingdom see the emergent Indo-Pacific region as an opportunity to develop commercial ties—hence the Johnson Government's interest in joining the Comprehensive and Progressive Agreement for Trans-Pacific Partnership (CPTPP) free trade agreement—and, more generally, as an important area for engagement in its quest to reinvent itself as 'Global Britain' (Policy Exchange, 2020).

While strategic priorities vary among state actors—Japan for example has prioritised multilateral free trade agreements, whereas India is much more ambivalent with respect to such schemes, withdrawing from the Regional Comprehensive Economic Partnership (RCEP) negotiations at the end of 2019 (Heiduk & Wacker, 2020, p. 29, see also Dolven & Vaugh, 2020)—they all highlight important and growing economic, geopolitical and security-related connections between the Pacific and Indian Ocean regions. Many states also share a preference for an Indo-Pacific region that is not dominated by China. As Medcalf (2020, p. 23) notes, 'the Indo-Pacific idea dilutes and absorbs Chinese influence. That is much of the point'. Previously, he had suggested that,

> [f]or those states concerned about managing the growth of China's power and interests, the use of the Indo-Pacific term is a coded way of indicating that this region must not be considered as a special sphere of Chinese influence and any attempts in that direction should, by implication, be resisted. (Medcalf, 2015)

However, not all states and regional entities employing the Indo-Pacific terminology would agree the main aim is to 'resist', or for that matter 'contain', China. Some of the current visions are more inclusive than others. What they all share, however, is the idea that the Indo-Pacific should not be a China-dominated or Sinocentric region but rather a diverse, perhaps multipolar space whose different parts should be respected—hence the emphasis in some papers on the 'diversification' of diplomatic and economic ties.

Not surprisingly, the People's Republic of China (PRC) has taken issue with the new Indo-Pacific terminology. The Chinese Foreign Minister Wang Yi was widely quoted as having at a press conference in March 2018 belittled strategies based on the Indo-Pacific concept, suggesting that they were 'like the sea foam in the Pacific or Indian Ocean: they may get some attention, but soon will dissipate' (FMPRC, 2018). While there are arguably strong Indo-Pacific dimensions to both the maritime part of China's Belt and Road Initiative (BRI), the 'Maritime Silk Road' first mentioned by State President Xi Jinping when visiting Jakarta in 2013 (Xi, 2013), and to the country's naval development strategies (see Medcalf, 2015), the government in Beijing basically sees the Indo-Pacific concept as a cover for strategies aimed at containing China. It has thus clung to the older 'Asia–Pacific' terminology (Heiduk & Wacker, 2020, pp. 31–34; He & Li, 2020) which is still being used by other states as well as China. In fact, many of the contributors to this volume use it, either because they take a historical perspective and/or because they prefer it to the Indo-Pacific terminology. We will discuss the rise of the Indo-Pacific as a strategic construct in more detail in the following section. As we deal in this volume with one specific dimension of Indo-Pacific dynamics, namely, diplomacy in and around the region, we highlight different perspectives on this question. We conclude this introductory chapter by sketching the individual contributions to the volume.

THE INDO-PACIFIC: EMERGING WORLD REGION OR STRATEGIC CONSTRUCT?

Since the end of the Cold War, the international order has been in transition or, more open-endedly, in flux. Taking a cue from democratisation research, 'transition' refers to the interval between one order and another (O'Donnell & Schmitter, 1986, p. 6). As students of democratisation and political transformation more generally know, transitions are idiosyncratic and uncertain processes, highly contingent on a plethora of factors that play out in specific contexts. Such transitions do not always follow a linear path leading to a clearly defined outcome. Just as the 'third wave' of democratisation, starting with political change on the Iberian Peninsula, and which gained momentum after the end of the Cold War, did not lead everywhere to self-sustaining, 'consolidated' liberal democracies, there is little evidence to suggest that the transition of the international order is destined to produce a well-defined end state. Many political regimes at the national level are characterised today, some decades after the onset of political transitions, by a form of hybridity involving a mixture of democratic and authoritarian elements. Such hybrid orders or regimes—we are using these two terms interchangeably here, referring to the formal and informal rules and norms guiding and stabilising the behaviour and expectations of the political actors affected by them—may seem unstable or unsustainable to outside observers. Yet hybrid orders have shown a remarkable staying power in many places. Nonetheless, such orders often remain contested, with some political actors preferring, and pushing for, a different kind of political regime.

The international order is also likely to stay contested, as the 'unipolar moment' of unrivalled US hegemony during the early years of the post-Cold War era has subsided in the face of conflicting pressures from deepening globalisation and intensified great-power rivalry. In what is increasingly called the Indo-Pacific, the impact of growing economic interdependence—powered by revolutions in communication and information technology—has combined uneasily with increasing competition between the United States and a resurgent China and generated significant effects on the political, economic and security complexion of the Indo-Pacific. This area is home to some 60% of the world's population and contains major economies such as China and India, which are often expected to be the world's two leading economies by 2050 (see PwC, 2017). Key economic and social indicators across the region continue to project an upward trajectory, and it is likely that significant parts of the Indo-Pacific will recover more quickly than the rest of the world from the immediate economic effects of COVID-19.

But does it really make sense to consider the Indo-Pacific as one coherent, unified world region? Martin Lewis and Kären Wigen (1997) provided a forceful reminder that meta-geographical concepts such as 'continents', 'Orient' and 'Occident', 'East' and 'West'—or, for that matter, 'Global North' and 'Global South'—are social constructions. Nearly all grand schemes of geographical demarcation have historically

been acts of imagination, often motivated and powered by particular (strategic) interests and certain biases, and sometimes prejudices.[2]
Regions are characterised as such for one purpose or another, including
to enhance order or at least to give a semblance of order. There are
simply no clear-cut political, economic, social, ethnic, topographic or
other criteria that can easily be applied in a consistent way to demarcate
different regions of the world.

Such problems of demarcation exist and are probably compounded at
the global level. Different ideas on how to conceptualise certain large-
scale regions persist and find expression in the contested popularising of
concepts such as 'Eurasia', 'Asia–Pacific' (sometimes known as 'Pacific
Asia' or the 'Pacific Rim') or, more recently, the 'Indo-Pacific' (initially
called 'Indo-Pacific Asia' by some observers: cf. Medcalf, 2015).[3] In some
cases, a label for a certain region gains currency, gets widely accepted and
is adopted. For instance, the term 'South East Asia', originally no more
than the denomination of a military command area of the Allies in World
War II, is a case in point. In other situations, new labels prove to be a
fleeting fad. Some new terms stick, if perhaps only for some time, because
they are persuasive, if not to everyone then at least perhaps to a dominant
coalition of actors, because these labels serve some shared interests and/or
because they persuasively capture a relevant development.

The 'Asia–Pacific' was for a while a fairly persuasive label. It gained
currency in the latter half of the 1980s and became increasingly institutionalised thereafter, not least because it captured the reality of increased
flows of goods, services, people and ideas across the Pacific Ocean and
within the Asian region after the end of the Cold War. It also seemed
to capture the increasing integration of China and other Asian socialist
countries into the global economy. The 'Asia–Pacific' concept became
closely identified with an era of globalisation, the advance of the neoliberal

---

[2] Of course, the geographical vantage points of those who conceive of and map relevant
large-scale areas also play a role. Thus, 'North Asia', 'North-east Asia' and 'East Asia' refer
basically to the same region, as do the 'Middle East', the 'Near East' and 'West Asia'.

[3] Wigen and Lewis (1997, Chapter 6) themselves make the case for differentiating
between more than a dozen or more 'world regions', based each on shared historical
legacies (e.g., former empires), shared ideational foundations (including religion) and ways
of communication (languages), and/or intensive interactions (flows of people, goods,
capital etc.) within these world regions. While the concept of world regions may be
preferable to existing meta-geographical schemes, it still entails arbitrariness in that there
are also no clear-cut criteria for demarcating one world region from another.

policy paradigm, and the rapid expansion of free trade agreements at the regional level and beyond. Organisationally and institutionally, regional economic co-operation was embodied by APEC—founded in 1989 at the initiative of Australia and Japan, with American support—and the incorporation of ASEAN, which had formalised its own (sub)regional integration process some three decades earlier, but now added new institutional layers such as the ASEAN Regional Forum (ARF), a security dialogue with a host of regional and extra-regional partners. From an initial 12 economies represented by the establishment of APEC in 1989, the list of members expanded to 17 by 1993 and 21 in 1998 while the organisation became internally more complex, adding new agendas and co-ordination mechanisms.

As Medcalf (2015) has noted,

> the Asia–Pacific concept could not last without coming to terms with two factors that emerged in the 1990s: 1) the rise of India as a substantial economic and military power with interests beyond South Asia; and 2) the increased connection between the economic powerhouses of East Asia and the Indian Ocean region, related especially to their demand for energy and other resources. These developments are major driving factors for turning the Indo-Pacific into the world's economic and strategic centre of gravity.

By mid-2019, even an initially resistant ASEAN embraced the term in the title of its report 'ASEAN Outlook on the Indo-Pacific'. Seeking to safeguard 'ASEAN centrality' in the wider scheme of things, the policy document looked upon the Indian and Pacific Ocean regions 'not as contiguous territorial spaces but as a closely integrated and interconnected region, with ASEAN playing a central and strategic role'. The document also argued for an inclusive approach, emphasising that dialogue and co-operation, not rivalry, should be at the centre of regional dynamics (ASEAN, 2019, p. 2). ASEAN's acceptance of the Indo-Pacific terminology led some observers to declare that the Indo-Pacific was now 'the shared geographic term for conceiving of this region' (Conley Tyler, 2019). Surely if ASEAN had come to terms with the Indo-Pacific term, it was here to stay, or so it seemed.

Regardless of where one stands on the issue of whether the 'Indo-Pacific' can be usefully understood as a region in geographical terms—and the different attempts at demarcation alert us to how problem-ridden such understandings are—the Indo-Pacific terminology is undoubtedly of strategic use to the actors employing it. As noted above, the use of such terms is rarely 'neutral' or 'value-free', but inherently political. Some of the strategic contexts have already been mentioned before. We can add that the use of a different term other than 'Asia–Pacific' makes intuitive sense because regional and global dynamics have changed dramatically in the last three decades or so. At the regional level, for the first time, four big powers—China, India, Japan and the United States—simultaneously seek to exert influence there. In particular, the rise of both China and India has had regional implications. As Medcalf (2015) notes in this context, '[t]he reality of an Indo-Pacific region has been brought about by a confluence of economic and strategic factors. A principal driver has been the rise of China and India as powers that have become increasingly outward-looking in their economic and military affairs'.

At the global level, the preceding era of policy liberalisation has clearly lost momentum since the Global Financial Crisis (GFC) of 2007–2008. Notwithstanding the conclusion of some major regional and cross-regional free trade agreements between 2017 and 2020, such as the EU-Japan Economic Partnership Agreement, the trans-Pacific CPTPP (not including China, India and the United States) and the less ambitious but large-scale RCEP (again excluding India and the United States, but including China), protectionism, nationalism and populism have been on the rise since at least the past decade, perhaps even longer. The idea that globalisation, and particularly free trade, brought benefits to everyone, had been questioned for some time—first by non-state actors, made very visible by the massive protests in Seattle in 1999 against the launch of a new round of trade liberalisation, and later by some national governments themselves. Tellingly, the Doha round of global trade negotiations, launched in 2001, could not be successfully concluded.

On reflection, the GFC marked an important turning point. It evidently challenged the global material and normative dominance of the United States, which had already been damaged by that country's disastrous military intervention in Iraq and, to a lesser degree, Afghanistan. The GFC brought into question the alleged superiority of the US politico-economic model and provided a significant boost to China's rise as a regional and global power. The emerging new era has been largely characterised by growing great-power competition between the United States and China—playing out most vividly in the Indo-Pacific where the recent closer alignment of the two other regional powers, India and Japan, as well as their increasing strategic interactions with a US ally, Australia, has added further impetus to the regional competition—and by increased efforts by the two superpowers to emphasise national interests (a trend which predated the Trump Administration but was accentuated by its arrival in office). At the same time, the Indo-Pacific has witnessed the return of geopolitical thinking (Kaplan, 2012, 2014) as well as the rise of geoeconomics (Rimmer, 2018, pp. 473–474).

The most momentous of these geoeconomic developments has been Beijing's ambitious BRI, Xi's signature foreign policy and connectivity initiative. The BRI is not so much a detailed master plan as a broad vision fuelled by tremendous resources, and potentially involving a multitude of actors in China and beyond. It builds on previous policies in the PRC to develop China's western provinces; aims to promote the 'going global' of China's state-owned and other enterprises; and seeks to productively recycle China's growing amounts of domestic savings and foreign exchange reserves. If that was not enough in itself, the BRI was and is also supposed to address a series of other, very diverse policy challenges. These included substantial overcapacity in sectors such as construction; the United States pivot to the Asia–Pacific—which before the Trump Administration included championing the Trans-Pacific Partnership free trade agreement; insufficient infrastructure and transport bottlenecks in the areas connecting China and its major markets; concerns about maritime 'choke points' in some of the waterways used to transport oil and other resources to China; and last but not least, realigning the regionalised world order in tune with China's rise. While other dimensions of 'connectivity' also loom large, at the centre of this major geoeconomic initiative with geopolitical repercussions is the building of local infrastructure financed by Chinese concessional loans.

Infrastructural development and concomitant financial needs in the Indo-Pacific region (and beyond) are huge, and China's offers have been welcomed by many governments in the region. This also applies to some countries in the South Pacific, which is now increasingly seen as part of the Indo-Pacific strategic landscape (Medcalf, 2020, p. 15; Sargeant, 2020, p. 29). Certainly, the extension of the Maritime Silk Road to the South Pacific and strategic responses by traditional regional powers, like Australia and New Zealand, have turned this part of the Indo-Pacific into another arena for geopolitical competition. In the South Pacific and elsewhere not every existing BRI project has been adequately financed or, for that matter, planned on a sustainable basis. However, claims that the

BRI is designed to ensnare Pacific Island states in a network of 'debt-trap diplomacy' seem wide of the mark. That is to say, all BRI projects involve push and pull factors. On closer inspection, even the case of Hambantota port in Sri Lanka, which is often is cited providing prime evidence of China's 'debt diplomacy', proves far more complicated than many observers initially thought or would like to believe (see Jones & Hameiri, 2020).

In any event, the BRI and concerns about China's intentions have sparked a host of new, regionally oriented infrastructure-related initiatives (as well as bolstering existing development programmes) in countries such as Japan, Australia, India, the United States and the European Union (EU). Infrastructure, Jeffrey Wilson (2020, p. 67) notes in a recent paper, has emerged as a source of geostrategic tension particularly in the Indo-Pacific 'as the region's major powers have begun using infrastructure initiatives as a tool in contests for leadership'. In the Indo-Pacific, no fewer than three large national programmes (including the BRI), two multilateral development banks and three regional dialogues are active in the domain of infrastructure provision (Wilson, 2020). If properly co-ordinated, the initiatives could go a long a way to addressing the region's infrastructure needs. Geopolitical competition could lead to an increasing 'clash of connectivity strategies' in the Indo-Pacific and elsewhere.

To sum up: while the 'Indo-Pacific' label does not capture a self-defined and coherent mega world region, the term describes a huge contested strategic space affected by a host of overarching geopolitical and geoeconomic dynamics and shared challenges that do not respect borders, such as COVID-19 and climate change. What happens in this emerging economic and strategic centre of gravity is of vital interest not only to the countries in the Indo-Pacific itself but also to other actors with global interests. By way of example, Medcalf (2015) notes that,

> [t]erritorial disputes in the South China Sea are being watched as a labo-ratory for how a powerful China behaves when it does not get its way. Trading nations everywhere have stakes in Southeast Asian shipping lanes, and many regional players have a deep interest in what developments in the South China Sea mean for the fate of a rules-based order.

At the same time, China's own economic success also depends on access to markets like the United States, Japan and the EU, and so Beijing may be constrained on how far it can press claims in places like the South China Sea without jeopardising its own global trade strategy. The Indo-Pacific remains an internally complex and diverse strategic space consisting of various subsystems with their own distinct dynamics: northeast Asia (including the two heavyweights China and Japan plus the Korean Peninsula and Taiwan, with their own specific security problematiques); Southeast Asia (encompassing the disputed South China Sea); South Asia (essentially the north-eastern part of the Indian Ocean and its littoral states); and the South Pacific, i.e. the arc of Pacific Island countries stretching from Papua New Guinea to New Zealand (Sargeant, 2020, pp. 26–27).

Thus, the Indo-Pacific region is a strategic space that needs to be navigated not only by the superpowers United States and China, now locked in a long-term struggle for global influence, but also regional powers like Japan and India (a prospective great power in its own right), secondary regional powers like Australia, the Republic of Korea or Vietnam, and a host of small powers and regional entities like ASEAN or the Pacific Islands Forum. While the relationship between the United States and China is expected to be a major factor in shaping the strategic environment in the Indo-Pacific, other countries and regional entities also exercise a major influence in the emerging Indo-Pacific strategic space, reflecting a redistribution of power across the system (Sargeant, 2020, pp. 28–29). Rivalry, competition and co-operation will be visible in different measure in policy areas ranging from (traditional and non-traditional) security and defence policy, to economic and trade policy, cultural policy and climate policy, not to forget infrastructure and connectivity-related policy areas.

While the great powers in particular show a certain preference for bilateral approaches and hub-and-spoke-like arrangements, small powers and some regional powers have a clear-cut preference for multilateral approaches and arrangements based on shared norms and rules of engagement ('amorphous, inconsistent and unevenly enforced' as these rules may be in practice: Byrne, 2020, p. 13). Moreover, the scope for effective unilateral action by the United States and China is limited. It is striking that during the COVID-19 pandemic neither of the superpowers have been able to demonstrate much international leadership in the Indo-Pacific and elsewhere in dealing with this deadly virus. So, while the Indo-Pacific is likely to remain a central site for contestation about the future of the international order generally—a contest that will have important implications for smaller actors in the region like New Zealand—it is also a contest in which states are increasingly confronted by critical problems which do not respect borders. Diplomacy will arguably play a central role in shaping Indo-Pacific dynamics, as it will be shaped by these dynamics. But what exactly is diplomacy? We turn to this topic in the following section.

PERSPECTIVES ON DIPLOMACY

In public and academic discourse, and even more so in everyday use, the terms 'foreign policy' and 'diplomacy' often get conflated or are used interchangeably (see also Cooper et al., 2013, p. 2). Some of the contributors to this volume also use the two terms synonymously, while others carefully distinguish the two. Whereas foreign policy denotes the full spectrum of externally oriented policies of national governments and regional entities, diplomacy refers, as Allan Gyngell (2019, p. 24) succinctly puts it, to the 'operating system' at the service of such policy. In a similar vein, Ronald Barston argues in his textbook on modern diplomacy that diplomacy,

> is concerned with the management of relations between states and between states and other actors. From a state's perspective, diplomacy is concerned with advising, shaping and implementing foreign policy. As such it is the *means* by which states through their formal and other representatives, as well as other actors, articulate, coordinate and secure particular or wider interests, using correspondence, private talks, exchanges of view, lobbying, visits, threats and other related activities'. (Barston, 2019, p. 1, emphasis added)

Diplomacy then may be conceived as an instrument through which state (and other) actors attempt to achieve national (or more particular) objectives. As Arnold Wolfers (1962, p. 59) noted many years ago, the pressure on diplomats to adhere to a 'nationalistic scale of values' does not always sit comfortably with the wider diplomatic task of promoting international co-operation.

From a slightly different perspective that focuses on the actors involved, one may distinguish between the formulation of foreign policy by political leaders (or 'principals' in agency-theoretical terms) and the execution of such policy by civil servants, including diplomats or relevant government 'agents'. But then, of course, such a distinction overlooks the possibility that such 'agents' often also have a crucial role in (foreign) policy formation themselves. A similar distinction between the activities of political leaders and their official representatives, including diplomats, is offered by Jeffrey Robertson (2019), who argues that diplomacy by political leaders does not constitute diplomacy per se. The background to this is that high-level political leaders can be very active in terms of pushing foreign policy initiatives and/or engaging in establishing, developing or promoting personal relations with political leaders in other countries or regional entities. This is also noted by Barston, who does not however draw a clear-cut analytical distinction between political leadership and diplomacy when he states that,

> [a]n important feature of modern diplomacy is the enhanced role of personal diplomacy by the head of state or government. The direct or indirect involvement of heads of government in central foreign policy issues has generally reduced the overall role and influence in many instances of foreign ministers, and is at times at the expense of the local ambassador. (Barston, 2019, p. 8, see also ibid., p. 101)[4]

A particularly extreme example of such political leadership in the diplomatic sphere has recently been provided by former US President Donald Trump. As Hal Brands notes with special reference to the long-serving 32nd US President Franklin Roosevelt (1933–1945), Trump was hardly the first president 'to put faith in leader-to-leader relations and the power of his own personality' (Brands, 2020). Brands notes that 'Trump, who personalizes nearly everything, [used] the same approach and made it a defining theme of his statecraft', especially concerning relations with North Korea's leader Kim Jong Un, but also with respect to Saudi Arabia, the Philippines, Turkey, China and Russia. Trump showed a particular penchant for media-saturated summits, some of which were not always well prepared and went against the traditional idea of finalising long negotiations at an operational level with summits. Such an approach gave political leaders the opportunity to negotiate final problems that could not be solved by their officials. The very patchy record of Trump's heavily personalised diplomacy confirmed 'that personal diplomacy is no magic

---

[4] The blurring of international and domestic affairs has led to the fact that only few issue areas these days constitute solely the prerogative of foreign ministers and their diplomats. In parliamentary democracies, the need for coalition governments may further complicate foreign policy formation and decision-making.

bullet. Diplomacy doesn't ultimately hinge on how leaders feel about each other. It hinges on whether their countries' interests align and what the fundamental power realities are' (Brands, 2020).

Beyond the question of who actually engages in diplomacy, many authors have approached the subject from a more functional perspective by seeking to pinpoint what diplomacy is about. Andrew Cooper, Jorge Heine and Ramesh Thakur note in the *Oxford Handbook of Modern Diplomacy* that,

> [d]iplomacy at its essence is the conduct of relationships, using peaceful means, by and among international actors, at least one of whom is usually governmental. The typical international actors are states and the bulk of diplomacy involves relations between states directly, or between states, international organizations, and other international actors. (Cooper et al., 2013, p. 2)

Yet they also note that an increasing number of actors have in recent decades become involved in the conduct of diplomacy (Cooper et al., 2013, pp. 1–2), be it subnational governments (including city governments), especially in federal systems of government, engaging in what is called 'paradiplomacy' (Kuznetsov, 2015; Paquin, 2020), or a host of other actors reflecting the specific configurations and contours of specialised, sectoral or issue-specific areas of diplomacy, be it climate diplomacy,[5] economic or trade diplomacy,[6] science diplomacy (Davis & Patman, 2015) or sports diplomacy (Kobierecki, 2020; Murray, 2018).

In a functional vein, different authors have also discussed the central aims and tasks of diplomacy and the main tools employed to achieve these ends. Adam Watson argues that 'the central task of diplomacy is not just the management of order, but the management of change, and the maintenance by continual *persuasion* of order in the midst of change' (Watson, 1984, p. 223, cited in Barston, 2019, p. 5, emphasis added). Louise Fréchette (2013, p. xxxii) makes a similar point: '[d]iplomacy is about persuasion, not coercion. It is about looking for and finding common

---

[5] See, for example, Barston (2019, Chapter 20) who focuses on the Paris Agreement.

[6] See also the respective chapters by Alan Bollard and Vangelis Vitalis in this volume. On trade diplomacy see also Barston (2019, Chapter 10) and Tussie (2013), who notes the vitality of regional sites and the roles played by non-governmental organisations in trade diplomacy.

ground, about forging agreement and achieving a balance of benefits that will allow each party to go home with at least some degree of satisfaction'. This is echoed, if in slightly different ways, by Robertson, who considers diplomacy to be 'the mediation of estranged entities by official *representatives*' (Robertson, 2019, emphasis in the original) and by Jörg Lau and Michael Thumann (2020) who see diplomacy as the 'transformation of opposition into processes, treaties, inspection regimes' (Lau & Thumann, 2020, own translation).

Important as some of these activities may be, William J. Burns, a former ambassador and designated to head the CIA in the Biden Administration, has argued that diplomacy is 'by nature an unheroic, quiet endeavour, often unfolding in back channels out of sight and out of mind. Crises averted are less captivating than military victories; diplomacy's preventive care is less compelling than the military's surgical feats' (Burns, 2019). Yet, while diplomacy may be more about the art of compromise, about resolving disputes (and about building relationships more generally) on a non-violent basis, this does not mean it entirely rejects coercion (Grace & Patman, 2020). Diplomacy is conducted by states (and other actors) in a relatively decentralised or anarchical international environment, and states have often sought to revise borders, control populations, or alter the access to material resources or terms of trade in their favour through the use of force or the threat of the force. Such coercion may involve the use of formal and informal sanctions of an economic or other type. Kofi Annan, a former United Nations Secretary General, once observed: 'You can do a lot with diplomacy, but with diplomacy backed up by force you can get a lot more done' (Annan, 1998, paragraph 14).

While diplomacy in practice has traditionally relied on personal interactions, gaining a personal rapport and trust-building, the COVID-19 pandemic has in recent times largely deprived political leaders and official representatives of the opportunity to engage in direct face-to-face discussions. It remains an open question whether the expanded use of 'digital diplomacy', 'online diplomacy', 'virtual diplomacy' or 'Zoom diplomacy' heralds a new age that will see the traditional focus on official visits and direct encounters being replaced by new technological, cost-efficient and time-saving alternatives (Robertson, 2020a, 2020b). Such new options may even allow more time for strategic reflections (Vimont, 2020). Or whether, given the apparent limits of digital meetings (Bland, 2020; Heath, 2020; Leithäuser, 2020), there will be, once the current pandemic subsides, a speedy return to the conventional and time-proven means of communications which make it easier to 'read between the lines by examining subtle tones and facial cues and then seek some middle ground in negotiations' (Sugiyama, 2020). Alternatively, and perhaps most likely, we may see a mixture of the two modes of diplomacy, depending very much on the occasion and purpose of the meeting in question, with 'virtual conversations dedicated to strategic dialogues or high-principled exchanges and direct physical meetings focussed on more detailed negotiations and drafting exercises' (Vimont, 2020).

Regardless of how the pandemic-induced digital shift will change in the longer term the channels in which diplomacy takes place, there are a number of other important global and regional trends that have been impacting diplomacy in the Indo-Pacific and will continue to do so in the foreseeable future. This leads us to the contributions to this volume.

THE CONTRIBUTIONS TO THIS VOLUME

As noted above, these contributions were written by a set of international authors, not only academics but also practitioners of regional diplomacy in different forms and shapes. We believe that this mix of authors not only accounts for the special flavour of the volume but, more importantly, helps to shed light on important insider perspectives. What also distinguishes this volume from others is that the authors do not focus, once more, on great-power relations or, for that matter, on a certain socially constructed group of states in the region, be it 'middle powers' or 'regional powers', but that they collectively give due attention to states with different international status and to various actors within them. We do not claim to cover all relevant actors in Indo-Pacific diplomacy, their ideas and interests, or the institutions they make use of (or subvert), or indeed the various and manifold issues that diplomacy in the region addresses or should address. Rather, this volume provides an assemblage, hopefully illuminating, of pertinent perspectives on diplomacy in the Indo-Pacific as it has unfolded and continues to unfold in the early decades of the twenty-first century.

Evelyn Goh begins the contributions to this volume by providing a big-picture appraisal of what she refers to as a regional transition to the 'age of uncertainty': an era where China has risen, the United States' resolve and commitment to the region are uncertain, and other regional powers with different political systems are resurgent. Goh demonstrates that we have transitioned into an era also in which traditional understandings of power, security and influence are challenged and where a much larger number of states and other actors than ever before are capable of exercising real agency in shaping the development of the Indo-Pacific. She distils the most important elements of our age of uncertainty, where globalised interdependence has created connectivity and vulnerability in equal measure. Goh then discusses the ways in which interconnections between economics and security need to be understood and managed in the Indo-Pacific if the region is to successfully navigate the ongoing transition.

Providing a practitioner's view, Alan Bollard's chapter complements Goh's overview by discussing the changing landscape of regional economic diplomacy. He argues that there has been a shift from economic to non-economic objectives across the region in recent years. Bollard points out that, while the earlier US-led rules encapsulated in policies such as the Washington Consensus helped bring about a trade-driven improvement in economic livelihoods in the region, recent structural changes have led to a breakdown of the neoliberal consensus. This development has helped to facilitate a growing challenge from nationalist forces and a shift to non-traditional and non-economic objectives of diplomacy in the region.

The following four chapters then address the regional diplomacy of different states in the Indo-Pacific. Kurt Campbell, whose own career showcases the close links between the realms of policymaking and think tanks in the United States, indicates that the American foreign policy paradigm has experienced significant shifts over recent decades and is now increasingly centred on the perceived challenge from China. He argues that, despite internal political divisions, there is a bipartisan consensus with respect to taking a more robust approach towards Beijing. While it remains to be seen what policies the new Biden Administration—which includes Campbell within its ranks—will adopt in relation to China and the wider region, it is clear the United States will need to re-evaluate and strengthen relations with some of its older allies and partners in the region.

Mingjiang Li analyses in his contribution recent changes in China's policy in the Indo-Pacific region. He maintains Beijing's growing assertiveness across the Asia–Pacific during the past decade was partially attributable to the limitations of Washington's 'strategic rebalance' policy in the region. Beijing's heavy-handed regional security policy in the 2010s had a markedly negative impact on China's relations with some of its neighbouring states. As Beijing moved to consolidate its presence in the East and South China Seas through various unilateral initiatives, a number of states in the region became visibly more apprehensive about the future of China's policy. Li argues that Washington's recent promotion of the concept of a Free and Open Indo-Pacific strategy seems to be more directly threatening to China's interests in the region than America's previous 'strategic rebalancing' approach.

Turning to Japan, Balazs Kiglics highlights in his chapter some of the major foreign policy strategies that Tokyo has formulated in the context of a rapidly changing Indo-Pacific during the last two decades. He focuses on the 'value-oriented diplomacy' that became a central element in the diplomacy of the two Abe Administrations. Kiglics contends such strategic initiatives are best understood as attempts to safeguard Japan's national interests at a time when the Indo-Pacific region is facing growing great-power rivalry between China and the United States. Such rivalry has prompted Tokyo to strengthen its co-operation with like-minded countries, a development that has required a more proactive Japanese diplomacy than at any time during the past seven decades.

Ian Hall examines Indian Prime Minister Modi's diplomacy, and argues past precedents and institutional shortcomings have contributed to a greater emphasis on prime ministerial engagement in international affairs than might be the case in many other countries. In his chapter, Hall explores somfve of the innovations of Modi's time in office, including the new emphases on religious diplomacy and diaspora engagement. According to Hall, Modi's embrace of personal diplomacy has been neither wholly new nor entirely positive. It represents an attempt to overcome long-standing institutional weaknesses, but has failed to deliver on many of the promises made.

Shifting the focus, Patrick Köllner's chapter compares Australia and New Zealand's diplomatic efforts to strengthen their relations with the Pacific Island countries, not least to counter China's growing 'footprint' in this region. Köllner contrasts the multilateral approaches of Australia and New Zealand in the region with China's preference for bilateral diplomacy. He argues that the Pacific Island countries have welcomed both China's growing engagement and the expanded regional engagement of New Zealand and Australia as these offer the prospect of a greater range of policy options and enhanced leverage. Köllner's chapter highlights the fact the South Pacific is no longer seen as a strategic backwater and that while the interest of external actors is growing, they will need to reckon with the increasingly complex dynamics in that region of the world.

Moving from the analysis of government-to-government diplomacy to New Zealand's experience with regional Track II diplomacy, James To examines New Zealand's national and international concerns in upholding a rules-based regional architecture across the Indo-Pacific in order to advance Wellington's economic, political and defence-related objectives. As other countries across the region have been looking for partners to deal with foreign policy challenges like intensified great-power rivalries, New Zealand policymakers have moved from a 'balance of power' to a 'balance of partners' model as well as a search for 'like-minded' countries—in order to navigate this increasingly complex environment.

Well-informed international affairs think tanks can contribute in important ways to influencing the conduct of diplomacy. In their contribution to this volume, Raphaëlle Khan and Patrick Köllner focus on the recent emergence of new foreign policy think tanks in India. They argue that the country's foreign policy think tank sector has significantly gained in visibility and vibrancy due to new demand in the wake of India's expanding international role. Khan and Köllner identify two distinct types of foreign policy think tanks: ones that are close to Indian businesses and/or connected to foreign think tanks which tend to promote a liberal world view, and those that are close to the ruling Bharatiya Janata Party and thus tend to contribute to a mainstream nationalist ideological narrative in foreign policy.

An ASEAN insider perspective on the Indo-Pacific is provided by Elaine Tan. She says that diplomacy among Southeast Asian countries must be used to develop a stronger sense of regional identity among the ten ASEAN member states. While ASEAN was able to transform relations among the state actors, Tan expresses the concern that such diplomacy was not making a major impact on ordinary peoples' lives: There has been a disconnect between ASEAN and its own citizens. Tan argues that building a sense of belonging to the region could foster a closer ASEAN identity and that in turn would strengthen the ASEAN Community.

The final three chapters in this volume connect the issues of peace, prosperity and populism to the study of diplomacy in the Indo-Pacific. David Welch considers threat perceptions in relation to the Korean Peninsula and the South China Sea by applying the concepts of confidence, trust and empathy to these cases. He argues that empathy could be the key to manage conflict in such disputes and shows how the failure to build empathy complicates and potentially threatens conflict management in what are two of the region's most serious flashpoints. Welch's chapter also explores the practical consequences of achieving a higher degree of empathy in both cases.

In another policy practitioner perspective, Vangelis Vitalis notes the 'Golden Weather' period for New Zealand trade policy is well and truly over. He argues that, like that of many other small countries, New Zealand diplomacy has been significantly challenged by a transition to a new global environment for trade—an era of increasing complexity characterised by a significant erosion of many previous assumptions about a rules-based international trading system. Vitalis's chapter situates New Zealand's trade policy within International Relations theory and provides an overview of the country's trade policy, including during the COVID-19 era. He concludes with a discussion of New Zealand's dynamic and evolving framework for navigating turbulent times for international trade policy.

The final chapter, authored by Aurora Javate de Dios, addresses the impact of profound political change in the Philippines: Rodrigo Duterte's 2016 electoral victory was followed by a significant reversal of the county's democratic tradition and the onset of 'authoritarian populism'. As president, Duterte has not only consolidated his power by highly controversial domestic policies but also reversed the Philippines' foreign policy direction. In doing so, he has shown little regard for human rights or the commitment to the rule of law in the South China Sea. De Dios argues that Duterte's maverick policies have significant implications for undermining stability and security across the region.

References

ABC [Australian Broadcasting Corporation]. (2021, January 12). *Previously secret details of Trump administration's IndoPacific strategy revealed.* https://www.abc.net.au/news/2021-01-12/details-of-trump-administrations-indo-pacific-strategy-revealed/13052216. Accessed 17 January 2021.

Annan, K. (1998, February 24). *Transcript of press conference by Secretary-General Kofi Annan at United Nations headquarters.* https://www.un.org/press/en/1998/19980224.SGSM6470.html. Accessed 21 January 2021.

ASEAN [Association of Southeast Asian Nations]. (2019, June 23). *ASEAN Outlook on the Indo-Pacific.* ASEAN Statements & Communiques. https://asean.org/asean-outlook-indo-pacific. Accessed 15 December 2020.

Barston, R. P. (2019). *Modern diplomacy* (5th ed.). Routledge.

Beeson, M., & Lee-Brown, T. (2021). Regionalism for realists? The evolution of the Indo-Pacific. *Chinese Political Science Review*. https://link.springer.com/article/10.1007/s41111-020-00163-0. Accessed 25 February 2021.

Bisley, N. (2020, July). Book review of Rory Medcalf's *Contest for the Indo-Pacific*. *Australian Foreign Affairs, 9*, 127–130.

Bland, B. (2020, August 31). The Limits of Zoom diplomacy in Asia. *The Interpreter*. Sydney: The Lowy Institute. https://www.lowyinstitute.org/the-interpreter/limits-zoom-diplomacy-asia. Accessed 5 September 2020.

Brands, H. (2020, April 4) Trump's personal diplomacy is dead, even if Kim isn't. *The Japan Times*. https://www.japantimes.co.jp/opinion/2020/04/24/commentary/world-commentary/trumps-personal-diplomacy-dead-even-kim-isnt/. Accessed 27 May 2020.

Burns, W. J. (2019, March 8). How to save the power of diplomacy. *The New York Times*. https://www.nytimes.com/2019/03/08/opinion/sunday/diplomacy-trump-state-department.html. Accessed 12 March 2019.

Byrne, C. (2020). Securing the 'rules-based order' in the Indo-Pacific. *Security Challenges, 16*(3), 10–15.

Conley Tyler, M. (2019, June 28). The Indo-Pacific is the New Asia. *The Interpreter*. https://www.lowyinstitute.org/the-interpreter/indo-pacific-new-asia. Accessed 4 July 2019.

Cooper, A. F., Heine, J., & Thakur, R. (2013). Introduction: The challenges of 21st century diplomacy. In A. F. Cooper, J. Heine, & R. Thakur (Eds.), *The Oxford handbook of modern diplomacy* (pp. 1–31). Oxford University Press.

Davis, L. S., & Patman, R. G. (Eds.). (2015). *Science diplomacy: New day or false dawn?* World Scientific.

Dolven, B., & Vaugh, B. (2020, January 30). *Indo-Pacific strategies of U.S. allies and partners: Issues for Congress*. CRS Report R46217. Washington: Congressional Research Service. https://www.everycrsreport.com/reports/R46217.html. Accessed 27 July 2020.

Envall, H. D. P. (2020). The Pacific islands in Japan's 'free and open Indo-Pacific': From 'slow and steady' to strategic engagement? *Security Challenges, 16*(1), 65–77.

Federal Foreign Office. (2020). *Policy guidelines for the Indo-Pacific*. Berlin: FFO. https://www.auswaertiges-amt.de/blob/2380514/f9784f7e3b3fa1bd7c5446d274a4169e/200901-indo-pazifik-leitlinien--1--data.pdf. Accessed 19 January 2021.

FMPRC [Ministry of Foreign Affairs of the People's Republic of China]. (2018, March 9). *Foreign Minister Wang Yi meets the press*. https://www.fmprc.gov.cn/mfa_eng/zxxx_662805/t1540928.shtml. Accessed 27 January 2021.

Fisher, D. (2020). The crowded and complex pacific: Lessons from France's Pacific experience. *Security Challenges, 16*(1), 37–43.

Fréchette, L. (2013). Diplomacy: Old trade, new challenges. In A. F. Cooper, J. Heine, & R. Thakur (Eds.), *The Oxford handbook of modern diplomacy* (pp. xxx–xxxv). Oxford: Oxford University Press.

Grace, P., & R. G. Patman. (2020). Diplomatic heroism and positive peace. In K. Standish, H. Devere, A. E. Suazo, & R. Rafferty (Eds.), *The Palgrave handbook of positive peace* (forthcoming). Cham: Palgrave.

Gyngell, A. (2019, October). History hasn't ended: How to handle China. *Australian Foreign Affairs, 7*, 5–27.

Hatakeyama, K. (2020). Roles of norms-based diplomacy in the Asian maritime order. *Security Challenges, 16*(3), 16–20.

He, K., & Li, M. (2020). Understanding the dynamics of the Indo-Pacific: US–China strategic competition, regional actors and beyond. *International Affairs, 96*(1), 1–7.

Heath, R. (2020, April 16). For global diplomats, Zoom is not like being in the room. *Politico.* https://www.politico.com/news/2020/04/16/zoom-diplomacy-coronavirus-188811. Accessed 21 January 2021.

Heiduk, F., & Wacker, G. (2020, July). *From Asia–Pacific to Indo-Pacific: Significance, implementation and challenges* (SWP Research Paper 2020/RP 09). Berlin: German Institute for International and Security Affairs. https://www.swp-berlin.org/fileadmin/contents/products/research_papers/2020RP09_IndoPacific.pdf. Accessed 4 August 2020.

Jones, L., & Hameiri, S. (2020). *Debunking the myth of 'debt-trap diplomacy': How recipient countries shape China's belt and road initiative* (Research Paper). London: Chatham House. https://www.chathamhouse.org/sites/def ault/files/2020-08-19-debunking-myth-debt-trap-diplomacy-jones-hameiri. pdf. Accessed 27 January 2021.

Kaplan, R. D. (2012). *The revenge of geography: What the map tells us about coming conflicts and the battle against fate.* Random House.

Kaplan, R. D. (2014, March 20). Geopolitics and the new world order. *TIME.* https://time.com/31911/geopolitics-and-the-new-world-order/. Accessed 26 January 2021.

Kobierecki, M. M. (2020). *Sports diplomacy: Sports in the diplomatic activity of states and non-state actors.* Lexington.

Kusnetsov, A. (2015). *Theory and practice of paradiplomacy: Subnational governments in international affairs.* Routledge.

Lau, J., & Thumann, N. (2020, January 23). In einer Welt voller „Frenemies" [In a world full of 'frenemies']. *Die Zeit*, 2.

Leithäuser, J. (2020, April 22). Im Auge des Betrachters [In the eye of the beholder]. *Frankfurter Allgemeine Zeitung*, 4.

Lewis, M. W., & Wigen, K. E. (1997). *The myth of continents: A critique of metageography.* University of California Press.

Medcalf, R. (2015, June 26). *Reimagining Asia: From Asia–Pacific to Indo-Pacific.* The ASAN Forum. http://www.theasanforum.org/reimagining-asia-from-asia-pacific-to-indo-pacific. Accessed 19 January 2021.

Medcalf, R. (2020). *Contest for the Indo-Pacific. Why China won't map the future.* La Trobe University / Black Inc.

Medcalf, R. (2021, January 12). Declassification of secret document reveals US strategy in the Indo-Pacific. *The Strategist.* Canberra: Australian Strategic Policy Institute. https://www.aspistrategist.org.au/declassification-of-secret-document-reveals-real-us-strategy-in-the-indo-pacific. Accessed 17 January 2021.

Ministère des l'Europe and des Affaires étrangères. (2019). *The Indo-Pacific region: A priority for France.* https://www.diplomatie.gouv.fr/en/country-files/asia-and-oceania/the-indo-pacific-region-a-priority-for-france. Accessed 19 January 2021.

Murray, S. (2018). *Sports diplomacy: Origins, theory and practice.* Routledge.

Nabbs-Keller, G. (2020). ASEAN centrality and Indonesian leadership in a contested Indo-Pacific order. *Security Challenges, 16*(3), 21–26.

O'Donnell, G., & Schmitter, P. (1986). *Transitions from authoritarian rule.* Johns Hopkins University Press.

Paquin S. (2020). Paradiplomacy. In T. Balzacq, F. Charillon & F. Ramel (Eds.), *Global diplomacy.* Cham: Palgrave Macmillan.

Peters, W. (2018, June 29). *Next steps.* Opening speech at the 53rd Otago Foreign Policy School. https://www.beehive.govt.nz/speech/next-steps. Accessed 19 January 2021.

Policy Exchange. (2020). *A Very British Tilt: Towards a new UK strategy in the Indo-Pacific region.* An interim report by Policy Exchange's Indo-Pacific Commission. London: Policy Exchange. https://policyexchange.org.uk/wp-content/uploads/A-Very-British-Tilt.pdf. Accessed 28 January 2021.

PricewaterhouseCoopers (PwC). (2017, February). *The World in 2050.* https://www.pwc.com/gx/en/research-insights/economy/the-world-in-2050.html. Accessed 22 February 2021.

Rimmer, P. J. (2018). Geopolitics and geo-economics in Eurasia and the Indo-Pacific. In S. Hua (Ed.), *Routledge handbook of politics in Asia* (pp. 472–489). Routledge.

Robertson, J. (2019, March 6). Political leadership versus diplomacy. *The Interpreter.* Sydney: Lowy Institute. https://www.lowyinstitute.org/the-interpreter/political-leadership-versus-diplomacy. Accessed 20 April 2020.

Robertson, J. (2020a, August 18). Diplomacy and global governance after COVID-19: Prepare for change. *The Interpreter.* Sydney: Lowy Institute. https://www.lowyinstitute.org/the-interpreter/diplomacy-and-global-governance-after-covid-19-prepare-change. Accessed 20 August 2020.

Robertson, J. (2020b, October 21). Diplomacy and global governance after Covid: No looking back. *The Interpreter.* Sydney: Lowy Institute. https://www.lowyinstitute.org/the-interpreter/diplomacy-after-covid-no-looking-back. Accessed 22 October 2020.

Sargeant, B. (2020). The Pacific islands in the 'Indo-Pacific.' *Strategic Challenges, 16*(1), 26–31.

Scott, D. (2020, March 18). New Zealand picks up on Indo-Pacific. *Asia Pacific Bulletin,* 502. Washington, DC: East–West Center. https://www.eastwestcenter.org/publications/new-zealand-picks-the-indo-pacific. Accessed 20 January 2021.

Strangio, S. (2020, November 18). Following France and Germany, the Netherlands pivots to the Indo-Pacific. *The Diplomat.* https://thediplomat.com/2020/11/following-france-and-germany-the-netherlands-pivots-to-the-indo-pacific/. Accessed 19 January 2021.

Sugiyama, S. (2020, May 7). In the age of COVID-19, world leaders struggle to adjust to online diplomacy. *Japan Times.* https://www.japantimes.co.jp/news/2020/05/07/national/politics-diplomacy/coronavirus-world-leaders-online-diplomacy. Accessed 27 May 2020.

Tussie, D. (2013). Trade diplomacy. In A. F. Cooper, J. Heine, & R. Thakur (Eds.), *The Oxford handbook of modern diplomacy* (pp. 625–641). Oxford University Press.

U.S. Indo-Pacific Command. (2018). USINDOPACOM area of responsibility. https://www.pacom.mil/About-USINDOPACOM/USPACOM-Area-of-Responsibility. Accessed 19 January 2021.

Vimont, P. (2020, September 2). *Diplomacy during the quarantine: An opportunity for more agile craftmanship.* Carnegie Europe. https://carnegieeurope.eu/2020/09/02/diplomacy-during-quarantine-opportunity-for-more-agile-craftsmanship-pub-82559. Accessed 3 September 2020.

Watson, A. (1984). *Diplomacy: The dialogue between states.* Methuen.

Wilson, J. (2020). Infrastructure choices and the future of the Indo-Pacific. *Strategic Challenges, 16*(3), 64–68.

Wolfers, A. (1962). *Discord and collaboration. Essays on international politics.* Johns Hopkins Press.

Xi, J. (2013, October 3). *Speech by Chinese President Xi Jinping to Indonesian Parliament.* ASEAN–China Centre. http://www.asean-china-center.org/english/2013-10/03/c_133062675.htm. Accessed 26 January 2021.

The Asia–Pacific's 'Age of Uncertainty': Great Power Competition, Globalisation and the Economic-Security Nexus

Evelyn Goh

CONTEXT: OUR AGE OF UNCERTAINTY

In a well-known trilogy of books on what he called the ages of revolution, empire and capitalism, the eminent historian Eric Hobsbawm (1962, 1975, 1987) analysed the pivotal 'long nineteenth century'. Hobsbawm's thesis was that two sociopolitical–economic revolutions—the French Revolution and the Industrial Revolution—catalysed modern European history, and—via colonialism and imperialism—world history.

This chapter is based on the author's Keynote Lecture for the University of Otago's 53rd Foreign Policy School on 30 June 2018, and was developed also from her 2018 Shedden Lecture at the Australian Department of Defence, and her Distinguished Public Lecture as the Ngee Ann Kongsi Professor of International Relations at the S. Rajaratnam School of International Studies, Singapore, in August 2018. For their insights, comments and help, she particularly thanks Scott Dewar, Ralf Emmers and the volume editors.

E. Goh (✉)
Australian National University, Canberra, ACT, Australia
e-mail: evelyn.goh@anu.edu.au

29

In a subsequent book about the period from the start of the Second World War to the fall of the Soviet Union, Hobsbawm (1994) saw the 'short twentieth century' as being characterised by the failures of state socialism, capitalism and nationalism.

Here, my thesis is that via a post-Cold War interregnum of US hegemony (*circa* 1991–2008; see Goh, 2013) we have now entered an 'age of uncertainty' characterised by unprecedented economic interdependence, and renewed and expanded great power competition, fuelled by globalisation and what some call the 'Fourth Industrial Revolution' (4IR). Economic interdependence and globalisation are not new phenomena. But nothing highlights our current extreme globalised interdependence more acutely than the COVID-19 pandemic which emerged in central China towards the end of 2019 and is still raging across the world at the time of writing. Facilitated by the spread of economic and technological means of rapid interaction, and global just-in-time production systems and networks, our webs of socio-economic interdependence create connectivity and vulnerability in equal measure (e.g. Goh & Prantl, 2020). Expressions of such concerns that prevailed in the post-Cold War context, for example about terrorism and cybersecurity, are now overshadowed by the intertwined threats to health, food and economic security, which even raise the spectre of social revolution at the heart of the Western democratic world.

In the Asia–Pacific context, a crucial element of our strategic landscape over the past decade has been renewed great power competition of the sort some analysts and policymakers expected would cease after the Cold War ended. Now, a power transition seems to be upon us: China, undoubtedly, has risen; US resolve and commitment are uncertain, especially during the Trump presidency; and other regional powers with different political systems are also resurgent (particularly India, Japan and Russia). Great power competition has correspondingly expanded in both scope and domain. Apart from the United States–China trade war that has preoccupied policymakers around the world since 2018, a strategic environment defined by great power contestation now routinely includes power play in troubled areas like Iran, frigates colliding in the South China Sea, new forms of political interference in others' domestic politics, and competition over issues spanning development financing to contributions to the World Health Organization.

Overlaying this are the promises and perils of the so-called Fourth Industrial Revolution (Schwab, 2016). Proponents see this as a revolution in the proper sense: a disjuncture from the previous phase of technological development, marked by new abilities to blur the divides between the physical, digital and biological. They project the cumulative impacts of rapid and greatly increasing technological breakthroughs in many diverse fields—including quantum computing, biotechnology, artificial intelligence (AI), robotics and nanotechnology—arguing that the synergies among these developments and the exponential speed at which these changes are happening will create unprecedented effects for industries, countries and human society. While the effects have been most obvious to those in specific sectors to date, the transformations in work, services and production engendered by the COVID-19 pandemic may prove to be the tipping point, after which the Fourth Industrial Revolution's transformative and disruptive impacts will become clearer across the system.

What is the upshot for scholars and policymakers who have to grapple with these uncertainties? First, this 'age of uncertainty' is marked by accentuated pluralism—put simply, there are *more actors, more factors and more vectors*. In the defence realm, after the Cold War we had already become more familiar with this pluralism in, for instance, the growing range of security actors, including informal combatants, mercenaries, terrorists, individual extremists and cyber hackers. We have also increasingly recognised 'non-traditional' security issues like environmental degradation, migration, poverty, systematic social alienation and pandemics. And defence establishments around the world have been absorbing and trying to leverage the impacts of AI, blockchain technology and other aspects of the 4IR for defence systems and operations. In the following sections, I demonstrate that this accentuated pluralism is a bigger, systemic condition, which generates cumulative impacts.

Second, we are faced with unavoidable complexity. In terms of the international order, we have transitioned from the structural overlay of the bipolar Cold War to a mash-up of 'unknown unknowns', butterfly effects, wild cards, black swans, even black elephants. The notion of complexity references (a) the high degree of connectivity between the individual components of a system; (b) fundamental disproportionality between cause and effect (a seemingly small trigger such as the collapse of Lehman Brothers in 2008 can generate non-linear, cascading effects such as the Global Financial Crisis or GFC); and (c) the quality of emergence—new phenomena can emerge from the interactions of the individual components of a complex system (see e.g. Mitchell, 2009). The latter quality is especially important: connections and interactions between parts of the system create outcomes that are inherently unpredictable *ex ante* and are revealed only when they occur, giving rise to apparent strategic surprises such as 9/11, or SARS, the first coronavirus epidemic that broke out in East Asia in 2003. It is no surprise that, from the 1990s, strategists increasingly adopted the management concept about dealing with a volatile, uncertain, complex and ambiguous ('VUCA') world (Bennis & Nanus, 1985).

When faced with complex problems, rather than fixating on the immediate manifestation of the issue, strategic policymakers need to think about the systemic context. Crucially, they need to focus on picking out key nodes and vital relationships; identifying entry points for significant leverage; and considering how to shape the system as a whole to build optimal diversity and resilience (Goh & Prantl, 2016, 2017, 2020). At the same time, today's strategic policymaking establishments need to possess collective knowledge about quite a lot of particular things. While this may sound daunting, especially to states with relatively fewer resources, this is a lesson already well learnt from post-Cold War counterterrorism, which turned out to require knowledge about religion, ideology and international finance, as well as the politics, sociology and criminology of multiple countries and regions. The rest of this chapter is an effort to highlight some key areas of—too often siloed—knowledge, which are essential for strategists working in the Asia–Pacific's age of uncertainty.

GREAT POWER COMPETITION AND INTERNATIONAL ORDER

In 2013 I published a book entitled *The Struggle for Order* that chronicled the short interregnum of US hegemony in East Asia. I analysed East Asian states' primary reasons for favouring US hegemony, and highlighted China's shortcomings in terms of the vital leadership functions of providing public goods and a compelling vision for a different regional order. However, the book ended by explicitly asserting that the result of the ongoing order transition was yet unclear. Since then, the picture has become clearer. The region is leading the world towards an international system with more actors, more factors and more vectors. We can observe 'disaggregated change in [the] different arenas' of security, economics and institutions as a direct result of great power competition and the forces of globalisation (Goh, 2019).

Great power competition is, by 2020, a fact of life in the Asia–Pacific. Sino-American discord, tension and conflict are evident in the daily news, whether in the trade, geopolitical, institutional or pandemic realms. More significantly, their strategic planning and thinking have shifted into competition mode. For example, as the Policy Planning Staff in the US Department of State reconceptualised strategy towards China, the then director warned that this is 'the first time that we will have a great power competitor that is not Caucasian ... a fight with a really different civilization and a different ideology ... [one that] the United States hasn't had ... before'. In contrast, the United States–Soviet Union Cold War was 'a fight within the Western family' (quoted in Gehrke, 2019). In May 2020, the Trump White House published a new document on the US 'strategic approach' to China which stated: 'To respond to Beijing's challenge, the Administration has adopted a competitive approach to the PRC, based on ... a tolerance of greater bilateral friction' (The White House, 2020). During the trade war with the United States, China's leaders felt sufficiently under pressure to depart from the Party line of peaceful and co-operative intent to promise to 'rise up' against US bullying and to engage in 'a new Long March' (Lee, 2018; Zhou, 2019). Beyond the rhetoric, strategists and analysts on both sides increasingly accept the inevitability of mutual competition, if not outright conflict, and are preparing for it (see, e.g. Berger, 2019; McMaster, 2020; Tellis et al., 2020; Wang, 2020; Zhao, 2019).

There are deeper, structural implications of this renewed great power competition. Fundamentally, it means the end of US preponderance in East Asia—it is no longer the only credible great power in town. Structurally, the region is moving from a security order that was based on a single pillar (US primacy centred on its hub-and-spokes alliance relationships), to one that rests on multiple stilts of different sizes and functions (akin to, say, the traditional architectural style favoured for houses in the tropics). I prefer this analogy to the popular alternatives involving poles or cinemas. To be clear: this does not mean that the United States disappears from the landscape, either in the region or the world. It *does* mean that the United States is no longer East Asia's *only* pillar, shelter or policeman. It may not even be *a* pillar, shelter or policeman in some issue areas. In normative terms, it means the end of US hegemony in this part of the world, with hegemony understood as authority stemming from the consent of followers (see Clark, 2011; Goh, 2013). The distinction is important, because consent is an intervening variable: it can be 'sticky' and prolong an order transition even after the incumbent hegemon has been materially overtaken by a rising challenger, or it can be 'fluid' and accelerate a transition in favour of a rising challenger even before the latter is willing to take up the mantle of leadership.

For the Asia–Pacific, more broadly, the end of US hegemony has generated two significant strategic trends, arising from the security choices being made by regional states during this time of uncertainty. First, the greater resort to self-help. This is best illustrated in north-east Asia, where the most exciting development of 2018–2019 was the spate of summitry initiated by the President of the Republic of Korea (ROK) Moon Jae-in. His determined pursuit of the progressives' agenda of détente with North Korea was facilitated by the uncertainties surrounding the Obama Administration's partial pivot to Asia, subsequently intensified with President Donald Trump's erratic attention span and demands for US allies to bear greater costs. Moon's landmark April 2018 summit with North Korean leader Kim Jong Un and brokerage of the Trump–Kim summits helped regain some Korean control over the peninsula's future. While this included risks—Moon had to absorb the blowback of Trump's shock cancellation of annual United States–ROK military exercises—and while Korean Peninsula issues still require China and the United States for management and resolution, inter-Korean relations and the ROK's role now constitute a stronger third leg. In Japan, Prime Minister Shinzō Abe, while working hardest at maintaining the US alliance under Trump, also had to deal with many other aspects of the relationship being damaged, including US withdrawal from the Trans-Pacific Partnership (TPP) regional trade agreement and growing doubts about US commitment to regional institutions. These uncertainties compelled Abe to seek rapprochement with China despite bilateral tensions over territorial and historical disputes. Abe found Beijing receptive to his overtures, doubtless due to Chinese leaders' growing concerns about the US economic threat. In 2018 and 2019, Abe and Chinese President Xi Jinping revived bilateral summits, with Xi's visit to Japan in April 2019 being the first visit by a Chinese president since 2010, at which summit they pledged to promote 'free and fair trade' and to be 'eternal neighbours' (Sim, 2019). The annual trilateral summit between China, Japan and South Korea was also revived in 2018, after a six-year hiatus.

Self-help has also included US allies in north-east Asia looking southwards and region-wide. In 2019, Moon's Administration elevated economic and political relations with Southeast Asia under the banner of his 'New Southern Policy' (Easley & Kim, 2019). Since 2013, Abe's Japan has led in reviving strategic interest in Southeast Asia, steadily growing its patchwork of economic and security assistance and co-operation with key countries, including those which have territorial and maritime conflicts with China, such as Indonesia, Vietnam and the Philippines (Arase, 2019; Buzan & Goh, 2020, pp. 171–173). Notably, Tokyo has more actively tried to articulate a vision of a broader regional order based on liberal principles separate from US leadership (see Koga, 2020; Tamaki, forthcoming).

Self-help is also evident in how the 'spokes' of the US alliance system have tried to join up, creating new relationships among the regional satellites rather than channelling their interactions only through the US hub. The most publicised example is the Quadrilateral Security Dialogue (Quad) involving Japan, Australia and India alongside the United States, spearheaded by Abe in 2007 and resurrected in 2017. While much debated, the Quad is notable for its explicit values-based framing, stressing co-operation between democracies committed to—another Abe administration initiative—a 'Free and Open Indo-Pacific'. Also significant is the plethora of 'mini-lateral' security co-operation among sub-combinations of the four member states, including military exercises and high-level dialogues (see e.g. Buchan & Rimland, 2020). A less widely advertised example is the Australia–Singapore Military Training Initiative signed in 2018 under their broader bilateral Comprehensive Strategic Partnership: A 25-year, A$2.25 billion agreement for the small Southeast Asian security partner to build facilities and increase the number of troops it has on rotation in Australia from 6,000 to 14,000 annually.[1] Some scholars go so far as to suggest that US allies and security partners in the Asia–Pacific are restructuring their pre-existing bilateral security relationships with the United States into a 'networked security architecture' (Dian & Meijer, 2020).

Second is the growing importance of regional dynamics now that the systemic preponderance of the United States is increasingly contested.

---

[1] Some information about this military co-operation is provided by the Australian Department of Defence at https://www.defence.gov.au/Initiatives/ASMTI (Accessed 30 May 2020).

We get competing regional imaginaries, not just competing great powers. For me, geopolitics is a way of looking at the world, one that considers the links between political power, geography and cultural diversity. It is about imagining and prioritising some form of connectivity: which parts of the system are connected to each other more importantly than with others? Thus, geopolitical competition is essentially a contest over which 'imagined community'[2]—created through forging ideational and material connections—is most important. In Asia today, there are three competing imagined regions: the 'Asia–Pacific'; the '(continental) Belt and (maritime) Road'; and the 'Indo-Pacific'. Of course, there are other sub- and trans-regional projects, but these three are most significant because of the resources committed to them.

The 'Asia–Pacific' is the trans-Pacific imaginary[3] comprising East Asia, Oceania and the Americas.[4] This meta-region is the classic imagined community transformed into reality through the determined application of enormous resources over time: since 1898, the projection of superior US military, political and economic power into the western Pacific has dramatically mediated what strategists call the loss-of-force gradient over a vast distance. The enormous scale of this enterprise is clear when we look at the Mercator projection map centred on the Pacific Ocean, which represents the US military's Pacific Command theatre of operations (Fig. 1). The lived reality of the constructed 'Asia–Pacific' imaginary is ensured by the reciprocal connections that East Asia and Oceania have forged with North America in particular in the post-war era (see Dirlik, 1992). This interdependence was institutionalised in APEC (Asia–Pacific Economic Cooperation), the post-Cold War world's first mega-regional trade forum. The 'Asia–Pacific' was the preponderant regional imaginary for much of the post-Cold War interregnum, even though we also saw

[2] Here, I am adapting Benedict Anderson's (1983) classic concept of 'imagined communities'.

[3] Borrowing from literary convention, I use the term 'imaginary' as a noun, to refer to a collective notion of an imagined political/security/economic community we can infer from a particular strategic project.

[4] In this chapter, I use 'Asia–Pacific' when referring to the trans-Pacific region comprising East Asia, Oceania and the Americas. When my discussion pertains to the region encompassing China, Japan, the two Koreas, Taiwan and the South East Asian countries, I use 'East Asia'.

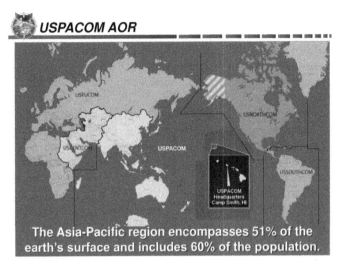

Fig. 1   US Pacific command theatre of operations (*Source* https://www.slides erve.com/dulcea/uspacom-global-basing-and-environmental-impacts)

the regional construction of the 'East Asia' imaginary from around the time of the 1997–1998 Asian Financial Crisis.

But it was China's full entry into the global economy after gaining World Trade Organization (WTO) membership in 2001, and its rapid rise as an economic power that propelled the major competing regional imaginary of our age. Centred on what has come to be called the 'Belt and Road Initiative' (BRI), this agglomeration of economic and geopolitical initiatives essentially aims to integrate China's economy with its peripheries and neighbours in the process of forging continental and maritime connections westwards through to the Middle East and Europe in effect (re-)creating a greater Eurasian imaginary. This is the key competing regional imaginary because enormous Chinese political resources and a high-level, whole-of-government effort have been poured into creating business, investment and political opportunities connecting all parts of China to old and new investors and markets (see Ye, 2020). Again, this enterprise acquires a lived reality because of the responses of others. On the one hand, multiple participating countries (including many US allies and partners) have made BRI possible by selling assets, co-operating with Chinese enterprises, receiving loans for infrastructure building and other forms of investment, or becoming members of the Asian Infrastructure Investment Bank (see Goh, 2019, pp. 633–635).

On the other hand, other countries and constituencies suspicious of the Chinese Government's intentions and practices have created a countervailing regional imaginary: the 'Indo-Pacific'. Its propagation within the Australian discourse might have created the impression that this two-ocean imaginary is mainly an allergic reaction to the BRI and opportunism by some Australia strategists trying to justify an Oceanic place in the evolving geopolitical great game. However, underlying the original idea is a palpable worry that the combination of US decline and China's rise, as well as India's re-emergence, compels new strategic thinking and co-operation to manage multipolar rivalry (see Medcalf, 2020). The Indo-Pacific imaginary looks likely to last, if only because significant others have bandwagoned with it: President Trump adopted the term from the 2017 US National Security Strategy onwards, and in May 2018 the US Pacific Command was renamed Indo-Pacific Command. Importantly too, two-time Japanese Prime Minister Abe has had the unique opportunity to resuscitate his idea of the confluence of the Pacific and Indian Oceans bringing about a 'broader Asia', tied to the 'Arc of Freedom and Prosperity' along the outer rim of the Eurasian continent his foreign minister advocated during his first tenure in 2006–2007. Both ideas were resurrected as Japan's 'Free and Open Indo-Pacific Strategy' in 2016,[5] which in turn has galvanised the Quad and also seen growing engagement from other regional actors such as ASEAN and Taiwan.

All three imaginaries will compete for the foreseeable future. But fundamentally, the geopolitical competition in our age of uncertainty will not be between binary continental and maritime great powers; it cannot be, simply because China is successfully blurring that divide and others wish to countervail or contain Chinese power where it spreads. So, instead, the competition will turn on how effectively these great powers integrate and leverage the interdependence between the maritime and continental aspects of power in Asia.

---

[5] For a useful insight into the Abe Government's iteration of a strategy developed over more than a decade, see the MOFA infographics page: https://www.mofa.go.jp/policy/page25e_000278.html (Accessed 30 May 2020).

GLOBALISATION AND DEEPER POWER SHIFTS

Indeed, in our globalised world, interdependence develops many new forms. At a basic level, intensifying economic interdependence creates greater connectivity among the different parts of the global system. However, the interdependence that has grown out of the unprecedented surge in global economic activity over the past three decades has also been asymmetrical, unevenly distributed and itself compelling redistributions. When we take into account the economic side of the story, it becomes evident that the great power dynamics discussed above belie a deeper power shift.

This crucial part of the story can be told in two steps. First, the rise of 'a more global South', as the 2013 United Nations Human Development Report put it. A significant number of developing countries—most notably, but not only, China—have used state intervention and tapped into global capital to spur their economies. They have generated remarkable new transboundary flows of goods, services and people; and global production 'is rebalancing in ways not seen for 150 years' (UNDP, 2013, p. 3). From 1980 to 2011, South–South trade as a proportion of world merchandise trade grew from 8 to 27%. During the same period, the proportion of North–North merchandise trade fell from 47 to 30%. The same report projected that, by 2050, the three key emerging economies of Brazil, China and India will together account for 40% of total global production, surpassing the projected combined production of the G7, which will fall to around 20%. This trend is influenced by the size of populations in developing countries, and—more importantly—by the rapid rise of their middle classes, with corresponding consumer spending power. An influential study (Kharas, 2017) showed that by 2015, there were over three billion people globally who fell into the middle-class category, roughly half of whom lived in Asia. *Circa* 2020, the middle class came to constitute a majority of the global population. In what is the most rapid expansion of the middle class the world has ever seen, almost 90% of the next billion entrants into the global middle class will be in Asia: 380 million Indians, 350 million Chinese and 210 million other Asians. At the time of Homi Kharas' updated study and prior to the COVID pandemic, middle-class consumption accounted for more than a third of the global economy, and was growing by about 4% annually, faster than the average GDP growth.

The second step in this story is the diffusion of economic power away from its previous concentration in the West. To be clear, I am not referring to an absolute decline of the West (yet). It is simply the 'rise of the rest', which has altered the relative distribution of global economic activity, be it production, consumption or investment. This is best captured in Danny Quah's (2011) modelling which showed the dramatic eastwards shift in the world's economic centre of gravity. Using GDP figures from 700 locations to calculate the average location of global economic activity, he placed the global economy's centre of gravity somewhere in the middle of the Atlantic Ocean *circa* 1980, reflecting the dominance of North American and Western European economies. By 2008, that centre of gravity had shifted to a location on the Eurasian continent, east of Helsinki and Bucharest. Extrapolating economic growth figures, Quah projected that, by 2050, the world's economic centre of gravity would relocate to a point midway between India and China. A 2012 McKinsey Global Institute report plotted longer-term data to reach a similar conclusion that, by 2025, the economic centre of gravity would return to the Asian continent, after a westward sojourn since around 1820 (Dobbs et al., 2012).

At a systemic level, this deep shift manifests as a marked reorientation of global trade, starting with significantly reduced dependency on Western or developed markets. A 2019 Bloomberg report indicated that, by 2017, 53% of all bilateral trade in the world involved at least one emerging market, up from 38% in 1997. The number of countries in the world whose majority of trade was with emerging markets rose from 19 to 64 during the same 20-year period (Tartar & Sam, 2019). In other words, producers in developing countries have loosened their previous dependence on demand from developed markets. These producers, along with producers from developed countries, are channelling more goods, services and employment to developing countries and emerging economies, where new consumer markets are growing dramatically. Put simply, the wealth of nations no longer primarily depends on Western consumption.

Thus, in the socio-economic realm, we find a clear parallel to the architectural shift I suggested is taking place in Asia–Pacific geopolitics. The result of the deeper economic power diffusion globally is, once again: more actors, more factors and more vectors. But unlike great power politics, in the economic arena, we also find fewer zero-sum games and a marked decline in binaries. This is especially so from the point of view of 'the rest'. Consider, for example, the proliferation of free trade agreements in the Indo-Asia–Pacific regions. Despite the popular perception that regional economies have had to choose between the United States-led TPP and a China-dominated Regional Comprehensive Economic Partnership (RCEP), the reality is that when the revised Comprehensive and Progressive Agreement for TPP came into effect at the end of 2018 without the United States, at least seven member states chose to be simultaneously part of RCEP.[6] The logic behind having a foot in both camps, as expressed by a prominent Singaporean diplomat, emphasises the positive-sum potential of the current choices, while hedging against uncertainties down the line:

> international relations are not sporting events in which a 'win' for one side is necessarily a 'loss' for the other. China's rise is not America's decline except relatively. In absolute terms, both will remain substantial powers. Neither is without weakness. Neither's future development is going to be described by a straight line trajectory either up or down .... (Kausikan, 2018)

Other regional countries may find it harder to abandon the binary thinking which served them well in the past. In recent years, for example, Australia has struggled between its dedicated security and identity ties with the United States and its growing economic dependence on China. As one leading politician put it though, the national discourse needs to go beyond treating security and economics as 'two disconnected camps', because they are now uncomfortably intertwined:

> [While] it is absolutely right that the defence, intelligence and security community be on the lookout for threats to Australia's sovereignty and well-being ... It's also [our] business ... to build Australia's economic strength, which is a key contributor to our national security. This means maintaining and expanding a robust trade and investment relationship with China .... (Wong, 2017)

---

[6] Australia, Brunei, Japan, Malaysia, New Zealand, Singapore and Vietnam.

THE ECONOMIC–SECURITY NEXUS

Thus far, I have concentrated on showing that the Asia–Pacific's age of uncertainty stems from the cross currents of rapid change in the geopolitical and socio-economic realms in recent decades. This creates a particular problem: how ought we—scholars and policymakers—usefully connect the security and economic parts of the story? In this final section, I identify three problematic intersections of economics and security that are most salient for our region, to highlight key challenges of the economic–security nexus that urgently need to be understood and managed during the ongoing transition.

The Economic Foundations of Hegemony

There is a myth that Australia can have the United States as a security provider on the one hand and China as an economic powerhouse on the other, in a cosy binary arrangement that will continue to fuel the Asia–Pacific's security and prosperity. Unfortunately, the post-war United States-led international order was built on the *nexus* between economics and security. The United States sustained the following bargain with its allies and supporter states: it provided access to its market and security guarantees, in exchange for supporter states' political, security and economic co-operation, including undervaluing their currencies and buying US debt. The latter facilitated massive US spending, including state spending on US military projection in East Asia. In economic terms, the United States could sustain massive deficits because its supporter states around the world accumulated surpluses. When China joined the capitalist world economy, it quickly became one of the most conspicuous United States-supporter countries, overtaking even Germany and Japan to hold the largest foreign government share of US debt in 2016. This is what we mean when we say that China's contemporary resurgence occurred within the US hegemonic order and was aided by the United States.

However, China's rise also occurred just as the US hegemonic bargain was proving itself unsustainable, and significantly exacerbated the attendant systemic problems. The United States-centric model of running the global economy had already been dealt a severe blow by the Asian Financial Crisis of 1997–1998, and the 2007–2008 GFC vividly brought the

point home to US markets and consumers, reinforcing the global redistribution of economic power away from North America and Western
Europe (see Kirshner, 2014). After the GFC, the surplus–deficit bargain
unravelled, as US leaders confronted the necessity of reducing US
domestic consumption and borrowing (Mastanduno, 2014). Since then,
the previous, Cold War era belief that the United States should maintain
an asymmetrically open economy because this would facilitate the strategic
purpose of strengthening its allies and supporter states has been increasing
questioned. Especially under the Trump Administration, the mantra now
is for 'more equal' economic relations and mutual access to goods, investment and ownership and 'stricter reciprocity', such that the United States
would 'treat other countries in the same way that they treat us' (see
Harris, 2017; Diamond & Schell, 2019). For its part, China—along with
other surplus countries such as Japan—has grown increasingly concerned
about its own domestic monetary stability, and potential entrapment and
losses in financing too much US debt (see Goh, 2019, pp. 23–25). Thus,
even as Washington becomes less tolerant of China's export-led growth
strategy, China has focussed on developing its own domestic consumer
market, diversifying its foreign reserves away from the US dollar and
internationalising its own currency.

The point here is that the United States–China trade war is but one
manifestation of a systemic crisis: the post-war US economic–security
bargain is broken, and we are all in the midst of groping towards a new
bargain. During this messy and uncertain transition, Asia–Pacific states
not only have to consider how to navigate the potential decoupling of
the US and Chinese economies; they also have to exert all domestic political and economic levers and regional institutional avenues in the process
of finding their place in this new global economic restructuring. It was
against this context that, at a critical juncture in the TPP negotiations in
mid-2015, Singapore's foreign minister bluntly reminded a Washington
audience that 'trade is strategy' and that 'if you don't do this deal, what
are your levers of power? … your only lever to shape the architecture,
to influence events, [will be] the Seventh Fleet and that's not the lever
you want to use' (Au-Yong, 2015). The Singaporean Government at the
time evidently considered the TPP a crucial instrument in negotiating a
new economic–security bargain that would keep the United States as a
vital player in the region. In this ongoing struggle, we can expect most
East Asian economies to pay serious attention to sharpening the tools of
industrial policy—making more effective state intervention in economic

and development policies (see e.g. Yeung, 2016)—and exploiting opportunities afforded by the 4IR to mitigate economic vulnerabilities and to shape comparative advantages.[7]

China's 'Connectivity Power'

In the midst of the dissolving hegemonic bargain, China under President Xi has invested heavily in building 'connectivity power', the influence a central government accrues through infrastructure projects that connect its domestic periphery and neighbouring states to the central core economy (Goh & Reilly, 2017). Together with the state-led push for Chinese enterprises and regions to increase their mutual investment with global capital, the numerous trans-regional projects gathered under the BRI umbrella highlight this. Since 2014, when the rest of the world began to take notice, China's growing connectivity power has had two major effects at the nexus of economics and security.

First, it is giving more flesh to the eastwards shift in the centre of global economic activity. China's investments in hard and soft infrastructure are capping the reorientation of its surrounding regions that had been under way as many of its neighbours took advantage of the past 30 years of China's rapid economic growth. But the BRI's main political effect is to elevate many regional peripheries, and to create alternative nodes and relationships within the system that were not there before. In Central, South and Southeast Asia, BRI projects emphasise many developing countries and peripheral states that have tended to be neglected, taken for granted or treated as mere arenas by other major powers. Stressing the developmental imperative that is deeply shared among these postcolonial developing countries, Beijing also emphasises how security is ultimately

---

[7] Key examples are found in north-east Asia: in 2016 the Abe Government launched the Japan Revitalization Strategy, stressing the need to harness 4IR technology to create a 'revolution in productivity' that would compensate for Japan's limited workforce, but also to develop new social and industrial structures in response to the 4IR (METI, 2016). South Korea, which has often led the pack in technological innovation, has a Presidential Committee on 4IR, which advocates the introduction of crypto-products into the financial system and recommends that Seoul should lead in developing international regulations for holding and exchanging crypto-assets (Yoon, 2020). Since 2016, the Taiwanese Government has introduced a raft of policies and incentives to stimulate the next generation of 'intelligent manufacturing' to help maintain the competitive edge for the island's vital electronics manufacturing industry (O'Meara, 2020).

assured by economic growth and the mutual benefits of regional development. While they may be sceptical of the relative distribution of benefits, many of these elites welcome Beijing's emphasis on political non-interference, bilateralism and statist forms of economic regulation, which help to safeguard their regime security (Goh, 2019). Critics of the BRI highlight valid sustainability concerns surrounding many projects, but they tend to miss the normative convergence between economic deals and regime security. There is also often the flawed assumption that these peripheries previously enjoyed an ideal, sustainable model of development that China's practices derailed.

Second, China's connectivity power vividly reminds us of some modes of international power that the Asia–Pacific may have forgotten during the interregnum of an offshore hegemon. Networks are, of course, channels of influence. As the stock of physical infrastructure—roads, railways, pipelines, electricity grids—come into use, these networks will create flows of goods, currency, investment, labour, energy resources, technology, intellectual property and so on. These are concrete means of intensifying interdependence with China, which as a primary consumer market wields enormous nodal structural power. Connectivity facilitates power projection for the entity that becomes the hub at the centre of the networks thus created, reinforcing the trend of 'all roads leading to China'. Existing economic ties with China have already caused many Asian states to pre-empt Chinese preferences when they make certain political choices, such as voting in the United Nations (e.g. see Foot & Inboden, 2016). The growing global shifts in trade, investment and energy patterns across the BRI regional imaginary will oblige more countries and corporations to take China's interests into account systematically in their policies, activities and planning. This is not new; Albert Hirschman's (1945, p. 29) classic study of German trade strategy in the interwar period alluded to how business interests profiting from relations with a foreign power would, in domestic politics, 'exert a powerful influence in favor of a "friendly" attitude toward the state to the imports of which they owe their interests'. The point is, these modes of influence do not require coercion; they operate through the reshaping of national interests as economic and thus political interdependence grows with China.

Moreover, China's growing role as a global node of production, investment and consumption brings with it governance requirements: whether we like it or not, Beijing is regulating the connectivity it is building, making rules and setting standards across the many domains implicated in the BRI and globalising its capital markets. These regulatory arenas include the terms of trade, legal frameworks, transport and communication, as well as new areas such as AI and other elements of 4IR development and usage. These areas of governance are not just regional; many have implications for evolving global practices and agreements. By growing its governance footprint, China is also developing its international role as a public goods provider. While this process will be difficult and controversial, it may prove to be vital to China becoming an indispensable global power at a time when the United States-led international order is challenged externally and undermined internally.

Globalisation's Discontents

The major factor undermining the post-war United States-led international order also resides at the nexus of security and economics. This is the threat posed from within, by those who feel alienated, dispossessed or marginalised by globalisation, and who also live in political systems that afford them opportunities to express their discontents and to generate resistance. There is a significant literature on a series of 'development traps' that poor countries are prone to, whether as a result of endemic conflict, natural resource endowments or weak governance (e.g. Collier, 2007; Easterly, 2006). All these pitfalls remain. But my concern here is with what I call the 'left-behind' trap in the developed and emerging economies. In his 2001 book, entitled *Globalization and Its Discontents*, Joseph Stiglitz memorably highlighted how globalisation exacerbated gross inequalities of income and production between the richest and poorest countries. By 2018, Stiglitz had updated his work to include analysis of how the systemic unfairness of globalisation had also 'doubled back to savage the middle classes in the very countries (the United States and western European states) who wrote the system's rules in the first place' (Hockenos, 2018). The downside of the shift and diffusion of global economic power over the past 30 years of globalisation is that the Western and developed world lost some of their economic share. As Stiglitz pointed out, significant proportions of middle- and lower-income wage earners in the most advanced industrial countries are now also the losers of globalisation, especially since the GFC. Depressed wages, low employment and skills training opportunities and regressive prospects for social mobility within developed economies have in turn fuelled the insurgencies of our time.

Trump's election, Brexit, and the rise of the European far right reflect what Pankaj Mishra (2017) calls an 'age of anger' on the part of those left behind—mainly disenchanted young men who fail to grasp the promised fruits of modernity—and seething with existential resentment. Looking back, the 11 September 2001 terrorist attacks in the United States and subsequent counterterrorism campaigns in Asia, the Middle East and Africa did alert many of us to the potential dire consequences of such existential resentment. Fuelled by partisan Western policies in the Middle East and elsewhere, transnational terrorism is a prominent consequence of uneven globalisation—and those both alienated by its liberal character and empowered by its instruments. In response, we witnessed the rise of the national security state and the securitisation of multiple aspects of surveillance and policing in national and foreign policy, creating a highly securitised 'ambient' atmosphere. On reflection, the fundamental attributes of extreme globalisation were already evident in the early 2000s: extreme interdependence and sensitivity, and enhanced polarisation. But now that we are grappling also with the uncertainties of a power transition, we may expect that the interaction between old geopolitical problems and new globalisation will generate complex outcomes that often include unintended consequences.

Looking across the Asia–Pacific, we may face a confluence of development traps. In some of the currently fastest growing economies in the Asia–Pacific, the left-behind trap may eventuate sooner than we expect, exacerbated by the much-discussed 'middle income trap'—industrialising countries that are unable to retain competitiveness because they cannot transition from resource-based growth to productivity-driven growth. While there is no easy solution, it is clear that the intertwining of economic and security concerns means that the relatively weak and marginal are nevertheless important. There is a Neapolitan saying to the effect that these three are powerful: the Pope, the King and the one who has nothing (in colloquial Italian: *tre sono i potenti: il Papa, il Re, e chi non ha niente*). Whether it is slum dwellers during a pandemic, or potential extremists among those left behind by globalisation, those who have nothing can still create disproportionate system effects. Development thus becomes about distributing globalisation's benefits and managing its discontents, for which a holistic notion of security is essential.

CONCLUSION

In mid-2017, when I gave the first version of a lecture on this topic, I assured an audience of defence policymakers that 'for now, it is not yet a brave, or scary, or completely new world: we are facing mainly an intensification of key existing tensions that generate new and often unexpected challenges. But we should expect accelerated innovation and exaggerated impacts not too far down the line'. In mid-2020, I feel that we are now some way down that line.

I am sure that the surface of debate will continue to focus for a while on questions of whether we are in a new United States–China Cold War, or whether and how to contain or 'stand up to' China. On this issue, I concur with Joseph Nye's (2019) observation that,

> with less preponderance and a more complex world, American exceptionalism in terms of its economic and military power should focus on sharing the provision of global public goods, particularly those that require 'power with' others … but America's place in that world may be threatened more by the rise of populist politics at home than the rise of other powers abroad.

At the same time, I am even more convinced that today, a wider range of states and actors than before can exercise real agency in making choices that can shape this region. I hope that the big-picture survey I have provided here helps to convey a wider sense of possibilities to our present and future strategic leaders too.

Returning to where we began, Hobsbawm's thesis that the long nineteenth century was shaped by twin political and economic revolutions seems remarkably relevant as we hang off the precipice of system change in the Asia–Pacific. I wonder about the emergent effects of the multiple revolutions that will determine the outcome of our own age of uncertainty.

REFERENCES

Anderson, B. (1983). *Imagined communities: Reflections on the origin and spread of nationalism*. Verso.

Arase, D. (2019). *Japan's strategic balancing act in Southeast Asia*. ISEAS Perspective No. 94. ISEAS-Yusof Ishak Institute. https://www.iseas.edu.sg/images/pdf/ISEAS_Perspective_2019_94.pdf. Accessed 1 May 2020.

Au-Yong, J. (2015, June 17). Shanmugam: US risks losing credibility in Asia. *The Straits Times*. https://www.straitstimes.com/singapore/shanmugam-us-risks-losing-credibility-in-asia. Accessed 1 May 2020.

Bennis, W., & Nanus, B. (1985). *Leaders: The strategies for taking charge*. Harper & Row.

Berger, D. H. (2019). *Commandant's planning guidance: 38th commandant of the [US] Marine Corps*. Misc. Publications. Marine Corps Publications Electronic Library. https://www.hqmc.marines.mil/Portals/142/Docs/%203 8th%20Commandant%27s%20Planning%20Guidance_2019.pdf?ver=2019-07-16-200152-700. Accessed 1 May 2020.

Buchan, P. G., & Rimland, B. (2020). *Defining the diamond: The past, present, and future of the quadrilateral security dialogue*. CSIS Briefs March 2020. The Center for Strategic and International Studies. https://www.csis.org/analysis/defining-diamond-past-present-and-future-quadrilateral-security-dialogue. Accessed 1 May 2020.

Buzan, B., & Goh, E. (2020). *Rethinking Sino-Japanese alienation: History problems and historical opportunities*. Oxford University Press.

Clark, I. (2011). *Hegemony in international society*. Oxford University Press.

Collier, P. (2007). *The bottom billion: Why the poorest countries are failing and what can be done about it*. Oxford University Press.

Diamond, L., & Schell, O. (Eds.). (2019). *China's influence and American interests: Promoting constructive vigilance*. Report of the working group on Chinese influence activities in the United States. Hoover Institution Press. https://www.hoover.org/sites/default/files/research/docs/diamond-schell_corrected-april2020finalfile.pdf. Accessed 1 May 2020.

Dian, M., & Meijer, H. (2020). Networking hegemony: Alliance dynamics in East Asia. *International Politics, 57*, 131–149.

Dirlik, A. (1992). The Asia-Pacific idea: Reality and representation in the invention of a regional structure. *Journal of World History, 3*(1), 55–79.

Dobbs, R., Remes, J., Manyika, J., Roxburgh, C., Smit, S., & Schaer, F. (2012). *Cities and the rise of the consuming class*. Report. McKinsey Global Institute. https://www.mckinsey.com/featured-insights/urbanization/urban-world-cities-and-the-rise-of-the-consuming-class. Accessed 1 May 2020.

Easley, L. E., & Kim, S. Y. (2019). New North-Southeast Asia security links: Defending, recentering, and extending regional order. *Australian Journal of Politics & History, 65*(3), 377–394.

Easterly, W. (2006). *The white man's burden: Why the West's efforts to aid the rest have done so much ill and so little good*. Penguin.

Foot, R., & Inboden, R. S. (2016). China's influence on Asian states during the creation of the UN Human Rights Council: 2005–2007. In E. Goh (Ed.), *Rising China's influence in developing Asia* (pp. 237–258). Oxford University Press.

Gehrke, J. (2019, April 30). State Department preparing for clash of civilizations with China. *Washington Examiner*. https://www.washingtonexaminer.com/policy/defense-national-security/state-department-preparing-for-clash-of-civilizations-with-china. Accessed 1 May 2020.

Goh, E. (2013). *The struggle for order: Hegemony, hierarchy, and transition in post-Cold War East Asia*. Oxford University Press.

Goh, E. (2019). Contesting hegemonic order: China in East Asia. *Security Studies, 28*(3), 614–644.

Goh, E., & Prantl, J. (2017). Why strategic diplomacy matters for Southeast Asia. *East Asia Forum Quarterly, 9*(2), 36–39.

Goh, E., & Prantl, J. (2020). *Covid-19 is exposing the complexity of connectivity*. EAF special feature series. East Asia Forum. https://www.eastasiaforum.org/2020/04/08/covid-19-is-exposing-the-complexity-of-connectivity. Accessed 1 May 2020.

Goh, E., & Prantl, J. (Eds.). (2016). Strategic diplomacy in Northeast Asia. *Global Asia, 11*(4), 1–64.

Goh, E., & Reilly, J. (2017, October–December). The power of connectivity: China's Belt & Road Initiative. *East Asia Forum Quarterly*, 33–34.

Harris, J. M. (2017). *Writing new rules for the U.S.–China investment relationship* (Discussion paper). Council on Foreign Relations. https://www.cfr.org/sites/default/files/report_pdf/Discussion_Paper_Harris_China_OR.pdf. Accessed 1 May 2020.

Hirschman, A. (1945). *National power and the structure of foreign trade*. University of California Press.

Hobsbawm, E. (1994). *The age of extremes: The short twentieth century, 1914–1991*. Penguin.

Hobsbawm, E. (1962). *The age of revolution: Europe 1789–1848*. Weidenfeld & Nicolson.

Hobsbawm, E. (1975). *The age of capital: 1848–1875*. Weidenfeld & Nicolson.

Hobsbawm, E. (1987). *The age of empire: 1875–1914*. Weidenfeld & Nicolson.

Hockenos, P. (2018). *Globalisation and its discontents revisited*. Book reviews. International Politics and Society. https://www.ips-journal.eu/book-reviews/article/show/globalization-and-its-discontents-revisited-2708. Accessed 1 May 2020.

Kausikan, B. (2018). *Thinking about geopolitics in East Asia*. Keynote address to the RAAF Air Power Conference. Air Power Development Centre. https://www.youtube.com/watch?v=rszViHCPY7c. Accessed 1 May 2020.

Kharas, H. (2017). *The unprecedented expansion of the global middle class: An update* (Global Economy & Development Working Paper 100). Brookings Institution. https://www.brookings.edu/wp-content/uploads/2017/02/global_20170228_global-middle-class.pdf. Accessed 1 May 2020.

Kirshner, J. (2014). *American power after the global financial crisis.* Cornell University Press.

Koga, K. (2020). Japan's 'Indo-Pacific' question: Countering China or shaping a new regional order? *International Affairs, 96*(1), 49–73.

Lee, A. (2018, October 10). China won't back down in trade war with US: Commerce Minister. *South China Morning Post.* https://www.scmp.com/economy/china-economy/article/2167715/china-wont-back-down-trade-war-us-commerce-minister. Accessed 1 May 2020.

Mastanduno, M. (2014). Order and change in world politics: The financial crisis and the breakdown of the US-China grand bargain. In G. J. Ikenberry (Ed.), *Power, order and change in world politics* (pp. 162–191). Cambridge University Press.

McMaster, H. R. (2020). How China sees the world and how we should see China. *The Atlantic.* https://www.theatlantic.com/magazine/archive/2020/05/mcmaster-china-strategy/609088. Accessed 1 May 2020.

Medcalf, R. (2020). *Contest for the Indo-Pacific: Why China won't map the future.* La Trobe University Press.

METI [Ministry of Economy, Trade and Industry, Japan]. (2016). *Vision of new industrial structure.* Interim report. Japan's Ministry of Economy, Trade, and Industry. https://www.meti.go.jp/english/policy/economy/industrial_council/pdf/innovation160427a.pdf. Accessed 1 May 2020.

Mishra, P. (2017). *Age of anger: A history of the present.* Macmillan.

Mitchell, M. (2009). *Complexity: A guided tour.* Oxford University Press.

Nye, J. S. (2019, January). The rise and fall of American hegemony from Wilson to Trump. *International Affairs, 95*(1), 63–80.

O'Meara, S. (2020). From plastic toys to Industry 4.0: How Taiwan is using science to upgrade its manufacturing. Briefing. *Nature.* https://www.nature.com/articles/d41586-020-00060-1. Accessed 1 May 2020.

Quah, D. (2011). The global economy's shifting centre of gravity. *Global Policy, 2*(1), 3–9.

Schwab, K. (2016). *The fourth industrial revolution.* World Economic Forum.

Sim, W. (2019, June 27). Japan and China vow to be 'eternal neighbours' at Abe–Xi summit meeting in Osaka. *The Straits Times.* https://www.straitstimes.com/asia/east-asia/japan-and-china-vow-to-be-eternal-neighbours-at-xi-abe-summit-meeting-in-osaka. Accessed 1 May 2020.

Stiglitz, J. (2002). *Globalization and its discontents.* W.W. Norton.

Stiglitz, J. (2018). *Globalisation and its discontents revisited: Anti-globalisation in the era of Trump.* W.W. Norton.

Tamaki, N. (forthcoming). Japan's quest for a rules-based international order: The Japan–US alliance and the decline of US liberal hegemony. *Contemporary Politics.*

Tartar, A., & Sam, C. (2019). *How the rise of developing countries has disrupted global trade.* Bloomberg New Economy Report. https://www.bloomberg.com/graphics/2019-bloomberg-new-economy/global-trade-developing-nations. Accessed 1 May 2020.

Tellis, A. J., Szalwinski, A., & Wills, M. (Ed.). (2020). *Strategic Asia 2020: U.S.–China competition for global influence.* National Bureau of Asian Research.

The White House. (2020, May 20). *US strategic approach to the people's Republic of China.* https://trumpwhitehouse.archives.gov/articles/united-states-strategic-approach-to-the-peoples-republic-of-china/. Accessed 10 June 2020.

UNDP [United Nations Development Programme]. (2013). *Human Development Report 2013.* Human Development Reports. United Nations Development Program. http://hdr.undp.org/sites/default/files/reports/14/hdr2013_en_complete.pdf. Accessed 1 May 2020.

Wang, J. S. (2020). *Xinguan yiqing xia de zhongmei guanxi* [China–US relations amid the Covid-19 pandemic]. Speech. National School of Development of Peking University. https://www.nsd.pku.edu.cn/sylm/gd/501976.htm. Accessed 1 May 2020.

Wong, P. (2017). *A new phase in Australia's relations with China.* Keynote speech to AIIA National Conference. The Australian Institute of International Affairs. http://www.internationalaffairs.org.au/news-item/aiia-national-conference-2019-senator-penny-wongs-keynote-speech. Accessed 1 May 2020.

Ye, M. (2020). *The Belt Road and beyond: State-mobilized globalization in China, 1998–2018.* Cambridge University Press.

Yeung, H. W. (2016). *Strategic coupling: East Asian industrial transformation in the new global economy history.* Cornell University Press.

Yoon, Y. S. (2020, January 6). Korea needs to allow financial companies to release cryptocurrency-related products, a presidential commission says. *Business Korea.* http://www.businesskorea.co.kr/news/articleView.html?idxno=39847. Accessed 1 May 2020.

Zhao, M. H. (2019). Is a new Cold War inevitable? Chinese perspectives on US–China strategic competition. *The Chinese Journal of International Politics, 12*(3), 371–394.

Zhou, X. (2019, May 21). Xi Jinping calls for 'new Long March' in dramatic sign that China is preparing for protracted trade war. *South China Morning Post.* https://www.scmp.com/economy/china-economy/article/3011186/xi-jinping-calls-new-long-march-dramatic-sign-china-preparing. Accessed 1 May 2020.

Economic Diplomacy and Diplomatic Economists in the Asia–Pacific

Alan Bollard

INTERNATIONAL ECONOMIC DIPLOMACY

This chapter looks at developments in international economic diplomacy in the Asia–Pacific, and argues that in recent years there has been a switch from economic to non-economic objectives, while still using economic policies, though more largely negative sanctioning tools. By the term *international economic diplomacy* we mean international discussions, strategy and negotiation that takes place both unilaterally and multilaterally, as part of both informal and formal multilateral agreements, typically with the aim of increasing economic welfare, which could include trade growth, economic growth, or other measures of well-being. Traditionally this has been used to promote economic integration, mainly using economic instruments, which could include tariffs, quotas and other border measures, or multilateral agreements such as free trade agreements, or other preferential arrangements, or unilateral moves like development aid, or negative reactive instruments such as sanctions and embargoes.

A. Bollard (✉)
Victoria University of Wellington, Wellington, New Zealand

R. Patman et al. (eds.), *From Asia-Pacific to Indo-Pacific*, Global Political
Transitions, https://doi.org/10.1007/978-981-16-7007-7_3

53

Before the Second World War the Western world went through cycles of globalisation driven by economic opportunities, and cycles of de-globalisation, mainly for domestic political or security reasons. In the period after 1945 there was a huge expansion in economic globalisation. During that time economic diplomacy and geopolitical diplomacy were often in lockstep, and economists were in the ascendency. Over the last decade this has been changing. Economic diplomacy and geopolitical diplomacy are heading in different directions, causing big challenges. Economic globalisation is being challenged in complex ways, most recently in the COVID-19 crisis. Economic tools are being used for non-economic objectives. Many of these tools are non-traditional ones, and are being used for sanctioning purposes.

INTERNATIONAL ECONOMIC THEORY

International economic policy has a long history of debate. This was most clearly seen in European economies as their trading patterns became increasingly globalised with the spread of colonisation and the subsequent shipments of commodities to Europe. The arguments were encapsulated in the debate on the Corn Laws in nineteenth-century Britain, where pressure from local farmers led to the imposition of high tariffs on imported grain. The proponents of such mercantilism argued that the benefits of these policies went beyond the vested interests of local producers, claiming that a country could become wealthier by imposing barriers to foreign imports through the value added in local production, or by the revenue earned from tariffs.

In contrast to this unilateralist approach, Adam Smith in *The Wealth of Nations* pointed to the advantages of increasing international trade. He was followed by David Ricardo, who in *On the Principles of Economy and Taxation* proposed the theory of comparative advantage. This showed that each country should specialise in that production where it held a relative competitive advantage, and that by doing this, both countries involved in trade could expect to benefit, a win–win outcome. This thinking held sway in the second half of the nineteenth century when colonial exploitation, naval advances and the industrial revolution led to a big increase in trade and investment by dominant European countries. The growth in internationalisation and wealth also brought increasing competition and the militarisation of European powers that collapsed into the First World War. The complicated aftermath of the war, the post-war imperial breakups, the volatility and inflation of the 1920s, the spread of Marxism-Leninism, the British Imperial Preference scheme, US isolationism, the 1930s Depression and restrictions on arms-related exports, all drove economic nationalism and a reduction in world trade. This lasted until the massive reflation through armaments production in the Second World War.

After the war, the geopolitical balance of the world changed, with the growth of two antagonistic political and economic blocs, the phenomenon which we now call the Cold War. It had a stark ideological and geographical division: the Soviet bloc in Eastern Europe driven by Marxist-Leninist ideology and centrally planned economies were positioned against the United States, Western Europe and their allies with largely democratic governments and market-driven economies. This political division was matched by different economic systems, different economic objectives and different economic instruments. The United States rebuilt their consumer economy, while also funding the Marshall Plan which offered significant aid to reconstruct Western Europe and rebuild Western-bloc trade, under the security umbrella of the North Atlantic Treaty Organization (NATO). The Soviets responded with their focus on heavy industry and the Council for Mutual Economic Assistance (Comecon) trading bloc, with their defence oriented around the Warsaw Pact.

The United States-led coalition constructed a new set of economic rules of the game. These were based on the 1944 Bretton Woods negotiations which established the International Monetary Fund and World Bank, followed in 1947 by the General Agreement on Tariffs and Trade (GATT), which developed into the World Trade Organization (WTO). Financial standards were regulated through the Bank for International Settlements and related bodies, overseen by G20 organisations. International payments were controlled through the SWIFT agreement. The United States and its European allies tightly controlled these institutions and for many years resisted the attempts of others to dilute them (e.g. G77 through the UN General Assembly, the Non-Aligned Movement through the United Nations Conference on Trade and Development (UNCTAD).

With the establishment of the Organisation for Economic Co-operation and Development (OECD) in Paris, the preferred recipe for prosperity in the Western alliance became clearly articulated: stabilising monetary and fiscal policy, market-driven allocations, defined property rights, limited government intervention in the case of market failure, the state providing a social safety net, and open to international trading conditions. This recipe delivered broad growth for Western trading partners for some decades, and at times spectacular growth for some developing economies under the US security umbrella.

Nevertheless there were some severe tension points in this arrangement: in the 1970s such as the pressures of the Vietnam War, the first Organisation of the Petroleum Exporting Countries (OPEC) crisis, significant inflation, and tensions among the Association of Southeast Asian Nations (ASEAN) countries; in the early 1980s pressures from fast East Asian growth and an uncompetitive US dollar led to the Plaza Accord and voluntary export restraints; and in the early 1990s the end of the Cold War, the entry of the Communist bloc into the world trading system, and China's entry to the WTO in 2001 helped globalise the labour force. Over this period, trade and investment patterns changed significantly, but United States-led geopolitical and economic patterns moved together and delivered clear growth dividends, especially in the Asia–Pacific. It was a system known as the Washington Consensus.

The post-war period saw an increase in the role of economists in policy and diplomacy as governments grew bigger. Foreign affairs and trade ministries recruited for economic skills and established economic divisions. In some countries economists took on the leading role as international trade negotiators and as designers of appropriate domestic policy. After the war there were many domestic arguments among economists as Keynesians clashed with Monetarists. But from an international policy viewpoint, there was broad agreement: policies in line with the Washington Consensus meant exports should follow comparative advantage and earn producer revenue, while imports should provide domestic competition and increase consumer welfare. This was considered to be a win–win situation.

Having enjoyed strong growth in the 1950s and 1960s, the New Zealand economy slowed in the 1970s as the UK market became more restrictive with British entry into the European Economic Community (EEC). In the 1980s New Zealand reviewed the Washington Consensus and decided its best prospects were as a rule-abiding internationalist, with unilateral liberalisation along GATT/OECD principles, an approach driven by economists, but supported at the time by many officials, businesspeople, politicians, farmers and unionists alike.

Across the region some of these policies (as in New Zealand) were entered into unilaterally. But there was also much regional and multilateral effort devoted to liberalising trading arrangements and other flows across borders, including the movement of capital. Initially agreements were modest and subregional in scope. Gradually they expanded their product and geographical coverage, and became more liberal and WTO-compliant in approach. Guidance for these developments came from the Asia–Pacific Economic Cooperation (APEC) body, itself a product of the post-Cold War world. It has promoted best practice arrangements in free and open trade and inclusive growth, largely assuming an economically liberal approach. As a consequence, there are now over 150 regional trading arrangements under way in the Asia–Pacific region. Some of these are mega-arrangements: the United States–Mexico–Canada Agreement in North America, the Comprehensive and Progressive Agreement for Trans-Pacific Partnership (CPTPP) in the Pacific Rim, the Pacific Alliance in Pacific Latin America, and the ASEAN Economic Community now expanding to the Regional Comprehensive Economic Partnership for East Asia (RCEP).

In the years leading up to the Global Financial Crisis (GFC), the drivers of internationalisation were changing. The entry of Chinese labour into world production had a major impact, with big growth in production, especially in East Asia. In addition, the development of sophisticated supply chains, strong economic growth, increasing debt on balance sheets, overheating economies from inflation, a big increase in home ownership, and growth in financial balance sheets and the role of banks, all had their effects. The GFC exposed the weaknesses and under-regulation of this over-leveraged system, with a major cross-Atlantic banking crisis that in turn sparked conventional and unconventional monetary and fiscal interventions, and resulted in slowing growth, exposing imbalances across the developed world. The financial crisis then morphed into a major economic recession with damage to homeowners in the United States, jobseekers in Europe and financial balance sheets across the world. These cyclical changes also masked some important structural developments that were under way, that have since resulted in a wave of anti-globalisation, and that have ultimately broken the post-war consensus which linked economic advancement and geopolitical security.

STRUCTURAL CHANGES AND THEIR IMPLICATIONS

Changing Trade Patterns

Until the last decade, merchandise trade growth has been the major driver of globalisation and the major driver of economic growth in the Asia–Pacific region. Resources from southern countries, the build-up of product components through ASEAN supply chains, financed by Japanese and US investment, assembled in China, consumed in North America—this was a model that produced a revolution in competitive production that helped to link the region together economically and also improve the lot of producers and consumers alike. In the period 1990–2015 a billion people were able to move from poverty towards middle income in the East Asia–Pacific region (ourworldindata.org/extreme-poverty).

Since the GFC, traditional merchandise trade growth has slowed substantially. Partly this is due to slower regional economies. Partly it is accounted for by China supplanting regional supply chains with domestic sourcing, moving production from the eastern coast to its lower-cost inland provinces as it has felt the winds of competition from cheaper South Asian and Southeast Asian producers. While Asia–Pacific merchandise trade growth has been slowing, there has been a big increase in services trade with the rise of digital technologies. More products are now ordered electronically, manufactured digitally and sometimes delivered remotely as well. China has been responsible for a huge growth in regional trade. Yet China's own economic position has not been easy—it has had to deal with a massive hangover following its US$1 trillion reflation at the time of the GFC, its growth rate has fallen, its corporates have indebted balance sheets, the country is ageing and its trading surplus is evaporating.

Socio-Economic and Demographic Change

When APEC was founded in 1989, the Asia–Pacific region was on balance rural, village-based, poor with pockets of the middle class and wealth, with a high degree of subsistence living and dependence on the family for financial support. Today the region is mainly urbanised, and much of this population lives in fast-growing megacities. The region is now mainly middle-income, with pockets of poverty and pockets of wealth. In addition, the growing middle-aged population is driving significant social change through the households of the region. People, especially women, are more likely to be tertiary-educated. They are more likely to have left their extended families and be living in new, smaller units on their own or in nuclear families, sometimes distant from their parents. East Asia has seen the highest demographic turbulence. Family sizes are smaller than ever, with fertility rates dropping and life expectancy rising. Countries like South Korea, Taiwan and Singapore have the lowest fertility rates in the world, Japan has the oldest population (second only to Monaco) and China has one of the lowest population growth rates. The younger millennials have higher incomes, are more likely to spend on consumption, including higher-priced, higher-quality imported products and services such as education, health or travel. Purchasing an apartment has become the signal aspiration for many, and such apartments dominate household balance sheets. These younger urban middle-class populations are also more demanding of new social and environmental services from government.

Another major demographic change is looming as a result of the longer life expectancies now found in the West and soon to follow in developing economies. In principle, older people in these countries might now routinely anticipate retirement periods of up to 30 years or more. Countries differ in their public and private provisions for retirement, but none appears to be in a comfortable position to fund this extended longevity. A corollary is that the legal age of retirement should lengthen with improving health. This is starting to happen, but is slowed by social acceptance, employer–employee attitudes and legal restrictions. Care of the elderly was traditionally the responsibility of extended families in lower-income Confucian, Islamic and Catholic societies. Nuclear family arrangements do not handle such support easily, and there is a looming problem with growing dependency ratios—there are many more elderly people, with fewer young to support them socially and financially.

Working-age populations (as traditionally defined) have now declined in developed economies and peaked in the Asia–Pacific. The strong economic growth of previous decades is partly due to the demographic dividend: the impact of half a billion additional workers in the two decades to 2014. In contrast, the next decade will bring a reduction in the region's labour force (tradingeconomics.com). This ageing and declining workforce impacts production capabilities at a time when advancing technology and automation are placing new demands on skills. Educating younger populations for a technologically disruptive world where many traditional job types are disappearing is complex. But it also needs to be handled alongside the reskilling of older workers who present different learning challenges altogether.

Technology

The evidence is mixed, but the region appears to be entering another period of technological disruption, popularly known as Industrial Revolution 4.0. It has been particularly difficult to assess the overall implications of this on jobs, on industries and on economic competitiveness. Digital technologies, artificial intelligence, machine learning, robotics and electronic commerce are combining to produce fundamentally different ways of meeting demand across a range of traditional industries as fundamental as car production, banking, communications and education. In some cases, such as the Uber and self-driving car revolution, digital technologies look like providing improved service with far less capital equipment required. In many cases, balance sheets are being reconstructed with less plant and equipment, and more value in intangibles such as data, IP and branding. A classic example is the smart phone, where manufacturing accounts for a very small part of final value. There are non-traditional producers, non-traditional technologies and non-traditional methods of production.

It is still too early to generalise about the impact that these changes will have: what will be produced and where, whether traditional-scale economies will persist or break down, and whether the current trend to vertical disintegration through sophisticated supply chains will persist. It is also unclear whether this will pose a relative advantage to more isolated economies like New Zealand, which industries will continue to rely on low costs, and how important access to markets will be. But the disruptions look to be large enough to assume that traditional patterns of international comparative advantage could be rewritten. What is already clear is that digitally enhanced e-commerce is changing trade. In both developed and developing economies a large proportion of consumables are now marketed, searched for, identified, ordered, paid for, tracked and sometimes delivered, electronically, disrupting traditional logistic, wholesale and retail channels and opening up a consumer revolution. In East Asia, particularly in China, most of these transactions are done on handheld smartphone devices and are ubiquitous across the region.

A further dimension to these developments is 'trade tech'. Remote tracking, e-quality certification, digital market platforms, global currencies, trade-related blockchain, e-logistics, machine learning of trade flows, e-trade finance, customer tracking satellites, and new land and ocean fibre networks—all these technologies make it easier and cheaper to locate, control, trade and deliver products. For a remote, biologically resourced country like New Zealand, this looks to have significant implications. For example, rather than shipping frozen meat carcasses, this allows for the transport and control of high-quality chilled cuts with full originating information, directly from farm to restaurant, cutting through many expensive traditional logistical barriers.

This trend has thrown into focus new cyber issues such as security, privacy and conductivity. The privacy problem has revealed significant differences in attitudes to property rights: in simple terms for example, personal data derived from social media is considered to be ultimately owned by consumers in Europe, by producers in the United States, and by the state in China. This has so far made it difficult to harmonise standards, ensure connectivity and move data between regions. In addition, attitudes to the internet differ fundamentally, with countries like China, Indonesia and India looking to separate national networks, and other East Asians like Singapore and Malaysia applying strict usage laws. Concerns about a 'splinternet' are being driven by such barriers.

The advantages of digital connectivity are increasingly being weighed against the risks from cybersecurity. This impacts personal data, company intellectual property and national security issues in complex ways. China's hacking of companies, Russian hacking of government systems and US hacking of what it views as 'rogue' states, is now routine. This is a key for the technologies, because standards and operating conditions for the fifth generation (5G) of wireless communications technologies networks are currently being established. In contrast to previous generations of telecommunications connectivity, 5G represents a major step forward in speed, latency and access and is expected to enable far greater application of the internet of things, with all its implications for remote access, remote control and remote delivery. This has proved a complex background for US and Chinese competing companies, competing technologies and competing standards.

Climate Change

The increasing evidence of climate change looks likely to have major implications on Asia–Pacific production and lifestyles. The impact is complex and uncertain, yet some trends are showing. Large tropical cities are under pressure from rising ambient temperatures, with water supply and flooding problems in large deltas, population displacement and increased pressures on migration. Agriculture is under threat from increased salinity and low-lying rice paddy fields, increased erosion of topsoil and other impacts on agricultural production, with rising temperatures impacting zones of crop production. All regions are being impacted by bush fires in Australia, rising sea levels are severely affecting Pacific islands, pressure from Himalayan ice melt is affecting the major river systems of East, South-East and South Asia, and strong volatility in wind and rainfall is causing coastal damage in North America.

These developments are leading to new pressures on international economic policy: increased pressure to convert fossil fuel usage to renewable energy production, increasing sustainability standards being demanded of traded production, environmental chapters added to trade agreements, pressure to agree reductions in international carbon emissions, and tougher standards on the growing and contentious regional trade in waste products. There are some market-driven developments to address these pressures. Many countries have evolving markets for trading carbon credits. The price of renewables has dropped significantly, and solar, wind and battery technologies are partially substituting for the traditional fossil fuel trade in oil, gas and coal. However, some economists argue that there is a social reluctance to apply potentially effective economic tools to climate change, an approach that could compensate for the major market failures.

Though complex, these climate pressures look likely to impact regional competitiveness in a major way. They are also already arousing significant international tensions with resource pressures and tensions across borders, and the millennial generation is blaming its predecessors for their environmental neglect. Climate change is a classic case of the problem of the commons, with the users of limited environmental resources not paying the full costs, leaving them to accrue to others. There is frustration on the part of developing countries that richer countries have developed off the back of environmental overuse, without paying its full cost, while they will be unable to do the same. The UN Conference of the Parties

(COP) has put this in stark terms. China is now the world's biggest carbon emitter, but understands it has to move to more expensive but lower-emitting energy, transport and industrial technologies. The United States has historically been the world's biggest polluter without directly bearing its full cost. The US administration has worsened these concerns by announcing both its withdrawal and subsequent stated intention to rejoin from the Paris Agreement on climate change mitigation within the space of four years.

Impacts on Economic Diplomacy

All these structural changes have implications for the nature of economic diplomacy. The huge growth in Asia–Pacific trade means it is an obvious target for further liberalisation but also a tool to exert diplomatic leverage. However, in today's trade patterns, action taken on imports of final goods will resonate right through the supply chain, sometimes with unwanted consequences. The growth of services trade and e-commerce rely on different tools (e.g. telecommunications policy). In addition, the growth of millennial middle-class, middle-income populations, who are far more likely to purchase foreign imports, is changing the political dynamics of trade.

China's huge trading growth has meant that the country now holds huge diplomatic power over its trading partners (as opposed to a large country like India whose economic growth is mainly domestic). New US fracking and oil shale technologies are turning that country from the world's biggest energy importer to a self-sufficient one, reducing international trade in oil and making it far less dependent on the Middle East, which has broad diplomatic consequences.

ANTI-GLOBALISATION

The developing economies of Asia–Pacific are mainly looking for continued economic growth through traditional trading patterns. But in developed economies an anti-globalisation agenda is taking root. These structural changes and evolving pressures in the globalisation process have led to significant pushback from some developed economies, where significant parts of the population have blamed globalisation for real and perceived problems that they face. The driving forces have differed among countries. In Great Britain, there has been a reaction against Brussels bureaucracy, in much of Europe a reaction against migrants, in Eastern Europe against Islamic pressures, in Australia against climate activism and Chinese foreign investment, and in Hong Kong against Mainland pressures.

However, it has been anti-globalisation in the United States that has had most domestic and international impact. In contrast to socio-cultural concerns in Europe, US anti-globalisation has been driven by economic concerns. The drivers have been factory closures and job losses in traditional manufacturing industries, static labour incomes, increased inequality and clouded intergenerational prospects, particularly among male blue-collar industrial workers without tertiary education. Most opinion surveys have blamed these developments on cheap foreign competition, especially from China. By contrast, most economic research acknowledges that this has been a significant pressure, but attributes greater weight to evolving automation and job displacement. A common thread has been a popular distrust of elites and a feeling of lost sovereignty.

Many countries with anti-globalisation pressures have reacted by electing new populist regimes, and these have implemented nationalistic policies, with greater use of economic nationalist policies. In the United States, these policies have typically been imposed unilaterally and focussed on win/lose outcomes; have been assertive, radical, short-term, disruptive and transactional; and have been communicated in populist terms. They have challenged or overthrown many of the accepted norms of traditional international behaviour, including the Washington Consensus, which itself was the product of US economic leadership. Experience of trade tensions, financial pressures, Chinese resurgence and pandemics suggest that some economic problems are best addressed multilaterally. It is too early to judge the longer-term trends of anti-globalisation, but currently the United States and to some extent Western Europe are stepping back from their traditional global leadership roles. Yet many of the Asia–Pacific countries remain committed globalists. China has offered them leadership through its regional trade initiatives, but has so far received only guarded support.

THE TRADE WAR

US Policies

This economic nationalism has been most evident with the US Administration under President Donald Trump from early 2017. He promoted a new vision, labelled as MAGA, 'Make America Great Again'. The main features were a focus on traditional manufacturing industries (coal, iron and steel, motor vehicles), a mercantilist approach to bilateral trading arrangements, and a unilateral approach to traditionally multilateral economic relations, resulting in a hub-and-spoke framework with the United States at the centre. The Trump style was distinctive: an assumption that negotiations will be win/lose (in contrast to Ricardo's theory), a willingness to disrupt traditional arrangements without a clear view of new outcomes (e.g. the WTO, the Trans-Pacific Partnership / TPP), and an unusually personalised, transactional and disruptive negotiating style. There was a mixing of economic and security instruments (e.g. the use of national security powers to override WTO undertakings on tariffs), a willingness to interfere politically with independent economic institutions (the Federal Reserve and Congressional Budget Office), and a target (the trade deficit) articulated in economic terms, but really for political purposes.

Despite Donald Trump being the only American president to have held an economics degree, this set of policies was not led by government economists in the US administration, nor did they use economic tools in a conventional way. State Department diplomats do not appear to have been particularly influential. Instead, there was rivalry between trade lawyers led by the US Trade Representative Robert Lighthizer and non-specialist (often inexperienced) appointees in the administration. The role of the US Treasury was been relegated to currency matters. As well as trade rebalancing, the US President seemed to regard buoyancy in the US share market as a measure of success.

Over the last few years this new US policy was targeted at a range of countries (both traditional allies and competitors alike) and at a range of multilateral institutions (exiting from the TPP, withdrawal from the Paris Convention, obstructing WTO dispute resolution, and making bilateral use of G20 events). However, increasingly the US focus has been on its bilateral relations with China. The US President was galvanised by a large and growing bilateral deficit in merchandise trade with China which he represented as a direct Chinese attack on the economic dominance of the United States.

The president's favourite measure was heavily criticised by traditional economists because it only included merchandise trade, and arbitrarily excluded services trade, an area of successful US dominance; it was measured in terms of final consumption, not in value added terms; and it did not include other current account components such as the earnings by US firms from their Chinese investments. From a policy viewpoint, it failed to take into account intra-industry trade or the complications of supply chains; it assumed China has been cheating with its low-cost structure and alleged stealing of US intellectual property and forced technology transfer. In addition, it assumed a causality most economists would not support, and it failed to recognise the reciprocal relationship with the US imbalance in its own savings and investment. Many economists would view a trade surplus as a political aim rather than an economic one.

With growing domestic political support, the Trump Administration focussed its policies on China, where protracted trade negotiations have become intermingled with political and security concerns. The negotiations do not appear to be the result of any grand economic or game theoretic design, but instead rely on the much larger Pacific trade flows eastwards, the US dominance in technologies and US sway over multilateral arrangements to apply negotiating pressures. The negotiations commenced with a series of accusations by the United States, followed by unilateral imposition of tariffs on China. These tariffs were broadened in scope and increased in magnitude as part of a long and confusing negotiating process. As well as tariffs, other instruments such as financial sanctions and technology licencing requirements were used. The US Administration also put in place domestic support arrangements in agriculture and some industries to counter the impact of retaliatory tariffs. The distributive effects of this process are complex, but economic analysis points to higher input prices and the disruption of offshore investment borne by US companies with Chinese links, and, as a result, US consumers facing higher retail prices. Most economic modelling concludes that the short-/medium-term impact on the US economy is negative.

China Policies

The United States pressures on China have come at a difficult time. Economic growth has persistently slowed, China's current account surplus with the world has almost evaporated, there is a hangover from the huge Chinese reflation during the Global Financial Crisis, many corporates have a heavy debt burden, and the demographic dividend is turning into a demographic burden. These economic pressures are combined with political pressures in Xinjiang, in Hong Kong and with Taiwan. While Chinese trade has slowed, its foreign footprint has expanded, led by the Belt and Road Initiative, the newly founded Asian Infrastructure Investment Bank (AIIB), the New Development Bank (the former BRICS Development Bank) and the large foreign investment flows funded by domestic Chinese development banks. These investments have been part of China's attempt to realign trade routes, broaden trading partners, reduce Chinese economic dependence, onshore some regional production, build markets in Central Asia, address strategic security concerns and respond to US trade moves.

China has specifically responded to US tariffs by imposing counter-tariffs on some US production, though this has been more limited in scope, and more cautious in application. In fact, China is tactically disadvantaged in the negotiations—it has fewer bilateral imports to sanction than does the United States, and some have very inelastic demand. The United States still has undoubted economic power over them. So far, the trade war has damaged both countries' economies, but China is more at risk. This comes at a time when China is under domestic pressure to achieve the targets laid out in Xi Jinping's 'China Dream' by 2021, by the centenary of the founding of the Chinese Communist Party in July 2021. China's own vision has been encapsulated as 'Made in China 2025'. This vision is being impacted not just by the trade war, but also by an evolving tech war.

The Tech War

The United States has extended its trade sanctions by imposing restrictions and prohibitions on the export of certain US technologies and the import of certain Chinese technologies. This comes at a crucial time in the preparation for 5G investments, and has become identified with the Huawei debate about US restrictions on a Chinese company that now holds key 5G technologies, that has allegedly benefited from US technology in the past, and that is close to the Chinese Government and therefore vulnerable to its security demands. The technology tensions have laid bare an important technology dependence of Chinese companies on US high-end semiconductors, and the use of Android smartphone software. Having identified these vulnerabilities, it is likely the Chinese Government will now promote major investment into their own domestic capabilities in this technology, effectively reinforcing the 'Made in China 2025' strategy.

The pressures are not all one-way: the United States also has some dependence on the Chinese economy, in particular its imports of specialised rare earth minerals, the low-cost assembly of products such as Apple iPhones, and access to the huge Chinese consumer market. It appears that both the United States and China have decided that these tensions must lead to an economic and technological decoupling from their current close economic interdependence. This decoupling has been compared with the two rival blocs of the Cold War, however the difference is that the modern trade war starts from a high degree of initial interdependence.

The Financial War

There is some risk that the next step after the tech war could be a financial war, with the United States moving to confront China's growing digital payments and finance industry (Alipay, WeChat Pay, UnionPay). For their part, Chinese corporates are struggling between the need to maintain market growth while tolerating tighter political control. For them this is not a new tension. China is a dominant holder of US debt. It is in a position to sell down Chinese holdings of US Treasury bonds, though it has not been keen to do this, disliking the financial instability that might result, and understanding that the value of their debt holdings would also decline. The prospects of a currency war worsened in August 2019 when the US Treasury (ignoring its previously declared criteria) labelled China a currency manipulator. The markets showed considerable nervousness, and the renminbi declined in value.

The financial markets have proved something of a restraint on precipitate administration action. The United States knows that if the renminbi drops further it could improve Chinese trade competitiveness, negating the impact of the US tariffs on exports. China knows that actions could damage the value of its overseas holdings. The United States has always been active in using the wide reach of its financial industry and their regulators to apply sanctions to prevent their own companies trading with declared miscreant regimes. The former Trump Administration was more activist in applying extraterritorial restrictions on other countries' companies. Most important in the trade war has been US sanctions aimed at preventing Chinese purchase of Iranian oil, and US sanctions preventing China providing North Korea with coal and other key supplies. Ultimately, these actions will reduce the attractiveness of the US dollar. But for now, the US dollar remains by far the most internationally traded currency, allowing the US latitude in using its reserve currency status in a way that China and other countries cannot aspire to.

The COVID-19 Pandemic

The COVID-19 pandemic arose out of China in early 2020. In contrast to earlier viral infections, COVID moved swiftly through the region and beyond, causing major medical problems in the United States and Europe. The responses so far have been nationally based, with limited multilateral support. The US response has been defensive and internally focussed, exemplified by their withdrawal from the World Health Organisation, a decision that was reversed in January 2021. The Chinese response has been to seek advantage by offering medical supplies in the region.

Commencing with the global lockdown, the ongoing economic implications will be major for the region, though at this stage we can only speculate just how bad. The pandemic has triggered a major rethink under way on the movement of people and freight across borders. There will probably be ongoing restrictions on travel and transport connectivity, for obvious health reasons. Some global supply chains, especially for medical supplies and food stocks, have proved more fragile than expected. Businesses are making their own commercial judgements about future sourcing, based on concerns about resilience of supply. At a national level, many countries are looking to policies to localise food and medical production and increase self-sufficiency. This is likely to see smaller countries raise trade barriers, especially in agriculture. These policies will be exacerbated by the impending world economic recession which will be likely to sharpen trade conflicts, increase bilateral tensions and put multilateral institutional arrangements under even more pressure.

Impacts on the Region

Third Countries

Third countries in the region are clearly worried by the trade war, but unlike the financial markets, they have limited ability to calm the large protagonists. The impacts of this trade/tech/financial war are now being felt through the region, though they differ widely. Companies are reassessing their regional supply chains to test where their dependences are. US companies know they are particularly vulnerable, and a large proportion report they are carrying out major changes to their supply chains, generally reducing their concentration in China.

A number of Chinese and Southeast Asian businesses are reinvesting in facilities to move Chinese production. Lower value added textiles are already on the move to Cambodia, Myanmar or Bangladesh, for competitiveness reasons. China is losing some (but by no means all) assembly operations to neighbouring countries. More worrying for China is that some high-end electronic production is being relocated to Vietnam and Malaysia, sometimes by Chinese investors, sometimes by local ones. There have also been reports of Chinese products for the US market being relabelled or rerouted through another country to escape US tariffs. Trade flows to the United States are seeking China-insulation in other ways. US trade data shows that tariff-targeted imports from China are declining. Southeast Asia expects more investment as a consequence, but some of this involves trade distortions, and overall trade flows are likely to decline.

In addition, bilateral United States–China tensions seem to have legitimised countries' mixing of political and economic tensions. A resurgence of wartime legacy tensions between Japan and South Korea has led them to apply mutual trade restrictions. The United States used domestic political concerns to leave the TPP. Now India has used political concerns to justify dropping out of the ASEAN-led RCEP. ASEAN countries are now keenly aware that they are caught in a difficult place: on the one hand they have increased economic dependence on China (through both production links and final consumption); on the other they have continued reliance on the US strategic umbrella, to counter Chinese assertiveness in the South China Sea and North Korean aggression further north. This is not new for them—balancing such tensions is something that they have had to do since the inception of ASEAN, but today both pressures are more intense.

New Zealand and APEC

Australia and New Zealand face a similar dilemma to the ASEAN countries, though in their cases they are considerably less experienced at handling such tensions. China is now New Zealand's biggest export market, while its security interests seem much more aligned to the United States. With its heavier export dependence on China and its active membership of ANZUS, the Five Eyes intelligence network, and its US military bases and spy satellite facilities, Australia is even more caught in the balancing dilemma.

The wider implication is that for the first time Australasia's economic interests and its geopolitical interests do not closely align. This means continued adherence to the Washington Consensus may become less regarded, but it is unclear what should replace it, how far national economic interests can be handled separately from security interests, what consensus there will be for international economic cooperation and continued integration, whether economic policies will remain basically benign, and whether economic instruments are going to be increasingly applied to non-economic objectives.

In late 2021, New Zealand is due to host and chair the APEC forum and related meetings. With the United States somewhat detached from international institutions during the Trump years and with the risk of other Asia–Pacific countries adopting economic nationalism, APEC with its non-binding informal nature presents a key opportunity to rebuild regional economic cooperation. Following the Bogor Goals' 2020 deadline, APEC has adopted a new pathway for the future, and it will be New Zealand's role to operationalise this. The new approach realigns the 'free and open trade' motto towards 'free and fair trade'. It promotes continued integration, but recognises more attention needs to be paid to its distributive effects.

The most pressing challenges for APEC in realigning the Asia–Pacific economic order would seem to be to identify problems in economic integration in advance, to devise policies that cushion the impact of change on affected parties, to design trade and investment outcomes that continue to drive employment and economic growth, and to rebuild a consensus for a new-look economic consensus. We will need both economic diplomats and diplomatic economists to achieve this. The history of economic internationalism in the Asia–Pacific has not been smooth, but the post-Cold War years have seen increasing globalisation. The region's policy and international economists have often promoted this, seeing it as having a broadly positive impact on livelihoods. However, over the last decade, trade tensions, competitive resurgences, financial stress, pandemics and many other structural changes have increased resistance to globalisation in some major economies, resulting in nationalist policies and reduced influence from market economists. Whether smaller open economies like New Zealand's can resist this trend is still to be seen.

America's Rebalancing Towards the Asia–Pacific in Retrospect and Prospect

Kurt M. Campbell

INTRODUCTION

Over the last three years, the United States has entered the most consequential rethink of its foreign policy since the end of the Cold War. Although Washington remains bitterly divided on many issues, a rare area of apparent consensus across the political aisle has emerged around the need to pursue a more robust approach when it comes to China. There is an uneasy sense, shared by Democrats and Republicans alike, that 'engagement' belongs to the past, but it is unclear what lies ahead.

With remarkable speed, the American foreign policy paradigm shifted from a focus on the Cold War and then the War on Terror to one now increasingly centred on the China challenge. The new paradigm is driven

---

The views expressed in the article are Kurt Campbell's personal views, drafted before joining the National Security Council; they are not intended to reflect current policy or strategy of the Biden Administration as it relates to the topic.

K. M. Campbell (✉)
The Asia Group, Washington, DC, USA
e-mail: burton@the-asia-group.com

by an urgent question: how should the United States compete and—where possible—co-operate with a China that is not merely rising, but, in critical respects, has already risen? That question, in turn, foregrounds Asia as the most critical theatre for the United States in the period ahead.

This is not the first time that the United States has turned its attention eastwards. During the Obama Administration, the US Pivot to Asia elevated the region in American foreign policy after nearly two decades, which hitherto focussed largely on the challenges of the Middle East. The Pivot directed resources and high-level attention towards strengthening US regional alliances and partnerships, engaging multilateral institutions, pursuing economic agreements, modernising the US military and its regional posture, defending liberalism and shaping the contours of China's rise (Campbell, 2016).

The Trump Administration had continued certain features of this approach but undermined others. While it deserves credit for refocusing American strategy from counterterrorism to great power ties—particularly China—it struggled at times to pursue a coherent Asia strategy despite the determined efforts of its Asia hands, with policies on key regional challenges varying widely. The causes of that policy volatility included President Trump's whims, his need for diplomatic triumphs to distract from domestic challenges, his fondness for authoritarian strongmen, and his long-standing scepticism of free trade agreements and alliances with Asian states which he believed took unfair advantage of the United States.

In the period ahead, American policy in Asia and with respect to China in particular will need to evolve from both the Obama and Trump approaches. In contrast to the Obama era, future policy will need to involve far greater leader-level attention to the China challenge. In contrast to the Trump era, Asia policy will require a clear-eyed understanding that Washington's greatest competitive equities lie in the very values, economic relationships, institutions and alliances that were sometimes neglected or dismissed by the Trump Administration. And in contrast to both eras, Asia policy will increasingly need to engage with questions—often domestic—that are central to American competitiveness: innovation, trade, state–market relations, industrial policy and the competition for the technologies that are likely to be central to the Fourth Industrial Revolution.

As China emerges as the organising principle for much of American foreign policy, the United States will have to resist the temptation to focus on China in strictly bilateral terms and will instead need to embed its

China strategy in a dense network of relationships and institutions in Asia and the rest of the world. The combined weight of these relationships can shape China's choices. While the Trump Administration alienated many of the United States' traditional friends with tariffs, demands of payment for military bases, and by abandoning key institutions like the World Health Organization, a Biden Administration will need to instead see its Asian allies and partners as assets to be invested in rather than costs to be cut (Campbell & Sullivan, 2014).

This chapter discusses the often inconsistent nature of US involvement in Asia before turning to the Obama Administration's Pivot, the Trump Administration's Asia policy and the future of American policy in Asia—particularly in light of intensifying competition with China.

Asia as the 'Secondary Theatre'

In Washington, Asia has often played a secondary role behind more pressing global or regional concerns. The American legacy of regional engagement has often been reactive, episodic and ambiguous, leaving behind a sense of uncertainty and a job half-finished.

At the end of the nineteenth century, the United States sought to steer clear of European affairs and involved itself more in Asia, with President Theodore Roosevelt declaring that the American future 'will be more determined by our position on the Pacific facing China than by our position on the Atlantic facing Europe' (quoted in Tuchman, 2001, p. 34). But that focus did not last, and by the end of the First World War, American attention returned to Europe. During the Second World War, the United States went into Asia to combat Japanese imperialism, but once again, relative disengagement followed victory and the United States did little when the Chinese Communist Party prevailed in the country's civil war. The Korean War took Americans by surprise and brought American focus on combatting the spread of communism—a focus that also motivated the Vietnam War—but both conflicts were followed by disengagement, with President Nixon announcing the 'Nixon Doctrine' to reduce US commitments towards Asia in the waning years of the Vietnam War. Afterwards, Soviet resurgence in the Pacific, Japan's economic ascent, efforts to contain North Korea's nuclear ambitions, and the 1996 Taiwan Strait Crisis drew US attention to Asia for brief periods, but the principal theatres remained elsewhere—particularly Europe and the Middle East.

Although these cycles of attentiveness and inattentiveness have been enduring in American statecraft in Asia that does not mean there has been no strategy—however imperceptible—guiding moments of American activism. As Henry Kissinger (2014, p. 233) writes, 'For over a century ... it has been a fixed American policy to prevent hegemony in Asia'. Accordingly, periods of American activism have driven by a belief that the country must wield its diplomatic, economic and military instruments to prevent the emergence of a hegemon in Asia, thereby making the region safe for a range of American pursuits that have, over the last two centuries, varied from trade and faith to democracy and military security. Washington's policymakers have consistently believed that if Asia does not fall under the domination of another power, trade will flow more freely, religious freedom will grow, liberal values will flourish, and US territory will be safe from menacing powers. It was this belief that animated the Open Door Policy in the late nineteenth century; President Theodore Roosevelt's involvement in the Russo-Japanese War; the struggle against Japanese imperialism in the Second World War; and the efforts to counter Soviet and Chinese regional influence during the Cold War. And it is this belief in the need to balance the rise of a potential hegemon in Asia that once again constitutes a major reason for Washington's greater focus on Asia today.

Today, that potential hegemon is China, and its rise could put Asia's balance of power increasingly out of balance. Many familiar with the rise of China on the global stage overlook its equally impressive rise *within* Asia. In what has long been the world's most economically dynamic region, China has grown the fastest, outpacing every other major Asian economy. China's share of Asia's combined GDP was a mere 7% in 1980; by 2020 that share will have risen to 50% (IMF, 2015). Already China's GDP is double the combined size of the next two largest economies, Japan and India. If China alone occupied one end of a scale, it would take every other Asian state to bring that scale into economic balance. On the military side, China's share of total defence spending in Asia is enormous—roughly half annually (IISS, 2015, pp. 201–211). China's success in emerging swiftly from the COVID-19 pandemic has further amplified these advantages. The question for Asia—and for the United States—is increasingly whether much of Asia will fall entirely out of balance and gradually become a part of Chinese order.

The question of Asia's power balance constitutes one major reason for greater US involvement in Asia, but it does not account for the totality of American interests. It is also the case that Asia is crucial to success for virtually every one of Washington's policy goals in the twenty-first century. The path to arresting climate change runs through Asia, already the producer of more carbon emissions than any other region. The prevention of nuclear proliferation will require the co-operation of Asian nuclear powers, some of whom have been active proliferators. The verdict on which economic principles and technology standards will become nodal—from artificial intelligence to quantum computing—will be reached in Asia, home to three of the world's four largest economies and much of its high-tech manufacturing. On so many issues central to the world's future, Asia is at the centre of the action.

The Pivot to Asia

These complex motivations—the rise of a potential hegemon in China as well as the indisputable importance of Asia for every American priority—helped drive the US Pivot to Asia.

'As the war in Iraq winds down and America begins to withdraw its forces from Afghanistan', began Hillary Clinton's October 2011 article in *Foreign Policy* magazine that broadcast the renewed focus on Asia, 'the United States stands at a pivot point' (Clinton, 2011). With that simple turn of phrase, the Obama Administration's Asia policy gained a name. Later, in her memoir, *Hard Choices*, Secretary Clinton explained that 'journalists latched on to [the word *pivot*] as an evocative description of the administration's renewed emphasis on Asia' (Clinton, 2014, pp. 45–46). The word, mentioned but three times in a 5,500-word article, was suddenly and indelibly affixed to US policy. Some felt the word 'Pivot' suggested a pivoting away from one region to the other, giving rise to the alternative phrase for the Obama Administration's Asia efforts, the 'Rebalance'.

The policies associated with the Pivot, or rebalance, were broad. As Secretary Clinton made clear in her *Foreign Policy* piece, '[o]ne of the most important tasks of American statecraft over the next decade will therefore be to lock in a substantially increased investment—diplomatic, economic, strategic and otherwise — in the Asia–Pacific region' (Clinton, 2011).

At the diplomatic level, the United States engaged South East Asian institutions more vigorously than had been the case before. It signed the ASEAN (Association of Southeast Asian Nations) Treaty of Amity and

Cooperation, joined the East Asia Summit, and dispatched senior officials to the ASEAN Regional Forum. After decades of strategic neglect, the United States re-engaged New Zealand as a friend and security partner. Importantly, it reopened ties with Myanmar to pull it from Beijing's orbit. Over the course of the Pivot, the United States successfully intensified its bilateral relationships with nearly every Asian state, from India to Vietnam and from Malaysia to Mongolia. On the economic side, the United States increased foreign aid in the region, boosted its exports, finalised a free trade agreement with South Korea negotiated under the previous administration, and negotiated the Trans-Pacific Partnership (TPP)—though the Trump Administration withdrew from the agreement. At the military level, the United States stationed 2,500 marines in Darwin, Australia, dispatched littoral combat ships to the Strait of Malacca, improved exercises with allies and partners, and shifted more of its forces to the Pacific.

The Pivot also involved a crisis response capability. After North Korean provocations, Washington bolstered South Korea with diplomatic assistance and military signalling. After Japan was ravaged by a tsunami and the most devastating civilian nuclear crisis ever to hit Asia, Washington provided extensive humanitarian resources and military support.

Finally, the Pivot involved steps to push US Government agencies and military services to focus more attention on Asia, especially in matters of personnel policy. The State Department, for example, created 70 new positions for specialists on East Asia and the Pacific, and a similar internal reprioritisation on Asia occurred in other parts of the executive branch (Brimley & Ratner, 2013, p. 180).

The Pivot to Asia nonetheless faced obstacles. Russia's invasion of Crimea and the rise of the Islamic State in the Middle East eventually pulled American attention back to Europe and the Middle East. Some of the Pivot's objectives, including retooling the US Government for an era where Asia will be at the centre, would continue to take years to achieve. And other goals of the Pivot, particularly in economic spheres, were complicated by growing concerns in both American political parties about the terms of free trade agreements.

TRUMP'S ASIA POLICY

The Trump Administration continued some aspects of the Pivot while curtailing others. For example, it continued to move US forces into the region; regularise some ties with Taiwan; steadily advance closer ties with states like Australia, India, Japan and Vietnam, and normalise freedom of navigation operations in areas such as the South China Sea.

The Trump Administration also made important contributions to US strategy. In its 2017 National Security Strategy (The White House, 2017), the administration elevated great power competition with China and Russia over a focus on counterterrorism; the document was criticised for failing to differentiate adequately between the challenges posed by Moscow and Beijing. The Trump Administration also elevated Japan's Indo-Pacific concept in US strategy documents, making India more central to US Asia policy. In addition, it pursued a Blue Dot Network, which sought high standards for infrastructure projects in terms of financial transparency, environmental sustainability and the impact on economic development with a view to shaping the contours of China's Belt and Road Initiative (BRI).

These areas of progress, however, must be weighed against some of the challenges that the Trump Administration introduced. President Trump's scepticism of trade agreements led him to withdraw the United States from the TPP Agreement and impose steel and aluminium tariffs on friendly economies like Japan, Australia and Taiwan—complicating a united front on efforts to deal with trade imbalances with China. His administration's efforts to engage North Korea produced little as Pyongyang continued to advance its nuclear programme. Meanwhile, whatever goodwill those efforts could have produced in Seoul was undermined by Trump's trade measures against South Korea, and, perhaps more critically, his blunt effort to force Seoul to pay more for the US troop presence within the country—which sharply undermined bilateral ties. And the Trump Administration did not adequately invest in the region's multilateral diplomacy, to the dissatisfaction of the region and to China's own advantage.

The Trump Administration also elevated competition with China as a central element of US foreign policy. In most cases, however, these efforts were stewarded by the administration's Asia hands despite contradictory signals sent by President Trump himself, and at times were assisted by bipartisan efforts from Congress. For example, on human rights matters, even as Congress pushed legislation on Xinjiang and Hong Kong and the Trump Administration pursued sanctions against China, President Trump personally told Chinese leader Xi Jinping to proceed with his repressive campaigns (Bolton, 2020). On Huawei, the Trump Administration launched an increasingly successful effort to persuade countries not to embed the company's telecommunications equipment in their 5G networks, but the President himself said publicly he would reconsider his efforts against it and privately told Xi he would reconsider these measures too, raising confusion (ibid.). The Trump Administration also launched a trade war against China, but, at the same time, President Trump sought and then signed a trade agreement with Beijing that addressed almost none of China's mercantilist practices threatening the American industrial base while essentially settling for greater commodity exports from the United States to China.

In some of these areas, Congress provided a welcome corrective (Brands, 2020). For example, Congress passed FIRRMA (Foreign Investment Risk Review Modernization Act) to better protect US industry from Chinese efforts to use investment to gain access to sensitive American technology, and has considered industrial policy to support the US semiconductor industry. It also passed the BUILD (Better Utilization of Investments Leading to Development) Act to increase US capacity for providing infrastructure assistance that could challenge China's BRI.

China and the New Foreign Policy Paradigm

If President Trump had not won the 2016 election, it is likely that US policy would nonetheless have moved in a more competitive direction towards China and that some of the key efforts his administration launched may have materialised in any case. This is, in part, because, even in what remains a time of great division within the United States, Americans are increasingly supportive of a more competitive approach to China. Public opinion now regularly demonstrates that most Americans see China as a top security threat and have an increasingly unfavourable view of Beijing's human rights record and economic challenge (Silver et al., 2020). These public sentiments are, if anything, lagging indicators that follow a hardening elite consensus on China that has proceeded with surprisingly little debate over the last three years. The watchword in elite discourses is 'strategic competition', and references to a second 'Cold War' are increasingly common and influential.

There is now a relatively clear consensus that competition will be at the centre of US–China policy in the period ahead, and that China policy will in turn be at the centre of US foreign policy. Even so, fundamental questions remain with respect to the objectives of the competition and the nature of the desired end state that Washington should pursue. While there is growing consensus on various elements of US strategy, critical questions also remain on how best to implement them, and the discussion as a whole has been slow to proceed from the level of generalities to that of concrete prescription.

The China challenge is also an unusual one for most policymakers because it touches virtually every aspect of foreign and domestic policy. It combines key elements of traditional and non-traditional foreign policy, ranging from some forgotten aspects of nineteenth- and twentieth-century great power competition to the twenty-first-century challenges posed by climate change, the coronavirus pandemic, emerging technologies and the management of the global economy.

Since the end of the Second World War, the United States has had two dominant strategic paradigms, and neither of these provides adequate preparation for competition with China. The first of these paradigms was the Cold War and the second was the Global War on Terrorism and the attendant military conflicts in the Middle East, North Africa and south-west Asia. This strategic history shaped the careers of most current American policy practitioners, and yet it provides less guidance for the period ahead than one might hope.

The first of these paradigms, the Cold War, is also the one most frequently invoked today. It is understandable that strategic elites would reach back to the only great-power competition they remember to make sense of the present one, and the analogy certainly retains intuitive appeal. China is a large, continent-sized great power with a repressive political system, and it poses a global long-term strategic challenge that will require significant US mobilisation.

But the similarities are limited. The United States–China relationship is not a bipolar contest of total victory and defeat. While the risk of conflict in Asia's hotspots is serious, it is by no means as high, nor is the threat of nuclear escalation as great, as it was in Cold War Europe, where American military doctrine envisioned the tactical use of nuclear weapons to offset Soviet conventional superiority. The present competition has not unleashed proxy wars or produced rival blocs of ideologically aligned states preparing for armed struggle.

Importantly, while the United States–China relationship is nowhere near as dangerous as the United States–Soviet rivalry, China represents a significantly more challenging competitive proposition, given that its economy is far larger, more technologically advanced and more dynamic than the Soviet economy. Beijing is also better able to wield its economic power for strategic influence, given its willingness to embrace the forces of globalisation and interdependence, though largely on its own terms. China is now the top trading partner for more than two thirds of the world's countries. Unlike the United States–Soviet relationship, Washington and Beijing are still connected by economic, people-to-people and technological linkages. These ties also exist between China and much of the world, which complicates a determination of whether particular states are aligned with the United States or with China.

For these reasons, the twenty-first century competition with China occurs on a fundamentally different scale and stage than that with the Soviet Union. China is a more creative and comprehensive competitor, and its weight is greatest in the economic and technological realms, in contrast to the arms races that defined the United States–Soviet rivalry. And given the wide-ranging influence of both the United States and China, the competition for influence runs not along the borders but through capitals, with middle powers playing critical roles in various 'swing states' and often the subject of contestation.

Second, US experience in the Middle East and South Asia also has limited utility in guiding us through the unique features of United States–China competition. The wars in Iraq and Afghanistan were largely waged apart from questions of great power competition, and they were fundamentally focussed on narrower questions of radicalisation, counterinsurgency and nation-building.

The challenges of the Middle East also led the United States to overlook the domestic foundations of its own power. Those conflicts came at a time of American pre-eminence when Washington took the sources of its influence for granted. Now, as those sources suffer from neglect and are increasingly matched by China—with some exceptions, such as in soft power, where Beijing lags far behind—the need to reinvest in them is greater. Unlike the Global War on Terror, the competition with China is as much about American rejuvenation as it is about foreign policy, and that requires a far more comprehensive approach.

The US focus on counterterrorism and nation-building produced a cadre of experts familiar with the various villages and valleys of the region and the complexities of the political struggles within it. But by contrast, the United States–China competition proceeds at an entirely different scale and scope and requires completely separate sets of expertise. Some of that expertise is regional, and the central theatre of United States–China rivalry—the Indo-Pacific—features prosperous economies, enormous trade flows and greater diversity than that in the Middle East, North Africa and south-west Asia. Some of the expertise will be functional, requiring fluency in the nuances of technology policy, domestic competitiveness and international economics. In both cases, that expertise is not readily abundant within the foreign policy community.

As with the arrival of any new foreign policy paradigm, the focus on China will require a considerable investment of American time, attention and resources. In many respects, the country is still at an early stage in determining how its China policy will evolve. But in the period ahead, one element is clear: any approach to China is more likely to be successful if it is embedded in the dense network of relationships and institutions the United States has built—particularly in Asia. China policy in many respects cannot be bilateralised but must be connected to American Asia policy.

Asia Policy in a New Administration

President Biden is well suited for this task and brings rich experience in Asian politics and diplomacy. During his Congressional career, he was involved in the recognition of China, the reconstruction of Cambodia, the establishment of an unofficial relationship with Taiwan, the diplomatic opening to Vietnam in the mid-1990s and the strengthening of the alliance with Japan. More recently, as Vice President, he was a frequent visitor to the region, with numerous stops and deep and sustained engagements with Japan, South Korea and Australia. He met frequently with then Vice President Xi, hosting him in the United States and reciprocating his visits with trips to China. He was also a proponent of the Obama Administration's Pivot to Asia.

Beyond his Asia experience, President Biden has assumed office with one of the most extensive résumés in foreign policy of any president. He served as vice president for eight years, was the most senior Democrat on the foreign relations committee for more than ten years, and was in the US Senate for 40 years. He has been a key voice in most American foreign policy debates throughout his career, as well as both a witness to history and an active participant in it. He saw the United States through the last painful stages of Vietnam, much of the Cold War, and the ongoing tribulations in Iraq and Afghanistan.

The Biden Administration has come into power at a time when there are many questions about the purpose and posture of the United States within the Indo-Pacific. For those who seek to understand what a Biden foreign policy might look like in Asia, his 2020 essay in *Foreign Affairs* and his recent campaign statements, as well as those of his senior staff, provide the foundations for a strategic approach both for the region and for an increasingly assertive China (Biden, 2020).

At the core of President Biden's philosophy is a recognition that Asia is a contested space facing a competitive challenge from China unique in the region's modern history. This is not a condition that can be solved but one that must be managed, and it will be an extraordinarily challenging task that will require the United States and its allies and partners to work together. While the United States has had enemies before like the Soviet Union, it has not faced a challenge that mixes deep structural and systemic competition with elements of profound economic, financial and technological interconnectedness. At the same time, there are undeniable areas where the United States and China—along with other states within Asia—must find ways to work together. These areas include climate change, the pandemic and nuclear non-proliferation, among others.

In many respects, Biden's approach to this challenge and to Asia more broadly is to blend traditional elements of American statecraft within the Indo-Pacific—such as commitments to trade, strong forward-deployed forces, purposeful support for human rights and democracy, close ties to US allies and partners, and re-engagement with institutions—with a series of new issues on the agenda ranging from climate change and health to technology standards and supply chains. To advance this agenda, a new administration would have several broad areas of focus.

First, a Biden Administration would seek to directly address the debate within Asia about American decline. This is not an entirely unfamiliar discussion, and the region has repeatedly had doubts about American power and commitment including during the Korean War, after American defeat in Vietnam, through the American malaise of the late 1970s and 1980s, and in the wake of the Global Financial Crisis. Each time, however, the United States was able to focus itself on reinvention and rejuvenation. In that tradition, a Biden Administration would begin with the recognition that the core of an effective approach is American competitiveness. Accordingly, President Biden will spend an inordinate amount of time making investments in education, technology, infrastructure, public–private partnerships and other foundations for American resilience. He understands that these areas have been neglected and that—in the wake of a devastating pandemic—there is both a need as well as an opportunity to 'build back better', as he said on his election campaign trail. He will also seek to link the China challenge to a more robust domestic agenda.

Second, President Biden's team understands that if the United States is to be effective within Asia and around the world, and if it is to properly manage the opportunities and challenges posed by a more powerful China, it must work far more effectively with close allies. At the top of that list is of course Japan, and there will also be a need for more sustained dialogue to forge common approaches together with other like-minded states: Australia, France, Germany, India, South Korea and the United Kingdom, among others. There is awareness within Biden's team that this co-operation will not be automatic and will require nimble adjustments and US humility, as well as adaptation and nuance. The United States will need to accept that there are more questions about it than in the past and that listening to its friends and allies will be an essential feature of a successful American journey in Asia. In addition, the United States has generally managed its different alliance systems in Europe and in Asia separately, with different dynamics and historical rationales in each region. Increasingly, however, the challenge to the United States will be to link these two alliance systems together, with Japan in particular as a key component of this effort.

Third, although democratic allies form the foundation for much of US policy in Asia, a new administration will also require broadening that approach to deal with countries that do not always fully share universal values or have democratic systems. Countries like Vietnam will be critically important to US strategy, and the United States will also need to find ways to work with others within the region, and particularly in South East Asia, with different government systems, such as Myanmar and Thailand. Most of these countries understand that the competition with China that is now emerging requires nuance. There are no clear and neatly delineated geographical lines separating a 'Chinese bloc' from an 'American bloc' as during the Cold War. The competition instead runs through capitals rather than along the borders, and most countries desire a balance between China and the United States that preserves their economic opportunity as well as their political autonomy. What is necessary is for the United States to be resolute and clear about the challenges posed by China and seek to summon the capacity among states to present China with a unified diplomatic position.

Fourth, the United States will seek to make progress on economic and technology issues, even if outside of formal institutions. Some of that agenda is domestic, and the kinds of Cold War-era public investments in science, infrastructure, industrial policies and education widely understood then to have salutary economic and strategic benefits will be important. But much of the agenda is also multilateral, and the United States will need to work with its allies and partners on shared efforts in clean energy, biotechnology, artificial intelligence and quantum computing, among other areas. It will need to co-ordinate with allied and partner efforts to selectively decouple with China, disengaging in sensitive technologies essential to national security while permitting regular interaction in trade and investment in those that are less sensitive. It will also need to work with allies and partners to reimagine global economic institutions and devise new ways to organise allies and partners across Asia and Europe—such as the 'D-10' arrangement proposed by the United Kingdom that might include the G7 democracies as well as Australia, India and South Korea. The ultimate purpose of these bodies would be to set rules for trade and standards for technology that can undergird free world approaches to geoeconomics.

Fifth, it is increasingly clear to most now that the military challenge China poses is qualitatively different from that to which the United States has grown accustomed since the end of the Cold War. The United States enjoyed uncontested dominance against its opponents in the Global War on Terrorism, but that era is fast receding. Now, Washington may even be operating from a position of relative weakness in the Indo-Pacific in light of China's investments in anti-access/area-denial capabilities. Accordingly, the United States will need to shift to a military posture focussed on deterrence rather than primacy, with asymmetric investments that could complicate Chinese amphibious operations across the Taiwan Strait or into the East and South China Seas. At the same time, more investment in risk reduction and crisis management—a well-developed aspect of United States–Soviet times that Beijing has sometimes been reluctant to pursue—will be important for reducing the risk of inadvertent conflict and escalation.

Sixth, while there is sometimes a tendency in American politics to discard everything one's predecessor did, there are a few areas where Biden would be wise to emulate President Trump's approach. President

Trump's highly personal diplomacy—including his leisurely meals and golfing sessions with then Japanese Prime Minister Shinzō Abe as well as other leaders like Indian Prime Minister Narendra Modi—was particularly effective in building rapport. There is a hope among many that President Biden will continue this brand of deeply personal diplomacy because face-to-face encounters are so important among leaders generally, and indeed this approach does come naturally to the former Vice President. In addition, President Trump rightly articulated some of the challenges posed by China on the trade and technology front, and said so forcefully and publicly. Much of Asia quietly rooted for Trump's continuing firmness in certain areas. It is fair to say that President Trump's team was not as effective or systematic in implementing this approach and that some Asian states were less pleased by some of its practical solutions, but the Trump Administration's overall scepticism of certain elements of how China treats the United States and the region was warranted and perhaps overdue.

Seventh, the Biden Administration will need to cultivate a cadre of strategic elites familiar with the politics of the Indo-Pacific, the arcana of the Chinese Communist Party and its grand strategy, and the economic and technological foundations of American competitiveness and power. It will need to develop and include in discussions at the very highest levels not only foreign policy practitioners but individuals from a wide swathe of society—academia, business and technology—who can inform all facets of US strategy, foreign and domestic. And it will need to cultivate the capacity for nimble and rapid strategic adjustment against a potentially dynamic and formidable competitor.

CONCLUSION

The Biden Administration's approach to Asia and to China will not be a restoration of the Obama-era approach. To beat back fears of American decline, cope with a steadily more powerful and assertive China, and make progress on traditional and emerging issues across the Asian landscape, President Biden's team will need a new strategy. Although there will be common and easily recognisable elements from previous periods of deep US engagement in Asia, there should be little question that Biden's team will also seek to field a policy that is uniquely suited to the times and developed in consultation with critical American allies. The Pivot to Asia—now nearing its tenth anniversary—was a major step down what still

remains a long and winding road to significantly reapportion US attention and resources towards Asia. Over the coming years, as the United
States seeks to rise to the China challenge, the incoming administration
will likely continue to take steps down that road.

REFERENCES

Biden, J. R. (2020). Why America must lead again: Rescuing U.S. foreign policy
after Trump. *Foreign Affairs, 99*(2). https://www.foreignaffairs.com/art
icles/united-states/2020-01-23/why-america-must-lead-again. Accessed 15
December 2020.
Bolton, J. (2020, June 17). The scandal of Trump's China policy. *The Wall
Street Journal.* https://www.wsj.com/articles/john-bolton-the-scandal-of-tru
mps-china-policy-11592419564. Accessed 15 December 2020.
Brands, H. (2020, July 28). Senate Republicans' China policy is better
than Trump's. *Bloomberg.* https://www.bloomberg.com/opinion/articles/
2020-07-28/senate-republicans-china-policy-is-better-than-trump-s. Accessed
15 December 2020.
Brimley, S., & Ratner, E. (2013). Smart shift: A response to 'The problem with
the pivot'. *Foreign Affairs, 92*(1), 177–181.
Campbell, K. M. (2016). *The pivot: The future of American statecraft in Asia.*
Twelve.
Campbell, K. M., & Sullivan, J. (2014). Competition without catastrophe:
How America can both challenge and coexist with China. *Foreign
Affairs, 98*(5). https://www.foreignaffairs.com/articles/china/competition-
with-china-without-catastrophe. Accessed 15 December 2020.
Clinton, H. (2011, October 11). America's Pacific century. *Foreign Policy.*
https://foreignpolicy.com/2011/10/11/americas-pacific-century. Accessed
15 December 2020.
Clinton, H. (2014). *Hard choices.* Simon & Schuster.
IISS [International Institute for Strategic Studies]. (2015). *The military balance.*
Routledge.
IMF [International Monetary Fund]. (2015). *World Economic Outlook 2015:
Uneven growth: Short-term and long-term factors.* International Monetary
Fund.
Kissinger, H. A. (2014). *World order.* Penguin Books.
Silver, L., Delvin, K., & Huang, C. (2020, August 13). *Americans fault China
for its role in the spread of COVID-19.* Pew Research. https://www.pew
research.org/global/2019/08/13/u-s-views-of-china-turn-sharply-negative-
amid-trade-tensions. Accessed 15 December 2020.
Tuchman, B. W. (2001). *Stilwell and the American experience in China, 1911–
1945.* Grove Press.

The White House. (2017, December). *National Security Strategy of the United States of America.* Washington, DC. https://trumpwhitehouse.archives. gov/wp-content/uploads/2017/12/NSS-Final-12-18-2017-0905-2.pdf. Accessed 15 December 2020.

China's Evolving Asia–Pacific Policy: From Asserting Chinese Interests to Coping with the Indo-Pacific Challenge

Mingjiang Li

Introduction

Many international relations experts believe that the top foreign policy priority of any major power is to build and secure strong influence on its neighbouring countries. In the case of China, some scholars even contend that Beijing regards its neighbouring regions as its 'backyard' (Chambers, 2008; Scobell, 2010). There are perhaps good reasons why China attaches great importance to its surrounding regions, including the Asia–Pacific. Historically, China enjoyed a predominant position in East Asian regional relations under the tribute system for many centuries. The sense of pride that comes with the 'central kingdom' mentality may not have completely vanished in the minds of many Chinese sociopolitical elites. Geographically, China is one of the few major powers in the world that have a large number of neighbours, and the relations between China and some of these countries are very complicated due to a multitude of reasons. Perhaps most importantly, from the Chinese perspective, Beijing is faced

M. Li (✉)
Nanyang Technological University, Singapore, Singapore
e-mail: ismjli@ntu.edu.sg

© The Author(s), under exclusive license to Springer Nature
Singapore Pte Ltd. 2022
R. Patman et al. (eds.), *From Asia-Pacific to Indo-Pacific*, Global Political
Transitions, https://doi.org/10.1007/978-981-16-7007-7_5

91

with an unusually challenging geopolitical environment in its neighbourhood. In the Asia–Pacific region, for instance, China has to deal with
US strategic supremacy, the Taiwan issue, various territorial and maritime
disputes in the region, and strategic rivalry with Japan.

Since the end of the Cold War, China has initiated a number of major
policies in the Asia–Pacific region. In the 1990s, Beijing adhered to
the 'low profile' strategy, which included active diplomacy to improve
relations with many neighbouring countries, participation in various
ASEAN-led multilateral institutions, and by and large displaying tolerance for the geopolitical status quo. In the 2000s, while continuing to
practise many elements of the 'low profile' strategy, China employed
a 'soft power' approach (a 'charm offensive') towards countries in the
Asia–Pacific through active diplomatic interactions, rhetorical persuasion,
sociocultural exchanges and, perhaps more importantly, strong economic
engagements (Kurlantzick, 2007; Teo, 2004). In particular, Beijing quite
effectively practised its economic statecraft in the region by using its
economic power to pursue various geopolitical and security interests. A
good example in this regard was the China–ASEAN Free Trade Agreement, the first such regional trade arrangement that created profound
strategic repercussions in the region. By the first half of the 2010s, China
began to pursue an ostensibly assertive regional strategy towards disputes
in the East and South China Seas, perhaps due to the dramatic growth
of its power, perceived success of its policy in the previous decade, and
various domestic sociopolitical changes.

Over time, the assertive behaviour had a major negative impact on
China's relations with a number of neighbouring states. As China consolidated its presence in the East and South China Seas through various
heavy-handed means, many regional states became more apprehensive of
the future of China's rise. In that context, the United States responded to
China's assertiveness with pushbacks and succeeded in building stronger
security ties with some regional countries under the policy framework of
'strategic rebalance to the Asia Pacific'. Under the Trump Administration,
Washington began to promote its Free and Open Indo-Pacific (FOIP)
strategy, a move commonly believed to be intended to further limit
Beijing's assertiveness and growing strategic influence in the Asia–Pacific
region.

Cognisant of the deterioration of its political ties with regional countries and the geopolitical challenges that a successful Indo-Pacific strategy
may entail, China has made significant amendments to its security strategy

in the Asia–Pacific in recent years. It replaced its erstwhile assertive activities in the region with more moderate actions. Beijing picked up its economics-for-politics strategy again. But this time, it made a much bigger geoeconomic move by launching the Belt and Road Initiative (BRI) in 2013, hoping to mend fences with neighbouring states and, more importantly, to compete with the US-led Indo-Pacific vision. For a few years after the BRI was announced, tensions in the South China Sea continued at a certain level, but the overall security situation in the region tended to be more stable after 2016. This chapter attempts to describe and analyse these changes in China's Asia–Pacific strategy.

Asserting Chinese National Interests in the Asia–Pacific

According to many analysts, China's assertiveness in the region has been evident in its handling of various territorial and maritime disputes with neighbouring countries since 2009. Its assertive actions significantly stirred up the tensions in the East China Sea, the South China Sea, and north-east Asia.

Conflict with Japan

China's heavy-handed approach to regional security was first evident in Sino-Japanese relations in the context of the East China Sea dispute. China has, for a long time, maintained a strong claim to sovereignty over the Diaoyu/Senkaku islands due to rising demand for natural resources, the history issue with Japan, domestic power struggles among the ruling elites, and considerations of national integration (Sato, 2019). The islands dispute also involves 'larger morally and emotionally charged struggles, over history, reputation, recognition, victimization, and status' (Hall, 2019).

Against this larger background, relations between China and Japan were saddled with a number of conflicts in the early 2010s. For example, in September 2010, a conflict arose when a Chinese trawler collided with Japan Coast Guard vessels in disputed waters near the Diaoyu/Senkaku islands. The collision and Japan's subsequent detention of the captain and other crew members of the Chinese fishing boat sparked political tensions between the two countries. After Tokyo rejected Beijing's demand for the release of the Chinese nationals, Beijing put all official meetings on hold at the ministerial level and above and even suspended the export of rare earth minerals to Japan (Bradsher, 2010). Beijing's response shocked many Japanese as the export ban demonstrated Beijing's tactic of linking economic relations to political tensions (International Crisis Group, 2013). Large-scale anti-Japanese demonstrations occurred in many Chinese cities (BBC, 2010).

Another Sino-Japanese conflict occurred in September 2012 after the Japanese Government announced the purchase of three islets of the Diaoyu/Senkaku group from a Japanese national. The government explained that the purchase was an attempt to prevent the then nationalist governor of Tokyo from acquiring them. Believing that Japan's decision was a unilateral change to the status quo, Beijing moved quickly to counter Japan's action: Chinese authorities declared territorial baselines around the Diaoyu Islands and deployed Chinese law enforcement vessels to waters near the islands to challenge Japan's decades-long de facto control of the area. For many months, the maritime patrol vessels of the two countries were engaged in numerous risky stand-offs. At one point in January 2013, both sides were on the verge of a military clash when a Chinese naval frigate made a dangerous move by locking its weapons-targeting radar on a Japanese destroyer near the disputed islands (Berkofsky, 2013). On 23 November 2013, Chinese authorities announced the establishment of an Air Defence Identification Zone (ADIZ), which overlapped with Japan's ADIZ in the East China Sea.

Amid rising tensions over the Diaoyu islands, some of the anti-Japanese demonstrations in China resulted in violence. Overall, these demonstrations severely damaged Japanese businesses in China. For example, Japanese carmakers saw their market share in China drop sharply from 23% in September 2012 to 14% within two months, prompting Japanese investors to move production to Southeast Asia (Berkofsky, 2013).

It took more than two years for the two countries to get over the conflict and take steps to stabilise their bilateral ties again. In November 2014, senior officials of the two countries reached a four-point consensus. The third point mentioned that 'the two sides have acknowledged that different positions exist between them regarding the tensions' over the disputed islands and waters in the East China Sea and that they 'agreed to prevent the situation from aggravating through dialogue and consultation and establish crisis management mechanisms to avoid contingencies'. The two sides also 'agreed to gradually resume political, diplomatic and security dialogue through various multilateral and bilateral channels and to make efforts to build political mutual trust' (PRC Ministry of Foreign Affairs, 2014).

Assertive Chinese reactions, which may have been partially aimed at driving a wedge in the United States–Japan alliance (Taffer, 2019), stoked fears in Japan of an increasingly powerful China. Japan reckoned that China would resort to 'bullying and ignoring the rules, using its military and economic might to assert its prerogatives in the region and beyond, and pushing Japan into its shadow' (Hall, 2019). After 2010, as the Abe Administration sought to avoid an all-out confrontation with China, partly because of Japan's economic stakes in its relations with China (Hosaka, 2013), it began to shift its defence attention away from the possibility of a northern invasion to safeguard its south-western islands and its maritime areas (Hornung, 2013).

Rising Tensions in the South China Sea

China's heavy-handed approach to regional security was particularly evident in the South China Sea dispute. In the larger context of China's maritime aspirations and the call by leaders in Beijing for stronger measures to protect China's maritime interests, China confronted other claimant states and various regional stakeholders on multiple fronts. Certainly, it would be useful to bear in mind the perspective that some of China's actions were 'reactive assertiveness', meaning that Beijing was simply responding to what other players did in the South China Sea (Turcsanyi, 2017).

In the early 2010s, Chinese maritime law enforcement agencies carried out a high-profile campaign of patrolling the waters within the nine-dash line (vaguely-located lines marking Beijing's territorial claims in the South China Sea) and challenging the maritime activities of other claimant countries. In the absence of an effective co-ordination mechanism, various agencies fought for greater portions of the 'budget pie'. For instance, the Bureau of Fisheries Management and the China Marine Surveillance agency tried to surpass one another's displays of assertive behaviour in the South China Sea. One study shows that 73% of the 70 major incidents in the South China Sea since 2010 involved at least one Chinese maritime law enforcement vessel (CSIS China Power Team, 2020). And other players such as national energy companies and the Hainan provincial government sought to advance their economic interests in the disputed maritime areas (International Crisis Group, 2012).

One particular Chinese move was the deployment of the Hai Yang Shi You 981 oil rig in a disputed area between the Paracels and Vietnam's coast in May 2014. The deployment immediately triggered the most serious security, political and societal conflicts between Vietnam and China since their naval conflict in 1988 in the Spratlys area. In response to China's move, Vietnam lodged strong protests and deployed as many as 29 naval and other ships to disrupt the oil rig's operations. For a few weeks, Chinese and Vietnamese ships were engaged in violent collisions and a dangerous stand-off. In Vietnam, virulent anti-China demonstrations and riots were widespread. Tensions subsided only when China finally withdrew its oil rig in mid-July, a full month before the announced date of completion of its drilling activities (Green et al., 2017).

China also had very negative encounters with the Philippines during the Benigno Aquino III Administration. A notable incident was the 2012 Scarborough Shoal stand-off, which was sparked by the Philippine Navy's attempt to arrest Chinese fishing vessels for carrying out allegedly illegal fishing. Beijing reacted very strongly by sending its maritime surveillance ships to rescue the Chinese fishing boats. Furthermore, Chinese law enforcement ships continued their presence in that area after the Philippine ships withdrew. The Scarborough Shoal has thus been put under China's de facto control. The Scarborough Shoal incident had a major impact on regional diplomacy involving ASEAN. At the ASEAN Foreign Ministers' Meeting, Cambodia (the chair of ASEAN in 2012) supported China by insisting that the Philippines–China conflict concerning territorial claims in the South China Sea should not be mentioned in the joint statement. As a result, ASEAN failed to release any joint statement, unprecedented in its 45-year history (Prak & Grudgings, 2012). This fiasco within ASEAN is an illustration of the effectiveness of China's divide-and-rule strategy in its relations with ASEAN in the context of the South China Sea dispute.

In light of China's intransigence and assertiveness, Manila decided to adopt an international legal approach by requesting an arbitral tribunal under the United Nations Convention on the Law of the Sea (UNCLOS) to make a ruling on its disputes with China in the South China Sea in 2013. The arbitral tribunal issued its ruling in July 2016, which was overwhelmingly in favour of Manila's position. In response to the legal proceedings and the arbitration result, Beijing announced its adoption of a non-participation, non-recognition and non-compliance policy. Inevitably, countries in the Asia–Pacific doubted Beijing's intent to comply with a rules-based regional order.

The most assertive Chinese activity in the South China Sea occurred when it began to undertake a massive land reclamation in December 2013. In the short span of about two years, China built eight artificial islands, with a total land area of about 3000 acres (1200 ha), on seven of its Spratly Island outposts. Beijing also deployed various military assets on these outposts, including missiles and radar systems (*South China Morning Post*, 2017a). Such island-building activity and military deployment has become a major contentious issue between the United States and China in recent years. In an official document, ASEAN countries also stated that the land reclamation has 'eroded trust and confidence and may undermine peace, security and stability in the South China Sea' (BBC, 2015).

Sino-South Korean Conflict

In July 2016, the United States announced its plans to deploy a Terminal High Altitude Area Defense (THAAD) missile system to South Korea to better defend the United States and its allies against possible North Korean ballistic missile attacks. In disagreement with the United States' proclaimed purpose, Beijing claimed that it was concerned that the THAAD system could cause an arms race in the Korean Peninsula, undermine China's nuclear deterrence and strengthen United States–South Korea–Japan trilateral security co-operation (Watts, 2018). Chinese security experts argued that the THAAD system would not serve the purpose of defending South Korea from a North Korean threat. They posited that Seoul's acceptance of US plans clearly demonstrated South Korea's inclination to side with the United States, aggravating tensions between Washington and Beijing (Zhao, 2016). They also forewarned that the deployment of this system could lead to the exacerbation of 'the security dilemma between the US and its allies on one side and China and Russia on the other' (Suh, 2017).

It was perhaps no surprise that China reacted to this United States–South Korean plan with outrage. Beijing quietly launched an economic campaign to punish South Korea. Its plan was to hit South Korea's tourism industry with tour bans. For a few months, Chinese travel agencies stopped organising group tours to South Korea. Jeju Island, a popular destination for Chinese tourists, saw the number of Chinese tourists decline by 87% between the harvest festivals in 2016 and in 2017 (*South China Morning Post*, 2017b). Moreover, Chinese media encouraged Chinese consumers to boycott South Korean products. The sales of South Korean cars and cosmetics in the China market were immediately affected. Sino-South Korean joint venture Beijing Hyundai saw its sales in China decline by 40% in the first eight months in 2017. Lotte Corporation was hardest hit. Between 2016 and 2018, its retail business in China experienced an operating loss of ₩140 billion (*Straits Times*, 2019).

It was only in late October 2017 that Beijing and Seoul decided to end their conflict. South Korea made the 'three noes' commitment to Beijing: no further anti-ballistic missile systems in Korea, no joining of a region-wide US missile defence system and no trilateral military alliance involving Korea, the United States, and Japan. China subsequently lifted all its coercive economic measures against South Korea. Pundits believe that China won this conflict 'without firing a shot' (Volodzko, 2017). Some of the consequences, in the words of Panda (2017), included the following: 'China has received considerable assurances about the scope of South Korean behaviour within its alliance with the United States' and 'effectively, by employing economic coercion, China has constrained the United States' relationship with a key ally in Northeast Asia'. One of the negative effects on Sino-South Korean relations was that China's policy on the THAAD issue was perceived as Chinese interference in Seoul's sovereign right to decide its national security policy (Hwang, 2019).

Deterrence Failure of US 'Strategic Rebalance to Asia–Pacific'?

The above are just a few notable examples of China's security conflicts with neighbouring countries in the 2010s. It is interesting to ask why China pursued those assertive regional security policies. There may be many reasons why China behaved assertively and why the United States could not stop China's assertiveness: for instance, rising nationalism and confidence in China after the financial crisis in 2008, and some of the new political dynamics in China after the 18th Party Congress. But one could also make the argument that US policy and strategy in the Asia–Pacific failed to constrain or deter China in the 2010s. This certainly does not mean that many regional states have become more receptive to China's growing influence.

It is common knowledge that the most important external factor influencing China's regional security policy has always been US power and strategy in the Asia–Pacific. China and the United States have fundamentally conflicting interests and policies on many regional security issues, ranging from the Korean Peninsula to the East China Sea, the Taiwan issue and the South China Sea disputes. For many years, Washington has maintained that its strong military presence and security ties with regional allies and partners were necessary for ensuring peace and stability in the region. Understandably, US military power and security strategy are targeted at preventing China's assertive actions from undermining the status quo in the Asia–Pacific.

Soon after taking office, former president Obama advocated his 'Pivot to Asia' policy, shifting US diplomatic, military and economic resources from the Indian subcontinent to Northeast Asia, in an attempt to reaffirm US leadership in Asia. The 'Pivot to Asia' was later renamed 'strategic rebalance to Asia–Pacific'. The latter was a mixed strategy of competition and engagement towards China. Through diplomatic means and freedom of navigation operations, the Obama Administration exerted significant pressure on China to change its stance on the South China Sea disputes. Washington strongly supported Japan during the Japan–China conflict in the East China Sea in 2010 and particularly in 2012 by making clear that the United States–Japan alliance treaty covered the disputed islands between Japan and China. It worked hard to get China's co-operation on the North Korean nuclear issue. It also made significant efforts to balance China's growing influence in the various ASEAN-led regional multilateral institutions, for instance the East Asia Summit. On the economic front, Washington played an active role in the Trans-Pacific Partnership (TPP) negotiations, hoping to use this trade arrangement to counter Beijing's expanding economic influence in the region. Obviously, these US countermeasures could not stop China's assertive actions in the Asia–Pacific in the 2010s.

But, there was also an element of strong 'engagement' with China in the strategic rebalance. Senior officials of the Obama Administration emphasised that one of the strategic objectives of the rebalance to the Asia–Pacific was to strengthen relationships with emerging powers including China, in addition to other objectives such as deepening US alliances in the region; facilitating economic growth and trade; improving good governance, democracy, and human rights; shaping a regional architecture; and preventing conflict (Yun, 2013). Former national security advisor Tom Donilon (2013) described one of the pillars of the US rebalance strategy as 'building a stable, productive, and constructive relationship with China'. He added, 'We do not want our relationship to become defined by rivalry and confrontation'. In reality, United States–China ties continued to deepen during the Obama era. The top political leaders met frequently, the successful visit of former Chinese president Hu Jintao to the United States in 2011 being a good example. Senior officials of the two countries had established dialogues on foreign policy, security, economics and trade, and culture and society. The militaries of the two countries also deepened their engagement. In this context, policy elites in Beijing constantly pushed for the establishment of a 'new type relationship between the two major powers' (*xin xing daguo guanxi*) (Chase, 2012).

A detailed examination of Chinese policy elites' analyses of US strategic rebalance to the Asia–Pacific would also reveal why China did not feel threatened by the US strategy. Chinese analysts believed that the US new strategy was aimed at constraining China's power. They understood the new US strategy as a complex balancing policy, which entails expanding US power, tapping into alliance resources, taking advantage of the regional maritime disputes and capitalising on various international rules. At the same time, they doubted the success of the new strategy because of the challenges posed by current US power, the security–economics dual structure in East Asia, the asymmetrical alliance relations, and China's counteroffensive capabilities (Liu & Li, 2014). As the United States had fallen from being the sole superpower in the world to a special major power and a swing power, Chinese policy elites believed that the rebalance strategy was formulated to preserve US hegemony. They argued that Washington did not have the financial resources for the implementation of such a grand strategy (Ruan, 2014). Instead, Chinese policy elites were confident that in the aftermath of the financial crisis in 2008, China's power in the economic, technological, military, as well as ideological (development model) arenas would quickly catch up with that of the United States. They argued that the increase of US military presence and activities in the Asia–Pacific region led many regional states to believe that the rebalance was targeted at China. But most regional states avoided taking sides between Washington and Beijing because they were keen to continue their economic co-operation with China. Thus Chinese policy elites concluded that the US rebalance strategy might not receive strong support from many regional countries (Liu, 2014).

It was a common view among Chinese analysts that the rebalance strategy was significantly flawed. Being aware of the many contradictions and imbalances of the strategy, they questioned whether the strengthening of alliances was a means to an end or an end in itself, and pointed out inherent contradictions between both. The rebalance strategy could instigate regional security conflicts in the Asia–Pacific, making it difficult for the United States to balance its role in conflicts in other parts of the world, particularly in the Middle East (Zhang & Liu, 2015). There could be subregional imbalance for the United States in the Asia–Pacific region as well. Traditionally, Northeast Asia has been a more important region for the United States. Under the rebalance strategy, Washington sought to shift some focus to Southeast Asia and South Asia. But whenever a crisis took place in the Korean Peninsula, US attention would be diverted away from these subregions (Yu, 2013). Another common view among Chinese policy analysts is that the US strategy, amid waning economic engagement and diplomatic dialogue, had overemphasised the military dimension, leading to a regional arms race and tensions in regional security (Wang & Gao, 2016).

The only major concern for China at that time was that a US strategic rebalance could embolden neighbouring countries to challenge China's position on various disputes. Japan, for instance, took advantage of the US strategy to escalate the disputes with China in the East China Sea to constrain China, strengthen Japan's military capability and expand Japan's security role in the region (Liu, 2015). Beijing also contended that the US rebalance strategy has led to the worsening of the security situation in the South China Sea, as seen in the increased US military presence and activities in the region, the emboldening of other claimant states, and the growing interference by other major powers in the disputes (Xi et al., 2017).

According to Chinese policy circles, the US strategic rebalance was basically a hedging strategy for America to deal with China in the Asia–Pacific (Yu, 2013). In the words of US analysts, Washington's responses to China's behaviour, for instance in the South China Sea disputes, 'have been insufficient' (Searight & Hartman, 2017). It may be plausible to argue that the deterrence failures of the US strategic rebalance at least partially encouraged Beijing to use tougher policies to assert its interests in the Asia–Pacific region in the 2010s. There were certainly other important factors too; for instance, a growing Chinese consciousness of enhanced economic and military might, nationalism in Chinese society and new dynamics in elite politics in China since 2012.

THE INDO-PACIFIC STRATEGY: A REAL CHALLENGE FOR CHINA?

The regional geopolitical environment for China's Asia–Pacific policy underwent rapid changes once Donald Trump became president in 2017. For example, bilateral relations between China and the United States as well as the US strategic approach to the region changed almost entirely. Sino-American ties were set to embark on a downward spiral and the two powers could have engaged in very serious confrontations, even in a new Cold War. The COVID-19 crisis deeply undermined the already fragile relations between Beijing and Washington. US political leaders' accusations of China's lack of transparency in handling the pandemic and Beijing's disinformation campaign significantly undermined trust between the two countries. Washington elites further advocated 'decoupling' from China in order to reduce dependence on China's supply of medical protection equipment.

Deterioration of Sino-American Relations

The US National Security Strategy, released in December 2017, describes China as a revisionist power and a competitor that 'seeks to displace the United States in the Indo-Pacific region, expand the reaches of its state-driven economic model, and reorder the region in its favor' (Trump, 2017). According to the 2018 National Defense Strategy, 'China is a strategic competitor using predatory economics to intimidate its neighbours while militarising features in the South China Sea' (Mattis, 2018, p. 1). The US Indo-Pacific Strategy Report states that China seeks Indo-Pacific regional hegemony in the near term by 'using economic inducements and penalties, influence operations, and implied military threats to persuade other states to comply with its agenda' (Department of Defense, 2019, p. 9). Details of the new competitive and whole-of-government approach towards China can be found in the official policy document titled 'United States Strategic Approach to the People's Republic of China' (White House, 2020).

Sino-American relations were plagued by conflicts in the past few years. The trade war that started in 2018 dramatically undermined bilateral economic relations, which for a long time had served as ballast for the strategic stability between the two powers. While delivering a China policy speech at the Hudson Institute in October 2018, Vice President Mike Pence proposed a comprehensive policy package to counter China (Hudson Institute, 2018). In the same month, security relations between the two countries took a turn for the worse. In October 2018, a Chinese destroyer, in an attempt to block US freedom of navigation operations in the South China Sea, moved within 41 metres of the USS *Decatur*. The two warships nearly collided (Wong, 2018). Disputes between the two powers over the Taiwan issue also became severe. The Taiwan Travel Act, signed by President Trump in March 2018, had the potential to significantly upgrade the interactions between officials of the United States and Taiwan, much to the anger of Beijing. Washington approved a US$2.4 billion sale of tanks and missiles to Taiwan in July 2019. US arms sales to Taiwan enabled leaders in Taiwan to negotiate with Beijing 'without a gun to their heads' (Magnier, 2020). Washington has also stepped up its efforts in helping Taiwan keep its diplomatic allies. The Taiwan Allies International Protection and Enhancement Initiative, which came into effect in March 2020, threatened to reduce US economic, security and diplomatic engagement with countries that take significant actions to undermine Taiwan's international status (Zhou, 2020). US interest in the internal affairs of China (namely, issues related to Xinjiang, Tibet and Hong Kong) has also significantly increased. Through legislation, Washington may decide to sanction Chinese officials who are believed to have violated the human rights of ethnic minority groups in Xinjiang (Byrd, 2020).

Chinese Perceptions of the Indo-Pacific Strategy

In the context of dramatically deteriorating bilateral ties, Washington has also rolled out its FOIP strategy as a main part of its effort to compete with China in the region. At the official level, Chinese leaders hardly mentioned the US Indo-Pacific scheme. Chinese foreign minister Wang Yi commented in 2018 that the Indo-Pacific idea may just resemble the ocean foam, which 'may get some attention, but soon will dissipate'

(Yong, 2018). More than a year later, Wang advised countries in the Indo-Pacific region to focus on co-operation and downplay geopolitical 'games' (PRC Ministry of Foreign Affairs, 2019).

The policy discussion in China took place in the wider policy community, involving analysts from various official think tanks. While Chinese policy analysts believe that the Indo-Pacific strategy may encounter a number of challenges (Chen & Yang, 2019), the vast majority of Chinese analysts believe that the strategy will significantly harm China's interests. They believe that the Indo-Pacific strategy is clearly aimed at containing China's maritime power and limiting the expansion of China's influence. They note that even its partial implementation would severely threaten China's national security and relations with neighbouring countries (Hu, 2019). The Indo-Pacific strategy is likely to be a scheme that forces China to compete for its place in the regional order (J. Zhang, 2018). With support from Japan, India and Australia, the United States can potentially turn its Indo-Pacific strategy into an Asian version of NATO (G. Zhang, 2019).

It is common knowledge among Chinese policy elites that the Indo-Pacific strategy is likely to create concrete serious consequences for China in the region. First of all, some Chinese analysts contend that the Indo-Pacific strategy is a response to China's BRI, a flagship international strategy that may help China expand its influence across the Eurasian continent and in the regions spanning the western Pacific to the western Indian Ocean region (Zhao, 2019). For the Indo-Pacific strategy to compete with China's BRI, the United States has already put forth various infrastructure financing plans for the region. It has already reformed its external investment and development assistance institutions, pledged to increase infrastructure financing for other countries, and started building partnerships with other major powers and the private sector to co-ordinate their international infrastructure investment decisions (F. Liu, 2019).

Second, the Indo-Pacific strategy is likely to worsen China's external environment: Washington may do everything possible to get many other countries (including Japan, Australia, India and ASEAN member states) to counterbalance China by more proactively intervening in the South China Sea disputes (Cai & Li, 2019). Japan's Indo-Pacific strategy, proposed in 2016, is basically a call for countries in the Pacific and Indian Ocean regions with similar values to strengthen co-operation for the purpose of addressing Japan's security challenges posed by China (Xue,

2020). Because Australia has had quite a number of conflicts with China in recent years, Beijing considers Canberra a strong supporter of the Indo-Pacific vision. India, another key player, embraces the concept of the Indo-Pacific, and not only because it conceptually highlights India's role in such regional strategic realignment, unlike the Asia–Pacific concept. More importantly, the new strategic concept offers India a policy tool to leverage the power of other players to balance China, especially in the Indian Ocean region (Lin, 2019). As the Indo-Pacific strategy will give India great strategic manoeuvrability against China, more uncertainties and complications will plague Sino-Indian ties in the coming years (Pang & Cui, 2019).

China is also wary of the inclinations of other, less crucial, players. The focus of Indonesia's Indo-Pacific vision is on ASEAN centrality and pan-Indian Ocean regional co-operation, and is quite different from the Indo-Pacific strategies of the other major proponents of the Indo-Pacific. But Chinese analysts believe that Indonesia's endorsement and participation in the Indo-Pacific scheme will inevitably further complicate the situation in the region (Y. Liu, 2019). Beijing is also concerned that United States–Taiwanese political and security co-operation is becoming more substantive. The Taiwan authorities, in particular, have a strong interest in leveraging the US strategy to counter pressure from mainland China. It is possible that Taiwan will behave as a 'troublemaker' or even a 'crisis maker' in cross-strait relations and in the East Asian region more generally (Zhong, 2019).

China also quietly acknowledges that ASEAN is currently marginally supportive of the Indo-Pacific vision. In June 2019, the 34th ASEAN Summit issued its ASEAN Outlook on the Indo-Pacific (AOIP). This policy document, which is an affirmation of the importance of ASEAN centrality, calls for inclusive co-operation on regional economic development, and emphasises the need for existing institutions. The positions stated in this document are fairly neutral in comparison to the major preferences of the Indo-Pacific strategy proponents. Yet India, Japan, Australia and the United States have immediately embraced the AOIP. In contrast, China has so far made no official comment on the AOIP. Given Washington's intent to use the Indo-Pacific to contain China's rise, Beijing is aware that ASEAN's acceptance of this concept will undermine China's interests. China's view is that the AOIP has displayed Washington's success in lobbying ASEAN countries to participate in the US-led network of security partnerships (J. Zhang, 2019), despite the fact that these regional states are primarily interested in maintaining ASEAN centrality in response to the Indo-Pacific vision. Moreover, ASEAN member states may have very different views on the Indo-Pacific concept.

China's Possible Policy Response to the Indo-Pacific Strategy

It is quite clear that Beijing has dire views of the US-led Indo-Pacific scheme. Chinese policy analysts have examined the potential consequences of various Chinese responses and made several suggestions. The first is that China abandon its current head-in-the-sand approach and consider joining the Indo-Pacific scheme. By doing so, China could reduce the other powers' obsessive treatment of it as the target of the Indo-Pacific strategy. Besides, China could attempt to offer its own proposals for resolving problems in the region. Should China dramatically reorient its policies related to security, economic engagement and diplomatic interaction with countries across the region, the United States and other leading players will assume that China is becoming more accommodating and less assertive. This policy proposal for China's participation in the Indo-Pacific is however a minority view in China. The mainstream official view is that Beijing should not officially engage in the Indo-Pacific strategy.

The second suggestion is that Beijing understand that the emergence of the Indo-Pacific scheme has to do with the growth of China's power and the security dilemma that exists between China and many neighbouring states. This means that China will need to improve its external communications to convince other countries of its goodwill and more importantly, exercise utmost self-constraint when handling the various regional territorial and maritime disputes, and improving crisis management and de-escalating conflicts. China can also provide more and better public goods in the Indo-Pacific region to support anti-piracy measures, the safety of sea lines of communication, and disaster relief (L. Zhang, 2019). This policy proposal appears to be in line with the official white paper on China's policy towards Asia–Pacific security co-operation (PRC State Council Information Office, 2017).

The third suggestion is to deepen co-operation with individual regional countries so that Beijing can exercise a divide-and-rule tactic. Much emphasis has been placed on the BRI. Under this, China and regional countries can further improve their connectivity in the areas of infrastructure, finance, trade, macroeconomic policy and sociocultural exchange to build an Asian 'community of common destiny' (PRC Ministry of Foreign Affairs, 2013). Beijing should seriously address some of the regional countries' objections about participating in the BRI by pursuing higher-quality projects in those countries. Elements such as cultural exchanges, poverty relief and various charitable causes could be further highlighted under the BRI. The key idea for the BRI is to synergise regional countries' development visions and plans so as to create regional co-operation for development. A key policy area for China is economic and trade co-operation in the Asia-Pacific. China should strive for the conclusion of a China-Japan-South Korea free trade agreement and for co-operation in various economic sectors in north-east Asia. In South East Asia, China can consider giving greater support to ASEAN-led multilateral institutions, while striving for an early signing of the Regional Comprehensive Economic Partnership to foster free trade among Asia-Pacific countries (Xu, 2019). China should do more to bring India into Asia-Pacific co-operation and explore the potential for third-party market co-operation with India under the BRI (Ding, 2019).

CONCLUSION

As a result of China's Asia-Pacific security policy, the region has experienced many years of Chinese assertiveness in the 2010s. On the other hand, Beijing has gained leverage in some ways: the creation of a new status quo in the East and South China Sea disputes, the expansion of its military and security presence beyond the first island chain, the first chain of islands off the East Asian coast, and sowing the seeds of doubt among some regional states about the credibility of US security commitments.

Sino-American relations and US strategic policy are the most important factors affecting China's regional policy in the Asia-Pacific. During the 2010s, Washington pursued a mixed policy of deterrence and engagement towards China. Under the 'Pivot to Asia' or 'strategic rebalance', US deterrence did not appear to be particularly threatening to China. Beijing also employed many 'grey zone' tactics, including the use of maritime law enforcement forces, maritime militia groups, state-owned energy enterprises and diplomatic coercion. These 'grey zone' tactics also rendered US deterrence strategy ineffective in dealing with China's assertiveness. The engagement aspect of US China policy, to some extent, reassured Beijing that China's assertive behaviour would not wreak havoc in its relations with the United States.

But China had to pay a very high price. Its regional image, which Beijing had worked hard to build, suffered. Some regional states have become more concerned about the uncertainties and disruptions that a more powerful China may create to the existing regional order. China's assertive behaviour alarmed Washington and threatened their relationship. And all these negative developments in China's neighbourhood provided fertile ground for the formation and gradual consolidation of the US-led Indo-Pacific strategy, as other major regional players including Japan, Australia and India sought to limit China's power. Fortunately for China, its regional strategic influence was not fundamentally weakened, due to its economic power and engagements with many regional states.

Now Sino-American relations have entered an era of fierce strategic rivalry. The Asia–Pacific and Indian Ocean regions now serve as theatres for such rivalry between the two major powers. China now considers the Indo-Pacific strategy a far worse threat than the 'strategic rebalance'. Will Washington's competitive approach to China's BRI and the evolving Indo-Pacific strategic realignments result in a moderate Chinese position on regional territorial and security disputes? Chinese policy analysts do suggest such a possibility. Very likely, China will reduce its heavy-handedness in handling regional disputes, continue to be proactive in pushing for regional economic co-operation, practise economic statecraft to deepen strategic partnerships with some regional states, and attempt to play a bigger role in dealing with regional non-traditional security challenges.

References

BBC. (2010, September 18). *Anti-Japan protests mark China anniversary*. https://www.bbc.com/news/world-asia-pacific-11354735. Accessed 2 March 2020.

BBC. (2015, April 28). *South China Sea island-building 'may undermine peace'—ASEAN*. https://www.bbc.com/news/world-asia-32476951. Accessed 12 March 2020.

Berkofsky, A. (2013, June). *Japan and China: Bitter rivals and close partners*. Asia Policy Brief, 3.

Bradsher, K. (2010, September 23). *China bans rare earth exports to Japan amid tension*. CNBC. https://www.cnbc.com/id/39318826. Accessed 17 April 2020.

Byrd, H. (2020, May 14). *Senate approves Uyghur human rights bill*. CNN. https://edition.cnn.com/2020/05/13/politics/uyghur-bill-senate-china/index.html. Accessed 15 May 2020.

Cai, Z., & Li, D. (2019). 'Yintai' zhanlue de yuanqi, benzhi ji qianjing [The origins, nature and prospects for the Indo-Pacific strategy]. *Zhanlue juece yanjiu* [Studies on Strategic Decision Making], 5, 57–73.

Chambers, M. R. (2008). The evolving relationship between China and Southeast Asia. In A. M. Murphy & B. Welsh (Eds.), *Legacy of engagement in Southeast Asia* (p. 298). Institute of Southeast Asia.

Chase, M. S. (2012). China's search for a 'new type of great power relationship'. *China Brief, 12*(17). https://jamestown.org/program/chinas-search-for-a-new-type-of-great-power-relationship/. Accessed 7 February 2020.

Chen, J., & Yang, J. (2019). Meiguo 'Yintai zhanlue' de yanjin jiqi qianjing tanjiu [The evolution and prospect of US Indo-Pacific strategy]. *Dangdai shijie* [Contemporary world], *10*, 36–43.

CSIS China Power Team. (2020). *Are maritime law enforcement forces destabilizing Asia?* https://chinapower.csis.org/maritime-forces-destabilizing-asia. Accessed 10 April 2020.

Ding, K. (2019). Yintai zhanlue: Diyuan zhanlue neihan, luoji yu sikao [The Indo-Pacific strategy: Its geo-strategic underpinnings, logics, and some thoughts]. *Guoji yanjiu cankao* [References of International Studies], 5.

Donilon, T. (2013). *Remarks by Tom Donilon, National Security Advisor to the President: the United States and the Asia-Pacific in 2013*. Speech delivered at the Asia Society, New York. https://obamawhitehouse.archives.gov/the-press-office/2013/03/11/remarks-tom-donilon-national-security-advisor-president-united-states-an. Accessed 7 March 2020.

Green, M., Hicks, K., Cooper, Z., Schaus, J., & Douglas, J. (2017). *Counter-coercion series: China-Vietnam oil rig standoff*. The Asia Maritime Transparency Initiative and the Center for Strategic and International Studies. https://amti.csis.org/counter-co-oil-rig-standoff. Accessed 7 July 2019.

Hall, T. (2019). *Why the Senkaku/Diaoyu Islands are like a toothpaste tube*. War on the Rocks. https://warontherocks.com/2019/09/why-the-senkaku-diaoyu-islands-are-like-a-toothpaste-tube. Accessed 7 February 2020.

Hornung, J. W. (2013). Japan's security policies a pragmatic response to changing Asia. *World Politics Review*. https://www.worldpoliticsreview.com/articles/13268/japan-s-security-policies-a-pragmatic-response-to-changing-asia. Accessed 7 July 2019.

Hosaka, Y. (2013). The Abe administration's domestic strategy and Northeast Asia. *SERI Quarterly, 6*(2), 30–39.

Hu, B. (2019). Meiguo 'Yindai zhanlue' qushi yu qianjing [US Indo-Pacific strategy: trends and prospects]. *Taipingyang xuebao* [Pacific Journal], *27*(10), 21–30.

Hudson Institute. (2018). *Remarks by Vice President Pence on the administration's policy toward China*. https://www.whitehouse.gov/briefings-sta tements/remarks-vice-president-pence-administrations-policy-toward-china. Accessed 12 March 2020.

Hwang, B. Y. (2019). Northeast Asian perspectives on China's Belt Road Initiative: The view from South Korea. *East Asia, 36*, 129–50. https://doi.org/10.1007/s12140-019-09310-0. Accessed 1 February 2020.

International Crisis Group. (2012). *Stirring up the South China Sea (1)*. Asia Report, 223. https://www.refworld.org/docid/4f992c9e2.html. Accessed 25 February 2020.

International Crisis Group. (2013). *Dangerous waters: China–Japan relations on the rocks*. Asia Report, 245. https://www.crisisgroup.org/asia/north-east-asia/china/dangerous-waters-china-japan-relations-rocks. Accessed 1 March 2020.

Kurlantzick, J. (2007). *Charm offensive: How China's soft power is transforming the world*. Yale University Press.

Lin, M. (2019). Yindu de 'Yintai zhanlue' zhengzai shengji? [India's Indo-Pacific strategy being upgraded?] *Shijie zhishi* [World Affairs], *20*, 74.

Liu, F. (2015). Lun Riben de Donghai zhengce jiqi dui Zhongguo de yingxiang [Japan's East China Sea policy and the impact on China]. *Riben yanjiu* [Japanese Studies], *4*, 25–31.

Liu, F. (2019). Meiguo 'Yindai' jichusheshi touzi jingzheng celue [US infrastructure investment competition strategy under the Indo-Pacific]. *Guoji wenti yanjiu* [International Studies], *4*, 1–20.

Liu, G. (2014). Meiguo 'Yatai zai pingheng' zhanlue mianlin de tiaozhan [Challenges for US strategic rebalance to Asia Pacific]. *Meiguo yanjiu* [American Studies], *3*, 97–102.

Liu, Y. (2019). 'Yinni Zuoke zhengfu de 'Yintai yuanjing' lunxi' [Indonesian Jokowi government's Indo-Pacific vision]. *Heping yu fazhan* [Peace and Development], *5*, 99–117.

Liu, Y., & Li, H. (2014). Meiguo Yatai zai pingheng zhanlue de zhiyue luoji [The constraining logics for the US strategic rebalance to the Asia Pacific]. *Taipingyang xuebao* [Pacific Journal], *22*(10), 48–60.

Magnier, M. (2020, January 17). Former US defence official calls us arms sales to Taiwan a catalyst for cross-strait dialogue. *South China Morning Post*. https://www.scmp.com/news/china/politics/article/3046468/former-us-defence-official-calls-us-arms-sales-taiwan-catalyst. Accessed 1 March 2020.

Mattis, J. N. (2018). *Summary of the 2018 National Defense Strategy: sharpening the American military's competitive edge*. Department of Defense. https://dod.defense.gov/Portals/1/Documents/pubs/2018-National-Defense-Str ategy-Summary.pdf. Accessed 7 January 2020.

Panda, A. (2017, November 13). China and South Korea: Examining the resolution of the THAAD impasse. *Diplomat.* https://thediplomat.com/2017/11/china-and-south-korea-examining-the-resolution-of-the-thaad-imp asse. Accessed 30 January 2020.

Pang, J., & Cui, L. (2019). 'Yindai zhanlue' shiyu xia de Zhongyin guanxi [Sino-Indian relations from the perspective of Indo-Pacific strategy]. *Nanya Dongnanya yanjiu* [South Asia and Southeast Asia Studies], *6*, 56–66.

Prak, C. T., & Grudgings, S. (2012, July 13). *SE Asia meeting in disarray over sea dispute with China.* Reuters. https://www.reuters.com/article/us-asean-summit/se-asia-meeting-in-disarray-over-sea-dispute-with-china-idUSBRE86 C0BD20120713. Accessed 1 March 2020.

PRC Ministry of Foreign Affairs. (2013, October 25). *Xi Jinping: Let the sense of community of common destiny take deep root in neighbouring countries.* https://www.fmprc.gov.cn/mfa_eng/wjb_663304/wjbz_663308/activities_663312/t1093870.shtml. Accessed 7 March 2021.

PRC Ministry of Foreign Affairs. (2014). *Yang Jiechi meets National Security Advisor of Japan Shotaro Yachi: China and Japan reach four-point principled agreement on handling and improving bilateral relation[s].* https://www.fmprc.gov.cn/mfa_eng/zxxx_662805/t1208360.shtml. Accessed 6 March 2020.

PRC Ministry of Foreign Affairs. (2019). *Wang Yi talks about Indo-Pacific concept.* https://www.fmprc.gov.cn/mfa_eng/zxxx_662805/t1685652.shtml. Accessed 1 March 2020.

PRC State Council Information Office. (2017). *Full text: China's policies on Asia–Pacific security cooperation.* http://english.www.gov.cn/archive/white_paper/2017/01/11/content_281475539078636.htm. Accessed 1 March 2020.

Ruan, Z. (2014). Meiguo 'zai pingheng' zhanlue qianjing fenxi [The prospect of US strategic rebalance to Asia Pacific]. *Shijie jingji yu zhengzhi* [World Economics and Politics], *4*, 4–20.

Sato, K. (2019). The Senkaku Islands dispute: Four reasons of the Chinese Offensive—A Japanese view. *Journal of Contemporary East Asia Studies.* https://doi.org/10.1080/24761028.2019.1626567. Accessed 7 March 2020.

Scobell, A. (2010). *China's geostrategic calculus and Southeast Asia—The dragon's backyard laboratory.* Testimony before U.S.–China Economic and Security Review Commission: China's activities in Southeast Asia and the implications for U.S. interests, 111–120. https://www.uscc.gov/sites/default/files/transc ripts/2.4.10HearingTranscript.pdf. Accessed 1 March 2020.

Searight, A., & Hartman, G. (2017). *The South China Sea—Some fundamental strategic principles.* CSIS. https://www.csis.org/analysis/south-china-sea-some-fundamental-strategic-principles. Accessed 10 March 2020.

South China Morning Post. (2017a). China builds new military facilities on South China Sea Islands, says US think tank. https://www.scmp.com/news/china/diplomacy-defence/article/2100667/china-builds-new-military-facilities-south-china-sea. Accessed 5 March 2020.

South China Morning Post. (2017b). Once crawling with Chinese tourists, a travel ban for South Korea leaves Jeju Island deserted. https://www.nst.com.my/world/2017/10/287844/once-crawling-chinese-tourists-travel-ban-south-korea-leaves-jeju-island. Accessed 5 March 2020.

Straits Times. (2019, March 13). South Korea's Lotte seeks to exit China after investing $9.6 billion, as Thaad fallout ensues. https://www.straitstimes.com/asia/east-asia/south-koreas-lotte-seeks-to-exit-china-after-investing-96-billion. Accessed 5 March 2020.

Suh, J. (2017). Missile defense and the security dilemma: THAAD, Japan's 'proactive Peace', and the arms race in Northeast Asia. *The Asia-Pacific Journal–Japan Focus, 15*(9), no. 5. https://apjjf.org/2017/09/Suh.html. Accessed 2 March 2020.

Taffer, A. (2019, September 6). China's Senkaku/Diaoyu Islands ploy to undercut the US-Japan alliance. *Interpreter*. https://www.lowyinstitute.org/the-interpreter/china-s-senkakudiaoyu-islands-ploy-undercut-us-japan-alliance. Accessed 1 March 2020.

Teo, E. C. C. (2004). *China's rising soft power in Southeast Asia*. PacNet, 19A, Pacific Forum CSIS, Honolulu, Hawaii. https://csis-prod.s3.amazonaws.com/s3fs-public/legacy_files/files/media/csis/pubs/pac0419a.pdf. Accessed 2 March 2020.

Trump, D. J. (2017). *National Security Strategy of the United States of America 2017*. https://trumpwhitehouse.archives.gov/wp-content/uploads/2017/12/NSS-Final-12-18-2017-0905-2.pdf. Accessed 2 March 2020.

Turcsanyi, R. Q. (2017, December 22). What's really behind Chinese assertiveness in the South China Sea? *Diplomat*. https://thediplomat.com/2017/12/whats-really-behind-chinese-assertiveness-in-the-south-china-sea. Accessed 2 March 2020.

US Department of Defense. (2019). *Indo-Pacific strategy report: Preparedness, partnerships, and promoting a networked region*. https://media.defense.gov/2019/Jul/01/2002152311/-1/-1/1/DEPARTMENT-OF-DEFENSE-INDO-PACIFIC-STRATEGY-REPORT-2019.PDF. Accessed 2 March 2020.

Volodzko, D. J. (2017, November 18). China wins its war against South Korea's US THAAD missile shield—Without firing a shot. *South China Morning Post*. https://www.scmp.com/week-asia/geopolitics/article/2120452/china-wins-its-war-against-south-koreas-us-thaad-missile. Accessed 2 March 2020.

Wang, H., & Gao, B. (2016). Meiguo Yatai 'zai pingheng' zhanlue de junshi dongxiang pingxi [Analysis of military trends in US strategic rebalance to Asia

Pacific]. *Guofang keji* [National Defense Science and Technology], *37*(6), 76–87.

Watts, R. C., IV. (2018). 'Rockets' red glare'—Why does China oppose THAAD in South Korea, and what does it mean for U.S. policy? *Naval War College Review, 71*(2), 79–107. https://digital-commons.usnwc.edu/nwc-rev iew/vol71/iss2/7. Accessed 20 March 2020.

White House. (2020). *United States strategic approach to the People's Republic of China.* https://trumpwhitehouse.archives.gov/articles/united-states-strate gic-approach-to-the-peoples-republic-of-china/. Accessed 28 May 2020.

Wong, C. (2018, October 3). US, Chinese warships within metres of collision in South China sea, leaked pictures show. *South China Morning Post.* https://www.scmp.com/news/china/military/article/2166849/us-chi nese-warships-within-metres-collision-south-china-sea. Accessed 2 March 2020.

Xi, D., Liu, J., & Zhou, Q. (2017). 'Yatai zai pingheng' zhanlue shishi yilai Meiguo zai Nanhai zhoubian junshi buju jiqi dui Nanhai wenti de yingxiang [US military activities in the South China Sea region in the context of the strategic rebalance to Asia Pacific]. *Yatai anquan yu haiyang yanjiu* [Asia Pacific Security and Maritime Affairs], *6*, 56–69.

Xu, W. (2019, November 5). Li urges RCEP to resolve outstanding issues. *China Daily.* https://global.chinadaily.com.cn/a/201911/05/WS5dc0d0d ca310cf3e355756ef.html. Accessed 28 March 2020.

Xue, L. (2020). Riben 'Yintai zhanlue' de jide weidu [Several dimensions of Japan's Indo- Pacific strategy]. *Shijie zhishi* [World Affairs], *1*, 31.

Yong, C. (2018, August 12). Scepticism over free and open Indo-Pacific strategy. *Straits Times.* https://www.straitstimes.com/asia/scepticism-over-free-and-open-indo-pacific-strategy. Accessed 2 March 2020.

Yu, Z. (2013). Meiguo Yatai zai pingheng zhanlue de shiheng [The imbalances of US strategic rebalance to Asia Pacific. *Guoji guanxi yanjiu* [Studies of International Relations], *2*, 3–12.

Yun, J. (2013). *Statement of Joseph Y. Yun, Acting Assistant Secretary Bureau of East Asian and Pacific Affairs, U.S. Department of State, before the Senate Committee on Foreign Relations Subcommittee on East Asian and Pacific Affairs: Democracy and human rights in the context of the Asia rebalance.* US Senate Committee on Foreign Relations. https://www.foreign.senate.gov/imo/media/doc/Yun_Testimony1.pdf. Accessed 6 March 2020.

Zhang, G. (2019). Yidaiyilu changyi yu Yintai zhanlue gouxiang de bijiao fenxi [A comparative analysis of the BRI and the Indo-Pacific strategy]. *Xiandai guoji guanxi* [Contemporary International Relations], *2*, 26–34.

Zhang, J. (2018). Hangshi Zhongguo fang'an yingdui Yatai zhixu zhizheng [Substantiating the Chinese solutions to compete for Asia Pacific order]. *Shijie zhishi* [World Affairs], *13*, 80.

Zhang, J. (2019). Dongmeng zhengshi jieshou le 'Yintai' gainian [ASEAN formally accepts the Indo-Pacific concept]. *Shijie zhishi* [World Affairs], *15*, 32–33.

Zhang, J., & Liu, L. (2015). Meiguo Yatai zai pingheng zhanlue zai pinggu [Revisiting US Asia-Pacific rebalance strategy]. *Nanyang wenti yanjiu* [Southeast Asian Affairs], *4*, 20–27.

Zhang, L. (2019). 'Yindai' zhanlue de jueding yinsu, fazhan quxiang ji Zhongguo yingdui [The decisive factors and trends of Indo-Pacific strategy and China's responses]. *Nanya yanjiu jikan* [South Asian Studies Quarterly], *1*, 1–7.

Zhao, M. (2019). Meiguo zheng fuyu 'Yintai zhanlue' shizhi neirong [The US substantiates the Indo-Pacific strategy]. *Shijie zhishi* [World Affairs], *5*, 55–57.

Zhao, T. (2016, August 30). *Zhong han dui 'Sade' de renzhi chayi* [The different perceptions of China and ROK on the 'THAAD' issue]. Carnegie–Tsinghua Center for Global Policy. https://carnegietsinghua.org/2016/08/30/zh-pub-64430. Accessed 2 March 2020.

Zhong, H. (2019). Yintai zhanlue Beijing xia Telangpu zhengfu dui Taiwan de juese dingwei jiqi yingxiang [Taiwan's role in Trump administration's Indo-Pacific strategy and its implications]. *Xiandai Taiwan yanjiu* [Contemporary Taiwan Studies], *5*, 42–49.

Zhou, C. (2020, March 27). Donald Trump signs TAIPEI Act to support Taiwan's international relations. *South China Morning Post*. https://www.scmp.com/news/china/diplomacy/article/3077192/donald-trump-signs-taipei-act-support-taiwans-international. Accessed 28 March 2020.

Japan's Asia–Pacific Diplomacy in the Twenty-First Century: Empty Rhetoric or a New Paradigm?

Balazs Kiglics

The Rise of Japan's Values-Based Diplomacy

During the Cold War and into the 1990s, Japanese foreign policy was characterised by its low-key diplomacy and high dependence on the US security umbrella (Akaha, 1991, pp. 324–325; Edström, 1999, pp. 8–25), in which period Tokyo was not known to be sensitive to democracy and human rights (Hasegawa, 2007, p. 65).[1] Even after the Japanese economy entered a prolonged period of stagnation in the early 1990s, while the Chinese economy continued to produce double-digit growth annually and globalisation accelerated in East and Southeast Asia, Tokyo's attitude towards the region continued to be relatively detached, as was shown, for instance, during the 1997–1998 Asian Financial Crisis. This was in contrast with Beijing's leadership in, and its successful handling of,

---

[1] For instance, while Japan–China relations were suspended soon after the Tiananmen Square protests to be in line with international sanctions, Japan soon embarked on a conscious policy that aimed to bring China back from its international isolation, and became the first major country to put relations back on track with China after 1989.

B. Kiglics (✉)
University of Otago, Dunedin, New Zealand
e-mail: balazs.kiglics@otago.ac.nz

© The Author(s), under exclusive license to Springer Nature
Singapore Pte Ltd. 2022
R. Patman et al. (eds.), *From Asia-Pacific to Indo-Pacific*, Global Political
Transitions, https://doi.org/10.1007/978-981-16-7007-7_6

the crisis, which caught the attention of many of the affected Southeast Asian countries. China was also able to further expand its influence across the region after attaining membership of the World Trade Organization (WTO) in 2001. At the same time, criticism towards Tokyo's 'check-book diplomacy' (Rose, 2000, p. 126; Tsuneo, 2000, p. 180) and Japan's growing domestic fiscal strains resulted in Japanese policymakers' questioning of Tokyo's Official Development Assistance as an effective foreign policy tool (Fukushima, 2000, p. 170). Japan's continued economic stagnation and China's rapidly growing regional economic influence had started to pose a significant challenge to the Japanese diplomacy by the beginning of the 2000s. Simply put, Tokyo could no longer rely on a passive and reactive economic diplomacy if it did not want to be left behind.

It was Beijing that first proposed a closer regional co-operation in the form of a free trade agreement (FTA) at the Association of Southeast Asian Nations (ASEAN) Plus China Summit in Manila in 1999. Surprising to many at the time, the proposal was quickly accepted by the ASEAN countries, and formal negotiations for the establishment of an ASEAN–China FTA were announced at the Brunei Summit in November 2001 (Cai, 2003, p. 396). Tokyo swiftly responded by putting forward the idea of an East Asian Community (EAC) at a meeting with ASEAN countries in Singapore in January 2002, when then Japanese Prime Minister Junichirō Koizumi proposed the creation of a regional community of nations that 'acts together and advances together' (MOFA, 2002). While Koizumi's speech placed a particular importance on Japan's relations with China, the occasion and place of his speech highlighted Tokyo's intentions that a Japan–ASEAN relationship should form the foundation of an EAC, based upon which engagement with other Asian countries like China should be built. A significant milestone in clarifying Tokyo's vision for regional co-operation came with the foundation of the Council on East Asian Community (CEAC),[2] an all-Japan intellectual platform funded by the Japanese Government. Interestingly, the CEAC was created in response to the China-led Network of East Asian Think-Tanks (Kim & Lee, 2017). China appeared open to the idea of the EAC, but a main

---

[2] The CEAC was headed by the ex-diplomat and political scientist Kenichi Itō, and was partly funded by former Prime Minister Yasuhiro Nakasone. Its membership consisted of representatives of public policy think tanks, business corporations, ex-bureaucrats, scholars, journalists and politicians. See http://www.ceac.jp/e/.

point of contention with Japan was around membership: Beijing preferred a closed type of regionalism that limited participation to the ASEAN Plus Three group,[3] while Tokyo insisted on an 'outward-looking' community welcoming countries outside the region as its members, particularly those that respected 'universal rules and principles' like Australia and New Zealand (MOFA, 2003, p. 5).

Sino-Japanese relations suffered a significant downturn in the early 2000s. The reasons included Prime Minister Koizumi's generally unapologetic attitude towards Japan's role in the Pacific during the Second World War, his annual visits to the controversial Yasukuni Shrine (Rose, 2008),[4] and territorial disputes regarding the ownership of the Senkaku/Diaoyu Islands. Amidst these tensions, Beijing strongly objected to Japan's bid for a permanent seat on the United Nations Security Council in 2004, which even triggered street protests across China (and South Korea). Some of these protests turned into anti-Japanese riots in a number of major Chinese cities, causing significant damage to Japanese business properties. In November 2004, a Chinese nuclear submarine intruded into Japanese territorial waters, an incident which prompted the Japanese Government to execute its Maritime Security Action Plan for only the second time in history (Ota, 2012, p. 101). Remarkably, between 2004 and 2005, the number of Chinese air force planes violating Japan's air defence zone had increased eightfold, from 13 times in 2004 to 107 times in 2005 (Ikegami, 2012, p. 113). As a result, Japan's National Defense Program Guidelines identified China as a potential threat to Japan's national security for the first time (MOD, 2004).

Growing tensions in Sino-Japanese relations were further highlighted by a sharp reduction in the expressions of mutual affinity in a public opinion poll conducted by the Japanese Government in 2004 and 2005. This polling indicated some of the lowest levels since the Pacific War (Bush, 2013, p. 385; Cabinet Office, n.d.). While Japan's GDP was nearly nine times bigger than that of China in 1990, this ratio had shrunk to only

---

[3] The ASEAN+3 consists of the ten members of ASEAN plus China, Japan and South Korea.

[4] The shrine is considered to be one of the strongest links to Japan's imperial past and wartime atrocities, particularly by China and the two Koreas. Koizumi started making annual visits to the controversial Yasukuni Shrine as prime minister in 2001. He made six visits during his six-year term, the last of which was arguably the most controversial due to its timing: 15 August is the commemorative day of Japan's Second World War surrender.

twice the size by 2005.[5] Bilateral tensions at the time were considered also to be a result of competition for regional leadership.

Enhanced competition with Beijing pushed Tokyo to further clarify its own vision for the region, in which a strengthened alliance with the United States and the promotion of 'universal values' came to play a central role. The first mention of such values appeared in the 2005 Joint Statement of the US–Japan Security Consultative Committee, which declared the advancement of fundamental values such as basic human rights, democracy and the rule of law in the international community as a top global common strategic objective (MOFA, 2005a). These values gradually became incorporated into Japanese strategic visions of regional community-building. For instance, in November 2005, Takio Yamada (2005, p. 1), then Director of the Regional Policy Division in the Asia and Oceanian Affairs Bureau at the Ministry of Foreign Affairs, argued that Japan should encourage a forward-looking transformation of East Asia and 'strive to create conditions where universal values like democracy are respected and can flourish throughout the entire region'.

A month later at the inaugural East Asia Summit (EAS), Japan made a strong case for the promotion of universal values and—despite explicit resistance from China—succeeded in convincing most of the participant countries to declare that the summit 'will be an open, inclusive, transparent and outward-looking forum in which we strive to strengthen global norms and universally recognised values' (MOFA, 2005b). The first EAS saw the further clash of Chinese and Japanese views on EAC participation. China (and Malaysia) firmly opposed expanding the scope of membership beyond the ASEAN Plus Three group,[6] while the Japanese delegation insisted on the inclusion of both Australia and New Zealand (Yoshimatsu, 2012, p. 364). Not being invited to the summit, Washington vehemently objected to any idea of East Asian regionalism that was exclusive of the United States (Tōgō, 2008, p. 175). Under these circumstances, there was little agreement on how to make progress

---

[5] The Chinese economy continued to produce two-figure growth annually, and overtook Japan's to become the world's second-largest economy by the end of 2010. For a detailed comparison, see https://data.worldbank.org/indicator/NY.GDP.MKTP.CD?end=2018&locations=JP-CN&page=2&start=1990.

[6] The group consists of the ten members of the Association of Southeast Asian Nations (ASEAN) and China, Japan and South Korea.

with regional community building, and the creation of an EAC eventually became a 'dead-end idea' (Hosoya, 2013, p. 149). The events of 2004–2005 drew the interests of Japan and the United States even closer to each other. References to shared universal values became frequent in their subsequent joint diplomatic statements, to the point that Koizumi referred to a 'value-alliance' (*kachi dōmei*) during his final trip to Washington as prime minister in June 2006. The subsequent United States–Japan Joint Statement declared that co-operation between Washington and Tokyo 'heralded a new US–Japan Alliance of Global Cooperation for the 21st Century' that was based on the 'advancement of core universal values such as freedom, human dignity and human rights, democracy, market economy, and rule of law' (GPO, 2006). This universal values-based alliance with the United States provided a new and essential pillar of Japanese diplomacy in the Asia–Pacific (and beyond) over the following years.

Tokyo's Values Diplomacy in Action

Before Shinzō Abe was inaugurated as Japan's prime minister in September 2006, he published a book entitled *Towards a Beautiful Country*, in which he explained his political philosophy and vision for Japan as a 'beautiful' and 'confident' country. His book argued that Japan needed to show leadership by contributing to the strengthening of universal values across the globe, and in Asia in particular. Abe also stated that it was necessary to convene summits or ministerial meetings among Japan, Australia, the United States and India, in order to achieve the strategic goal of promoting such values across the region (Abe, 2006). In line with that thinking, Abe's foreign minister, Tarō Asō, in his November 2006 speech at the Japan Institute of International Affairs, referred to a value-oriented diplomacy, which emphasised the active promotion of universal values as a new strategic initiative (MOFA, 2006). To identify Japan's main target region for its value-oriented diplomacy, Asō introduced the concept of an 'Arc of Freedom and Prosperity', which covered an area that broadly consisted of the outer rim of the Eurasian landmass, and where Tokyo hoped to help democratic nations come together and support the active strengthening of universal values in and among them (MOFA, 2007a) (Fig. 1).

Soon after Asō's initiative, in a policy speech to the Japanese Diet in early 2007, Abe introduced the concept of 'proactive diplomacy' and

Fig. 1 The 'Arc of Freedom and Prosperity' (*Source* 'A new Pillar for Japanese Diplomacy: Creating an Arc of Freedom and Prosperity', Diplomatic Bluebook 2007, Ministry of Foreign Affairs of Japan, n.d. http://www.mofa.go.jp/policy/other/bluebook/2007/html/h1/h1_01.html)

described Japan as 'a country that will serve as a new role model in the international community of the twenty-first century' (Cabinet Office, 2007). The first of the three pillars of Abe's proactive diplomacy was aimed at strengthening partnerships with countries that share the fundamental values of freedom, democracy, basic human rights and the rule of law. By that time, Abe had already embarked on deepening co-operation with like-minded countries in the region. One of his visits as prime minister was to New Delhi, where he and the Indian Prime Minister, Manmohan Singh, signed the 'Joint Statement towards Japan–India Strategic and Global Partnership'. The document declared that India and Japan were 'natural partners as the largest and most developed democracies of Asia', and that the two countries shared a 'common commitment to democracy, open society, human rights, rule of law and a free market economy' (MEA, 2006). Abe and the Australian Prime

Minister, John Howard, agreed to enter into formal talks about a bilateral economic partnership agreement in their first meeting in December 2006, which led to the signing of the Japan–Australia Joint Declaration on Security Cooperation in March the following year. The declaration affirmed that the two countries' strategic partnership was based on democratic values, a commitment to human rights, freedom and the rule of law, and committed to the continuing development of their strategic partnership to reflect shared values and interests (MOFA, 2007b). This was followed by a number of high-level bilateral meetings and other agreements that eventually led to the signing of the Memorandum on Defence Cooperation in December 2008, which aimed to strengthen national security co-operation in a trilateral framework between Japan, Australia and the United States (MOD, 2008). This agreement also aimed at expanding trilateral co-operation in regional multilateral frameworks such as the ASEAN Regional Forum, a key forum for security dialogue in Asia in which the three countries participate as dialogue members.[7]

The start of Japan's proactive diplomacy coincided with NATO's global partnerships initiative, which aimed at reaching beyond its traditional partners and establishing deeper relations with countries such as Australia and Japan, and regions such as Central Asia (NATO, 2006). In January 2007, Abe became the first Japanese prime minister to visit the NATO headquarters in Brussels. In his speech there, Abe pointed out that Tokyo was a natural partner in terms of sharing and protecting universal values and that Japan and NATO must 'elevate democracy in places where it is emerging; consolidate respect for human rights where it is suppressed' (NATO, 2007). After Abe's visit, Foreign Minister Asō went on to actively pursue the strengthening of universal values in bilateral and multilateral settings in the 'Arc countries' across Eurasia. He also sought to deepen co-operation in other existing multilateral frameworks such as the 'Central Asia Plus Japan' dialogue, the 'Visegrád Four and Japan' talks, Tokyo's dialogue with the GUAM countries (Georgia, Ukraine, Azerbaijan and Moldova), and co-operation with the South Asian Association for Regional Cooperation. Asō's visits and concluding joint statements always emphasised the pursuit of universal values and common goals as areas of common co-operation. However, and somewhat unexpectedly, Japan's coalition government was defeated in the July 2007 House of

---

[7] For an overview of the ASEAN Regional Forum, visit http://dfat.gov.au/internati onal-relations/regional-architecture/Pages/asean-regional-forum-arf.aspx.

Councillors (the Japanese Diet's Upper House) elections, after which Abe was forced to reshuffle his Cabinet, which resulted in Asō's resignation as foreign minister. Just three months later, Abe also resigned, citing health issues. These changes meant that Japan's value-oriented diplomacy lost its two main figures, and the concept of Arc of Freedom and Prosperity literally vanished from Japan's foreign policy strategy. The continued stagnation of the Japanese economy and prolonged internal political struggles meant that seven different governments were formed under seven different prime ministers in the next six years, including three formed by the Democratic Party of Japan, the main opposition to Abe's long-reigning Liberal Democratic Party between 2009 and 2012. Each successive prime minister had his own foreign policy and placed varying degrees of importance, if any, on the promotion of universal values.

THE DEEPENING SINO-JAPANESE CONFLICT

Hopes for a brighter chapter in Japan–China relations (Gao, 2008) were dampened by the fact that their bilateral relations continued to be more competitive than co-operative. Persistent tensions over different interpretations of history and territorial disputes had in fact further deepened, steering Sino-Japanese relations towards confrontation. The threat of conflict became imminent in 2010, when a Chinese fishing boat rammed into a Japan Coast Guard ship near the disputed Senkaku/Diaoyu Islands in the East China Sea. The incident resulted in the Japan Coast Guard's arrest of the captain of the Chinese boat. Tokyo then issued a statement saying there were no territorial issues surrounding the Senkaku/Diaoyu Islands as they were an inherent part of Japan's territory. In response, China's foreign ministry issued a statement claiming that Japan's actions 'seriously infringed upon China's territorial sovereignty and violated the human rights of Chinese citizens'. Furthermore, Premier Wen Jiabao stated that the islands were a part of China's 'sacred territory', and that the arrest of the captain was unlawful (Ross, 2013, p. 87). In response, China arrested four Japanese businessmen, introduced a trade ban on the export of rare earth elements to Japan and suspended the exchange of people from the ministerial level to the high-school student level (Kitaoka, 2011, p. 7). Japan yielded to pressure from China (as well as from the United States), released the Chinese captain and dropped all charges against him, but the incident and its outcome prompted Tokyo to further strengthen its relationship with Washington. Japan's December

2010 National Defense Program Guidelines stated that China's military modernisation and growing maritime activities caused 'concern for the regional and global community' and that the Japan–United States alliance remained 'indispensable in ensuring the peace and security of Japan' (MOD, 2010). Foreign Minister Seiji Maehara declared that 'an unshakeable Japan–US alliance will be essential' for the security of Japan and for peace and stability in the Asia–Pacific (MOFA, 2011). In the same year, Washington confirmed it would pay more attention to territorial disputes in Asia, declaring that the United States had a 'national interest in freedom of navigation' and in the 'open access to Asia's maritime commons' (Clinton, 2010). The Obama Administration went on to announce 'America's Pacific Century', which also meant a strengthened military presence in East and Southeast Asia that became known as the 'pivot' or 'rebalance' to Asia (Clinton, 2011).

Sino-Japanese tensions erupted again in 2012, when the former Governor of Tokyo, the right-wing politician Shintarō Ishihara, started a fundraising campaign to buy some of the Senkaku/Diaoyu Islands. In an attempt to prevent that, the Japanese Government announced the purchase of three islets in the area. Beijing reacted by stepping up its military presence in the East China Sea and sent six surveillance ships that carried out a 'patrol and law enforcement mission' near the disputed territories. China's Ministry of National Defense openly accused Japan of 'playing with fire' (Takenaka, 2012) and an editorial in the Chinese *Global Times* (2012)[8] argued that, under the new circumstances, 'backing off was no longer an option' for China. The Chinese Government issued a White Paper in the same month, which stated that the islands were 'China's inherent territory in all historical, geographical and legal terms', and that the country enjoyed 'indisputable sovereignty' over the islands (State Council, 2012). Washington, which for a long time occupied a neutral position regarding the islands, decided to throw its weight behind Tokyo. In December 2012, the US Senate passed a defence policy bill that guaranteed that the Senkaku/Diaoyu Islands were covered by the existing security treaty between the United States and Japan (Japan Daily Press, 2012).

---

[8] The *Global Times* is a nationalist tabloid owned by the *People's Daily*, the official newspaper of the Chinese Communist Party. The *Global Times* is one of China's largest English-language newspapers, and a major platform for commenting on international news from a Chinese perspective. Its website claims to have 15 million visits a day.

Meanwhile, the Liberal Democratic Party came back to power with a sweeping victory in the upper house elections, and Abe embarked on his second term as prime minister. A stronger United States commitment to Japan as well as a new conservative government in Tokyo only led to more friction in Japan–China relations. Beijing announced the establishment of its National Security Commission and stepped up its economic and military activities in the East China Sea. Despite a 2008 agreement between Japan and China, Beijing unilaterally started the development of the Shirakaba natural gas field in an area where territorial boundaries were disputed by both countries (Asia Daily Wire, 2013). In response to the new US defence policy bill, Beijing announced the establishment of an Air Defence Identification Zone (ADIZ) in the East China Sea that also covered the disputed islands. China's new ADIZ went as far as up to some 480 km beyond China's territorial sea, and, more importantly, overlapped with Japan's decades-long ADIZ in the same region (Vanhullebusch & Wei, 2016, p. 122). Between 2013 and 2015, Beijing also stepped up its military presence by building artificial islands with ports capable of sustaining military activities across the South China Sea in areas that were claimed by a number of ASEAN countries. These activities and China's declaration of territorial sovereignty over these areas further escalated tensions and raised significant security concerns across East and Southeast Asia.[9]

'Proactive Pacifism' Abe-Style

After returning to office, Abe's Administration went to great lengths to strengthen Japan's national security. He successfully pushed to reinterpret Article 9 of the Japanese Constitution by extending the scope of self-defence to that of collective self-defence. This move opened up the possibility for the Japan Self-Defense Forces to join the US military, and other partner countries, in combat outside Japan's own territory. In line with that, the Abe Administration renewed the Guidelines for Japan–U.S. Defense Cooperation. The new guidelines extended the areas where Tokyo could cooperate with Washington, with a focus on military contingencies that might directly affect Japan (Lande, 2018). Then,

[9] For an analysis with further links, see https://www.uscc.gov/sites/default/files/Res earch/China's%20Island%20Building%20in%20the%20South%20China%20Sea_0.pdf; for a visualisation, visit China Island Tracker at https://amti.csis.org/island-tracker/china.

in August 2013, on the anniversary of the Hiroshima atomic bombing, the Maritime Self-Defense Force launched the *Izumo*, Japan's newest and largest flat-top destroyer, sparking Beijing's accusations of a military escalation (Firn, 2013).[10] In November the same year, a large joint Japan–US naval exercise was held near the Senkaku Islands. During his first term as prime minister, Abe had consciously refrained from visiting the Yasukuni Shrine. In a sharp contrast to his earlier policy, Abe paid an unannounced visit to the shrine on the first anniversary of his re-election in December 2013, which move triggered a new wave of protest from Beijing (and Seoul). At the same time, his government hastily pushed the highly controversial State Secrets Protection Law (SSL) through the Japanese Diet. The SSL allowed for the Japanese Government to designate information as a state secret in areas such as defence, foreign policy and intelligence-gathering on behalf of a foreign power (Cabinet Secretariat, n.d.). Article 18 of the SSL granted full rights to Abe, as prime minister, to set the standards of classifying and declassifying state secrets,[11] and placed strict penalties on whistle-blowers. Still in the same month, Abe established the National Security Council, adopted Japan's first National Security Strategy and approved Japan's new National Defense Program Guidelines.[12] A main strategic adviser to Abe, Shinichi Kitaoka (2014b), explained that it was necessary for Japan to upgrade its defence forces to counter an increasingly assertive China (and respond to North Korea's progress in developing missiles and nuclear weapons), labelling Japan's

[10] While Tokyo said that the flagship will take part only in Maritime Self-Defense Force missions and will not be used as an aircraft carrier, Beijing's criticism of the move pointed out that *Izumo* was also the name of the Japanese battleship that led the country's invasion of China in the 1930s.

[11] Although the prime minister is required to consult an advisory committee, that committee does not have authority over the prime minister's final decision; its recommendations are non-binding. Also, when a government agency decides to destroy any designated state secret, it only has to obtain the approval of the prime minister before doing so. In the process, it is not required to consult other agencies, including public ones. A group of 24 prominent Japanese scholars issued a declaration against the bill before it was passed. They criticised it as being unconstitutional and threatening fundamental human rights. Over 80% of Japanese opposed the bill at the time, with street protests drawing crowds of up to 10,000 people in Tokyo. For the petition (in Japanese), see http://blog.livedoor.jp/nihonkokukenpou/archives/51748396.html.

[12] All these were preceded by the Chinese Government's announcement of the establishment of its National Security Commission and the creation of an ADIZ in the East China Sea that overlapped with that of Japan.

new defence strategy 'proactive pacifism'. Kitaoka (2014a) argued that the idea of passive pacifism had been mistaken in light of the continued expansion of the Chinese military. He added that, while Japan's self-defence budget had remained nearly flat in the preceding 25 years, China's annual military spending had increased 33-fold during the same period. The essence of proactive pacifism was to shore up Japan's defence capabilities and to continue to strengthen relations with like-minded countries based on a perception of shared values, particularly with India and the United States. Abe's new government also went on to lift Japan's decades-long self-imposed ban on arms exports in April 2014, replacing the highly restrictive and decades-long 'Three Principles' on weapons and military technology export with more permissive guidelines (MOFA, 2014).

In a speech during his first visit to Washington into his second term, Abe maintained that 'doors are always open on my side for the Chinese leaders' (MOFA, 2013). Accordingly, Japan's 2013 National Security Strategy called for the strengthening of co-operation with China under the principle of a 'Mutually Beneficial Relationship Based on Common Strategic Interests', including in the fields of politics and security (Cabinet Secretariat, 2013, p. 25). In reality, however, no significant effort was made by either Tokyo or Beijing to improve bilateral relations. Instead, both countries' leaderships appeared to be passively open and waited for the other side to initiate talks. This resulted in the two countries' leaders' failure to meet for nearly two years. When Abe and President Xi Jinping finally met on the sidelines of the Asia–Pacific Economic Cooperation (APEC) summit in Beijing in November 2014, their conversation was reported to have lasted for only 25 minutes, during which time both leaders appeared to be reserved. The outcome of their meeting was a 'vaguely worded statement' in which both sides recognised their 'different views' of history and territorial disputes (*Japan Times*, 2014). Despite these tensions, however, lawmakers on both sides continued to work on economic co-operation. Over the following years, it was groups like the Japan–China Economic Association and the Japan Business Federation that played a central role in Japan's relations with China, leading business delegations there and meeting with Chinese policymakers.

While failing to meet with his Chinese counterparts for two years, Abe visited leaders of a 'quarter of the world' (Panda, 2014) during the period: he flew to 49 countries, including the ASEAN countries, Mongolia, a number of Middle Eastern countries, Africa, Europe, South

America and North America, including two visits to the United States—during all of which trips he frequently made references to the importance of shared values. In other words, Abe's earlier value-oriented diplomacy was back in full swing. He also held a series of bilateral meetings with the Indian Prime Minister, Narendra Modi, including when he attended India's Republic Day parade as its chief guest in 2014. In July the same year, India invited Japan's Maritime Self-Defense Force to participate in Exercise Malabar, an annual joint military exercise with the US Navy. The exercise reflects its participants' shared perspectives on Indo-Pacific maritime security. Japan became a permanent Malabar member in 2015, and has taken part in the trilateral exercise every year since then.[13] In September 2014, Abe and Modi signed a number of key agreements, including one which upgraded the Japan–India relationship to a 'Special Strategic and Global Partnership' (MOFA, 2017). A major reason for the enhanced co-operation between New Delhi and Tokyo—what some refer to as 'Asia's most strategic friendship' (Miller, 2017)—was a shared strategic anxiety about China's rise and its implications for the Indo-Pacific. The Abe Administration's strategy to forge closer co-operation among like-minded countries in the region was highlighted by the first Japan–Australia–India trilateral dialogue in New Delhi in 2015, after which the three countries began to meet regularly—both trilaterally and in multilateral settings. Abe and Modi have since held 12 summit meetings and agreed to expand co-operation to 2 + 2 meetings for foreign and defence ministerial dialogues; Tokyo and Canberra have also held eight 2 + 2 meetings, where the two countries worked towards strengthening co-operation in a wide range of areas that included security, economic issues and regional affairs.

Abe preferred to view this trilateral co-operation as a part of an Asian 'Democratic Security Diamond' (DSD), which involves four prominent Asia–Pacific maritime democracies—Japan, Australia, India and the United States—with geographic lines between them forming a diamond-like shape across the region (Lee & Lee, 2016). It was during Abe's first term when the four nations began the so-called Quadrilateral Security Dialogue (Quad) with the aim to safeguard the maritime commons, address Chinese influence in the region, conduct joint exercises and defend the freedom of navigation. The DSD was basically a resurrection

---

[13] Japan first joined the exercise in 2007, at the time of the first Abe Administration.

of the Quad, which Abe announced just one day after assuming office in his second term in December 2012. Tokyo has also been a member of the United States–Japan–Australia Trilateral Strategic Dialogue. Established in 2002 to deal with joint security threats, the trilateral dialogue involves co-operation in the fields of intelligence, surveillance and reconnaissance, undersea warfare and missile defence, as well as developing greater interoperability. In 2017, Tokyo and Canberra agreed to conduct bilateral security exercises and operations separately as well. Closer co-operation between like-minded countries in the region was a part of Abe's concept of a 'Free and Open Indo-Pacific', which to an extent was the resurrection of his earlier administration's Arc of Freedom and Prosperity initiative, and aimed at promoting the stability and prosperity of a region that stretched from the Asia–Pacific through the Indian Ocean to the Middle East and Africa, with the aim of securing a free and open international maritime order in that region (MOFA, 2020; see also MOFA, 2019, p. 180).

Values Diplomacy and the United States–China Rivalry

Over the past years, three major economic co-operation frameworks have emerged in the region: the initially ASEAN-driven, but later China-dominated, Regional Comprehensive Economic Partnership (RCEP),[14] the China-centred Belt and Road Initiative (BRI), and the Trans-Pacific Partnership (TPP) agreement, the last of which is now referred to as the Comprehensive and Progressive Agreement for Trans-Pacific Partnership (CPTTP). Japan is a member of both the RCEP and the CPTPP, but not the BRI. The BRI is Beijing's own development initiative. It is based on bilateral agreements with some 125 countries and 29 international organisations (Belt and Road Portal, 2019) and focuses on expanding infrastructure, investment and trade networks by positioning China at its centre.[15] Beijing has used the BRI to strengthen its position as both

[14] For an overview of the RCEP, visit https://www.mfat.govt.nz/en/trade/free-trade-agreements/agreements-under-negotiation/regional-comprehensive-economic-partnership-rcep/rcep-overview.

[15] It was first announced as Beijing's 'One Belt One Road' (OBOR) initiative, but was changed to BRI in 2016 after criticisms of the emphasis on the word 'one'. However, OBOR (*yīdài yīlù*) is still used in Chinese-language media.

a regional and global leader and deepen ties with possible allies across the Eurasian continent.[16] Parallel to the BRI, and closely aligned with it, China initiated two new international financial institutions: the Asian Infrastructure Investment Bank and the New Development Bank.

Of these three initiatives, the CPTPP seems to be the most comprehensive economic partnership agreement, which includes not only trade and investment, but also e-commerce, state-owned enterprise reform and protection of intellectual property rights. Negotiations between its 12 members started during the Obama Administration, and were driven mainly by the United States–Japan tandem. However, Washington's attitude took a significant change with the 2016 election of President Donald Trump, whose 'America First' policy—which defined American interests in a much narrower nationalistic context—signalled a radical departure from a firm US commitment to multilateralism, as well as a much less enthusiastic leadership, if at all, in international organisations.[17] Trump made his intentions clear by withdrawing the United States from the TPP, his predecessor's signature trade deal, on his first day in office on 23 January 2017. While Tokyo was hit hard by losing the United States as its main trade ally in the TPP, the Abe Government stepped up and went on to lead negotiations among the remaining 11 countries. Tokyo's efforts resulted in the signing of the CPTPP. Japan also signed a multilateral trade agreement with the European Union, after talks were unsuccessful in finalising its Transatlantic Trade and Investment Partnership with the United States. With a new confidence, the Abe Government also strengthened engagement with a number of regional fora, including APEC, ASEAN, the ASEAN Plus Three and the ASEAN Regional Forum (MOFA, 2019).

While a growing sense of rivalry in the Sino–United States geopolitical and strategic competition predated the Trump Administration, tensions escalated to a new high with the outbreak of a trade war in 2018. In his State of the Union Address that year, Trump declared that China was one of the two US 'rivals that challenge our interests, our economy,

---

[16] See a compilation of analyses of the BRI at https://www.worldbank.org/en/topic/regional-integration/brief/belt-and-road-initiative.

[17] At the 2019 UN Summit, for instance, President Trump declared that the 'future does not belong to globalists, the future belongs to patriots.' See https://www.bloomberg.com/amp/news/articles/2019-09-24/trump-uses-un-speech-to-hit-china-over-trade-weeks-before-talks.

and our values' (The White House, 2018).[18] The Trump Administration then went on to impose a number of new tariffs on Chinese imports in response to what it referred to as China's continued unfair trade practices. Beijing reacted by imposing tariffs on a range of US goods. With neither side willing to back down, United States–China trade tensions erupted into a full-blown trade war. In May 2020, the total value of US tariffs applied to Chinese goods stood at US$550 billion, while Chinese tariffs imposed on US goods amounted to US$185 billion (China Briefing, 2020). It must be noted that, in the US President's view, 'trade equals military' in the Chinese context (The White House, 2019).

At the conclusion of the G20 Summit in Osaka in June 2019, assessments of the global economy increasingly identified the United States–China trade dispute as the main danger to its stability (see for example IMF, 2019). Having the fourth-largest export economy of the world, Japan has also been significantly affected by the spill over from the trade war: its exports fell by 8.2% year on year in August 2019, particularly to China, a decrease that exceeded the deceleration of the Chinese economy (Shane, 2019). Several major Japanese corporations, including Nintendo, Sony, Sharp, Ricoh and Kyocera, announced plans to move their production out of China in the same year (Sese, 2019). Another consequence of a deepening conflict between the United States and China was that Japan overtook the latter to become the second-largest user of the Panama Canal after the United States. In the month of the Osaka Summit, Japan also surpassed China as the main holder of US Treasury securities, and the gap between these two major holders of US foreign debt has been increasing ever since (Department of the Treasury, 2020).

United States–China tensions have also escalated in the national security and military domain. In May 2019, the US Department of Commerce added China's Huawei Technologies to the Bureau of Industry and Security's Entity List. The list imposes strict limitations and regulations on foreign businesses, governments, people and institutions that pose a national security risk. Over the following months, the list was expanded to include an additional 46 Huawei affiliates, bringing the total to over 100 persons and companies with Huawei ties. During the same time, the US Department of Defense (2019) released its new Indo-Pacific Strategy Report, which asserted Beijing sought to 'reorder the region to

---

[18] The other rival President Trump referred to was Russia.

its advantage by leveraging military modernization, influence operations, and predatory economics to coerce other nations'. The continued militarisation of sea lanes in East and Southeast Asia was highlighted by the fact that the navies of both the United States and China conducted a high number of drills in those regions in 2019. For instance, US Navy ships frequently carried out 'freedom of navigation' operations (FONOPs) in contested territories in the East and South China Seas, including around the Spratly Islands and the Taiwan Strait. On a number of these occasions, Beijing issued démarches to the US Navy, which in turn asserted in its statements that these FONOP passages demonstrated the United States' 'commitment to a free and open Indo-Pacific', and called on China to 'cease its bullying behaviour' towards other nations in the region. (Bose, 2019). In addition, the United States sold two arms packages to Taiwan, totalling over US$10 billion, in 2019, which included tanks, missiles and fighter jets.[19] In July 2019, China issued its first white paper on national defence for seven years. The document stated that, with its 2016 deployment of the Terminal High Altitude Area Defense system in South Korea, the United States had 'severely undermined the regional strategic balance' in the Asia–Pacific (Xinhuanet, 2019).

During recent years, Japan's annual defence white papers have continued to point to China's 'unilateral, coercive attempts' (MOD, 2019, p. 17) as a challenge to the existing regional order, and Beijing's expanding and intensifying military activities as a serious national security concern. As a consequence, Tokyo updated both of its major defence planning documents in December 2018: the National Defense Program Guidelines for policy guidance, and the Mid-Term Defense Program for acquisition. In addition, Japan's defence ministry budget for the period from 2019 to 2023 permitted a significant strengthening of Japan's defence capability in all domains, including the goals of reaching superiority in space, cyberspace and the electromagnetic spectrum (MOD, 2018). Accordingly, Japan's defence budget has increased by 1.2% to a

---

[19] United States–China tensions further escalated in June 2020, when a US Navy aircraft conducted a rare flight over Taiwan, which prompted Beijing to send some of its fighter jets near the island. Chinese experts in a subsequent *Global Times* article argued that Beijing sent a 'powerful warning and demonstrated how much the [Chinese army] was determined and prepared for war.' See https://www.globaltimes.cn/content/1191065.shtml.

record ¥5.32 trillion (approx. US$50.5 billion) in 2019 (Kelly, 2019). While singling out China as its major security concern, Japan's latest defence and diplomatic white papers reconfirmed that a close alliance with the United States continues to be the cornerstone of Japan's national security and diplomacy (MOD, 2019, p. 4; MOFA, 2019, p. 16).

In May 2019, President Trump became Tokyo's first official state guest in *Reiwa*, Japan's new imperial era. His visit was deliberately designed to symbolise the significance of the Japan–United States relationship. A few weeks later, the president flew back to Japan to participate in the G20 Summit in Osaka. While talks during these events reconfirmed the continued importance of the bilateral alliance, they also shed light on considerable tensions between the new US Administration and Tokyo. During both visits, Trump expressed his disappointment with Tokyo on two of his pressing alliance issues: the US trade deficit with Japan and what the US President perceived as a lack of alliance reciprocity, with Trump pressing for significant increases in Japan's share of the burden. There also appeared to be a disconnect between Washington and Tokyo over the issue of North Korea: Trump repeatedly dismissed his Japanese counterparts' concerns over North Korea's short-range missile tests, arguing that they should not be taken as a serious threat (Johnson, 2019). In contrast to that, the China–Japan–South Korea summit, which was resurrected in 2018 after a nearly three-year hiatus, emphasised the promotion of free trade (as opposed to Trump's protectionist agenda) and voiced a shared desire for the complete denuclearisation of the Korean Peninsula (Osaki, 2018).

As a result of an increasingly fraught United States–China relationship as well as considerable tensions within the United States–Japan alliance due to the Trump Administration's growing demands and unpredictable commitment towards Tokyo, the long-troubled Japan–China relationship has experienced a thaw over the past few years. In 2018, reciprocal visits were conducted by Prime Minister Abe and Premier Li Keqiang. Li's visit to Tokyo marked a Chinese premier's first official trip to Japan since 2010. During his visit, Li stated that Japan–China relations had returned to their normal track, while Abe claimed that relations had now transitioned from competition to collaboration. Following that, Abe flew to China in what was the first visit to Beijing by a Japanese prime minister in nearly seven years. The Japanese leader held talks with President Xi and Premier Li, and his visit resulted in the signing of 12 international agreements and memoranda involving various regional and global issues, including the fields of politics, security and foreign affairs (MOFA, 2019, p. 49). While these meetings signified a positive turn in Sino-Japanese relations, deep and persisting tensions over history, disputed maritime territories and China's military expansion prevailed. Leading up to the 2019 G20 Summit in Osaka, a *Global Times* opinion piece described the thaw in China–Japan relations as lacking substance, and urged Abe to 'steer Japan into a true partnership with its neighbor', describing China as 'the last hope for Abe to gain brownie points in diplomacy' (Jiao, 2019). A few days later the same paper argued that Japan need no longer 'play second fiddle' to the United States on the world stage, and could exercise international leadership provided it developed a 'healthy relationship with China'. The article concluded that the two countries have the potential to work together in global and regional governance (Zhang, 2019). In an interview with Japan's *Asahi* newspaper, Liu Mingfu, author of the controversial book *The China Dream*, argued that Japan should move away from being a 'client state strictly controlled by the United States in terms of foreign affairs and national security' and instead 'cooperate with China to create a new order' in the region (Minemura, 2019). While Tokyo makes its alliance with the United States the cornerstone of its foreign policy, it also increasingly needs to cooperate with China to manage present and future uncertainties. These messages suggest that Beijing also expects a much closer strategic co-operation from Japan, although on not very clear terms. Simply put, Tokyo has in the past few years found itself caught in the middle of a superpower-style struggle where it increasingly faces the necessity to navigate, and perhaps to a considerable extent manage, the trilateral.

JAPAN'S VALUES-BASED DIPLOMACY: EMPTY RHETORIC OR A NEW PARADIGM?

Over recent years, Japanese foreign policy has unfolded predominantly in the context of a growing Japan–China and United States–China rivalry as well as an American foreign policy that became less credible, more erratic and less committed to its traditional post-war alliances than ever before. This has forced Japan to continue to invest heavily in the creation of a regional security architecture, coupled with robust economic networks across the Asia–Pacific region (Katagiri, 2019, p. 17). By partnering with a rising power in India and a middle power like Australia, the

Abe Government has consciously brought together a group of strategically like-minded countries. This co-operation is likely to continue to strengthen as China's influence grows and a US commitment to the region continues to be uncertain. To be sure, Japan's alliance with the United States will remain a cornerstone of its foreign policy in the foreseeable future. But it is also likely that Tokyo will conduct a more independent and proactive foreign policy, as its leadership on the CPTPP indicates. In August 2020, Abe stepped down as prime minister for the second time. One of his most significant legacies is the Free and Open Indo-Pacific initiative, but it remains to be seen to what extent his successor, Yoshihide Suga, will pursue the concept further.

Despite being promoted as values-based, Tokyo's foreign policy has, in reality, continuously downplayed democratic values and human rights: the Abe Administration had very little, if anything, to say about the democracy protests in Hong Kong, the Uyghur 're-education' camps or the ethnic cleansing of Tibetans, which, if at all, may have further emboldened Beijing. Tokyo never openly criticised President Duterte's illegal war on drugs against his own civil society, raised its voice to protect ethnic Papuans' rights in Indonesia, or taken action against the Rohingya ethnocide, to name a few significant human rights violations in the region. Japan's reluctance to squarely address its own war crimes in the first half of the twentieth century also impedes its efforts to pursue a foreign policy based on liberal democratic values. While honestly facing its past could cause enormous domestic political problems for Tokyo, it might bolster relations with China and, more importantly, significantly boost relations with a liberal democratic South Korea. The fact that Japan and South Korea have had such strained relations in recent years shows that Japan's more independent and values-based approach may have only a selective appeal unless it is accompanied by a greater willingness to come to terms with its own past. Japan's values-oriented diplomacy has served as a tool to counterbalance China's growing economic power and political influence, to strengthen the United States–Japan relationship, as well as to hedge against future uncertainties in Tokyo's alliance with Washington during the Trump Administration. Through a value-oriented diplomacy, both Abe-led governments aimed to mitigate China's growing influence in the Asia–Pacific, and went to great lengths to strengthen co-operation with possible allies to build a 'free and open' region where universal values are more respected. Among deepening conflicts with China, the second Abe Administration significantly bolstered Japan's national security and self-defence capabilities, even at the cost of going against Tokyo's widely promoted universal values. Simply put, narrowly defined geopolitical and geoeconomic interests, rather than a genuine pursuit of shared and universal values, seem to have been defining Japanese foreign policy in recent years.

In less than a generation, the Asia–Pacific has undergone a remarkable transformation and has now entered a new era—one that features a more assertive yet more internally turbulent China, and a fracturing American alliance system with a relative power projecting capability that is now less dominant than it has ever been in the post-Second World War era. The unfolding picture is that of a rules-based international system under severe strain, where countries are facing increased pressure to take sides in the rivalry between Washington and Beijing.

In addition, recent projections indicate that, due to the COVID-19 pandemic, a major crisis in the global economy is could unfold—a crisis that is likely to rival or exceed that of any recession in the past 150 years.[20] This, combined with the ongoing climate crisis, will result in sociopolitical consequences never experienced before. Globalisation has made even the United States and China, the two superpowers of our time, much more vulnerable than any great powers in history. What Tokyo—and in fact many other states—seems to understand better than Beijing and Washington is that the challenges the Asia–Pacific is facing at the moment are not—and will never be—within the problem-solving capacity of any single country or partisan alliance. What really should matter is not who leads, but what norms, values and principles lead the evolution of today's Asia–Pacific/Indo-Pacific. A paradigm shift in foreign policy strategies is thus increasingly needed, but that will not happen without a deeper understanding of universal values, based on which a genuinely value-focused diplomacy can be formed. While it is becoming increasingly difficult, Japan can still choose to be at the forefront of establishing such a diplomacy.

---

[20] While China is expected to see a GDP rise of just 1%, forecasts for many other countries are severe: both the US and Japanese economy are facing a decrease of 6.1%, the Eurozone 9.1%, and, for instance, India 3.2%. See https://www.worldbank.org/en/publication/global-economic-prospects.

REFERENCES

Abe, S. (2006). *Utsukushii Kuni e* [Towards a beautiful country]. Bungei Shunju.

Akaha, T. (1991). Japan's comprehensive security policy: A new East Asian environment. *Asian Survey, 31*(4), 324–340.

Asia Daily Wire. (2013, July 4). Japan 'gravely concerned' over China's gas exploration. *Asia Daily Wire.* http://www.asiadailywire.com/2013/07/japan-pro tests-chinas-natural-gas-exploration-in-east-china-sea. Accessed 9 September 2015.

Belt and Road Portal [of the Government of China]. (2019, April 16). *China says Belt, Road will not get involved in territorial disputes.* https://eng.yidaiy ilu.gov.cn/home/rolling/85859.htm. Accessed 15 June 2020.

Bose, N. (2019, July 21). U.S. State Department says concerned by reports of Chinese interference in South China Sea. *Reuters.* https://www.reu ters.com/article/us-usa-china-southchinasea/u-s-state-department-says-con cerned-by-reports-of-chinese-interference-in-south-china-sea-idUSKCN1U F0EM. Accessed 15 June 2020.

Bush, R. C. (2013). *The perils of proximity: China-Japan security relations.* Brookings Institution Press.

Cabinet Office [of the Government of Japan]. (2007, January 7). *Policy Speech by Prime Minister Abe Shinzo to the 166th Session of the Diet.* http://japan. kantei.go.jp/abespeech/2007/01/26speech_e.html. Accessed 21 November 2017.

Cabinet Office. (n.d.). *Seron Chōsa: Chūgoku ni Kansuru Shinkinkan* [Public opinion survey: Affinity towards China]. http://survey.gov-online.go.jp/ h25/h25-gaiko/zh/z10.html. Accessed 15 June 2020.

Cabinet Secretariat [of the Government of Japan]. (2013, December 17). *National Security Strategy.* https://www.cas.go.jp/jp/siryou/131217anzenh oshou/nss-e.pdf. Accessed 15 June 2020.

Cabinet Secretariat. (n.d.). *Tokutei Himitsu ni Kansuru Hōritsu* [Specially Designated Secrets Protection Act]. http://www.cas.go.jp/jp/tokuteihimitsu/hou ritu108.pdf. Accessed 23 November 2017.

Cai, K. G. (2003, December). The ASEAN-China Free Trade Agreement and East Asian regional grouping. *Contemporary Southeast Asia, 25*(3), 387–404.

China Briefing. (2020, May 13). *The US-China trade war: A timeline.* https:// www.china-briefing.com/news/the-us-china-trade-war-a-timeline. Accessed 15 June 2020.

Clinton, H. R. (2010, July 23). *Remarks at press availability.* https://2009- 2017.state.gov/secretary/20092013clinton/rm/2010/07/145095.htm. Accessed 15 June 2020.

Clinton, H. R. (2011, October 11). America's Pacific century. *Foreign Policy.* http://foreignpolicy.com/2011/10/11/americas-pacific-century/. Accessed 15 June 2020.

Department of the Treasury [of the United States]. (2020, May 15). *Major foreign holders of treasury securities.* https://ticdata.treasury.gov/ Publish/mfh.txt https://www.bloomberg.com/news/articles/2019-08-15/ china-loses-status-as-u-s-s-largest-foreign-creditor-to-japan. Accessed 15 June 2020.

Edström, B. (1999). *Japan's evolving foreign policy doctrine: From Yoshida to Miyazawa.* St. Martin's Press.

Firn, M. (2013, August 7). Chinese anger as Japan launches biggest warship since WWII. *The Telegraph.* http://www.telegraph.co.uk/news/worldnews/ asia/japan/10227465/Chinese-anger-as-Japan-launches-biggest-warship-since-WWII.html. Accessed 23 November 2017.

Fukushima, A. (2000). Official Development Assistance (ODA) as a Japanese foreign policy tool. In T. Inoguchi & P. Jain (Eds.), *Japanese foreign policy today* (pp. 152–174). Palgrave Macmillan.

Gao, H. (2008, November). The China–Japan mutually beneficial relationship based on common strategic interests and East Asian peace and stability. *Asia-Pacific Review, 15*(2), 36–51.

Global Times. (2012, September 15). *Backing off not an option for China.* http://www.globaltimes.cn/content/733253.shtml. Accessed 15 June 2020.

GPO [United States Government Publishing Office]. (2006, July 3). Joint statement by President George W. Bush and Prime Minister Junichirō Koizumi of Japan: The Japan-U.S. alliance of the new century. *Presidential Documents, 42*(26), 1247–1249. https://www.govinfo.gov/content/pkg/WCPD-2006-07-03/html/WCPD-2006-07-03-Pg1247.htm. Accessed 4 May 2018.

Hasegawa, T. (2007). Japan's strategic thinking toward Asia in the first half of the 1990s. In G. Rozman, K. Tōgō, & J. P. Ferguson (Eds.), *Japanese Strategic thought towards Asia* (pp. 57–77). Palgrave Macmillan.

Hosoya, Y. (2013, November 1). Japan's two strategies for East Asia: The evolution of Japan's diplomatic strategy. *Asia-Pacific Review, 20*(2), 146–156.

Ikegami, M. (2012). Taiwan's strategic relations with its neighbors: A countervailing force to rising China. In J. Damm & P. Lim (Eds.), *European perspectives on Taiwan* (pp. 107–124). Springer VS.

IMF [International Monetary Fund]. (2019, June 9). *IMF Managing Director Lagarde calls for cooperation to support global growth.* https://www.imf.org/ en/News/Articles/2019/06/09/pr19205-imf-managing-director-lagarde-calls-for-cooperation-to-support-global-growth

Japan Daily Press. (2012, December 5). *U.S. Senate approves bill labeling Senkakus covered by Japan-US security pact.* http://japandailypress.com/u-s-senate-approves-bill-labeling-senkakus-covered-by-japan-us-security-pact-051 9350/. Accessed 9 September 2015.

Japan Times. (2014, November 10). Abe meet Xi for first China-Japan summit in more than two years. https://www.japantimes.co.jp/news/2014/11/10/

national/politics-diplomacy/abe-xi-meeting-likely-monday-sources/#.VoL AE0-REWh. Accessed 24 November 2014.

Jiao, K. (2019, June 23). Japan needs to end its two-faced China policy. *Global Times*. http://www.globaltimes.cn/content/1155408.shtml. Accessed 15 June 2020.

Johnson, J. (2019, August 28). Trump's de facto blessing of North Korea's missile tests sends ominous message to Japan. *Japan Times*. https://www.jap antimes.co.jp/news/2019/08/28/national/trump-blesses-north-korea-tests-japan/#.XuFnXmozYUR. Accessed 15 June 2020.

Katagiri, N. (2019, May 16). Shinzo Abe's Indo-Pacific strategy: Japan's recent achievement and future direction. *Asian Security*, https://doi.org/10.1080/14799855.2019.1607304. Accessed 15 June 2020.

Kelly, T. (2019, August 30). Japan's military seek eighth straight annual hike in defense spending. *Reuters*. https://www.reuters.com/article/us-japan-def ence-budget/japans-military-seek-eighth-straight-annual-hike-in-defense-spe nding-idUSKCN1VK0D2. Accessed 15 June 2020.

Kim, H. J., & Lee, P. P. (2017). China and the network of East Asian think tanks: Socializing China into an East Asian community? *Asian Survey, 57*(3), 571–593.

Kitaoka, S. (2011, December). A new Asian order and the role of Japan. *Asia-Pacific Review, 18*(2), 1–13.

Kitaoka, S. (2014a, February 6). Japan's new national security policy based on 'proactive pacifism'. *Nikkei Asian Review*. https://asia.nikkei.com/Politics/Japan-s-new-national-security-policy-based-on-proactive-pacifism. Accessed 23 November 2017.

Kitaoka, S. (2014b, April 2). The turnabout of Japan's security policy: Toward 'Proactive Pacifism'. *Nippon.com*. http://www.nippon.com/en/cur rents/d00108. Accessed 23 November 2017.

Lande, E. (2018). Between offensive and defensive realism—The Japanese Abe Government's security policy toward China. *Asian Security, 14*(2), 172–92. https://www.tandfonline.com/doi/full/10.1080/14799855.2017.1323882. Accessed 15 June 2020.

Lee, L., & Lee, J. (2016, August). Japan–India cooperation and Abe's demo-cratic security diamond: Possibilities, limitations and the view from Southeast Asia. *Contemporary Southeast Asia, 38*(2), 284–308.

MEA [Ministry of External Affairs, Government of India]. (2006, 15 December). *Joint statement towards India-Japan strategic and global partnership*. http://mea.gov.in/bilateral-documents.htm?dtl/6368/Joint+Sta tement+Towards+IndiaJapan+Strategic+and+Global+Partnership. Accessed 21 November 2017.

MFAT [Ministry of Foreign Affairs and Trade, New Zealand]. (n.d.). *RCEP overview*. https://www.mfat.govt.nz/en/trade/free-trade-agreements/agr

eements-under-negotiation/regional-comprehensive-economic-partnership-rcep/rcep-overview. Accessed 15 June 2020.

Miller, J. B. (2017, November 15). How Abe and Modi can save the Indo-Pacific: Asia's most strategic friendship. *Foreign Affairs*. https://www.foreig naffairs.com/articles/japan/2017-11-15/how-abe-and-modi-can-save-indo-pacific. Accessed 15 June 2020.

Minemura, K. (2019, May 28). Interview: Liu Mingfu: China dreams of over-taking U.S. in 30 years. *Asahi Shimbun*. http://www.asahi.com/ajw/articles/AJ201905280016.html. Accessed 15 June 2020.

MOD [Ministry of Defense, Japan]. (2004, December 10). *National Defense Program Guidelines, FY 2005–*. http://www.mod.go.jp/e/d_act/d_policy/pdf/national_guidelines.pdf. Accessed 16 November 2017.

MOD. (2008, December 18). *Memorandum on defence cooperation between Ministry of Defense, Japan and Department of Defence, Australia*. http://www.mod.go.jp/e/press/release/2008/12/18b.html. Accessed 21 November 2017.

MOD. (2010, December 17). *National Defense Program Guidelines for FY 2011 and beyond*. https://www.mod.go.jp/e/d_act/d_policy/pdf/guideline sfY2011.pdf. Accessed 15 June 2020.

MOD. (2018, December 18). *Medium Term Defense Program (FY 2019–FY 2023)*. https://www.mod.go.jp/j/approach/agenda/guideline/2019/pdf/chuki_seibi31-35_e.pdf. Accessed 15 June 2020.

MOD. (2019). *Defense of Japan 2019*. https://www.mod.go.jp/e/publ/w_p aper/pdf/2019/DOJ2019_Full.pdf. Accessed 15 June 2020.

MOFA [Ministry of Foreign Affairs, Japan]. (2002, January 14). *Speech by Prime Minister Junichirō Koizumi: Japan and ASEAN in East Asia—A sincere and open partnership*. http://www.mofa.go.jp/region/asia-paci/pmv0201/speech.html. Accessed 4 May 2018.

MOFA. (2003, December 12). *Tokyo Declaration for the dynamic and enduring Japan–ASEAN partnership in the new millennium*. http://www.mofa.go.jp/region/asia-paci/asean/year2003/summit/tokyo_dec.pdf. Accessed 4 May 2018.

MOFA. (2005a, February 19). *Joint statement, U.S.–Japan Security Consultative Committee*. http://www.mofa.go.jp/region/n-america/us/security/scc/joint0502.html. Accessed 20 November 2017.

MOFA. (2005b, December 14). *Kuala Lumpur Declaration on the East Asia summit*. http://www.mofa.go.jp/region/asia-paci/eas/joint0512.html. Accessed 4 May 2018.

MOFA. (2006, November 30). Speech by Mr. Tarō Asō, Minister for Foreign Affairs on the Occasion of the Japan Institute of International Affairs Seminar: 'Arc of Freedom and Prosperity: Japan's Expanding Diplomatic Horizons'.

http://www.mofa.go.jp/announce/fm/aso/speech0611.html. Accessed 20 November 2017.

MOFA. (2007a, March). *Diplomatic Bluebook 2007.* http://www.mofa.go. jp/policy/other/bluebook/2007/html/h1/h1_01.html. Accessed 15 June 2020.

MOFA. (2007b, March 13). *Japan–Australia joint declaration on security cooperation.* http://www.mofa.go.jp/region/asia-paci/australia/joint0703.html. Accessed 15 June 2020.

MOFA. (2011, January 6). *Opening a new horizon in the Asia Pacific.* Foreign Policy Speech by H.E. Mr. Seiji Maehara, Minister for Foreign Affairs of Japan at the Center for Strategic and International Studies. https://www.mofa. go.jp/region/n-america/us/juk_1101/speech1101.html. Accessed 15 June 2020.

MOFA. (2013, February 22). *Japan is back, by Shinzo Abe, Prime Minister of Japan.* http://www.mofa.go.jp/announce/pm/abe/us_20130222en.html. Accessed 15 June 2020.

MOFA. (2014, April 1). *The three principles on transfer of defense equipment and technology.* http://www.mofa.go.jp/press/release/press22e_000 010.html. Accessed 24 November 2017.

MOFA. (2017, September 25). *Japan–India relations (basic data).* http://www. mofa.go.jp/region/asia-paci/india/data.html. Accessed 24 November 2017.

MOFA. (2019). *Diplomatic Bluebook.* https://www.mofa.go.jp/files/000527 162.pdf. Accessed 15 June 2020.

MOFA. (2020, May 20). *Free and open Indo-Pacific.* https://www.mofa.go.jp/ policy/page25e_000278.html. Accessed 15 June 2020.

NATO. (2006, April 27). *NATO looks to global partnerships.* https://www.nato. int/docu/update/2006/04-april/e0427c.htm. Accessed 14 June 2020.

NATO. (2007, May 22). *Japan and NATO: Toward further collaboration.* Statement by Prime Minister Shinzō Abe to the North Atlantic Council. https:// www.nato.int/docu/speech/2007/s070112b.html. Accessed 15 June 2020.

Osaki, T. (2018, May 9). Japan, China and South Korea are 'in sync' on North Korea, Japanese official says. *Japan Times.* https://www.japantimes.co.jp/ news/2018/05/09/national/politics-diplomacy/japan-hosts-leaders-china-south-korea-summit-north-korea/#.XuVjBGozYUQ. Accessed 15 June 2020.

Ota, F. (2012). Lessons learned by the Japanese navy and coast guard from maritime security operations. In B. F. Uzer (Ed.), *Maritime security and defence against terrorism* (pp. 93–102). IOS Press.

Panda, A. (2014, September 11). Shinzo Abe has visited a quarter of the world's countries in 20 months: Why? *The Diplomat.* https://thediplomat. com/2014/09/shinzo-abe-has-visited-a-quarter-of-the-worlds-countries-in-20-months-why. Accessed 24 November 2014.

Rose, C. (2000). Japanese role in PKO and humanitarian assistance. In T. Inoguchi & P. Jain (Eds.), *Japanese foreign policy today* (pp. 122–135). Palgrave Macmillan.

Rose, C. (2008). Stalemate: The Yasukuni Shrine problem in Sino-Japanese relations. In J. Breen (Ed.), *Yasukuni, the war dead, and the struggle for Japan's past* (pp. 23–45). Columbia University Press.

Ross, R. S. (2013). The domestic sources of China's 'assertive diplomacy', 2009–2010: Nationalism and Chinese foreign policy. In R. Foot (Ed.), *China across the divide: The domestic and global in politics and society* (pp. 72–93). Oxford University Press.

Sese, S. (2019, August 5). Japan Inc. to speed up China exit in response to more tariffs. *Nikkei Asian Review*. https://asia.nikkei.com/Economy/Trade-war/Japan-Inc.-to-speed-up-China-exit-in-response-to-more-tariffs. Accessed 15 June 2020.

Shane, D. (2019, September 19). Japan exports fall for ninth month in a row. *Financial Times*. https://www.ft.com/content/2d6e0fda-d9a6-11e9-8f9b-77216ebe1f17. Accessed 15 June 2020.

State Council [of the People's Republic of China]. (2012, September). *White Paper: Diaoyu Dao, an inherent territory of China*. http://english.gov.cn/official/2012-09/25/content_2232763.htm. Accessed 9 September 2015.

Takenaka, K. (2012, September 11). Japan buys disputed islands, China sends patrol ships. *Reuters*. https://www.reuters.com/article/us-japan-china/japan-buys-disputed-islands-china-sends-patrol-ships-idUSBRE88A0GY20120911. Accessed 23 November 2017.

The White House. (2018, January 30). *President Donald J. Trump's state of the Union address*. https://trumpwhitehouse.archives.gov/briefings-statements/president-donald-j-trumps-state-union-address/. Accessed 15 June 2020.

The White House. (2019, September 20). *Remarks by President Trump and Prime Minister Morrison of Australia before bilateral meeting*. https://trumpwhitehouse.archives.gov/briefings-statements/remarks-president-trump-prime-minister-morrison-australia-bilateral-meeting/. Accessed 15 June 2020.

Tōgō, K. (2008). Japan and the security structures of Asian multilateralism. In K. E. Calder & F. Fukuyama (Eds.), *East Asian multilateralism: Prospects for regional stability* (pp. 168–197). Johns Hopkins University Press.

Tsuneo, A. (2000). US.–Japan relations in the post-Cold war era: Ambiguous adjustment to a changing strategic environment. In T. Inoguchi & P. Jain (Eds.), *Japanese foreign policy today* (pp. 177–193). Palgrave Macmillan.

US Department of Defense. (2019, June 1). *Indo-Pacific strategy report: Preparedness, partnerships, and promoting a networked region*. https://media.defense.gov/2019/Jul/01/2002152311/-1/-1/1/DEPARTMENT-OF-DEFENSE-INDO-PACIFIC-STRATEGY-REPORT-2019.PDF. Accessed 1 July 2020.

Vanhullebusch, M., & Wei, S. (2016, February). China's air defence identification zone: Building security through lawfare. *China Review, 16*(1), 121–50.

Xinhuanet. (2019, July 24). *Full text: China's national defense in the new era.* http://www.xinhuanet.com/english/2019-07/24/c_138253389. htm. Accessed 15 June 2020.

Yamada, T. (2005, November 15). *Toward a principled integration of East Asia: Concept of an East Asian community (3).* CEAC Commentary, 1–3.

Yoshimatsu, H. (2012, December). Identity, policy ideas, and Asian diplomacy: Japan's response to the rise of China. *International Area Studies Review, 15*(4), 359–376.

Zhang, Y. (2019, June 26). With increased confidence, China and Japan can lead on world stage. *Global Times.* http://www.globaltimes.cn/content/115 5801.shtml. Accessed 15 June 2020.

Narendra Modi and the Remaking of Indian Diplomacy

Ian Hall

Narendra Modi has embraced diplomacy like no Indian prime minister before him, with the obvious exception of the first holder of that office, Jawaharlal Nehru.[1] Since May 2014, Modi has travelled more widely and more frequently than all his predecessors, including Nehru, establishing himself as India's 'diplomat-in-chief' (Chaulia, 2016, pp. 27–53). This jet-setting has been criticised—not least for the expense it incurs[2]—but for many of Modi's supporters, his energetic engagement in international relations has helped to restore pride to India. For them, the apparent ease with which Modi relates to foreign leaders and the respect in which he appears to be held are seen to have paid dividends, elevating the country's standing in the eyes of others and—just as crucially—making his

---

[1] This chapter draws upon my recent book on Modi's attempted reinvention of Indian foreign policy (Hall, 2019a). I am grateful to Robert Patman and the organisers of the 2018 Otago Foreign Policy School for their kind invitation to travel to Dunedin.

[2] At the end of 2018, the cost of Modi's travel was estimated at more than ₹20 billion (2000 crore rupees), or almost US$290 million (Shrivastava, 2018). For a bracing, if not always on target critique of Modi's diplomacy, see Karnad (2018).

I. Hall (✉)
Griffith University, Nathan, QLD, Australia
e-mail: i.hall@griffith.edu.au

© The Author(s), under exclusive license to Springer Nature Singapore Pte Ltd. 2022
R. Patman et al. (eds.), *From Asia-Pacific to Indo-Pacific*, Global Political Transitions, https://doi.org/10.1007/978-981-16-7007-7_7

143

fellow Indians feel more confident and secure than ever before. In the eyes of Modi's backers, he has remade India's diplomacy, rendering it a 'leading power' as well as an attractive place to do business—and done so largely by force of personality.[3] This chapter interrogates these claims, focusing especially on Modi's personal diplomacy, and argues that its results have been patchier and less impressive than is often claimed. For context, it briefly addresses the role of prime ministers in diplomacy in India, observing that both by design and as a result of significant institutional shortcomings, they have long played a larger role in conducting international relations than they might. It then looks at Modi's diplomacy since his National Democratic Alliance (NDA) Government, led by the Bharatiya Janata Party (Indian People's Party or BJP), first came to power. It observes some of the innovations of Modi's conduct of apex leader diplomacy, including his attempt to give it a more religious character and his concerted effort to woo India's large and diverse diaspora. In the second half, it focuses on Modi's efforts to forge relationships with other key leaders, with particular regard to two challenging cases: the leaders of China and Pakistan. With Xi Jinping and with Nawaz Sharif, Modi invested heavily in personal diplomacy, but in both cases, I argue, it was not sufficient to bring about improvements in bilateral ties. The conclusion addresses what these cases might imply for India's international relations in the Modi era.

PRIME MINISTERS AND INDIAN DIPLOMACY

India's Constitution makes foreign policymaking and implementation the responsibilities of the core executive of the Union (that is, federal) Government in New Delhi, but subject to parliamentary oversight. The executive is bound by the Constitution, which—unusually—includes so-called Directive Principles of State Policy meant to guide its formulation. These principles address foreign policy as well as domestic areas and echo the United Nations (UN) Charter. They enjoin governments to 'promote international peace and security', 'maintain just and honourable relations

---

[3] See especially Ganguly and Chauthaiwale (2016), Chaulia (2016) and Tremblay and Kapur (2017). For more critical assessments of the direction, success and novelty of the Modi government's approach, see Hall (2015, 2016), Basrur (2017), Chatterjee Miller and Sullivan de Estrada (2017), and Ganguly (2017).

between nations', uphold international law and treaties, and peacefully settle disputes (Constitution of India, Article 51, 1950).

It is moot, of course, whether or not these Directive Principles have been followed in practice. What is not in dispute is that soon after independence, the prime minister—and by extension the officials and advisers of the Prime Minister's Office (PMO)—came to dominate both foreign policy and diplomacy, with little scrutiny from parliament, and indeed often little involvement from other Cabinet ministers.[4] In part, this was due to Nehru's energy, interest and knowledge of the area; in part too, it was a function of lack of capacity. In the 1940s and 1950s, few if any Indian politicians had travelled as much as Nehru, still less read as much or thought about international affairs as he did. Ground was thus ceded to him by others—and was eagerly taken. Nehru took for himself the job of external affairs minister and held it throughout his prime ministership, until his death in 1964 (Brown, 2003, pp. 244–245).

In diplomacy, Nehru led from the front, travelling widely and exercised a high degree of control, personally appointing foreign-service officers in the early years and nominating family members and close confidants to key embassies. He provided an ideological framework for Indian foreign policy and diplomatic conduct, laying out the principles of what became known as 'non-alignment' and encouraging an activist approach that saw India, despite its relative weakness, involved a series of major disputes, including the Korean War and the Congo crisis.[5] And although Indian voters, then as now, took little direct interest in foreign policy, Nehru's international statecraft burnished his reputation as a leader, at least until the disaster of the 1962 border war with China, in which India was humiliated.[6] Prime ministerial dominance in foreign policy continued long after Nehru's demise, though his successors provided far less in the way of new thinking. Under Indira Gandhi, his daughter—who ruled from 1966 to 1977, then again from 1980 until her assassination in 1984—the prime minister and PMO continued to direct strategy and pick key personnel, with the Ministry of External Affairs (MEA) largely

---

[4] For contemporary analyses, see Bozeman (1958) and Power (1964). For a measured assessment, see Rana (1976).

[5] On the ideological tradition Nehru established, and the foreign policy of his era more broadly, see Bandyopadhyaya (1979, pp. 69–80 and 286–320).

[6] For a critical assessment of the origins of the war and Nehru's missteps, see Maxwell (2015).

focused on implementation. Important decisions with significant consequences for India's international relations—such as the order to test a nuclear device in 1974—were taken without even informing the whole of Cabinet, let alone all parliamentarians. Nehru's successors did break from his practice in appointing others as foreign ministers, but for the most part, prime ministers still led the way on major issues. Under Indira Gandhi, one authority concluded, the external affairs and other relevant ministers 'played a relative[ly] unimportant role in decision-making'—the big choices were made by the prime minister (Bandyopadhyaya, 1979, p. 331). Questions of foreign policy did sometimes exercise members of parliament (MPs), as they did during the Pakistani Army's attempted suppression of the Bangladeshi independence moment, and India's subsequent military intervention, but rarely did they take sustained interest. Instead, Indira Gandhi and her successors were often able to use foreign policy as a means of consolidating domestic dominance—as she herself did, indeed, by launching the 1971 war and playing midwife to the birth of Bangladesh. Only occasionally did an international issue surface as a political threat to a government, like it did, for example, during the passage of the United States–India nuclear deal through parliament in 2008 (see Mistry, 2014, pp. 151–175).

A number of factors account for persistently high level of control exercised by Indian prime ministers over foreign policy and diplomacy. One was and remains the low level of knowledge and engagement with international affairs evident among ordinary parliamentarians compared to the few that have risen to be prime minister. Like her father, Indira Gandhi had far more experience of diplomacy and the outside world than the majority of her Cabinet, let alone the majority of MPs (Bandyopadhyaya, 1979, pp. 329–331). The same could also be said of her son, Rajiv Gandhi, who was also educated abroad, became an airline pilot, and married an Italian, Sonia Maino. And a similar story can be told of Atal Bihari Vajpayee, who took a keen interest in international affairs from the 1950s onwards, and served as prime minister from 1998 to 2004, and of his successor, the Cambridge graduate and international trade economist Manmohan Singh.

Another factor is the relative—and growing—strength of the PMO compared to the MEA and other relevant departments, arising from practice and a series of institutional changes brought about since independence in 1947. The first—evident during Indira Gandhi's tenure, in particular—was the emergence of a series of key lieutenants within the

PMO who could provide counsel or engage in quiet diplomatic missions. P. N. Haksar and D. P. Dhar played these roles in the late 1960s and early 1970s (Dixit, 2004, pp. 166–169). The new post of Principal Secretary to the Prime Minister was even created for Haksar in 1971, to keep him close (Ramesh, 2018); later it was held by figures like Brajesh Misra, who exercised much influence over foreign policy in Vajpayee's Government, which ruled from 1998 to 2004. The founding of the Research and Analysis Wing, an external intelligence agency, in 1968 was also an important change: its secretary reports directly to the prime minister and serves as an alternative source of information and advice to the MEA. A further factor, significant for similar reasons, was the creation of the post of National Security Advisor (NSA) in 1998, with an attendant bureaucracy located within the PMO. Under successive governments, the NSA has served as a key adviser and as an envoy and negotiator, sitting alongside and arguably supplanting, at least in part, the External Affairs Minister and the head of the MEA, known as the Foreign Secretary (Gupta, 2018).

Taken together, the high-profile role that Nehru established for prime ministers in setting foreign policy agendas and conducting apex diplomacy, the relative weakness of both Cabinet and parliamentary oversight, and the institutional competition faced by the MEA from other actors and departments have long combined to give Indian leaders considerable leeway in the conduct of the country's international relations. And one more factor has reinforced this tendency: state capacity, specifically in the MEA, as well as in other relevant ministries, including Commerce and Defence. The small size, heavy workloads and uneven skills of India's diplomats can generate circumstances in which it is necessary for leaders to take on diplomatic roles in order to pursue their objectives and make the deals they seek.

It has long been recognised that India's state capacity is severely limited at every level of government.[7] It is also well recognised that India has a particular problem in those parts of government that conduct its international relations (Bajpai & Chong, 2019). The Indian Foreign Service (IFS) has nurtured many fine diplomats, but it is tiny. Its present strength is 960 so-called Band A officers, supported by another 1500 technical specialists, and about 4500 lower-ranked and skilled Band B personnel—about 7000 in total (MEA, 2019a, pp. 18–19). These staff

---

[7] For a classic study, see Rudolph and Hoeber Rudolph (1987), and for a new one, Ganguly and Thompson (2017).

are distributed—thinly, by necessity—between the MEA, other departments in New Delhi, and India's 162 foreign missions. The IFS is now recruiting more than it historically did, in order to build numbers, but its annual intake of probationers is still only about 30–35 (MEA, 2019b). But the MEA as a whole remains under-strength, with almost 2000 posts unfilled in 2019 (MEA, 2019a, p. 19).

Capacity constraints imposed by inadequate staffing are compounded by a number of other difficulties. A major one is a lack of financial resources. The MEA's budget has increased under Modi's administration. In 2014–2015, the MEA received about US$2.4 billion.[8] In 2019–2020, it was allocated US$2.6 billion.[9] But these raw numbers mask a number of issues. One is salary costs, which have risen significantly, as civil service pay has increased. Another is the effect of inflation, which has run at more than 4.5% every year since 2014, and which eats into the MEA's budget as it does with any other part of government. A third is the increase in overseas development assistance and technical support to South Asian and Indian Ocean states, which is allocated to the MEA for distribution. And one more is the ever-rising cost—in terms of time devoted and money spent—of MEA consular and diaspora activities, which under Modi's government became a bigger focus of the ministry.

PACE AND INNOVATION

During Modi's first term in office, from May 2014 to May 2019, he embarked on as many state visits, bilateral meetings, summits and conferences as Singh, his immediate predecessor, had managed over a decade in government. Moreover, Modi went to places no Indian prime minister had ever been before, like Fiji or Mongolia, as well as to places where none had set foot for decades, like Australia or the Philippines. And over the course of Modi's first five years in office, the pace of his travel actually accelerated, with no fewer than 23 trips packed into 2018, prior to the

---

[8] In rupees, the figure was just over 147 billion. The rupee to US dollar exchange rate had fluctuated since 2014, so this figure is calculated at the 1 January 2014 exchange rate of 62 rupees to the US dollar.

[9] This figure is calculated at the 1 January 2019 rate of 69 rupees to the US dollar.

long campaign for re-election in the first five months of 2019 that kept him, for the most part, back in India.[10]

It was not just the pace of Modi's travels that marked him out from his predecessor, it was also what he did when abroad. For a start, he gave Indian diplomacy a more religious character, consistent with how Hindu nationalists believe that it ought to be conducted.[11] Significant religious sites were included on itineraries and featured heavily in the coverage of his visits on both traditional and social media. Hindu and Buddhist sites were particularly favoured, for different reasons. Early in Modi's time in office he went to the Pashupatinath temple in Kathmandu in Nepal, for example, and then, in the same month (August 2014), to the Buddhist To-ji temple in Kyoto in Japan. Visits to Hindu sites were designed largely to play to domestic audiences, to reinforce Modi's image as a robust defender of that religion, although in the special case of Nepal, the concern to strengthen bilateral relations with that Hindu nation also loomed large. Visits to Buddhist sites had a different purpose. They were intended to emphasise India's status as the birthplace of that religion and its past cultural links to other parts of Asia, including China, Japan, Mongolia, Sri Lanka and Southeast Asia. To those ends, in the space of less than a year in 2014–2015, Modi went to the Da Xingshan temple in Xi'an, to the Ganda monastery in Mongolia and Anuradhapura in Sri Lanka. In 2017, he visited the Shwedagon pagoda in Myanmar, and the following year, the Buddha Tooth Relic Temple in Singapore. Moreover, he made a point of delivering distinctively Hindu gifts, notably copies of the Bhagavad Gita, to some of his hosts, including Shinzo Abe and Barack Obama (Hall, 2019b, p. 11).

These kinds of visits were not unprecedented and nor were the appeals to India's rich cultural and religious inheritance. But there has been a concerted push under the Modi Government to emphasise it more and to engage deeper in inter-religious dialogue, especially with Buddhist groups. These efforts were again consistent with Hindu nationalist ideology, but also formed part of a push to accumulate 'soft power' than might be used to India's advantage across the Indo-Pacific (see

---

[10] Modi managed only one foreign trip—to South Korea—between the start of 2019 and the end of the election campaign, in late May. After his victory at the polls, he quickened the pace of his travels still further, making fifteen visits by the end of December.

[11] On Hindu nationalist thinking about international relations and Indian foreign policy, see Hall (2019a, pp. 41–60).

Hall, 2017). They have involved his government sponsoring events like Ravi Shankar's World Culture Festival, held near Delhi in March 2016, which brought together both political and religious leaders from India and overseas, and which the organisers claimed was attended by three and a half million people. In parallel, BJP-affiliated think tanks—notably the Vivekananda International Foundation, which used to be run by Modi's NSA, Ajit Doval—have co-organised projects like the Samvad Global Hindu Buddhist Initiative on Conflict Avoidance and Environmental Consciousness, held in India in 2015 and in Myanmar in 2017 (Hall, 2019b, p. 12). Beyond Buddhist groups, the Modi Government has also sponsored the World Sufi Forum, which the prime minister addressed in March 2016, and an India–Indonesia Interfaith Dialogue, launched by Modi and Indonesian President Joko Widodo in October 2018 (Hall, 2019a, p. 91).

The other significant innovation in the practice of diplomacy was Modi's very high-profile—and at times controversial—outreach to India's diaspora. This reflected, in part, the long-standing links between parts of that far-flung community and the Hindu nationalist movement, including the BJP (see Jaffrelot & Therwath, 2007, as well as Kinnvall & Svensson, 2010). India has, of course, a large and diverse diaspora—some long established in their host countries, and some only abroad for short periods, as temporary migrant workers—today numbering about 18 million people (Rooney, 2019). Many have flourished abroad. In the United States, Indian-Americans and Indian immigrants are the 'Other One Percent'—a highly educated, on average, entrepreneurial, successful and influential group of about four and a half million (Chakravorty et al., 2017). Elsewhere, the diaspora's fortunes are more mixed. There are now about eight million in the Gulf region, up from two million in the mid-2000s, spread mostly between Kuwait, Oman, Saudi Arabia and the United Arab Emirates (Rooney, 2019). Some are well-paid professionals, but a large number are low-paid temporary workers vulnerable to mishaps, exploitation and abuse. There is a similar mix in Southeast Asia, especially in Singapore, as well as sizeable populations of people of Indian origin, in varying circumstances, in Australia, Malaysia and Fiji.

Together the diaspora presents opportunities and challenges, both generating demands on the MEA. On the one hand, the wealthy and talented are a tempting source of inward investment and—for India's political parties, including the BJP—campaign donations and influence, both at home and abroad. On the other, poorer migrant workers and students, while a crucial source of remittances and future know-how, can put pressure on consular services and create diplomatic headaches in relations with host countries. Lost passports, stolen wages, assaults and arrests, deaths and illnesses all create problems, with migrant workers sometimes unable to resolve them without extensive help, including disbursements of emergency payments or even—as has happened several times over the past decade—physical evacuation. In 2015, for example, India was compelled to assist more than 4500 of its citizens stranded in Yemen, amidst an escalating civil war, using both specially chartered civilian and military aircraft, and naval vessels. At the same time, the proliferation of mobile phones and widespread use of social media mean that news of migrant worker distress or any other misfortune befalling a person of Indian origin overseas rapidly becomes public, and frequently a political issue.

Successive Indian governments have responded to these evolving pressures, generated by the diaspora and its diverse needs, in different ways. Historically, attitudes towards the diaspora were mixed. Educated Indians who emigrated to Britain or the United States were the objects of both resentment (because they had chosen to take their knowledge and skills abroad) and pride (because they had succeeded in making better lives for themselves and their families). New Delhi took less interest in them than in people of Indian origin in difficult circumstances—Indians living in South Africa under the racist apartheid regime, for example, who were the subject of official concern during the 1950s. By contrast, a 'certain distance' was maintained by Indian governments from the generally wealthier Indians in the West, fearful as they were about the effect of 'brain drain', despite the value of the remittances they sent back to the country (Varadarajan, 2010, p. 90). From the 1980s onwards, however, official interest grew, as governments sought out potential sources of inward investment. A scheme was proposed to facilitate investment by so-called Non-Resident Indians (NRIs), but it fell victim to persistent concerns about the effects of 'foreign' money on the economy and society (Varadarajan, 2010, pp. 93–101).

Since then, both Congress and BJP-led governments have pursued diaspora capital and know-how. They created new government departments and organisations to better connect India to the diaspora, and vice versa—most obviously the Ministry of Overseas Indian Affairs, set up in 2004 and merged into the MEA in 2016, and the Pravasi Bharatiya Divas ('Non-Resident Indian Day') conference run in India and outside it since

2002. They have also tried—to varying degrees of effect—to improve the consular services available to both wealthy members of the diaspora in the West and less well-off migrant workers in the Middle East and Southeast Asia (Rana, 2009). In parallel, the BJP in particular has worked hard to build up support within the diaspora that might provide it with funds to fight elections, skills to improve its campaign tactics and online outreach to voters, and influence abroad, among people of Indian origin and in the broader host societies.[12] Under Modi, this effort became more overt and more extensive. The most obvious sign of the step-up was the series of rallies of the diaspora he addressed overseas, with thousands or tens of thousands in attendance. At New York's Madison Square Garden in September 2014, Sydney's Allphones Arena in November 2014, London's Wembley Stadium a year later, Yangon's Thuwunna Stadium in September 2017, and most obviously at the Howdy Modi! event at Houston's NRG Stadium, Modi revelled in diaspora adulation, thanked Indians overseas for their backing, and exhorted them to keep giving (Chaulia, 2016, pp. 54–83). In the background, the BJP and its various affiliates, including the Rashtriya Swayamsevak Sangh (RSS), the quasi-paramilitary organisation to which Modi has belonged since he was a child, also intensified its outreach to the diaspora. Senior BJP officers like Vijay Chauthaiwale travelled widely to connect with branches of the Overseas Friends of the BJP (OFBJP), while RSS leader Mohan Bhagwat went to the United States, along with India's Vice President Venkaiah Naidu, to call for what he called 'Hindu unity' at the World Hindu Congress in Chicago in September 2018 (Outlook, 2018).

The increasingly religious character of some of the Modi Government's diplomacy and the push by the BJP and RSS to tap diaspora political and financial support reinforced each other. And to supporters, they lend credence to the argument that Modi himself was reinventing Indian foreign policy, shifting it away from an inherited Nehruvian approach, portrayed as secular and shaped by Western thinking, towards one more in keeping with India's traditions and beliefs, and in the interests of Indians wherever they found themselves (see Hall, 2019a). For them, as the BJP's 2015 resolution on foreign policy put it, the 'Prime Minister has restored pride in Bharat's [that is, India's] civilisational identity and cultural traditions and drawn global attention to [them] in a manner that befits this

---

[12] See, for example, Zavos (2010) on the work of the Vishva Hindu Parishad in the United Kingdom.

oldest civilisation of the world' (BJP, 2015). Modi was personally credited by the BJP and—if one poll taken prior to the 2019 election is
any measure—voters agreed that his government had bolstered India's
standing in the world. Dissatisfied with its management of the economy
though they were, voters still praised it for improving India's image in the
world.[13]

SUMMITRY AND PERSONAL DIPLOMACY

Modi has certainly been deft and assiduous in using personal diplomacy as
a means of burnishing his—and supposedly by extension India's—reputation. After coming to power, he quickly established himself as a regular
attendee of the minilateral and multilateral leaders' summits that prolif-
erated in the second half of the 2000s. These included the East Asia
Summit, first held in 2005, which Modi attended every year after winning
office; the Group of 20 (G20), which held its inaugural leaders' meeting
during the Global Financial Crisis of 2008 and every year thereafter; and
the annual gatherings of the leaders of the BRICS (Brazil, Russia, India,
China and South Africa) that began in 2009. Modi also went to the
opening session of the UN General Assembly in 2014 and 2015, and
then again after his re-election in 2019. Beginning in 2016, in advance
of the granting of full membership to India the following year, Modi also
attended the annual Shanghai Cooperation Organisation (SCO) summit.
When it was possible to convene them, he went to the South Asian
Association for Regional Cooperation (SAARC) and Bay of Bengal Initiative for Multi-Sectoral Technical and Economic Cooperation (BIMSTEC)
summits. The only gathering Modi avoided, indeed, was the Non-Aligned
Movement (NAM) summit, long a fixture for Indian Prime ministers, but
one closely associated with Nehru. In his stead, he sent Vice President
Mohammad Hamid Ansari to the NAM meeting in Venezuela in 2016,
and then Ansari's successor, Naidu, to the next iteration in Azerbaijan in
2019 (Ganguly, 2017, p. 132).

During both visits and summits, Modi devoted much energy to cultivating other apex leaders and indeed demonstrating to public audiences
his closeness to like-minded partners and his robustness in managing

---

[13] The CSDS Lokniti prepoll survey (Lokniti, 2019, pp. 24–25) reported 48.6% of
voters thought India's image had improved under Modi, 17.9% thought it had remained
the same and 16.9% thought it had worsened. The remainder did not express a view.

rivals. On the first, he inflicted bear hugs and swapped cheery messages on Twitter. Barack Obama, François Hollande, Shinzo Abe and Vladimir Putin were early recipients of what began known as the 'Modi hug', later extended to Donald Trump, Benjamin Netanyahu and, indeed, Mark Zuckerberg. With Australian Prime Ministers Malcolm Turnbull and Scott Morrison, as well as many others—including, somewhat surprisingly Chinese Premier Li Keqiang—Modi also took 'selfies' and posted them on various social media platforms. The leaders of key strategic partners were also honoured with invitations to attend India's Republic Day parade of military hardware down the Rajpath in New Delhi, beginning with Obama in January 2015, followed by Hollande, the Crown Prince of the United Arab Emirates, Mohammed bin Zayed Al Nahyan, the ten heads of state of the Association of Southeast Asian Nations (ASEAN), and, in 2019, South Africa's President Cyril Ramaphosa.

With China's President Xi, however, and with Pakistan's leaders, Nawaz Sharif and Imran Khan, Modi's personal diplomacy was very different. Both of these countries' leaders provided difficult tests of his approach. Both provided opportunities for Modi to appear strong and respected, but both also challenged him and his efforts to ensure he and India attained and maintained the standing it deserved.

Seeing Xi

Modi's Government came to power both wary of the People's Republic as a potential political and military threat and—because it sought to quickly boost economic growth—keen to explore whether it might provide or facilitate greater investment in India. To explore opportunities and to allow the Indian Prime minister to get the measure of the Chinese leader, who had come to power at the end of 2012, New Delhi invited Xi for a three-day-long state visit in September 2014. The centrepiece was a trip to Gujarat, Modi's home state. An elaborate show was contrived, including a photo opportunity in which Modi and Xi sat together on a gilded swing, with the Chinese leader wearing an Indian jacket. The meeting was not, however, without tensions. An alleged incursion of a unit of the People's Liberation Army (PLA) across the disputed border into what India claims as its territory prompted Modi to make a rare public rebuke of Chinese behaviour, pointedly delivered alongside Xi at a press conference (Bajpai, 2017, p. 81). Moreover, the quantum of inward investment promised by Beijing was lower than some expected—and lower than some Chinese diplomats had earlier hinted. Only US$20 billion was put on the table, a long way short of a mooted US$100 billion (Bajpai, 2017, p. 80).

Thereafter, Modi's interactions with Xi were more markedly more formal and, at times, tense, reflecting broader disagreements—some new and some long-standing—with the People's Republic and a desire to take a stronger public stance. His visit to China in May 2015 was overshadowed by the signing of the Belt and Road Initiative-linked China–Pakistan Economic Corridor (CPEC) project by Sharif and Xi during the latter's visit to Islamabad a month earlier. Because part of CPEC involves Pakistani-administered Kashmir, New Delhi issued a formal protest. At the same time, Indian officials and ministers re-emphasised India's claim to Arunachal Pradesh, which Beijing contests (Bajpai, 2017, p. 82). Although Modi's trip to China sealed another US$20 billion or so in bilateral business deals, its lasting image was of the prime minister, on his own and in a pair of dark glasses, staring down some of the terracotta warriors in Xi'an—a photoshoot that launched a thousand social media memes in India (Pandey, 2015).

Modi met Xi three times during 2016, at the SCO, G20 and BRICS summits. Each interaction highlighted differences, notably over China's refusals to allow India to join the Nuclear Suppliers Group (NSG) and to allow the UN Security Council to list Pakistan-based Jaish-e-Mohammed leader Masood Azhar as a terrorist. Their meetings in 2017, however, were even more strained. In May 2017, New Delhi issued a thoroughgoing critique of the BRI, making the statement public on the eve of Xi's inaugural Belt and Road Forum (MEA, 2017a). A month later, Indian troops confronted PLA forces building a road through a disputed area of Bhutan at Doklam (or Donglang, in Mandarin), leading to a nine-week-long stand-off during which Beijing made multiple threats to use force against India (Ganguly & Scobell, 2018). Modi met Xi immediately prior to Doklam at an SCO meeting at Astana in Kazakhstan; during the stand-off at the G20 in Hamburg in Germany, but only for a sideline talk and not a formal bilateral one; and then at Xiamen in China at the BRICS in September, where the two sat down for a scheduled conversation after the confrontation had been defused.

While substantive differences remained—notably over the border, BRI, Pakistan, India's relationship with the international nuclear order and the two countries' relationships with other states across the Indo-Pacific—Doklam did bring about a diplomatic innovation: the so-called 'informal summit'. In late April 2018, Modi joined Xi in Wuhan in China for the first of these meetings. In contrast to the earlier state visits and summit bilaterals, this conversation was not accompanied with the announcement of multibillion dollar business deals or rafts of new people-to-people interactions, still less a formal joint statement. Instead, it was presented as an opportunity for the two leaders to discuss matters of mutual concern and sources of conflict. And what it produced was a short, 11-point readout couched very much in generalities, with a promise 'to strengthen the Closer Development Partnership in a mutually beneficial and sustainable manner' and 'enhance efforts to build on the convergences through the established mechanisms in order to create the broadest possible platform for the future relationship' (MEA, 2017b). Importantly, it also allowed Modi to be seen interacting with Xi as an apex leader on a par with him, despite the Doklam stand-off, and as a statesperson apparently able to uphold India's honour and safeguard its security even when challenged by the country's most powerful rival.

Wuhan set a precedent of sorts. In November 2018, Modi held another informal summit, this time with Russian President Putin, in the southern Russian resort of Sochi. Almost a year later, in October 2019, following the BJP's triumph in the general election six months earlier, Modi held one more with Xi, this time near Chennai, in India. Both occasions were presented to the public as opportunities for the leaders to exchange views on matters of concern and their respective visions about how they might be tackled. Neither led to joint statements or announcements of investment. The 'Chennai Connect', as it was spun by New Delhi, did however produce many photographs and much film of Modi and Xi, seemingly relaxed in each other's company and communicating with ease, as well as a promise to have another such meeting in China.

Sharif and Khan

In the first two years of his government, Modi made several attempts to make some diplomatic progress with Islamabad with some eye-catching personal diplomacy. First, in May 2014, he invited Prime Minister Sharif to New Delhi to attend his swearing-in ceremony. The invitation was accepted, and Modi greeted Sharif with a smile and a handshake. The two exchanged gifts for each other's mothers—a shawl and a sari. The mood soured, however, when the Pakistani High Commissioner to India met Kashmiri separatist leaders in August. India responded by cancelling planned bilateral talks between officials. Sharif reportedly tried to make amends by sending boxes of mangoes to Modi and other Indian leaders, but to little effect (Buncombe, 2014). The two then sparred in their respective speeches to the opening session of the UN General Assembly in late September 2014 but did not meet. Two months later, Modi and Sharif sat together on the podium at the SAARC summit in Kathmandu. They did not however acknowledge one another or shake hands until the following day (PTI, 2014).

Bilateral relations deteriorated the following year. Modi and Sharif met again at a cricket match in February. The next month, he sent his Foreign Secretary, Subrahmanyam (conventionally, 'S.') Jaishankar to Pakistan to discuss restarting talks, and on the sidelines of the SCO Summit in July, the two leaders agreed that their national security advisers should meet. That dialogue was derailed, however, by a Pakistani attempt to have Kashmir put on the agenda, and two terrorist attacks in India. In November, however, Modi and Sharif met once more, this time at the Paris climate summit, and resolved to hold more talks. Then came a piece of characteristic drama: on the way back from Afghanistan, Modi made an unannounced visit to Sharif's residence in Lahore, where the Pakistani leader was holding a wedding party for his daughter, leaving a present to the bride (Bajpai, 2017, p. 74). Whatever goodwill this gesture generated quickly dissipated, however. In January 2016, terrorists attacked an Indian airbase at Pathankot in Kashmir, Punjab. New Delhi pointed the finger of blame at Islamabad, refused to proceed with further official talks, and Modi did not again attempt similar personal diplomacy with Sharif.

Bilateral relations worsened still more during the remainder of 2016. A planned SAARC summit in Pakistan was cancelled after India indicated it would boycott the event, with Bangladesh and Bhutan following suit. Another terrorist attack, at Uri in Jammu and Kashmir in September, saw India not just issue diplomatic protests, but also dispatch its special forces across the Line of Control in Kashmir to destroy an alleged training camp. Thereafter, ties did not improve, even after Sharif's departure from office in late July 2017. At the only occasion at which Modi's path crossed with his successor, Shahid Khaqan Abbasi—the Commonwealth Heads of Government gathering in London in April 2018—the two declined to meet. In July, Abbasi then lost the general election to Khan. Although Modi had granted Khan an audience in December 2015, just a couple of weeks before his impromptu visit to the Sharif family wedding, he did not offer another meeting after the former cricketer took office. Nor did he seek one at the multilateral summits that followed. The cancellation of the

2018 SAARC summit, also meant to be held in Islamabad in September of that year, removed one opportunity. The SCO summit in mid-June 2019 and the opening of the UN General Assembly a few months later provided others, but at both, Modi and Khan neither shook hands nor spoke to one another.

CONCLUSION

Modi has repeatedly been compared to other 'strongmen' of the era—to Recep Tayyip Erdoğan, Vladimir Putin, Donald Trump and to Xi Jinping (see Carpenter, 2017 or Drezner, 2017). This is not unreasonable: his domestic policies have been authoritarian and sometimes divisive; his rhetoric, especially with Indian audiences, can be fiery and hard line. But his diplomatic style is distinct. Some Indian critics argue Modi has been too quick to hug and flatter Western leaders especially, and too emollient abroad, even with Chinese and Pakistani leaders (see especially Karnad, 2018). This does not quite capture the purpose or character of Modi's personal diplomacy. Certainly, as we have seen, he embarked swiftly and determinedly to build relationships with key leaders—and to be seen to be doing this, especially in the eyes of the domestic audience. This was deliberate, and as I have argued elsewhere, part of the reinvention of his image during his first term in office, as he sought to move from being a state chief minister to a statesperson (see Hall, 2019a). Certainly too, Modi's personal diplomacy often did not bear fruit. The effort spent in building rapport with Xi and Sharif, as we have seen, did not lead to more benign attitudes towards India in Beijing or Islamabad. In both cases, indeed, bilateral relations deteriorated during Modi's first term in office, leading to a military stand-off with the PLA in mid-2017 and military action against Pakistan in 2016 and again in February 2019, when the Indian Air Force attacked targets across the international border, not just the Line of Control within Kashmir.

This should all be a matter of concern. If a leader's personal diplomacy fails, especially in an era in which 'strongmen' and their relationships seemingly dominate international affairs, and in which apex summitry is so regular, then the effects could well be significant. Of course, when it comes to India's relations with both China and Pakistan, there are long-standing and complex challenges, not easily resolved by bonhomie. But it is not clear, I have argued here, that Modi's attempt to remake India's diplomacy in his own image has brought about promised improvements where they need to be made.

REFERENCES

Bajpai, K. (2017). Narendra Modi's Pakistan and China policy: Assertive bilateral diplomacy, active coalition diplomacy. *International Affairs, 93*(1), 69–91.

Bajpai, K., & Chong, B. (2019). India's foreign policy capacity. *Policy Design and Practice, 2*(2), 137–162.

Bandyopadhyaya, J. (1979). *The making of India's foreign policy* (2nd ed.). Allied Publishers.

Basrur, R. (2017). Modi's foreign policy fundamentals: A trajectory unchanged. *International Affairs, 93*(1), 7–26.

Bharatiya Janata Party (BJP). (2015, April 3) *Resolution—1* (Foreign Policy). https://www.bjp.org/en/articledetail/226430/Resolution-1-Foreign-Policy. Accessed 3 March 2021.

Bozeman, A. B. (1958). India's foreign policy today: Reflections upon its sources. *World Politics, 10*(2), 256–273.

Brown, J. (2003). *Nehru: A political life.* Yale University Press.

Buncombe, A. (2014, September 5). Pakistan Prime Minister Nawaz Sharif sends mangoes to Indian counterpart Narendra Modi to sweeten relations ahead of possible New York meeting. *The Independent.* https://www.indepe ndent.co.uk/news/world/asia/pakistan-prime-minister-nawaz-sharif-sends-mangoes-to-indian-counterpart-narendra-modi-to-sweeten-9714790.html. Accessed 3 March 2021.

Carpenter, T. G. (2017). The populist surge and the rebirth of foreign policy nationalism. *SAIS Review of International Affairs, 37*(1), 33–46.

Chakravorty, S., Kapur, D., & Singh, N. (2017). *The other one percent: Indians in America.* Oxford University Press.

Chatterjee Miller, M., & Sullivan de Estrada, K. (2017). Pragmatism in Indian foreign policy: How ideas constrain Modi. *International Affairs, 93*(1), 27–49.

Chaulia, S. (2016). *Modi doctrine: The foreign policy of India's Prime Minister.* Bloomsbury Publishing.

Dixit, J. N. (2004). *Makers of India's foreign policy: Ram Mohan Roy to Yashwant Sinha.* HarperCollins.

Drezner, D. W. (2017). The angry populist as foreign policy leader: Real change or just hot air? *The Fletcher Forum of World Affairs, 41*(2), 23–43.

Ganguly, A., & Chauthaiwale, V. (2016). *The Modi doctrine: New paradigms in India's foreign policy.* Wisdom Tree.

Ganguly, S. (2017). Has Modi truly changed India's foreign policy? *The Washington Quarterly, 40*(2), 131–143.

Ganguly, S., & Scobell, A. (2018). The Himalayan Impasse: Sino-Indian rivalry in the wake of Doklam. *The Washington Quarterly, 41*(3), 177–190.

Ganguly, S., & Thompson, W. (2017). *Ascending India and its state capacity: Extraction, violence, and legitimacy*. Yale University Press.

Gupta, A. (2018). *How India manages its national security*. Penguin.

Hall, I. (2015). Is a 'Modi doctrine' emerging in Indian foreign policy? *Australian Journal of International Affairs, 69*(3), 247–252.

Hall, I. (2016). Multialignment and Indian foreign policy under Narendra Modi. *The Round Table: The Commonwealth Journal of International Affairs, 105*(3), 271–286.

Hall, I. (2017). Narendra Modi and India's normative power. *International Affairs, 93*(1), 113–131.

Hall, I. (2019a). *Modi and the reinvention of Indian foreign policy*. Bristol University Press.

Hall, I. (2019b). Narendra Modi's new religious diplomacy. *International Studies Perspectives, 20*(1), 11–14.

Jaffrelot, C., & Therwath, I. (2007). The Sangh Parivar and the Hindu diaspora in the west: What kind of 'long-distance nationalism'? *International Political Sociology, 1*(3), 278–295.

Karnad, B. (2018). *Staggering forward: Narendra Modi and India's global ambition*. Penguin Viking.

Kinnvall, C., & Svensson, T. (2010). Hindu nationalism, diaspora politics and nation-building in India. *Australian Journal of International Affairs, 64*(3), 274–292.

Lokniti. (2019, March). *All India prepoll NES 2019—Survey findings*. https://www.lokniti.org/media/PDF-upload/1570173782_98991600_download_report.pdf. Accessed 3 March 2021.

Maxwell, N. (2015) *India's China war* (Revised and updated ed.). Natraj.

Ministry of External Affairs (MEA). (2017a, May 13). *Official Spokesperson's response to a query on participation of India in OBOR/BRI Forum*. https://mea.gov.in/media-briefings.htm?dtl/28463/Official+Spokespersons+response+to+a+query+on+participation+of+India+in+OBORBRI+Forum. Accessed 3 March 2021.

Ministry of External Affairs (MEA). (2017b, April 28). *India–China informal summit at Wuhan*. https://mea.gov.in/press-releases.htm?dtl/29853/IndiaChina_Informal_Summit_at_Wuhan, Accessed 3 March 2021.

Ministry of External Affairs (MEA). (2019a). *Detailed demands for grants of Ministry of External Affairs for 2019–2020*. http://mea.gov.in/Uploads/PublicationDocs/31715_DDG_2019-20.pdf, Accessed 3 March 2021.

Ministry of External Affairs (MEA). (2019b). *Indian foreign service: A backgrounder*. https://www.mea.gov.in/indian-foreign-service.htm, Accessed 3 March 2021.

Mistry, D. (2014). *The US–India nuclear agreement: Diplomacy and domestic politics*. Cambridge University Press.

Outlook. (2018, September 8). *Hindus don't oppose anybody, allow even pests to live, says RSS Chief Mohan Bhagwat*. https://www.outlookindia.com/web site/story/world-hidu-congress-hindus-dont-oppose-anybody-allow-even-pests-to-live-says-rss/316250. Accessed 3 March 2021.

Pandey, V. (2015, May 26). Narendra Modi: India's 'social media' PM. *BBC News*. https://www.bbc.com/news/world-asia-india-32874568, Accessed 3 March 2021.

Power, P. F. (1964). Indian foreign policy: The age of Nehru. *The Review of Politics, 26*(2), 257–286.

Press Trust of India (PTI). (2014, November 27). Modi, Sharif exchange pleasantries during SAARC retreat. *The Hindu*. https://www.thehindub usinessline.com/economy/policy/modi-sharif-exchange-pleasantries-during-saarc-retreat/article23171492.ece, Accessed 3 March 2021.

Ramesh, J. (2018). *Intertwined lives: P. N. Haksar and Indira Gandhi*. Simon and Schuster.

Rana, A. P. (1976). *The imperatives of nonalignment: A conceptual study of India's foreign policy strategy in the Nehru period*. Macmillan.

Rana, K. (2009). India's diaspora diplomacy. *The Hague Journal of Diplomacy, 4*(3), 361–372.

Rooney, K. (2019, September 30). India's record-breaking diaspora in numbers. *World Economic Forum*. https://www.weforum.org/agenda/2019/09/india-has-the-world-s-biggest-diaspora-here-s-where-its-emigrants-live, Accessed 3 March 2021.

Rudolph, L. I., & Hoeber Rudolph, S. (1987). *In pursuit of Lakshmi: The political economy of the Indian state*. University of Chicago Press.

Shrivastava, R. (2018, December 29). 92 nations in 55 months: PM Modi's travel costs hit Rs 2,021 crore. *India Today*. https://www.indiatoday. in/india/story/92-nations-in-55-months-pm-modi-travel-costs-hit-rs-2021-crore-1419337-2018-12-29, Accessed 3 March 2021.

Tremblay, R. C., & Kapur, A. (2017). *Modi's foreign policy*. Sage.

Varadarajan, L. (2010). *The domestic abroad: Diasporas in international relations*. Oxford University Press.

Zavos, J. (2010). Situating Hindu nationalism in the UK: Vishwa Hindu Parishad and the development of British Hindu identity. *Commonwealth and Comparative Politics, 48*(1), 2–22.

Australia and New Zealand's South Pacific Diplomacy: Seeking to Balance China's Regional Engagement

Patrick Köllner

INTRODUCTION

China's ties with the South Pacific — development assistance, trade, investment, involvement in the Belt and Road Initiative (BRI), and more—have grown substantially since the early years of the twenty-first century. Australia and New Zealand, the traditional dominant powers in this region, have recently upped their game in order to balance Chinese activities. In this chapter I discuss and compare the two Australasian allies' diplomatic efforts to build stronger ties with Pacific Island countries

This chapter grew out of a briefing paper of the German Institute for Global and Area Studies (Köllner, 2020). The author would like to thank the many interviewees in Wellington who gave so generously of their time in March 2020. He is grateful to Balazs Kiglics and Robert Patman for helpful comments on an earlier draft. The author would also like to thank the Department of Politics at the University of Otago for hosting him in February 2020.

P. Köllner (✉)
GIGA and University of Hamburg, Hamburg, Germany
e-mail: patrick.koellner@giga-hamburg.de

(PICs). I start by noting the ways in which the South Pacific matters in global terms. I then trace and outline China's growing engagement in the region. This engagement has provided an important impetus for Australia and New Zealand's recent diplomatic initiatives towards the region, the 'Pacific Step-up' and the 'Pacific Reset'. I identify both the similarities between the two initiatives and the differences that set them apart. By way of conclusion, I discuss what growing geopolitical competition means for the South Pacific.

THE SOUTH PACIFIC: AN IMPORTANT OCEANIC WORLD REGION

The South Pacific—or simply 'the Pacific' in Australian and New Zealand parlance—is a huge but sparsely populated world region. The Pacific covers nearly a third of the Earth's surface and offers plenty of blue-economy resources—some of which already require protection against depletion (such as tuna) and others of which have not even been fully explored yet (deep-sea mining). The Pacific is of tremendous importance for the planet's climate and is a showcase of what climate change can lead to. Whereas the nations and territories in the South Pacific produce collectively only around 0.03% of global greenhouse gases (GHGs) (SPREP, 2016), some of the region's microstates face physical extinction due to rising sea levels. Tropical storms are bound to grow in intensity. Climate-related problems can exacerbate some of the traditional developmental challenges faced by many PICs and are likely to lead to greater migratory pressure. Whereas the South Pacific may constitute a dream destination for tourists, many Pacific Islanders have headed in the other direction. Pulled there by job and educational opportunities, many thousand Pacific Islanders live, for example, in New Zealand, which offers a number of permanent residence visas to citizens of Fiji, Tonga, Kiribati and Tuvalu every year. In the case of some states and territories, more Pacific Islanders actually live overseas than on their home islands.[1] Australia aside, no more than 17 million people in total live in the 17 other member states and

---

[1] According to a 2013 census, close to 30,000 Niueans and more than 7000 Tokelauans (who are both also New Zealand citizens) then lived in New Zealand, compared to 1500 people on Niue and 1400 on Tokelau. Also, more than to 140,000 Samoans lived in New Zealand in 2012 (Ratuva and Brady 2019, pp. 148–150), while Samoa's own current population stands at 198,000.

territories belonging to the Pacific Islands Forum (PIF),[2] the region's premier regional organisation, set up in the wake of late decolonisation in this region. Population-wise, Papua New Guinea (PNG), with its nearly nine million inhabitants, and Fiji, with its close to one million, are the heavyweights among the core PICs, while the region's microstates include Tuvalu and Palau, with their respectively fewer than 20,000 inhabitants each. Together with Tonga, PNG and Fiji are also the only PICs with standing armies. Yet, despite their small populations and land masses, the PICs are a force to be reckoned with. They constitute 12 members of the United Nations and have developed their 'Blue Pacific' narrative—an evocative framing of the importance of the Pacific Ocean for its inhabitants, and for humankind more generally (see e.g. Tukuitonga, 2018).

Since the coming into force of the UN Convention on the Law of the Seas (UNCLOS) in 1994, the PICs have also called some of the world's largest Exclusive Economic Zones (EEZs) their own (see Fig. 1). For example, Kiribati, with its 120,000 inhabitants, has an EEZ of more than 3.5 million km^2. To sum up: While the South Pacific is a sparsely populated world region composed of island states and self-governing territories scattered over vast expanses, it is also a world region that matters globally in terms of climate issues, political representation and economic resources. What is more, geopolitical competition has entered the picture (again) in recent years, especially with China's growing regional presence and the reaction thereto of Australia and New Zealand.

---

[2] Although both Australasian countries belong to the PIF, New Zealand's claim to being a Pacific nation rings truer, given its geographic position, its constitutional obligations to the Cook Islands, Niue and Tokelau, plus its *Pasifika* population, estimated to reach 10 per cent by 2026. MPs with roots in the Pacific Islands are well represented in New Zealand's parliament, especially in the current coalition government (cf. New Zealand Parliament 2019). Finally, there is New Zealand's sizeable Maori population with its own ancestral links to the region. While there is thus substance to New Zealand's Pacific identity claims, such claims may have even greater strategic utility outside of the region and international fora, as Anna Powles (2018, p. 181) notes. Australia, for its part, borders not only the South Pacific but also Southeast Asia and the Indian Ocean region—one reason why it has eagerly embraced the 'Indo-Pacific' concept in recent years.

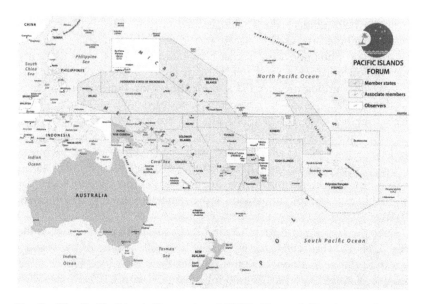

Fig. 1 The Pacific Islands Forum (as of 2015) (*Source* © iStock.com / Rainer Lesniewski *Note* French Polynesia and New Caledonia became full PIF members in 2016; Tokelau became an associate member in 2016, and Wallis and Futuna in 2018)

China's Growing Regional Engagement

Concerns shared by the region's traditional powers, Australia and New Zealand, about external forces are nothing new. In the 1980s, there were worries about the Soviet Union's increased interest in the region, which manifested itself most notably in fishing agreements with Kiribati and Vanuatu (Thakur 1991, pp. 18–19; Willis, 2019). The Soviet threat, real or imagined, disappeared in the late 1980s however; concerns about Libya's romance with the postcolonial regime in Vanuatu and the independence movement in New Caledonia (CIA, 1987) had also largely dissipated by that time. What remained was the rivalry between the People's Republic of China (PRC) and Taiwan, the key protagonists of geopolitical competition. Decolonisation in the South Pacific, starting with (Western) Samoa in 1962 and ending, for now, with Palau in 1994, provided Beijing and Taipei with opportunities to boost their international legitimacy by befriending countries that would recognise them diplomatically.

The emerging marketplace for diplomatic recognition led Beijing and Taipei to engage in chequebook diplomacy, offering development aid—presented in the case of the PRC as 'South–South cooperation'—in exchange for diplomatic recognition (Atkinson, 2010). By 1988, the PRC had established diplomatic relations with five countries in the region and Taiwan with four. By 2008, when mainland China and Taiwan declared a truce, the ratio remained about the same, with the PRC maintaining diplomatic relations with eight countries and Taiwan with six. The rivalry picked up steam again when the mainland-friendly Kuomintang party lost the presidential election in Taiwan in 2016. By that time, it had become clear that this was a race that Taiwan could not ultimately win. In 2019, the Solomon Islands and Kiribati cut ties with Taiwan, leaving it with only four small diplomatic allies in the region (out of then 16 worldwide)—the Marshall Islands, Nauru, Palau and Tuvalu.

While there has been much talk over the years about the destabilising effects and potential of the two Chinas' competition for diplomatic recognition, it is effectively unclear whether corruption or, for that matter, domestic political strife would have been much lower without the PRC–Taiwan tussle. Ill-gotten gains on the part of local politicians schmoozing up to Beijing and/or Taipei aside, the diplomatic competition certainly brought attention and aid with it that otherwise would not have been there—or at least not to the same degree (Atkinson, 2010, pp. 419–420). Hundreds of millions of US dollars have been spent by mainland China and Taiwan on courting the PICs. Joel Atkinson (2010, p. 412) notes that PRC and Taiwanese aid packages have been 'considerably more focused on meeting the requirements of Pacific Island politicians than aid from Western donors'. Certainly, fewer government and parliamentary buildings across the region would have been built without the diplomatic rivalry.

Both China and Taiwan have been welcome partners for the PICs, providing them with alternatives to Western aid. 'While traditional donors emphasise conditionality and a rigid process of approval and monitoring', as Denghua Zhang and Stephanie Lawson (2017, p. 203) note,

> Chinese aid is faster to negotiate and to proceed ... China also concentrates on government-to-government channels, and does not impose any

conditions in areas such as democratic institutional building and good governance. This practice gives more discretion to the recipient governments on the use of Chinese assistance, and is welcomed by many PIC officials. China's emphasis on building infrastructure projects is also welcomed where infrastructure improvement remains an important task.'

For a country like Fiji that lost access to Western aid after the 2006 military coup, Chinese assistance was particularly useful—both in terms of funding and to show traditional partners that other options were available (see Hamiri, 2015, pp. 645–648).

While a number of PICs are no longer considered least developed countries, or will soon cease to be considered as such, the South Pacific is on a per capita basis the most aid-dependent region worldwide. Chinese aid to the region grew significantly in the 2010s. According to the Lowy Institute's Pacific Aid Map, the PRC provided US$1.62 billion in aid to PICs between 2011 and 2019, making it the largest donor behind Australia and ahead of New Zealand (Lowy Institute, n.d.). Well over 70 per cent of Chinese overseas development assistance (ODA) has taken the form of concessional loans, thus having to be repaid at some point. What also sets Chinese ODA apart is that there is a huge difference between funds committed and funds spent. In geographical terms, China's ODA is concentrated on the more resource-rich Melanesian PICs, i.e. PNG (receiving one-third of the funds), the Solomon Islands, Fiji and Vanuatu. Regional institutions and initiatives in the South Pacific have also received a significant amount of funding, but most Chinese ODA in the region is bilaterally oriented.

The PRC has by now a fairly extensive diplomatic presence in the region. Since 1989, it has been an official dialogue partner of the PIF. In this millennium, the PRC has three times so far convened the China–Pacific Island Countries Economic Development and Cooperation Forum, a 'multi-bilateral grouping' (Taylor, 2019), in which China engages with its diplomatic partners and announces aid packages. The first such forum took place in Suva (Fiji) in 2006, when Chinese Prime Minister Wen Jiabao visited the region. In 2013 it was held in Guangzhou and in 2019 it returned to the South Pacific, being held in Apia, Samoa. China's rising profile in the region in the past few years has been highlighted by two visits by President Xi Jinping. In November 2014, he became the first Chinese head of state to visit the PICs, more precisely

Fiji, where he met with the leaders of China's then eight diplomatic partners among the PICs. Four years later he visited PNG, which hosted the Asia–Pacific Economic Cooperation (APEC) summit at the time (see also Chen, 2019).

Apart from the competition with Taiwan, there have also been other factors behind Chinese engagement in the region. Business opportunities and broader economic motivations have clearly played a role. Some scholars emphasise the strategic nature of it, seeing such engagement as part of China's longer-term plan also to become the leading power in this part of the Pacific. Others have argued that China's interest is mostly commercial.[3] While local markets are not huge, they do provide opportunities for many small entrepreneurs active in the PICs' retail sectors and beyond. There are no reliable statistics concerning the number of Chinese traders and the broader Chinese diaspora in the PICs. Available numbers differ widely, ranging from 80,000 to 200,000, and many Chinese have been active in the region for a long time. Anti-Chinese sentiment has been an issue at times, taking extreme forms, for example most recently in 2009 when Chinese-owned businesses in PNG were looted and torched. The activities of small traders, but also many other Chinese companies operating in the PICs, have not been state-guided. This may even apply to some of the bigger, often state-owned companies that have engaged, for example, in construction projects—building roads, bridges, ports, hydroelectric plants, official buildings and sports stadiums—either as part of Chinese development co-operation activities or as part of their own 'going global' ones.

The PICs' huge EEZs and the stocks of migratory fish—tuna in particular—in them have also drawn Chinese fishing fleets (including illegal operators) to the region. So have the natural resources in PNG (such as nickel, cobalt and chromite) and Fiji (gold, bauxite, ironsand), where Chinese companies have invested in the respective mining sectors (see Hannan & Firth, 2015, pp. 869–870). The South Pacific has thus helped to feed China's hunger for natural resources. Certainly, China is overall an attractive market for the PICs. Manufactured goods are flowing the other way. China has become a key trading partner for PICs in recent years, competing in some for the number one spot (Dornan & Muller,

---

[3] See, for example, Hayward-Jones (2013), Hameiri (2015, pp. 638–643), and Wesley (2020, pp. 197–199). Zhang and Lawson (2017, p. 201) provide an overview of the debate.

2018). The volume of Chinese tourists has also increased over the past decade, with Beijing having granted 'approved destination' status to its South Pacific allies. In 2018, close to 125,000 Chinese tourists visited the South Pacific, accounting for around 6 per cent of total visitors in that year (South Pacific Tourist Organisation, 2019). For PICs interested in diversifying their relationships, this is mostly good news.

China's increased engagement has, however, also led to problems. Concessional loans have certainly increased the debt burden of some PICs. As of 2019, six PICs were indebted to the PRC. But, as a Lowy Institute report (Rajah et al., 2019) notes, only PNG and Vanuatu had taken on new Chinese loans since 2016. Tonga, Samoa and Vanuatu are the countries in the region that are most indebted to China in proportion to their gross domestic products. Tonga's debt to China amounts to nearly two thirds of its overall debt, and close to a third of the country's GDP. In August 2018, then Tongan Prime Minister Akilisi Pohiva called on China to write off its loans to South Pacific nations, as they imposed too much of a burden on governments. Apart from another deferral of Tongan debts to China, nothing came of this, as Pohiva's colleagues from Samoa and elsewhere did not agree with the assessment (AFP, 2018). And, as Denghua Zhang (2018) notes, it is anyway difficult for China to write off concessional loans (as opposed to the small category of interest-free foreign aid loans: cf. Brautigam, 2020). While there are thus real issues in terms of debt for some PICs, China is not necessarily the driver and the only source of this. Claims of Chinese 'debt diplomacy' do not—at least not recently—withstand close scrutiny in the case of the South Pacific (see also Fox & Dornan, 2018).

Many of the bigger Chinese activities in the South Pacific in recent years, such as a new terminal at Samoa's Faleolo International Airport, have been carried out as part of China's BRI. When Xi visited Fiji in 2014, he invited the PICs to participate in the '21st Century Maritime Silk Road', i.e. the maritime part of the BRI. A year later, the South Pacific had officially become one of the maritime centres of the BRI. By early 2019, nine PIF members had signed memoranda of understanding to participate in the BRI—Fiji, Samoa, Tonga, Vanuatu, the Cook Islands, the Federated States of Micronesia, PNG, Niue and New Zealand (Taylor, 2019). Especially in the Oceania core of the PIF, China's greater presence and the options it provided has been welcomed. As the Secretary General of the PIF, Dame Meg Taylor, noted in 2019,

[i]n general, Forum members view China's increased actions in the region as a positive development, one that offers greater options for financing and development opportunities — both directly in partnership with China, and indirectly through the increased competition in our region.

China offered, the Secretary General added, '[a]ccess to markets, technology, financing, infrastructure'. Clearly, the emergence of China as a major player in the region has endowed PICs with greater agency, and helped to reduce their dependence on traditional development partners.

Australia 'Steps up' Its Regional Engagement

Australia and New Zealand worry that China's more opaque and unconditional financial support undercuts the good-governance approach of their own ODA programmes focused on the region. Other perceived problems include the mixed quality of some of the Chinese infrastructure projects there, the lack of maintenance of existing facilities, and the fact that it is mostly Chinese workers who participate in these projects (Zhang & Lawson, 2017, p. 204). Finally, strategic circles in Canberra worry that the debt burdens of individual PICs will become unsustainable and that China might transform its leverage in this regard into political capital or even use it as a pretext to assume control of assets in the PICs (some of which might ultimately be used for military purposes).

This leads to the heart of security and geostrategic concerns that have animated relevant discourses in Australia. The South Pacific is far away from current or potential trouble spots in the Indo-Pacific and is unlikely to become itself a genuine hotspot for militarised confrontation. The region matters, however, in strategic terms in the increasing geopolitical competition between China and the United States (and the latter's regional ally, Australia). The ability—or presumed inability—of PIC governments to remain free of Chinese influence has emerged as a significant concern for strategic circles in Australia. This is connected to earlier, long-standing concerns about state fragility and internal security issues in the PICs and their ramifications for Australia. These concerns triggered a number of Australian-led 'co-operative interventions' from the late 1980s—usually jointly with New Zealand—in places such as the Bougainville region of PNG or the Solomon Islands (see Wallis, 2017a, chapter 3). Australia's 'age of intervention' in what has been called an 'arc of instability' (see Ayson, 2007) only came to a close in 2017 with the end of the multibillion, 14-year-long Australian-led Regional Assistance Mission to the Solomon Islands (RAMSI), an initiative to stabilise the country and to rebuild key state institutions there.

However, Australian governments continue to see a 'special responsibility' to manage the region in security terms—sometimes described by political leaders in Canberra as 'our patch' (for a critical appraisal see Lilford, 2019, pp. 16–19). Likewise, there is the expectation in Washington and beyond that Australia (together with New Zealand) assumes this responsibility (see Wesley, 2020, pp. 193–194). In recent years, strategic circles in Australia—and by extension in the US—have worried that China will set up a military base in the South Pacific. While such a base would arguably be of limited military value, it would signal that China defied the status quo in this world region and tried to assert itself as a maritime player in this part of the Pacific as well. As Hugh White (2019, p. 16) argues, such a base would signal 'intention and resolve' and thus be strategically important. Australia has, in conjunction with New Zealand, long followed a policy of 'strategic denial', trying to make sure that no (potentially) hostile power gains a foothold in the South Pacific (Herr, 1987; Wallis, 2017a, pp. 39–45). This policy can be traced back to colonial times, and is also a legacy of the Second World War, when heavy fighting occurred in the region (especially in 1942 and 1943 at Guadalcanal in the Solomon Islands). In early 1942, Japanese imperial forces even carried out a massive bombing raid on Darwin in Australia's Northern Territory, an event sometimes called Australia's 'Pearl Harbor'. A slew of further attacks followed later that year and in 1943.

Seventy-five years later, in April 2018, front-page newspaper articles in Australia reported that China had approached Vanuatu, one of the countries most heavily indebted to it, with a view to setting up a naval base there (e.g. Wroe, 2018a). The reports were vehemently denied by governments in Beijing and Port Vila. Other PICs, including PNG, have been mooted as possible locations for 'dual use' bases (see Lilford, 2019, pp. 10–11). Regardless of whether these were just rumours, or amounted to more, they prompted the Australian Government to take action. At the 2018 APEC summit in Port Moresby, Australian Prime Minister Scott Morrison announced that this country, together with the PNG and the United States, would redevelop a former wartime US naval base on Manus Island. This announcement was a part of a broader policy initiative of Australia towards the South Pacific. What started as the announcement of a 'step change' towards the region by Morrison's predecessor, Malcolm Turnbull, in 2016, and got spelt out in Australia's 2007 Foreign Policy White Paper, became known as the 'Pacific Step-up'—a fully fledged foreign policy programme under Morrison (Harris Rimmer, 2019, pp. 646–647).

The government in Canberra likes to emphasise that the initiative is not directed at any one country but constitutes a positive contribution to the region—Australia's 'Pacific family' (see, e.g. Wroe, 2018b). Yet, it is clear that the Step-up seeks to balance China's growing engagement there. Arguably, it is also about signalling to Washington that Canberra is doing something to counter that engagement (Wesley, 2020, p. 202). Australian governments had long liked to believe that it was possible to enjoy the best of both worlds by benefiting from China's economic rise while also being an ally of the United States. Under Turnbull, Canberra finally came to the conclusion that it needed to push back both against Chinese inter-ference in domestic politics and public life (see Köllner, 2019; Medcalf, 2019) and against China's growing influence in the region—which might undermine the PICs' sovereignty. The domestic pushback, culminating in the Espionage and Foreign Interference Act of 2018 and the Pacific Step-up are thus two sides of the same coin.

The Step-up consists of measures ranging from the announced redevelopment of the Manus Island naval base to the promotion of people-to-people exchanges, for example among churches—Christianity is widespread in the South Pacific—and also involving sports-related exchanges. Some of the main activities and plans (see DFAT, n.d.; Harris Rimmer, 2019, pp. 646–647; Zhou & Walsh, 2020) include:

- substantially raising ODA to the South Pacific, reaching AU$1.4 billion in the 2019/20 financial year
- building an ODA-financed underwater internet cable in the Coral Sea which links the Solomon Islands and PNG to Australia (outbid-ding China's Huawei telecommunications company)
- establishing the Australian Infrastructure Financing Facility for the Pacific, which can draw on A$1.5 billion in loans and A$500 million in grants. To better compete with China on infrastructure, the government has also made available A$1 billion for Export Finance Australia, the remit of which got extended to overseas infrastructure projects
- introducing a new Pacific Labour Scheme which builds on the Seasonal Worker Programme established in 2012 and allows low-

and semi-skilled persons from the South Pacific to work for three years in rural Australia;

- launching the Australia Pacific Security College, currently based at the Australian National University and devoted to the training of mid- and senior-level officials from the region
- making available a semi-mobile infantry unit and, in the future, a large-hulled vessel for humanitarian and disaster relief missions in the region
- new diplomatic posts in the region and a new co-ordinating 'Office of the Pacific' within the Department of Foreign Affairs and Trade
- significantly intensifying high-level visit diplomacy

Symbolically, Morrison's first overseas visit as PM took him to the Solomon Islands—where he announced a ten-year, A$250 million bilateral infrastructure programme (Osborne, 2019). Arguably, Morrison, who has family connections to the South Pacific, is the most regionally engaged Australian prime minister since Bob Hawke (1983–1991).

Overall, the Pacific Step-up represents a fairly substantial and comprehensive policy initiative. Australia will remain the biggest donor to the region, contributing around 45 per cent of all ODA going there, and will also remain the region's primary partner with respect to (traditional) security co-operation. It remains to be seen, however, how sustained this all will be. In the past, Australia's engagement in the South Pacific has been cyclical, with episodes of strong engagement alternating with ones of benign neglect (Schultz, 2014). Moreover, Australia's spending on diplomacy and ODA has dwindled in recent years, from an inflation-adjusted A$8.3 billion in the 2013/14 financial year to A$6.7 billion six years later, with ODA going down by 27 per cent in real terms since 2013, standing relative to GNP at a miserly 0.2 per cent (Conley Tyler, 2019, p. 110). While the PICs will welcome the increased aid to their region, it comes at the expense of Australian aid going elsewhere. Australian ODA increasingly follows diplomatic and security objectives. In Morrison's second cabinet, sworn in May 2019, the minister for international development and the Pacific has notably also served as assistant defence minister.

New Zealand also 'Resets' Its Pacific Engagement

Australia's 'principal strategic partner' in the South Pacific is New Zealand (see Wallis, 2017b, p. 9; Wallis & Powles, 2018, p. 3). A few months after coming to power, the centre-left coalition government in Wellington, led by Prime Minister Jacinda Ardern (Labour Party) and Foreign Minister Winston Peters (New Zealand First), also embarked on a major regional initiative. Peters, a veteran politician who had already served as foreign minister between 2005 and 2008, announced the 'Pacific Reset' in Sydney in March 2018, indicating the need for collective regional efforts by the two Australasian allies. Later on, he also implored the United States to reinforce its activities in the South Pacific (Peters, 2018b). Although Peters did not cite China by name and merely spoke about the South Pacific as an 'increasingly contested strategic space, no longer neglected by Great Power ambition' (Peters, 2018a), China's growing regional engagement and the challenge this poses to the traditional dominance of Australia and New Zealand provided an, if not the most, important motivation for the Reset. Differences in relative size and available resources notwithstanding, the Reset shares some characteristics of Australia's Step-up: it involves a substantial increase of ODA to the region—to be increased over four years by NZ$714 million, the establishment of no fewer than 14 new diplomatic and development posts in the region and, to co-ordinate development policies, also in Beijing, Brussels, Tokyo and New York, plus a substantial increase in high-level diplomacy (Cabinet Office, 2018).

In some ways, the South Pacific has thus regained the importance in New Zealand foreign policy that it had in the 1970s and 1980s, when New Zealand first embraced its Pacific identity. Whereas Australia has traditionally a strong focus on Melanesia, given its geography and PNG's history as a former colony, New Zealand has an equally strong focus on Polynesia. This is also easily explained by a combination of geographical and historical factors, as well as by constitutional obligations to the Cook Islands and Niue—which are self-governing but in free association with New Zealand—and Tokelau, a dependent territory. New Zealand also has a special relationship with its former trust territory Samoa, which includes a preferential immigration regime. The Reset does stretch beyond Polynesia however, for example in terms of ODA. Similar to Australia, New Zealand's ODA spending had declined under conservative governments between 2008 and 2017. Even with the new outlay, New Zealand's ODA will only go up, in relation to GDP, to something like 0.28 per cent in 2021 (Walters, 2018). Past National Party-led governments were more focused on creating free trade agreements (FTAs)—though with limited success—in the South Pacific. An upgraded FTA linking Australia and

New Zealand ('PACER Plus') with many PICs was signed in 2017, but regional heavyweights PNG and Fiji decided to opt out as they felt that the FTA overly favoured Australian and New Zealand interests.

DIFFERENCES BETWEEN THE APPROACHES OF AUSTRALIA AND NEW ZEALAND: CLIMATE POLICY AND BEYOND

Differences between Australia's and New Zealand's approach to the Pacific extend beyond regional foci or, for that matter, diplomatic styles. New Zealand's Pacific policy is overall less 'securitised' and geopolitical in orientation than Australia's. There are various reasons for this. For one, New Zealand spends—even in relative terms—less on defence than Australia (see Thomson, 2018, pp. 22–23). Being sheltered by Australia, it can afford a military more geared towards peacekeeping operations than territorial defence. Since the mid-1980s, New Zealand is also no longer a formal ally of the United States—though security and intelligence ties have increased again in the past decade. Furthermore, New Zealand's focus on Polynesia means that it is mainly concerned with the part of the region that has experienced fewer problems in terms of state fragility and internal security than Melanesia, Australia's focus. New Zealand's views of the South Pacific thus tend to be more benign than Australia's (see also Howe, 2000, esp. p. 6).[4]

Still, security issues are integral to the Reset. Most prominently, in terms of the operational readiness of the NZ Defence Force, the South Pacific has been placed on the same level as New Zealand's own territory. That matters, for example, with respect to responding to requests for help from PICs hit by cyclones. Climate change, one of the 'complex disruptors' affecting regional security (New Zealand Government, 2018a, p. 6), will likely lead to higher-intensity cyclones and the need for more humanitarian and disaster relief operations. New Zealand military procurement priorities, as outlined in the 2019 Defence Capability Plan (New Zealand Government, 2019a), thus include increased air and sealift capabilities as

---

[4] The geopolitical character of Australian policy towards the South Pacific might also explain why human rights issues in the Pacific do not rank that highly in Canberra. New Zealand policymakers, on the other hand, believe they cannot turn a blind eye to human rights issues in the South Pacific without getting some sort of domestic backlash, particularly from Maori and Pacific Islanders in New Zealand. The author is grateful to Robert Patman for this insight.

well as improved aerial and maritime domain surveillance capacity. The latter will come courtesy of four state-of-the-art Boeing P-8A Poseidon maritime patrol aircraft. The biggest New Zealand defence procurement in decades, coming with a price tag of NZ$2.4 billion, will also increase interoperability with Australia and other core security partners.

Every official New Zealand defence document published since 2018 has featured climate change prominently, discussing what it means for the posture of the NZ Defence Force, its equipment, co-operation with partners in the Pacific and so on (see New Zealand Government,). This focus reflects a comprehensive understanding of security. It also helps to explain why the Green Party in New Zealand has lent its support to the government's defence policy and, by New Zealand standards, the massive investments that it entails. In 2019, the New Zealand Parliament passed, with bipartisan support, the 'Climate Change Response (Zero Carbon) Amendment Act'. This bill sets the framework for cutting net emissions of all GHGs (except biogenic methane) to zero by 2050 (Parliamentary Counsel Office, 2019). In sum, the current New Zealand Government is singing from the same hymnsheet as the PICs when it comes to climate change policy.

For PICs, climate change constitutes the single biggest security threat. The Boe Declaration on Regional Security, issued at the 2018 PIF summit, captures this reality. It reaffirmed that 'climate change remains the single greatest threat to the livelihoods, security and well-being of the people of the Pacific and our commitment to progress in the implementation of the Paris Agreement' (Pacific Islands Forum Secretariat, 2018). The declaration has served to increase security-related co-operation between Australia, New Zealand and the PICs. It is, however, also a reminder that not every party is on the same page when it comes to related priorities. For the Australian Government, the challenge from China constitutes the most prominent security issue. China's growing regional 'footprint' also animates discussions among strategic circles in New Zealand—but it is still possible to discuss South Pacific issues in Wellington without necessarily referencing the East Asian country.

Australia was once instrumental in setting up the Green Climate Fund, a key body under the Paris Agreement to support climate action in developing countries—including in the South Pacific (Merzian, 2019). But that was then. Josh Frydenberg, Treasurer under Prime Minister Morrison, declared in 2018 that 'Australia would not damage its economy in pursuit of climate goals' and was opposed to a 'recklessly high target' for GHG reduction (Crowe & Hunter, 2018). The government clings to coal exports, and in 2019 gave the green light to the construction of the huge and hugely contested Carmichael mine in Queensland, run by the Indian Adani Group. Moreover, Australia is the only advanced country that planned to use 'carryover credits'—carbon credits accrued from the Kyoto Protocol—to meet its Paris Agreement targets. By doing so, Australia sought to meet its 2030 reduction target mostly based on a mere bookkeeping exercise (Merzian, 2019; Zhou & Walsh, 2020).

Australia also blocked an ambitious climate statement coming out of the 2019 PIF summit in Tuvalu. PIC leaders were not impressed by the consolation prize of a five-year, AU$500 million climate and resilience regional support package and heavily criticised Australia for placing the interests of an industry above the welfare of its 'Pacific family' (Handley, 2019). They have also not forgotten that Australia has used the region as a dumping ground for unwanted refugees, having put them for years under its 'Pacific Solution' and 'Operation Sovereign Borders' policies in detention camps on Nauru and Manus Island. Australia might be a superpower in the South Pacific, whose resources are vital and welcome. Generating goodwill and trust in the region—the very basis for influence—will, though, need more than what the Step-up might ultimately be able to deliver. As Richie Merzian (2019) notes, stepping up in the Pacific and stepping back on climate action are difficult to reconcile (see also Hayward-Jones, 2019).

The COVID-19 pandemic has seen both China and the Australasian partners provide the PICs with medical supplies and other humanitarian assistance (see e.g. Australian Government, 2020; Pryke & McGregor, 2020). What might be even more important in the medium term, given that most PICs (except for some Melanesian countries) are heavily dependent on tourism and remittances and are thus hard-hit by the pandemic, would be an extension of the planned trans-Tasman COVID-safe travel zone. Australians and New Zealanders account for nearly two thirds of the tourists visiting PICs annually, while seasonal worker programmes have seen thousands of Pacific Islanders employed in agricultural and horticultural jobs in both countries, sending much-needed remittances home (Cook, 2020). If the number of infections in all countries concerned were to be reduced to around zero and stringent health and travel protocols established, an extension of the planned COVID-safe travel zone could help cushion the economic effects of the pandemic on the region and become an exemplar of Australian and New Zealand regional leadership.

CONCLUSIONS

China is today the most important non-traditional power in the South Pacific and it is there to stay. The PRC's rise in the region is owing to the long-standing diplomatic competition with Taiwan, the 'going global' of Chinese entrepreneurs and companies, and the concerted efforts of the Chinese Government, recently under the label of BRI, to bring the region into a closer orbit of the Middle Kingdom. Australia and New Zealand have been quite active in the past two decades when it came to security interventions and free trade initiatives, but have—ODA aside—not treated the South Pacific as a foreign policy priority. Their more recent large-scale initiatives towards the region are welcomed by PICs as they further increase these countries' options. Australia and New Zealand's initiatives are aimed at making sure that China does not become a hegemon in the South Pacific. In that, they might well succeed. Together, the two Australasian partners still account for more than half of ODA going to PICs, and their support for the region generally contrasts with China's preference for bilateralism. Also, Australia seems destined to remain the primary (traditional) security partner of the PICs. Yet the Australian Government's climate policy (or lack thereof) limits its potential for regional influence. If circumstances allow, Australia still has the potential to provide, in conjunction with New Zealand, regional leadership during the current pandemic by extending their planned COVID-safe travel zone to the South Pacific.

Strategic circles in Australia and beyond have viewed China's growing engagement in the South Pacific with equally growing suspicion. PICs themselves, however, have generally welcomed China's burgeoning profile—as they welcome the engagement of other external actors such as the European Union or Japan. The more players that are active in the region, the more agency and options are available for the PICs. Increasing geopolitical competition has thus been, so far, a good thing for PICs as it has increased interest in, and available funds for, the region. Yet there are also risks and unwelcome outcomes. A militarisation of geopolitical competition in the South Pacific is the last thing that PICs would like to see. The military base issue in PNG is a timely reminder that such militarisation is not as far-fetched as it may seem. Also, PICs might be confronted in the future more often with the reality that in international relations there is (often) no such a thing as a free lunch. PICs that recognise China and benefit from its largesse might be pressured to side with the PRC in international fora or, perhaps more likely, at the regional level when it comes to the treatment of Taiwan in the PIF and beyond. This, in turn, might led to greater discord among PICs.[5] In a worst-case scenario, the integrity of the PIF would be undermined and its hard-earned gains in terms of collective agency be threatened. Such an outcome would also be in the interests of Australia and New Zealand. As comparatively resource-rich countries that are able to offer job-related and educational opportunities, these two countries have plenty to offer to PICs. Stoking direct, militarised competition with China would be counterproductive. Certainly, the South Pacific is no longer a strategic backwater. External actors need to take note of the complex unfolding dynamics in this world region.

References

AFP [Agence France-Press] (2018, August 20). China must not write off Pacific island debts, says Samoan leader. *South China Morning Post*. https://www.scmp.com/news/china/diplomacy-defence/article/2160429/china-must-not-write-pacific-island-debts-says-samoa. Accessed 29 July 2020.

Atkinson, J. (2010). China-Taiwan diplomatic competition and the Pacific Islands. *The Pacific Review, 23*(4), 407–427.

Australian Government. (2020). Partnerships for recovery: Australia's COVID-19 development response. Department of Foreign Affairs and Trade. https://www.dfat.gov.au/sites/default/files/partnerships-for-recovery-australias-covid-19-development-response.pdf. Accessed 22 June 2020.

Ayson, R. (2007). The 'arc of instability' and Australia's strategic policy. *Australian Journal of International Affairs, 61*(2), 215–231.

Brautigam, D. (2020, April 15). Chinese debt relief: Fact and fiction. *The Diplomat*. https://thediplomat.com/2020/04/chinese-debt-relief-fact-and-fiction. Accessed 29 July 2020.

Cabinet Office. (2018). The Pacific reset: The first year. Minute of Decision, ERS-18-MIN-0028. Cabinet External Relations and Security Committee. https://www.mfat.govt.nz/assets/OIA/R-R-The-Pacific-reset-The-First-Year.PDF. Accessed 25 February 2020.

CIA [Central Intelligence Agency]. (1987). Libyan Activities in the South Pacific. Partly declassified report. https://www.cia.gov/library/readingroom/docs/CIA-RDP90T00114R000200270001-7.pdf. Accessed 9 June 2020.

---

[5] For a discussion of some early signs in that regard, see Wesley (2020, p. 212).

Conley Tyler, M. (2019, October). Solving Australia's foreign affairs challenges. *Australian Foreign Affairs*, 7, 109–115.

Cook, S. (2020, May 21). Now is the right time to bring Fiji into trans-Pacific bubbles talks. *The Interpreter*. Lowy Institute. https://www.lowyinsti tute.org/the-interpreter/now-right-time-bring-fiji-trans-pacific-bubble-talks. Accessed 25 May 2020.

Chen, X. (2019). China, the United States and the changing South Pacific regional order in the 2010s. *China International Strategic Review*. https:// link.springer.com/content/pdf/10.1007%2Fs42533-019-00022-x.pdf. Accessed 27 May 2020.

Crowe, D., & Hunter, F. (2018, August 28). Morrison climate deal test. *The Age*, 1.

DFAT [Department of Foreign Affairs and Trade, Australia]. (n.d.). Stepping-up Australia's Pacific engagement. https://dfat.gov.au/geo/pacific/engage ment/Pages/stepping-up-australias-pacific-engagement.aspx. Accessed 3 July 2020.

Dornan, M., & Muller, S. (2018, November 15). The China shift in Pacific trade. DevPolicyBlog. https://devpolicy.org/china-in-the-pacific-aus tralias-trade-challenge-20181115. Accessed 9 June 2020.

Fox, R., & Dornan, M. (2018, November 8). China in the Pacific: Is China engaged in 'debt-trap diplomacy'? DevPolicyBlog. https://devpolicy.org/is-china-engaged-in-debt-trap-diplomacy-20181108. Accessed 9 June 2020.

Handley, E. (2019, August 16). Australia accused of putting coal before Pacific 'family' as region calls for climate change action. https://www.abc.net.au/ news/2019-08-16/australia-slammed-watering-down-action-climate-change-pacific/11420986. Accessed 2 July 2020.

Hannan, K., & Firth, S. (2015). Trading with the Dragon: Chinese trade, investment and development assistance in the Pacific Islands. *Journal of Contemporary China*, 24(95), 865–882.

Hameiri, S. (2015). China's 'charm offensive' in the Pacific and Australia's regional order. *The Pacific Review*, 28(5), 631–654.

Harris Rimmer, S. (2019). Issues in Australian Foreign Policy January to June 2019. *Australian Journal of Politics and History*, 65(4), 638–652.

Hayward-Jones, J. (2013). Big enough for all of us: Geo-strategic competition in the Pacific Islands. *Analysis*. Lowy Institute. https://www.lowyinstitute. org/publications/big-enough-all-us-geo-strategic-competition-pacific-islands. Accessed 26 May 2020.

Hayward-Jones, J. (2019, June). Cross purposes: Why is Australia's Pacific influence waning? *Australian Foreign Affairs*, 6, 29–50.

Herr, R. A. (1987). Regionalism, strategic denial and South Pacific security. *The Journal of Pacific History*, 21(4), 170–182.

Howe, K. (2000). New Zealand's twentieth-century Pacifics: Memories and reflections. *New Zealand Journal of History, 34*(1), 4–19.

Köllner, P. (2019). Australia and New Zealand recalibrate their China policies: Convergence and divergence. *The Pacific Review.* https://www.tandfonline.com/doi/full/10.1080/09512748.2019.1683598. Accessed 29 July 2020.

Köllner, P. (2020). Australia and New Zealand face up to China in the South Pacific. *GIGA Focus Asia*, 3/2020. German Institute for Global and Area Studies. https://www.giga-hamburg.de/en/publication/australia-and-new-zealand-face-up-to-china-in-the-south-pacific. Accessed 3 July 2020.

Lowy Institute. (n.d.). Lowy Institute Pacific Aid Map. Lowy Institute. https://pacificaidmap.lowyinstitute.org. Accessed 27 July 2020.

Lilford, O. (2019). Australia's Pacific 'step-up': A legitimate engagement? Working Paper No. 13. School of Government, Development and International Affairs, University of the South Pacific. https://www.usp.ac.fj/filead min/files/Institutes/piasdg/SGDIA/SGDIA_WP_Series_2017/SGDIA_Wor king_Paper_13_-_Oliver_Lilford.pdf. Accessed 29 May 2020.

Medcalf, R. (2019). Australia and China: Understanding the reality check. *Australian Journal of International Affairs, 73*(2), 109–118.

Merzian, R. (2019, July 27). Our climate inaction will destroy our Pacific neighbours. *Canberra Times.* https://www.canberratimes.com.au/story/629 5355/our-climate-inaction-will-destroy-our-pacific-neighbours. Accessed 24 June 2020.

New Zealand Government. (2018a). Strategic Defence Policy Statement 2018. Ministry of Defence. http://www.nzdf.mil.nz/downloads/pdf/public-docs/2018/strategic-defence-policy-statement-2018.pdf. Accessed 5 July 2018.

New Zealand Government. (2018b). The Climate Crisis: Defence Readiness and Response. Ministry of Defence and Defence Force. https://www.defence.govt.nz/assets/Uploads/66cfc96a20/Climate-Change-and-Security-2018.pdf. Accessed 3 March 2020.

New Zealand Government. (2019a). Defence Capability Plan 2019. Ministry of Defence. https://www.defence.govt.nz/assets/Uploads/03acb8c6aa/Def ence-Capability-Plan-2019.pdf. Accessed 28 May 2020.

New Zealand Government. (2019b). Advancing Pacific Partnerships. Ministry of Defence. https://www.defence.govt.nz/publications/publication/advancing-pacific-partnerships-2019. Accessed 3 March 2020.

New Zealand Parliament. (2019). Pacific Island MPs in the New Zealand Parliament, 1993 onwards. https://www.parliament.nz/en/visit-and-learn/mps-and-parliaments-1854-onwards/pacific-island-mps-in-the-new-zealand-parliament-1993-onwards. Accessed 19 June 2020.

Osborne, P. (2019, June 3). Pacific step-up means showing up: PM. AAP Australian News Wire. Accessed 25 April 2020 via EBSCOhost.

Pacific Islands Forum Secretariat. (2018). Boe Declaration on Regional Security. https://www.forumsec.org/2018/09/05/boe-declaration-on-regional-security. Accessed 30 June 2020.

Parliamentary Counsel Office. (2019). Climate Change Response (Zero Carbon) Amendment Act 2019. http://www.legislation.govt.nz/act/public/2019/0061/latest/LMS183736.html. Accessed 2 July 2020.

Peters, W. (2018a, March 1). Shifting the dial. Speech to Lowy Institute. https://www.beehive.govt.nz/speech/shifting-dial. Accessed 5 May 2018.

Peters, W. (2018b, December 15). Pacific partnerships — Georgetown address. https://www.beehive.govt.nz/speech/pacific-partnerships-geo rgetown-address-washington-dc. Accessed 6 July 2020.

Powles, A. (2018). New Zealand's strategic influence and interests in an increasingly Global Pacific. In R. G. Patman, I. Iati, & B. Kiglics (Eds.), *New Zealand and the World: Past, Present and Future* (pp. 169–185). World Scientific.

Pryke, J., & McGregor, R. (2020, April 23). China's Coronavirus Aid to Pacific Countries is Part of Geopolitical Game. Commentary. Lowy Institute. https://www.lowyinstitute.org/publications/china-coronavirus-aid-pacific-islands-part-geopolitical-game. Accessed 5 May 2020.

Rajah, R., Dayant, A., & Pryke, J. (2019). Ocean of debt? Belt and road and debt diplomacy in the Pacific. *Analysis.* Lowy Institute. https://www.lowyinstitute.org/publications/ocean-debt-belt-and-road-and-debt-diplomacy-pacific#_edn20. Accessed 9 June 2020.

Ratuva, S., & Brady, A.-M. (2019). Neighbours and cousins: Aotearoa-New Zealand's relationships with the Pacific. In A.-M. Brady (Ed.), *Small states and the changing global order: New Zealand faces the future* (pp. 145–165). Springer.

Schultz, J. (2014). Theorising Australia-Pacific island relations. *Australian Journal of International Affairs, 68*(5), 548–568.

South Pacific Tourist Organisation. (2019). 2018 Annual Visitor Arrivals Report. SPTO. https://pic.or.jp/ja/wp-content/uploads/2019/07/2018-Annual-Visitor-Arrivals-ReportF.pdf. Accessed 11 June 2020.

SPREP [Secretariat of the Pacific Regional Environment Programme]. (2016). Six Pacific Islands Ratify The Paris Climate Accord. https://www.sprep.org/news/six-pacific-islands-ratify-paris-climate-accord. Accessed 11 June 2020.

Taylor, Dame M. (2019, February 8). The China alternative: Changing regional order in the Pacific Islands. Keynote address. https://www.forumsec.org/key note-address-by-dame-meg-taylor-secretary-general-the-china-alternative-cha nging-regional-order-in-the-pacific-islands. Accessed 29 May 2020.

Thakur, R. (1991). Introduction to the South Pacific. In R. Thakur (Ed.), *The South Pacific: Problems, issues and prospects* (pp. 1–33). Macmillan.

Thomson, M. (2018). *New Zealand, Australia and the ANZUS alliance: Interests, identity and strategy.* Special Report. February 2018. Australian Strategic Policy Institute. https://www.aspi.org.au/report/new-zealand-australia-and-anzus-alliance-interests-identity-and-strategy. Accessed 3 July 2020.

Tukuitonga, C. (2018). Looking to 2019: The Blue Pacific narrative will be key for our region. Pacific Community. https://www.spc.int/updates/blog/2018/12/looking-to-2019-the-blue-pacific-narrative-will-be-key-for-our-region. Accessed 27 July 2020.

Wallis, J. (2017a). *Pacific power? Australia's strategy in the Pacific Islands.* Melbourne University Press.

Wallis, J. (2017b). *Crowded and complex: The changing geopolitics of the South Pacific.* Special Report. April 2017. Australian Strategic Policy Institute. https://www.aspi.org.au/report/crowded-and-complex-changing-geopolitics-south-pacific. Accessed 6 July 2020.

Wallis, J., & Powles, A. (2018). *Australia and New Zealand in the Pacific Islands: Ambiguous Allies.* Discussion Paper. Strategic Defence Studies Centre, ANU College of Asia & the Pacific. http://sdsc.bellschool.anu.edu.au/experts-publications/publications/6508/australia-and-new-zealand-pacific-islands-ambiguous-allies. Accessed 6 July 2020.

Walters, L. (2018, July 4). New fund to help grow influence. *The Dominion Post*, 11.

Wesley, M. (2020). Oceania: Cold war versus the Blue Pacific. In A. J. Tellis, A. Szalwinski, & M. Wills (Eds.), *Strategic Asia 2020: U.S.–China Competition for Global Influence* (pp. 199–215). National Bureau of Asian Research.

White, H. (2019, July). In denial: Defending Australia as China looks south. *Australian Foreign Affairs, 6,* 5–27.

Willis, J. (2019). When the 'tuna wars' went hot: Kiribati, the Soviet Union, and the fishing pact that provoked a superpower. *Pacific Dynamics: Journal of Interdisciplinary Research, 1*(2), 264–281.

Wroe, D. (2018a, April 9). China eyes Vanuatu military base in plan with global ramifications. *Sydney Morning Herald.* https://www.smh.com.au/politics/federal/china-eyes-vanuatu-military-base-in-plan-with-global-ramifications-20180409-p4z8j9.html. Accessed 6 July 2020.

Wroe, D. (2018b, November 9). Pyne pledges new navy ship in South Pacific 'pivot'. *Sydney Morning Herald,* 14.

Zhang, D. (2018). Chinese Concessional Loans Part 2 — Pacific Indebtedness. *In Brief* 2018/29. Department of Pacific Affairs, Australian National University. https://openresearch-repository.anu.edu.au/bitstream/1885/154727/1/ib2018_29_chinese_concessional_loans_part_2_-_pacific_indebtedness.pdf. Accessed 29 July 2020.

Zhang, D., & Lawson, S. (2017). China in Pacific regional politics. *The round Table, 106*(2), 197–206.

Zhou, C., & Walsh, M. (2020, January 17). Australia pledged to 'step up' in the Pacific amid growing Chinese influence, but are we on track? ABC News. https://www.abc.net.au/news/2020-01-18/australia-pacific-step-up-in-review/11863150. Accessed 12 February 2020.

Navigating the 'New Normal': New Zealand Track II Diplomacy and the Shifting Dynamics in Asia

James To

INTRODUCTION

New Zealand's present and future—economically, culturally and socially—have been and will continue to be firmly tied to Asia. As such, there is a strong need to establish a deliberate and considered approach for engagement with the region so that New Zealanders can thrive in this environment. In seeking to advance this objective, the Asia New Zealand Foundation Te Whītau Tūhono runs a suite of programmes to help build New Zealanders' confidence, knowledge and networks for making the most of the opportunities presented across its neighbourhood.[1]

To grow New Zealanders' understanding of Asia, the foundation leads a series of bilateral and regional Track II exchanges with leading

---

[1] The Asia New Zealand Foundation's activities cover more than 20 countries and territories across Asia — see map on page 17 of Asia New Zealand Foundation (2019) *New Zealanders' Perceptions of Asia and Asian Peoples 2018 Annual Survey.* https://www. asianz.org.nz/assets/Uploads/PerceptionsofAsia_2018Final_Online.pdf.

J. To (✉)
Asia New Zealand Foundation, Wellington, New Zealand
e-mail: JTo@asianz.org.nz

think-tank partners, commentators and academics throughout the Asia–Pacific. These informal, non-governmental and unofficial dialogues offer an insight into how the great powers, medium-sized and smaller countries are dealing with strategic, foreign, security and trade policy issues. The topics discussed and debated are often consequential and have an impact on the discussants and who they represent—whether these be political, economic, military or cultural in nature. Participants enjoy free and frank discussions that are relevant and useful for everyone around the table. Track II dialogues are an opportunity to share diverse perspectives about what is going on and why; to identify areas of contrast, convergence and priority—especially in a dynamic and shifting environment—and come away with a more nuanced appreciation of what is driving the thought and policy processes throughout Asia and the wider region. This chapter summarises some of the leading topics of conversation drawn from the foundation's recent Track II discussions, and presents an assessment, opinion and commentary regarding some of the implications for New Zealand's international relations.

A 'New Normal'?

Although the title of this chapter refers to navigating the 'New Normal' and managing the shifting dynamics in Asia, there is nothing new in the observation that there has been a redistribution of regional and global power over the last couple of decades—particularly the shift of pre-eminence towards Asia, and more so within Asia. Rather, the 'New Normal' refers to a geostrategic environment reflecting the disruption to international relations over recent years. Under the Trump Administration, Washington has taken a unilateral approach to trade policy, for example; selectively applied rules and tariffs; and abandoned multilateral organisations and regional agreements. At the same time, a more confident People's Republic of China (PRC) has flexed its economic (and military) muscle in looking to reassume its pride of place in the region and beyond.

These changes in great-power relations have required a new set of calculations and game plan design. Policymakers have had to think deeply about how their governments and political masters should position themselves throughout this process. What have been some of the key issues of concern under this 'New Normal'? Is this turbulence in global politics just a temporary aberration, or does it reflect an exit from a period of remarkable stability? Indeed, the existing architecture has been under stress of late—the European Union (EU), the Paris Agreement (within the United Nations Framework Convention on Climate Change)—just to name a couple of examples. The post-war Bretton Woods system and alliances have been tested—the World Trade Organization (WTO), its disputes resolution process and the appellate body in crisis were a case in point. Institutions that were established in the twentieth century have shown themselves to be less fit for purpose in the twenty-first.

Across the world there has been a rise in populism, nationalist politics and revisionist tendencies. In the Asia–Pacific, there has been the emergence of the Indo-Pacific, the Belt and Road Initiative (BRI) and escalating tensions in the South China Sea. And having looked at how the Association of Southeast Asian Nations (ASEAN) countries, Australia and others have dealt with these challenges—New Zealand has also found itself to have been pushed and pulled about in ways that it did not have to concern itself with previously.

President Donald Trump's barrage of tweets added to a surprising and often confused read of how the United States has responded to international affairs. Concerns about an America in decline and withdrawing from the world order have been a major talking point for many analysts and policymakers, both domestically and abroad (Ayson & Capie, 2020; Bennhold, 2020). This was quite a departure from the previous administration, where there was at least some clarity and reassurance on what the role was for the United States in the region.

New Zealand has not been alone in this—none of the foundation's think-tank partners reported much success in getting coherence out of Washington during the Trump era. The one consistent theme that came across loud and clear, however, was that no matter whether it was Democrat/Republican, academic, economic or military, there was a union of voices critical of China. This was the one bipartisan issue on Capitol Hill. Accordingly, there has been a lack of optimism around the region—terms like 'decoupling' and 'unravelling' have been used more often. Prominent experts such as Hugh White of the Australian National University have argued for a 'Plan B' in the event Canberra can no longer rely on Washington's commitment to the region and protection—as an alliance partner (White, 2019). And what has been the outlook from Wellington on these developments? How have these views impacted New Zealand's foreign policy calculus? One thing that has been certain—alliances and allegiances have been shifting, and small countries have been increasingly looking to each other for support as they balance their major power interests.

NAVIGATION OF NEW ZEALAND'S RELATIONSHIPS WITH THE UNITED STATES AND CHINA

Almost twenty years ago (and about four months before the 9/11 attacks) the then Prime Minister of New Zealand, Helen Clark, famously articulated that New Zealanders lived in an 'incredibly benign strategic environment' (Catley, 2017, p. 137). This was partly an attempt to justify a significant reduction in and change of focus regarding New Zealand's defence spending, but also spoke to some practical considerations as well: New Zealand has never been at war with a neighbour. Indeed, New Zealand has had little to worry about when it comes to being attacked on its own soil by enemy forces. One Swedish assessment argued that because of its geographical isolation, the size of its territory and the difficulty of its terrain, any attempt to invade New Zealand would be 'a logistical nightmare' (Svenska Dagbladet, 2018).

Yet now New Zealand has found itself to be in a part of a world that is hotly contested by the two great economic and military powers: the PRC and the United States. Throughout the foundation's Track II discussions, finding a balance between these two important relationships for New Zealand has increasingly been pitched as a choice between economy and security. Many interlocutors have recognised that this is a false dichotomy—that it is not necessarily a choice; rather New Zealand policymakers have attempted to navigate their way through specifically so that they *do not have* to choose. The diplomatic process of such balancing is the 'New Normal'. No longer does Wellington necessarily take the black-and-white positions that it once held, but instead has learned to 'live with grey'—which, as a sweeping generalisation, New Zealanders generally do not like. Equally, the thought of having to make a 'choice' may be deeply troubling for New Zealand policy thinkers and politicians—New Zealand has hugely significant equities in these relationships.

Some context might be useful here. New Zealand was a founding member of the United Nations (UN), the WTO and the Organisation for Economic Co-operation and Development (OECD). When people refer to 'the West' they mean countries like New Zealand. New Zealand is part of the 'Other' in the Western European and Others Group.[2] Language, values and shared history have made those countries more natural partners in a reflexive sense for New Zealanders.

Despite some rocks in the road when New Zealand scrambled to diversify its trading markets following the entry of the United Kingdom into the European Economic Community in 1973, and a significant cooling with Washington from 1985 to 2006 when Wellington promoted a non-nuclear policy, New Zealand's security outlook was basically informed by the two world wars and our past alliances with the United Kingdom, Australia and the United States. New Zealand's membership in the Five Eyes intelligence sharing arrangement ensured that high-level strategic and security interactions with Western partners remained uninterrupted.

So in navigating its way through the probability of increased tensions between major powers, New Zealand's instinct or 'muscle memory' would usually have looked to Australia and the United States in the first instance. Note, 'looked to' not 'followed'—these are different things which have an important distinction. After all, New Zealand has prided itself on forging an independent foreign policy, but in close concert with friends.

In days past, it was easier to advance the trade relationship with China. Since New Zealand officially recognised Beijing in 1972, that relationship with the Middle Kingdom has not had to endure much tension. But the hopeful premise that the West could bring China into the 'Western-led fold' through greater neoliberal engagement has not come to fruition. While China played by the rules of the liberal order when it was in its selective interests, an increasingly confident China has since demonstrated that the dragon will not and cannot be tamed by the West. Indeed, China's assertive behaviour has been much more pronounced of late: patrolling near disputed territories such as the Diaoyutai/Senkaku Islands, major port development in Sri Lanka and lobbying of New Zealand's Pacific neighbours, for example. Given these developments, what is the role of China as a rising power? The bigger question is how should the world view China, and what are the risks in engaging? The PRC has a legitimate role to play in the world, so how to best identify and respond to that? Do countries need to recalibrate their China relationship? New Zealand is not looking at making a choice with China, but views

---

[2] This is one of five unofficial Regional Groups in the United Nations.

making more connections and convergences through partnering as the way forward. Prime Minister Jacinda Ardern has said that New Zealand would look to cooperate with China in promoting regional stability and development—consistent with New Zealand's values of openness, transparency and the rule of law (Ardern, 2018b).

The problem however, is that New Zealand has found itself dealing with competing ideas about the rule of law—not necessarily everyone holds that international law is 'objective and established'. China has applied different interpretations by promoting and explaining its concepts of maritime law and the rules-based order. Take Beijing's refusal to accept the Permanent Court of Arbitration's ruling over disputed territories in the South China Sea, and maintaining its sovereign claims by historic right along the nine-dash line, as notable examples. In talking about China during Track II exchanges, mention of maritime terminology such as Freedom of Navigation Operations (FONOPS) and Exclusive Economic Zones (EEZ) have been raised frequently. These conversations have tended to revolve around territorial disputes, the expanding role and reach of China, and what this has meant for its neighbours and mitigating tensions by way of a South China Sea Code of Conduct.

New Zealand has tended to see things from a different perspective and according to its own national interests. 'Where you stand depends on where you sit' goes the old adage — also known as Miles' Law. And where New Zealand stands, when it looks north it sees a vast expanse of water and some small islands; when it looks west it sees Australia; to the south is ice and to the east—more water. So when New Zealand has been talking about maritime issues, the focus has fallen on a much wider set of largely maritime-based and non-traditional security challenges—such as illegal fishing, transnational crime, trafficking, rising sea levels, pollution, environmental degradation and piracy. New Zealand has also been active in counterterrorism and cybersecurity, as well as humanitarian assistance and disaster relief efforts—all of which require regional co-operation. And with one of the largest EEZs in the world, New Zealand's scope of interest has encompassed the vast expanse of the Pacific and Southern Oceans right down to Antarctica. To engage in the region, and to get its voice heard, New Zealand has relied heavily on regional architecture and institutions to ensure a more level playing field. It has looked to others to help support those structures too.

LIKE-MINDEDNESS

The term 'like-minded' has also cropped up in many of the foundation's Track II conversations. Whether it has been with commentators from Vietnam, the Republic of Korea (ROK) or Japan, there have been some similar threads regarding how countries have related to each other. Historically, 'like-minded' meant sharing neoliberal values and enjoying open economies (Jain, 2013; The Economist, 2018). The term has since evolved to describe the more common challenges that nations face in the turbulent 'New Normal'—one of which continues to be commitment to the international rules-based order. Once again, the United States' recent position—in closing its economy, applying tariffs, abandoning multilateral organisations and regional agreements and selectively applying rules— has made it one of the biggest contradictions ... not just China (which has perhaps been more threatening than contradictory). With regard to this, New Zealand has looked at who are also 'like-minded' on these kinds of issues—including those countries who have had to navigate more thoughtfully in their relationships with Washington and Beijing.

Apart from the obvious concern for a military or far-reaching economic confrontation between the two great powers, almost of more concern for New Zealand has been the undermining of the post-Second World War rules-based system. Here New Zealand can learn from its Asian partners. ASEAN countries (particularly Vietnam) have had to contend with these issues for some decades now, and they have accumulated a wealth of useful perspectives about their relationships in the region—particularly with China. One of ASEAN's strengths is its diversity of membership, so finding others to help in response to the changing and challenging nature of New Zealand's security and economic outlook ahead will be in the common interest. Countries across the region will all have the same things to contend with when it comes to handling their major power relations, and on this each brings its own unique baggage—which should be viewed as useful assets for how to engage. The bigger questions are 'how will countries work together in shaping rules and institutions that will be to their mutual benefit?' and 'do countries see value in that engagement, and are they maximising that value?'

COMMITMENT TO MULTILATERALISM

Peace and security in the Asia–Pacific region are based upon multiple strands of bilateral, diplomatic, economic, social and military relationships—much of them by participation in overarching regional institutions. These relationships and commitments change as nations rise and fall in terms of their relative power, and as national interests and interdependencies shift—and especially when new leaders take or retake power.

Some countries may attempt to use their influence and align the rules and institutions in order to serve their own interests and capacities; and, if unable to do so, choose to assert their sovereignty and take a more autonomous stance. Over the last couple of years, there has been a surge in unilateral approaches to international relations—Beijing's BRI, Washington's tariff war on China, its withdrawal from the Trans-Pacific Partnership (TPP) and failure to support other regional and global trade architecture, were all examples of a trend towards autonomous/one-sided/individual action. This behaviour is typical of bigger powers who wish to signal their dissatisfaction with or their rejection of the current system and international rules. In the past, smaller countries (like New Zealand) have tended to be the losers in these kinds of environments.

While some Track II dialogue partners in Southeast Asia have felt that a direct bilateral approach may be more likely to yield results, New Zealand's tactic (especially as a smaller power with limited resources and influence) has been to work with others. No doubt, bilateral relationships will always have their place in multilateral diplomacy. But in the current era, they cannot always be relied upon to deliver. From its point of view, as an export-led trading island nation, New Zealand has sought effective and fair global regulation for advancing its economic prosperity and safety. New Zealand is not a major power; it is remote from its markets; it is highly dependent on the openness of international trade, freedom of movement of people and goods, and competitive advantage and enhancing capabilities through technology transfers and education. The political, economic and social rights that New Zealanders value, and the independent foreign policy that it has enjoyed, are tested when multilateral institutions and international law are challenged. So when it has engaged with its partners, New Zealand has done so with a strong sense of commitment to multilateralism. Its best outcomes have come through working with a whole mix of powers, be they big, medium or small. That said, New Zealand's small size has also limited its bandwidth—and New

Zealanders have a predisposition not to invest resources into new structures that duplicate those already in existence. That in part speaks to the importance New Zealand has placed on its membership in plurilateral organisations and its commitment to the rules-based international order.

At the same time, multilateral and plurilateral objectives have often conflicted with more realist, national interests. But there has been a sweet spot for New Zealand—although in its political rhetoric it may have sought to portray itself as a 'good' international citizen, it has often been more in New Zealand's self-interest to advance its economic, political and defence objectives in concert with others. Having benefited from the international rules-based order, as others have too, New Zealand needs to preserve what it has, adapt it for the new situation, and find others with whom it can work together in support of the common good (and not simply abandon it). Wellington policymakers accept that rules-based institutions like the UN Security Council, WTO, World Health Organisation (WHO) and International Monetary Fund need to adapt to the modern realities and whatever lies ahead. But what they do not accept—and cannot accept—is that those institutions are broken beyond repair. And it is not just about post-war architecture. It is also about how nations shape the next generation of rules. What does it mean for regulations and governance of emerging issues like artificial intelligence/cyber/nanotechnology? These are consequential security concerns for everyone and require a degree of multilateral engagement. Governments will each have their own policies governing these matters, but in the absence of multilateral frameworks, should the policies of bigger countries invariably dominate?

For countries like New Zealand that have relied heavily on the rules-based order, the fear is that if the rules are gone and the institutions have collapsed, it is hard to see how they could ever come back. These institutions and rules were set up in a post-war environment that no one should ever want to see again. The first sentence of the UN Charter, underlines that the whole concept of multilateralism is for 'We the peoples ...' It is useful to recall its very first words: 'We the peoples of the United Nations determined to save succeeding generations from the scourge of war, which twice in our lifetime has brought untold sorrow to mankind'. (United Nations, 1945).

'Asia–Pacific' vs 'Indo-Pacific': What's in a Name?

As times have changed and relationships shifted throughout the international arena, new groupings have formed, evolved and grown. Over the years New Zealand has had to think long and hard about joining such institutions, many of which have had a regional dimension to them. In general, Wellington has preferred to influence changes as a partner or member from the outset—rather than hoping to join later when it will be likely to lack leverage. Part of New Zealand's values-based foreign policy is to foster inclusiveness when it comes to international and regional architecture, rather than exclusiveness. One assessment of this narrative is that it sends the message of 'count us in, unless you are trying to count someone else out'. Or more colloquially, 'if you are not at the table, you are on the menu'.

As a smaller player it is in New Zealand's national interests to be a rule-maker rather than a rule-taker. The Asian Infrastructure Investment Bank (AIIB) and the BRI are both initiatives where Wellington sought to be inside the tent early rather than staying outside and trying to join later on. For the AIIB, although New Zealand was initially criticised by its Western partners for signing up, it was later complimented for its early move once it was clear it could help shape the rules and structure. New Zealand's participation during its establishment meant it could also push for things like better governance and improved transparency. On the BRI, New Zealand's Memorandum of Arrangement with China is non-binding and has to do with symbolising the importance attached to a 'deliverable' for its wider relationship (which, in 2019, was the New Zealand–China free trade agreement upgrade).

For the last couple of years, officials have been talking more about the 'Indo-Pacific' concept—a topic that has featured consistently in Track II exchanges too. There have been a range of articulations, descriptions and pitches as to what the Indo-Pacific means (including geographic, strategic and economic interpretations—even some with an ideological twist) from a variety of interlocutors around the world. And despite much discussion and debate, there still remain fundamental differences on exactly what the term 'Indo-Pacific' refers to. For some countries, it has been a logical description of their physical geography; others have contextualised it with the rise of India and its re-integration into a broadened and diversified regional matrix; New Delhi has viewed it as an opportunity to make its mark on the world stage as an emerging power; others have seen it through a defence prism—for example, the United States renamed its Pacific Command (PACOM) the Indo-Pacific Command (INDOPACOM) in an effort to pull others into the region. The narrative has been increasingly clear that the United States' Indo-Pacific strategy is about countering the parts of China's rise that Washington has found threatening. The elephant in the room, of course, has been where China fits into all of this, and the implications for those countries in the region.

In attempting to get more buy-in, Japan has moved from initially describing the 'Indo-Pacific' as a 'strategy' to the more inclusively framed 'Free and Open Indo-Pacific vision'—making the tone and language much more agreeable to its neighbours. Similarly, ASEAN announced its own 'Outlook on the Indo-Pacific' in 2019—with the emphasis on the word 'Outlook'. Drawing from conversations with Track II colleagues across the region, the 'Indo-Pacific' concept was getting too 'security-heavy' when referred to as a 'strategy' and put pressure on ASEAN member states to choose sides. Calling it an 'outlook' has been typical of ASEAN—a way of achieving a consensus of views, yet remaining non-committal and preserving internal differences to save face.

The New Zealand government's thinking about the 'Indo-Pacific' was officially articulated by foreign minister Winston Peters at the opening of the 2018 University of Otago Foreign Policy School (Peters, 2018b). He noted that such a concept would have to embrace some fundamental aspects and working principles that mattered most to New Zealand regarding its engagement throughout the world:

1. Recognising the rules-based order to support peace and prosperity
2. Promoting free and open trade and investment, and enhanced connectivity
3. Ensuring good governance, democratic values and sustainability
4. An open international commons (sea/air/cyber)
5. Climate change
6. ASEAN centrality (a cornerstone)

In general, New Zealand has supported initiatives that embrace inclusive, transparent, rules-based principles and values that work towards achieving peace and prosperity under sustainable and democratic good governance. In that context, New Zealand has interests across the Indo-Pacific region; yet with all of this in mind, foreign minister Peters still favoured the term 'Asia–Pacific' over 'Indo-Pacific'. It was a conscious and considered choice to use one over the other. Why? The answer lies in New Zealand's surroundings. New Zealand has invested a lot in the Pacific and building close relations with its ASEAN and wider Asian neighbourhood. For most New Zealand interactions, the Asia–Pacific still makes sense. Further afield, and certainly where the Indian Ocean is concerned, the Indo-Pacific comes more into frame. And of course, the term 'Pacific' is used with regard to New Zealand's more immediate neighbours and local community. The technical diplomatic term for this approach is 'constructive ambiguity' which puts New Zealand in quite a different place to the rest of its traditional allies who have embraced more positional language.

By taking this line, New Zealand might be seen as a bit of an anomaly or an outlier. One of the things often noted about New Zealand's foreign policy is that having options is important for a small country (Ayson, 2018). In other words, it has had to spread its bets by backing several horses in a race to increase the chances of a win. But the problem has been that in today's regional environment, although the United States and China are not the only horses in the race, as two of the leading contenders they are certainly running in different directions: the BRI has essentially been about cementing China's rise, while the 'Indo-Pacific' is currently minus China.

The Importance of ASEAN

New Zealand will support any institutional arrangements where the United States, China and others can continue to engage with medium and smaller powers in order to articulate regional perspectives and promote sustainable development. It makes sense, therefore, to do more together to strengthen organisations such as ASEAN. In 2017, ASEAN— a diverse community of ten members that came together at different times in different circumstances—celebrated its 50th anniversary. This was a reminder of what ASEAN represents, its role in global affairs, and the challenges it has faced to remain united yet flexible in a dynamic environment.

ASEAN has brought architecture to a region without regionalism. But even after more than five decades, its members are still discussing the basic issues concerning the association's existence. Moreover, mutual trust has not been fully established as part of the ASEAN Way,[3] as political grievances and divergent national interests remain a factor of difference. Among the ASEAN membership, domestic politics, personalities and priorities have often loomed large. There is a maritime ASEAN and a continental ASEAN. There are the original founding members, and more recent ones—each with its own competing agendas and objectives. At the same time, ASEAN has had to demonstrate a collective response to the big issues and challenges as defined by its peoples—only in that way has it remained relevant in this day and age. So on sensitive issues, such as the South China Sea, while there may be differing perspectives from individual member countries, there remains a general commitment to uphold a united voice.

New Zealand recognises the importance of shared values and norms as enshrined in the ASEAN Charter and the Treaty of Amity and Cooperation in Southeast Asia, as well as ASEAN centrality and leadership in the evolving regional architecture. While a solid, unified response to the sensitive issues might not always be expected, countries can and should cooperate in those areas where there is agreement and alignment. The ASEAN Way remains a concerted way of approaching problems in the most inclusive manner.

New Zealand has been heavily invested in ASEAN because a strong ASEAN has been in New Zealand's interests too. Wellington has looked to this regional grouping for support with its trade and security policies, as well as to foster connectivity and achieve shared objectives. New Zealand has seen ASEAN and the ASEAN-led organisations as being at the centre of a rules-based order for engaging with regional actors. The East Asia Summit (EAS), the ASEAN Regional Forum (ARF) and the ASEAN Defence Ministers' Meeting-Plus (ADMM +) are all forums that have put both great and small powers all in the same room. These have been spaces in which to engage and socialise ideas, and provide a conducive environment for talking to each other. The convening power is what has counted most. The Asia–Pacific middle powers (including Japan, the ROK or Australia for example), together with smaller powers in the region, such as New Zealand, should be working to do more together to strengthen ASEAN centrality and to persuade Beijing and Washington

---

[3] The 'ASEAN Way' is characterised by an informal and personal approach that aims at conflict prevention, often not demonstrated in public. It is also important to not embarrass members or compromise their sovereignty.

not to discard old rules and norms—and also to work together to mitigate and manage regional tensions and conflicts.

WHERE DOES NEW ZEALAND FIT INTO ALL OF THIS?

There is a depth and traction that New Zealand has had with ASEAN—serving as a ballast in the choppy waters that Wellington policymakers have been trying to navigate. That speaks to the importance of building upon mutual trust by banding together with others in the region on those issues that matter, and where countries can cooperate. The challenge ahead is to develop commonality of intent between politicians, bureaucracy and the public to work together on this. During Track II conversations, ASEAN member countries have tended to talk themselves down when it comes to the value of ASEAN and the importance of ASEAN centrality. In fact, ASEAN colleagues have pointed out that New Zealand cares more about ASEAN than ASEAN does itself. There has been a level of evangelism for ASEAN in New Zealand because it has served as an important hook for New Zealand's engagement with the region.

One of the questions ASEAN interlocuters have often asked is how New Zealand has viewed its role and identity in Southeast Asia and the wider Asia–Pacific, and, in turn, how New Zealand has been viewed by its Southeast Asian counterparts. Is New Zealand seen as a regional stakeholder or an external player? What is expected of New Zealand? What might ASEAN gain from closer engagement with New Zealand? And what might New Zealand gain from closer engagement with ASEAN? The response has been that New Zealand is both and neither a regional stakeholder or an external player. Because, ultimately, does it really matter what the labels are? Has it not been more about national interests? With ASEAN, New Zealand has had skin in the game and forged strong relations for a while now—and that has shown what matters most. Those interests have reflected who New Zealand is, what it wants, and what it needs. That same self-interest has explained why New Zealand is so committed to ASEAN.

There may be a lack of strong regional institutions inside the Asia–Pacific that are addressing and co-ordinating multilateral security agreements as topics of importance, so New Zealand has placed strong support for ASEAN centrality in the evolving regional architecture. New Zealand has been an active contributor to ASEAN-centric security forums, such as the ARF Defence Officials' Dialogue. New Zealand has supported many other ASEAN initiatives—such as the Southeast Asia Nuclear Weapon-Free Zone Treaty. New Zealand has also demonstrated support of disarmament and arms control as part of the ASEAN–New Zealand Strategic Partnership. And Wellington has done this because it has been in its best interests to invest more in ASEAN. The trick is knowing exactly what those best interests are. And where can New Zealand deepen that engagement? The Regional Comprehensive Economic Partnership (RCEP), Comprehensive and Progressive Agreement for Trans-Pacific Partnership (CPTPP) and WTO reform are good starters. And that is where the ASEAN–Australia–New Zealand free trade agreement (AANZFTA) matters so much. This agreement could be given more attention. It tends to lack the airtime and profile it deserves. AANZFTA is a high-quality and ambitious partnership that New Zealand, Australia and ASEAN share together in addressing some of the trade and economic challenges that lie ahead.

New Zealand's Ministry of Foreign Affairs and Trade officials have proposed different ways New Zealand's relationship with ASEAN could be strengthened. New Zealand has been a dialogue partner of ASEAN since 1975. Forty years of relations were celebrated in 2015 with a commemorative summit held in Kuala Lumpur, where ASEAN and New Zealand committed to deeper regional integration and the realisation of a politically cohesive, economically integrated, socially responsible, rules-based, people-oriented and people-centred ASEAN—as reflected in the ASEAN Community Vision 2025. New Zealand marked another major relationship milestone in 2020—the 45th anniversary of ASEAN–New Zealand relations. This anniversary has provided an opportunity to seek more high-level engagement and refresh the two partners' Plan of Action.

The ASEAN region has been home to a relatively young population of more than 650 million, and its fast-growing middle class is increasingly demanding the food and goods that New Zealand can help supply. As of July 2019, ASEAN was New Zealand's fourth-largest trading partner, representing 12 per cent of New Zealand's goods trade; two-way trade has grown by 66 per cent since 2010.[4] But this relationship has not just been about trade and selling more goods. Through academic

---

[4] ASEAN-NZ Trade Figures as of July 2019. https://www.mfat.govt.nz/en/countr ies-and-regions/south-east-asia/association-of-south-east-asian-nations-asean/. Accessed 7 January 2020.

exchanges, capacity-building and development programmes such as the Colombo Plan, New Zealand has enjoyed the fruits of its investment in fostering a plethora of people-to-people links. New Zealand has been well placed to offer other forms of support in the region over its 45 years of partnership. What has been its 'value-add' beyond the transactional connections? Co-operation and mutual interest over the years have helped foster a solid partnership, leading to the NZ Inc ASEAN Strategy[5]— a government/non-government/industry-wide initiative that has worked towards more engagement, integration and co-operation based on shared history, trade, development and security interests. The strategy has sought to help New Zealand:

1. Become better connected and more influential in ASEAN countries.
2. Become better integrated with the ASEAN community.
3. Boost investment and trade and economic returns from the region to grow our exports from 30% to 40% of GDP by 2025.

In periods of relative uncertainty in the region, there has always been a role to be played by non-threatening, credible powers like New Zealand in raising a moderate voice—a voice that does not put a high premium on geopolitics and the use of force to realise domestic goals; a voice that reminds countries to stay calm, and to resolve disputes in a way that unites rather than divides our interests.

Conclusion: New Zealand's Foreign Policy — Balancing Interests, Values and Partnerships

Speeches from New Zealand's current prime minister and foreign minister have heavily referenced New Zealand's values and principles, and where it has stood on significant foreign policy issues. For example, Prime Minister Ardern has talked about how 'reputation' has been the central pillar of New Zealand's economic relationships (Ardern, 2018b). 'When we speak, it is with credibility; when we act, it is with decency' (Ardern, 2018a). In his 'Pacific Reset' speech, foreign minister Peters clearly articulated a 'collective ambition' with regional partners on shared objectives, and

---

[5] NZ Inc ASEAN Strategy. https://www.mfat.govt.nz/en/trade/nz-inc-strategies/asean-strategy. Accessed 7 January 2020.

for sustainable goals (Peters, 2018a). Those values have been something that New Zealanders can be proud of, and are rightly used to set their country apart from others. These values have spoken to the transparency, accountability and responsibility of a small nation that has relied on being honest, consistent and reliable in order to earn the trust and respect of its partners. Being 'independent' should also be added into that mix as well—New Zealanders have often made efforts to distinguish themselves from Australia and the United States.

But balancing between these values and national interests has been something that New Zealand has to face up to more and more as it looks at its place within and without regional constructs. Interests and values do not always align (Ayson & Capie, 2020). With that becoming more contested and disrupted by players who are looking to set the rules for governance, New Zealand will be articulating its national value proposition for making Wellington's views known, recognised and hopefully accepted and accommodated across the region and the rest of the world.

This is paramount for New Zealand as it recovers and rebuilds post-COVID-19. The novel coronavirus and its ramifications have caused massive upheaval everywhere—widespread social, economic and political disruption adding to the domestic, regional and international dilemmas governments were already grappling with. Geopolitically, Trump had been taking the United States on an inwardly spiralling course anyway, criticising not just competitors like China, but also the United States's traditional partners and allies (including the ROK and the EU) long before the outbreak. In an already fragile international environment, Trump's call to abandon organisations like the WHO, while looking for scapegoats to blame, only served to consolidate concerns about Washington's retrenchment from responsible global leadership and the multilateral system. In the face of this turbulent transition, like-minded countries such as New Zealand have sought more partnerships to mitigate further deterioration of the rules-based order. For Wellington, embracing and investing in global connections, architecture and systems in order to deal with these shared challenges has become more important than ever.

Some of those taking a realist perspective might interpret New Zealand's approach as a vain attempt to resist the return of great-power rivalry and the implications of such competition for the Asia–Pacific; that a rules-based order simply constrains the autonomy of sovereign states—especially the great powers—and therefore a 'balance of power' is inevitable. It has been notable to see that New Zealand policy thinkers have moved from a discussion of 'balance of power' to a 'balance of partners'. The diplomatic directive has been to 'create more choices'. This has been something that ASEAN has managed successfully for decades, and policymakers can learn from those experiences.

In this globalised and interdependent world, the speed with which Asia gets back up on its feet will be vitally important for New Zealand's own eventual recovery. To help spur this effort, New Zealand and its partners all have a shared commitment to deepening domestic, regional and international connections, to grow knowledge, nurture collaborations and, most importantly, come up with more options for navigating the uncharted territory that lies ahead: a new 'New Normal'.

REFERENCES

Ardern, J. (2018a, February 27). Speech to New Zealand Institute of International Affairs. https://www.beehive.govt.nz/speech/speech-new-zealand-institute-international-affairs-2. Accessed 30 April 2020.

Ardern, J. (2018b, May 14). Speech at China Business Summit. https://www.beehive.govt.nz/speech/china-business-summit. Accessed 7 January 2020.

Asia New Zealand Foundation. (2019). *New Zealanders' Perceptions of Asia and Asian Peoples 2018 Annual Survey.* https://www.asianz.org.nz/assets/Uploads/PerceptionsofAsia_2018Final_Online.pdf. Accessed 22 April 2020.

Ayson, R. (2018). The Ardern Government's Foreign Policy Challenges. *Policy Quarterly, 14*(2), 18–24. https://www.victoria.ac.nz/__data/assets/pdf_file/0020/1500833/Ayson.pdf. Accessed 21 April 2020.

Ayson, R., & Capie, D. (2020, April 29). Geopolitics after Covid-19: Who can NZ trust? *Newsroom.* https://www.newsroom.co.nz/ideasroom/2020/04/29/1148171/geopolitics-after-covid-19-who-can-nz-trust. Accessed 29 April 2020.

Bennhold, K. (2020, April 20). 'Sadness' and disbelief from a world missing American leadership. *The New York Times.* https://www.nytimes.com/2020/04/23/world/europe/coronavirus-american-exceptionalism.html. Accessed 28 April 2020.

Catley, R. (2017). *The American challenge: The world resists US liberalism.* Routledge. https://www.taylorfrancis.com/books/9781351147842. Accessed 20 April 2020.

Jain, A. (2013). Working paper: Like-minded and capable democracies — A new framework for advancing a liberal world order. Council on Foreign Relations. https://cdn.cfr.org/sites/default/files/pdf/2012/11/IIGG_WorkingPaper12_Jain.pdf. Accessed 20 April 2020.

Peters, W. (2018a, March 1). Shifting the dial. Speech to Lowy Institute. https://www.beehive.govt.nz/speech/shifting-dial. Accessed 7 January 2020.

Peters, W. (2018b, June 29). Next Steps. Speech to Otago Foreign Policy School. https://www.beehive.govt.nz/speech/next-steps. Accessed 7 January 2020.

Svenska Dagbladet. (2018, May 17). Dessa är de svåraste länderna att invadera [These are the most difficult countries to invade]. https://www.svd.se/vilka-ar-de-svaraste-landerna-att-invadera. Accessed 7 January 2020.

The Economist. (2018). Keeping it together: Countries team up to save the liberal order from Donald Trump. *The Economist*. https://www.economist.com/international/2018/08/02/countries-team-up-to-save-the-liberal-order-from-donald-trump. Accessed 20 April 2020.

United Nations. (1945). Charter of the United Nations. https://www.un.org/en/sections/un-charter/preamble/index.html. Accessed 27 February 2020.

White, H. (2019, August 13). How to defend Australia. East Asia Forum, https://www.eastasiaforum.org/2019/08/13/how-to-defend-australia. Accessed 7 January 2020.

The Rise of New-Generation Foreign Policy Think Tanks in India: Causes, Contours and Roles

Raphaëlle Khan and Patrick Köllner

INTRODUCTION

Under Narendra Modi, prime minister since 2014, foreign policymaking in India has undergone an important evolution, adding to longer-term trends. Somewhat paradoxically, India has seen both a greater centralisation of foreign policy decision-making and the simultaneous rise of a newer generation of foreign policy think tanks. While traditionally marginalised, India's foreign policy think-tank sector has gained in visibility and vibrancy due to India's expanding international stakes and new

An earlier version of this chapter was published as a briefing paper of the German Institute of Global and Area Studies (Khan & Köllner, 2018). Raphaëlle Khan would like to thank Mélissa Levaillant for their discussions on foreign policy think tanks in India.

R. Khan
City University of New York, New York City, NY, USA

P. Köllner (✉)
GIGA and University of Hamburg, Hamburg, Germany
e-mail: Patrick.Koellner@giga-hamburg.de

© The Author(s), under exclusive license to Springer Nature
Singapore Pte Ltd. 2022
R. Patman et al. (eds.), *From Asia-Pacific to Indo-Pacific*, Global Political
Transitions, https://doi.org/10.1007/978-981-16-7007-7_10

demand from the Indian Government and other stakeholders. Yet few academic works have focused on the evolution and roles of such think tanks in India (e.g. Mathur & Mathur, 2007; Mathur, 2013; Thakur & Davis, 2017; Bhatnagar & Chacko, 2019; Bhatnagar forthcoming).

Understanding the evolution and diversity of Indian foreign policy think tanks today can help us to assess trends in Indian foreign policy and to identify (emerging) political dynamics in New Delhi. In the following we first put these think tanks in global context and address some conceptual issues. We then examine the profiles of the newer foreign policy think tanks and how they differ from older organisations in terms of access to funding and information. We also clarify how these organisations engage with stakeholders, notably the Indian Government, and what their respective roles are. Lastly, we focus on the political orientation of these think tanks in the domestic context.

THINK TANKS IN GLOBAL COMPARISON AND CONCEPTUAL PERSPECTIVE

Examining Indian foreign policy think tanks is timely and important. As part of the recent growth of such organisations Asia-wide, the number of think tanks in India has—at least according to one count—more than quadrupled from 121 in 2007 to 509 in 2019 (McGann 2008–2020). According to the data collected by James McGann and his collaborators, in 2019 India hosted the second-highest number of think tanks after the United States (1,872), on a par with China (507) and very much ahead of the United Kingdom (321) (McGann, 2020, p. 43). The delayed wave of think tank expansion in Asia follows the surge in think tanks that occurred in Europe and the United States during the 1980s and the 1990s. The number of Indian think tanks focusing on foreign policy has also increased substantially in recent years, and their earlier image as marginalised political actors corresponds less and less to the reality on the ground. Although one needs to handle these think-tank rankings with caution in view of major conceptual and methodological problems (Köllner, 2013), it is noteworthy that some Indian think tanks have recently ranked relatively high in them, indicating growing international visibility.[1] When we speak of foreign policy think tanks in this chapter we refer to think tanks that focus either on international affairs or on defence and security issues.[2] Such think tanks may, depending on the individual circumstances, perform a host of roles. Beyond the production of new research and the repackaging and synthesising of policy knowledge, think tanks may also, or indeed mainly, focus on other roles, such as providing opportunities for interactions among scholars, policymakers and other practitioners ('salon' function); engaging in Track II exchanges ('informal diplomacy' function); legitimising the emerging and extant policy positions of the government ('intellectual cheerleader' function); providing content for the media ('pundit' function) or training practitioners and young academics ('capacity-building' function).[3]

The term 'think tank' itself is a slippery one and definitions differ. We define think tanks as organisations whose main mission is to inform and influence public policy on the basis of research and analysis. We thus concur with Hartwig Pautz (2011) and earlier arguments by Diane Stone (2004, pp. 4–5) that certain attributes that have been used to capture the essence of think tanks, such as their non-profit character or their 'independence', should either be dropped altogether or at least be analytically disentangled. Indeed, it is important to remember that, despite their often-professed public purpose orientation, think tanks are organisations that are guided by interests and depend on particular sources of funding (see Ladi, 2011). Consequently, although often presented as

---

[1] For instance, in McGann's 2019 report the Observer Research Foundation (ORF) was ranked 15th among top non-US think tanks, while the Manohar Parrikar Institute for Defence Studies and Analyses (IDSA) was ranked 37th (McGann 2020, pp. 59–60). In the same report, in the worldwide ranking of think tanks, Brookings India was first among the Indian think tanks (placed at 23rd) before ORF (27th) and IDSA (41st) (ibid., pp. 66–67)—indicating both the visibility of these think tanks and the problems with this ranking exercise.

[2] We exclude here Indian think thanks that work only indirectly on foreign policy issues, such as those focusing on economic affairs (such as the Indian Council for Research on International Economic Relations or the Research and Information System for Developing Countries) and on the environment (such as the Centre for Science and Environment or the Energy and Resources Institute).

[3] See Köllner (2011, pp. 5–6) and the literature cited therein.

bridges between power and knowledge, think tanks are arguably a 'manifestation of the knowledge/power nexus' and may help to serve the interests of dominant elites (Stone, 2007, p. 276).

Do think tanks also matter in other respects, and how can we understand their development?[4] As 'ideas organisations' and 'knowledge brokers', think tanks are involved in shaping the production of political knowledge, not least due to their participation in public and policy-related discourses and networks. Knowledge production always involves the articulation of perspectives and is part of a competition between distinct interests, including those of think-tank funders. Think tanks are arguably not objective or impartial knowledge brokers but rather contribute to the blurring of the boundaries between interest and knowledge. Certainly, as Marco Gonzalez Hernando, Pautz and Stone (2018, p. 126) argue, think tanks need to be taken seriously as political actors, given that (a) such organisations have reached a critical mass in many countries; (b) they are established with the explicit mission to inform or influence, either directly or indirectly, government policy and (c) they seek to 'establish themselves as indispensable repositories of expertise, technical skill, professional experience, rational thinking and policy opinion, providing solutions for [policymakers], and content for the media'.

With respect to the development of think tanks, context matters. More specifically, individual think tanks and the think-tank systems they form a part of are greatly influenced by the specific political context in which they exist. Not only do the political contextual factors that impact the trajectories and traits of think-tank landscapes vary between countries but also they operate at different interactive levels: (a) at the level of the international and transnational context within which think-tank sectors develop; (b) at the level of domestic governmental systems and their openness to external policy advice and other think-tank services and (c) at the level of individual political leaders interested in engaging with think tanks or using them to push their agendas. In view of the potential complexity of these interactions, generalisations about the impact of political context on think-tank development are fraught with danger—hence the need for context-sensitive analyses. In the following we will examine the development of foreign policy think tanks in India and illuminate the context in which the recent rise to prominence of newer think tanks has occurred.

---

[4] The following two paragraphs draw on Köllner et al. (2018, pp. 6, 22–23).

INDIA'S NEW-GENERATION
FOREIGN POLICY THINK TANKS

Unlike their economic affairs counterparts, Indian international affairs and security and defence think tanks have traditionally faced a number of difficulties which have curtailed their significance: a lack of funding (partly due to a lack of investment of the state and a lack of alternative sources from the corporate sector); a lack of qualified human resources, as well as the dominance of retired civil servants in senior positions and restricted access to information, hindering—with some notable exceptions—the production of relevant research and the formulation of timely policy recommendations.[5] Since Jawaharlal Nehru's time as India's first prime minister and minister of external affairs (1947–1964), foreign policymaking has largely remained the preserve of the Prime Minister's Office and the National Security Council, while the Ministry of External Affairs (MEA) has traditionally been in charge of policy implementation. The MEA has traditionally not sought research or analysis from external institutions (Chatterjee Miller, 2013). This, at least, seems to have been the case since the 1970s.[6] Thus, except for a very few high-profile think-tank leaders, think tanks and other external providers of policy advice have not been influential in shaping Indian foreign policy (Markey, 2009; Mattoo & Medcalf, 2015; Kumar, 2015).

Furthermore, only a few think tanks have traditionally been active in New Delhi. The initial few publicly funded and government-related think-tanks—the Indian Council of World Affairs (ICWA) and Manohar Parrikar Institute for Defence Studies and Analyses (IDSA) were followed over the years by a handful of more diversified and privately funded think tanks, notably the Centre for Policy Research (CPR) and the Delhi Policy Group.[7] The landscape of foreign policy think tanks started to markedly evolve in the first decade of the twenty-first century, when

[5] For details, see Goyal and Srinivasan (2013), Celestine (2012).

[6] Considering for instance the major role that the Indian Council of World Affairs (ICWA) played in the organisation of the Asian Relations Conference of 1947, India's Government's relations with some think tanks were arguably strong when Nehru was prime minister. The close relationship with the ICWA partly reflected the government's desire to promote the development of scholarship on international affairs in India. M. S. Rajan, the Administrative Secretary of the ICWA in 1948, set up the Indian School of International Studies in 1955 on Nehru's suggestion (Vivekanandan 2010, 103).

[7] For a short historical background on think tanks in India, see Ravichander (2018).

active and retired high-ranking military leaders established specialist think tanks to produce knowledge on defence-related topics. In 2001–2002, Air Commodore Jasjit Singh created the Centre for Air Power Studies, staffed with retired top brass and ambassadors. In 2004 Lieutenant General Vijay Oberoi, a former vice chief of army staff, set up the Centre for Land Warfare Studies (CLAWS) to promote strategic thinking and new ideas in this security domain. In 2005 then defence minister Pranab Mukherjee launched the National Maritime Foundation (NMF), which seeks to enhance dialogue on maritime security, formulate policy advice, mould public opinion and influence the national security elite on issues involving India's maritime security interests. Lastly, in 2007, the Centre for Joint Warfare Studies was set up by the Ministry of Defence. These think tanks organise numerous events annually in their respective fields, with the NMF being particularly active in this regard.

Towards the end of the first decade of the new millennium, new foreign policy think tanks with a broader focus emerged and became active and visible in the public sphere. First, the Vivekananda International Foundation (VIF) and the India Foundation (IF) were founded in 2009 by personalities close to the Hindu nationalist Bharatiya Janata Party (BJP)—the party of Prime Minister Modi.[8] The VIF and the IF present themselves as independent organisations, unlike the lesser-known and openly Hindu nationalist Dr Syama Prasad Mookerjee Research Foundation, which is affiliated to the BJP. Yet both these organisations' members and programmes closely align with the BJP's. According to Edward Anderson and Arkotong Longkumer (2018), 'soft neo-Hindutva' organisations like the IF tend to avoid explicit linkages with Hindu majoritarian politics.[9] IF and VIF are the most visible examples of a larger trend noted by Walter Andersen and Sridhar Damle (2019, p. 71) of several 'RSS [Rashtriya Swayamsevak Sangh] think tanks' burgeoning in Delhi after the BJP lost the 2004 parliamentary elections, before becoming major players in the think-tank world after the BJP victory in 2014.

Second, the Brookings Institution India Center was created in 2013, and Carnegie India was opened in 2016. They are international centres of the prominent US think tanks the Brookings Institution and the Carnegie

---

[8] The journalist Prashant Jha (2015), who noted the rise of the think tanks with close party affiliations, provides additional details about IF and VIF.

[9] In contrast to 'hard neo-Hindutva' groups which do not conceal their connections to Hindu nationalism. On the concept of 'neo-Hindutva', see Anderson (2015).

Endowment for International Peace, but they are legally independent, and their founding members are mostly Indian. Third, several think tanks developed through business initiatives have emerged or been recently set up. Although founded in 1990 as a Reliance Industries initiative, the Observer Research Foundation (ORF) has become particularly prominent in the past few years. The Aspen Institute India was created in 2004 through the collaboration of the Aspen Institute (United States) and the Confederation of Indian Industry. In 2006 it was renamed the Ananta Aspen Centre. It has an Indian board and receives Indian funding. Outside Delhi, the Mumbai-based Gateway House: Indian Council on Global Relations was founded in 2011. Its founding members include prominent companies such as the Mahindra Group, Suzlon Energy and TVS Motor Company. The size and means of these think tanks vary greatly. ORF is the largest organisation and one of the best funded (see Table 1).

The emergence of new think tanks contributed to a (limited) regional spread of these organisations in India, as several of them were set up outside Delhi. The right-wing Centre for Strategic Studies, which launched a Centre for Public Policy Research, was set up in 2004 in Kochi.[10] The Center for the Study of Science, Technology and Policy was founded in Bengalore in 2005, the Chennai Centre for China Studies was set up in 2008, and Gateway House was established in Mumbai in 2009, while the Takshashila Institution was created in Bangaluru in 2010. In 2012, the publishers of *The Hindu* group of newspapers launched in Chennai the Hindu Centre for Politics and Public Policy, which also addresses international issues (see *The Hindu*, 2012).

As indicated by the above-mentioned rankings, some of these think tanks have become quite visible internationally. This is partly because they have developed effective communication techniques involving the internet, social media and international networks. More fundamentally, these think tanks have become visible because they are less constrained by the hurdles faced by older think tanks.

---

[10] The institute is a partner of the libertarian Atlas Network which promotes free-market policies across the globe.

Table 1 India's Foreign Policy Think Tanks[11]

Name	Year of establishment	Current heads and their personal background	Declared funding sources and budget (latest available year)[12]
The United Service Institution of India (USI)	1870	Major General B.K. Sharma, Ret. (director)	n.a
Indian Council of World Affairs (ICWA)	1943	Dr. T. C. A. Raghavan (director general), former High Commissioner to Pakistan / M. Venkaiah Naidu (president of council), Vice President of India	Central Government, 2020/21: €1.97 m
Manohar Parrikar Institute for Defence Studies and Analyses (IDSA)	1965	Amb. Sujan R. Chinoy (director general), former ambassador to Japan and Mexico/ Rajnath Singh (president of the executive council), Minister of Defence	Ministry of Defence, n.a
Centre for Policy Research (CPR)	1973	Yamini Aiyar (president and chief executive), expert on social policy and development	Indian Council for Social Science Research, other grants from foundations, corporate philanthropy, governments, and multilateral agencies, 2018: €4.5 m 2019: €3.7 m

11 This table does not provide an exhaustive list of India's think tanks addressing foreign affairs or security issues, but rather identifies the most prominent ones today and the most representative ones for our study.

12 The exchange rate of ₹1 = €0.012 as of April 2020 has been used to convert Indian rupees into Euros.

Name	Year of establishment	Current heads and their personal background	Declared funding sources and budget (latest available year)
Observer Research Foundation (ORF)	1990	Sunjoy Joshi (chairman), former senior civil servant, former joint secretary in the Ministry of Petroleum and Natural Gas / Samir Saran (president), former vice president of Corporate Affairs at Reliance Industries Ltd	Combined incomes and funds of €5.1 m by the end of March 2019
Delhi Policy Group	1994	Amb. Hemant Krishan Singh (director general), former ambassador to Japan and Indonesia	Declared foreign contributions of €140,000 in 2018 and approximately €17,000 in 2019
Institute of Peace and Conflict Studies (IPCS)	1996	Lt. Gen. Arvinder Singh Lamba (president), former Vice Chief of Army Staff	n.a
Centre for Air Power Studies (CAPS)	2001	Air Marshal K.K. Nohwar, Ret. (director general) / Air Chief Marshal **S. P. Tyagi**, Ret. (chairman of the executive committee), Former Chief of Air Staff	n.a
Centre for Land Warfare Studies (CLAWS)	2004	Lt. Gen. (Dr.) Vijay Kumar Ahluwalia (director), commander-in-chief of the Strategic Forces Command	n.a

(continued)

Table 1 (continued)

Name	Year of establishment	Current heads and their personal background	Declared funding sources and budget (latest available year)
National Maritime Foundation	2005	Admiral Sunil Lanba, Ret. (chairman) / Vice Admiral Pradeep Chauhan, Ret. (director general)	n.a
Ananta Aspen Centre	2006	Kiran Pasricha (executive director), former deputy director general of the Confederation of Indian Industry	n.a
India Foundation (IF)	2009	Several directors incl. Shaurya Doval, son of the current National Security Advisor, and Ram Madhav, BJP National General Secretary	n.a
Gateway House: Indian Council on Global Relations	2009	Manjeet Kripalani (co-founder and executive director), former India Bureau chief of *Businessweek* magazine, and Neelam Deo (co-founder and director), former ambassador to Denmark and Ivory Coast	n.a
Vivekananda International Foundation (VIF)	2009	Arvind Gupta (director), Indian foreign-service officer, former deputy national security advisor and secretary, former director of IDSA / Ajit Doval (founder), current national security advisor	Declared donations of €0.78 m Euros in 2018

Name	Year of establishment	Current heads and their personal background	Declared funding sources and budget (latest available year)
Brookings India	2013	Vikram Singh Mehta (executive chairman), former senior civil servant, former chairman of the Shell Group of Companies in India	Declared combined foreign and domestic grants of €0.31 m in 2018 and €0.81 m Euros in 2019
Carnegie India	2016	Rudra Chaudhuri (director), senior lecturer at King's College London / C. Raja Mohan (founding director), leading strategic thinker and analyst of India's foreign policy	Donations and grants, n.a
Dr. Syama Prasad Mookerjee Research Foundation (SPMRF)	n.a	Anirban Ganguly (director), member of the BJP Policy Research Department and former research fellow at the VIF	n.a

Sources: Authors' own compilation based on institutes' websites, annual reports and newspaper articles

More Funding and Better Access to Information

The new generation of foreign policy think tanks have more funding, as well as more diverse sources thereof, and increased access to information, due to a more supportive government and the fact that the MEA has become more open to external expertise (Bagchi, 2016a). On the one hand, powerful Indian businesses have become increasingly interested in India's foreign policy. In the context of economic liberalisation and globalisation, economic and political issues have been increasingly interlinked. Additionally, India's emergence as a rising power has increased India's stakes internationally. Accordingly, some corporations have been increasingly involved in funding think tanks since the 1990s.

On the other hand, the Modi Government's attitude of active engagement vis-à-vis selected think tanks has partly lowered the barriers to access to information for these organisations and increased their visibility. As Stuti Bhatnagar and Priya Chacko (2019) note, the Indian Government's engagement with civil society in foreign policymaking can be traced back to the Congress Party-led United Progressive Alliance Government in the 2000s. This engagement was partly the result of the combined effect of economic liberalisation and political fragmentation, which led to a process of state transformation and enabled think tanks to play a role in the peace process started in 2004 with Pakistan. However, it was only during Modi's first term as prime minister that the government openly expressed the desire to increase its engagement with think tanks. In June 2014, Modi indicated his openness to fresh thinking, arguing that 'the input of intellectual think tanks' should be substantially enhanced for a better policy framework (PIB, 2014).

Think tanks were thus officially recognised as sources of policy advice or, at least, as providers of relevant expertise. In practice, some organisations have come to enjoy better access to information than others. In parallel, the MEA and the government have also become increasingly open to external expertise. Foreign Secretary Subrahmanyam Jaishankar announced in 2015 that the policy planning and research division of the ministry sought to employ external experts; the government subsequently advertised the possibility of three-year stints at the MEA (see Haidar; Jha, 2015; Sen, 2015). In 2016, the Union Parliament's Standing Committee on External Affairs recommended to expand such openings 'to increase the information base and expertise of the Ministry in handling emerging and challenging issues in the field of geopolitics, [and] environ-mental/commercial diplomacy' (Bagchi, 2016b). It suggested to open lateral entry in the ministry to 'academia, think tanks, NGOs and the Private Sector' (Lok Sabha Secretariat, 2017, pp. 28–29). By 2017, the MEA had started to implement the recommendations of the committee by engaging academic consultants with expertise in International Rela-tions for its Policy Planning Division, although on a contractual basis (ibid.). In October 2017, the ministry also put a call out for consultants fluent in Chinese for a new MEA think tank that would help to formulate policies concerning China (Mitra, 2017).

The MEA's growing interest in working with think tanks, as promoted by Jaishankar, has led the ministry to collaborate with and provide funding for select organisations, which, for example, organise events for it (Gogna, 2016). Its change of attitude is, to a degree, explained by the growing needs of the overstretched Indian Foreign Service (see Markey, 2009). In a context of increasing policy complexity and high workloads, the government has started to tap into the expertise, services and added value that think tanks can provide. As C. Raja Mohan, the director of Carnegie India, has noted, 'given the complexity of policy, there's scope for outside people contributing to it' (Mohan, 2016).

Yet the MEA's opening up to outside sources of expertise and services remains limited. For instance, the new channels of communi-cation between the ministry and some select think tanks are based on trust relations between individuals rather than on clearly demarcated insti-tutionalised links between the MEA and these organisations. Moreover, funding is based on informal contacts as there is no official process to apply for ministerial grants. While the current situation constitutes a clear improvement in terms of funding compared to earlier decades, the lack of formal funding options does not allow for open competition among foreign policy think tanks for financial government support. The journalist Jyoti Malhotra (2017) has suggested that decisions on MEA's funding to think tanks close to the BJP and the related RSS get taken directly in the Prime Minister's Office.

THE MULTIPLE ROLES OF THINK TANKS

The greater presence and visibility of India's new foreign policy think tanks reflects their greater engagement with stakeholders, notably the government. As noted above, foreign policy think tanks across the globe can perform a multitude of roles. In the Indian context one can distinguish at least five such roles. First, some think tanks provide expertise and assistance for designing specific policies—in some cases, they can shape policy. ORF, for example, helped with India's cyber framework agreement with the United States, which provided a basis for much of its cyber diplomacy subsequently. Additionally, ORF provided inputs to the MEA on its foreign assistance policy, drawing from other examples such as Japan, South Korea, Germany and the United Kingdom. Studies conducted by Brookings India were also used by India's Ministry of Coal, NITI Aayog, the Ministry of Railways and the Ministry of Health and Family Welfare as a basis for policy, such as mining targets and public health investments.[13]

Second, some think tanks provide platforms for political dialogue among foreign policy actors from India and abroad, such as governments, policymakers and the strategic community. In this respect, the VIF and the IF have played an increasingly important role by organising small exclusive gatherings and meetings with high-profile guests. In 2015 the *Economic Times* reported that the closed-door sessions hosted by the IF on Wednesdays had come to replace the Saturday Club meetings at the India International Centre as the 'Delhi establishment's prime talk shop' (Tripathi, 2015). The IF has also been involved in organising Prime Minister Modi's diaspora events during his visits abroad. Organisations like ORF have also organised large annual policy conferences with the collaboration or participation of the MEA. The annual Raisina Dialogue in New Delhi, a joint MEA–ORF initiative established in 2016, serves to showcase India's regional ambitions and leadership and helps the government convey its perspectives to the world. The 2016 ORF annual report presents the Raisina Dialogue as 'India's flagship conference engaging with geopolitics and geoeconomics'. The 2017 Raisina Dialogue was opened by Prime Minister Modi and involved 800 participants including many high-level guests and 120 speakers from 65 countries. According to ORF president Samir Saran (2020), its 2020 version was to bring together over 600 speakers and official delegates from over 100 countries. The event has been positioned as a South Asian complement, and even a potential alternative, to the annual high-level security conference in Singapore, the Shangri-La Dialogue.[14]

---

[13] Interview by one of the authors with Dhruva Jaishankar, April 2020, via email.

[14] Other notable large annual events supported by the MEA and organised in partnership with think tanks are the Indian Ocean Conference (with the India Foundation), the

Third, some think tanks have utilised and further expanded their networks for engaging in informal diplomacy and developing India's international presence. At one level, ORF in particular is greatly involved in Tracks 1.5 and II diplomacy. The organisation is India's representative to the BRICS Think-Tanks Council set up in 2013 and the official Track II co-ordinator for the BRICS Forum, which sets the agenda for the discussions among the member states at their governmental meetings (Saran & Mohan, 2018). The Aspen Institute India was also originally created to promote such dialogue with US partners. Its successor, the Ananta Aspen Centre, has organised Track II exchanges with partners in various countries, including Japan, Israel, Singapore and China. The past years have also seen an increasing number of joint initiatives in which Indian think tanks have taken part. In relation to European countries, for instance, an EU–India Think Tanks Annual Conference has brought together think tanks from India and the EU since 2016 to discuss EU–India relations and to identify areas to strengthen their strategic partnership. Since 2015, the EU–India Think Tanks Twinning Initiative, launched by the delegation of the EU in India, has fostered co-operation and networking between Indian and European think tanks. Notably, ORF also set up a regional office in Washington in 2019—a first for an Indian think tank.

Fourth, some think tanks have developed youth networks that socialise and train a young generation, some of them openly along ideological lines. Since 2010, ORF has hosted a Raisina Young Fellows Programme, an annual ten-day policy workshop also called the 'Asian Forum on Global Governance' (Saran, 2020, p. 13). The Hindu nationalist-oriented Vision India Foundation, launched in 2014 with its Centre for Strategic and Foreign Relations, focuses specifically on developing summer schools, fellowships and 'policy boot camps'.[15]

Fifth, in a context where the government carefully manages information, some think tanks have become 'platforms for the dissemination of information' by the government (Malhotra, 2017). This is notably the

Global Technology Summit (with Carnegie India), the India–US Forum (with the Ananta Centre) and the West Asia Conference (with IDSA).

[15] Other Hindu nationalist think tanks are specialised in training, such as the older Rambhau Mhalgi Prabodhini (RMP), run by BJP Vice President Vinay Sahasrabuddhe. RMP provides training to politicians, their staff, government officials, and more generally RSS and BJP workers (Mohan 2015).

case of the Dr Syama Prasad Mookerjee Research Foundation (SPMRF), which hosts a page entitled 'PM Modi's vision' on its website (SPMRF n.d.). Modi's abolition of the media adviser post in his office led to the creation of new channels for passing on relevant information to journalists. Think thanks close to the government have come to function as significant nodes of information exchange. They also offer new platforms for the Modi Government to present its views and defend its positions through panel discussions and lectures (Shukla & Pandey, 2019).

THE BLURRING OF POWER AND IDEAS

The growth of new-generation foreign policy think tanks in India has been mostly limited to two distinct types of advocacy and research organisations: those close to Indian businesses and/or connected to foreign think tanks and those that are ideologically close to the ruling Hindu nationalist BJP and the RSS. This evolution seems to denote the increasing power of Hindu nationalism and of business groups in India—rather than a general pluralisation of the landscape of think tanks—and has several implications regarding the level of autonomy and the roles of these think tanks.

On the one hand, the foreign policy think tanks that are close to Indian businesses and/or connected to foreign think tanks have contributed to the diversification of the Indian think-tank sector by promoting world views that tend to be in agreement with a liberal international order and by representing the interests of major corporate actors (Sarkar, 2017, 2018, 2019). These think tanks also place great emphasis on their high-quality expertise and new thinking. Carnegie India appointed first C. Raja Mohan—a prominent strategic thinker—as its founding director, with the King's College London academic Rudra Chaudhuri also joining the institute. Brookings India selected the internationally renowned Dhruva Jaishankar and Johns Hopkins University-educated Constantino Xavier to run its international affairs and security-related activities. Harsh V. Pant, professor of International Relations at King's College London, joined ORF as head of its Strategic Studies Programme.[16] These think tanks have

---

[16] CPR, from an older generation of think tanks, strengthened its expertise in international affairs through recognised experts, including historian Srinath Raghavan (a former senior fellow), foreign affairs analyst Zorawar Daulet Singh, Professor Rani Mullen (senior visiting fellow) and Professor Brahma Chellaney.

contributed to developing expertise on international affairs and India's foreign policy and diffusing it to a wider public.

On the other hand, the think tanks that are ideologically close to the ruling Hindu nationalist BJP and the RSS have contributed to the mainstreaming of a Hindu nationalist discourse in foreign policy, in line with the government's ideological agenda. For instance, on its website the IF presents itself as a '[f]oundation [that] believes in understanding contemporary India and its global context through a civilizational lens of a society on the forward move. [...] It seeks to articulate [an] Indian nationalistic perspective on issues'. (India Foundation n.d.) The IF has also established the Centre for Study of Religion and Society, while the VIF has set up its Historical and Civilisational Studies programme. Both organisations have used new platforms to disseminate their ideas. For instance, the VIF has organised with partners in Japan and Myanmar the Samvad Civilisational Dialogue, a global Hindu–Buddhist initiative based on a culturalist ideology and designed to 'adopt principles of Asia's age-old spiritual teachings of Hinduism and Buddhism to address modern-day issues threatening human civilisation' (VIF, 2017). Modi promoted the format after a meeting with Japanese Prime Minister Shinzō Abe. The IF has held its Dharma–Dhamma Conference annually since 2012 to promote the idea of India's interconnectedness with neighbouring countries, in particular in Southeast Asia, through Buddhism.[17] By financing and co-operating with advocacy think tanks such as the IF and the VIF, the MEA has effectively contributed to mainstreaming the ideological tenets they share with the government, contributing to a substantial blurring of power and ideas (and their carriers).

This blurring also extends to lateral links between the IF and the VIF, on the one hand, and the government and the ruling party (in terms of leading personnel), on the other. For example, Ram Madhav, BJP National General Secretary and the RSS's head of public relations, also serves as IF director. Another IF director, Shaurya Doval, is partner in a financial services company and the son of the current National Security Advisor, Ajit Doval, who himself founded the VIF. Both the IF and the VIF has provided personnel to the Modi Government, with several of their members taking up positions within the government and the National Security Agency (Shukla & Pandey, 2019).

---

[17] See also the chapter by Ian Hall in this volume.

There are also numerous links in terms of leading personnel among India's foreign policy think tanks. To cite only a few examples, the current head of the SPMRF, Anirban Ganguly, used to work as a research fellow at the VIF and is also a member of the BJP's Policy Research Department. The VIF's current head, Arvind Gupta, served first as director general of the IDSA (2012–2014) and as Deputy National Security Advisor under Modi until 2017. The former director of the CLAWS, Major General Dhruv C. Katoch, is now an IF director. A closely-knit elite network thus connects the realms of India's foreign policy think tanks and the incumbent government, with powerful individuals serving as 'boundary spanners'.

Policy Impact and Funding Issues

Their proximity to power surely lends visibility and prominence to the newer Hindu nationalist think tanks. Yet it is difficult to assess the extent to which these think tanks are truly influential as organisations, and what forms and manifestations this influence might take. Certainly, think tank visibility does not equal policy impact, and impact is also hard to measure (see Köllner, 2013). Recent years have clearly witnessed the rise of some new-generation foreign policy think tanks in India; however, political access (sometimes even political office) and direct leverage are tied to individual power brokers. This seems to confirm the conclusion of Amitabh Mattoo and Rory Medcalf (2015, p. 279) that 'the story of Indian foreign policy is more about the influence of certain individuals rather than institutions'.

In this context there has also been a contradictory trend towards more visible yet non-transparent politics. On the one hand, the introduction of new agendas, the creation of new high-profile platforms and the engagement of the MEA with several think tanks have created an environment propitious for more open policy debates. On the other hand, the conspicuous lateral links between some of the high-profile new think tanks and the incumbent government—as well as between the think tanks themselves—reinforce not only the risk of uniformity and orthodoxy of and among the think tanks concerned but also the opacity of their operations.[18]

[18] On the issue of conflict of interests in the case of the India Foundation, see Chaturvedi (2017).

Furthermore, while some think tanks are today more at ease finan- cially, the state has restricted funding for organisations such as think tanks in new ways. During its first term, the Modi Government drastically curbed external funding for non-governmental organisations (NGOs). The Foreign Contribution (Regulation) Act (FCRA) of 2010, which regulates the use of foreign funding for 'organisations of a political nature', was amended and made stricter by Parliament in 2016. Since 2011, the home ministry has cancelled the licences of more than 20,000 Indian NGOs,[19] notably human rights NGOs, which meant they could no longer receive foreign funding. Most cancellations of licences have happened under the Modi Government.[20] Although the government argued that the cancellations of licences were justified by the fact that the NGOs concerned had breached the legal requirements of the FCRA, this move has been interpreted as targeting critical voices,[21] and was condemned as such by the United Nations (2016).

The Hindu, a well-established newspaper, also reported that the MEA cut funding to the Association of Asia Scholars and discontinued its annual funding of ₹10 million to the Institute of Chinese Studies (ICS) in early 2017, replacing this grant with a project-based funding model. The ICS had been initially funded by the Vajpayee Government in the 1990s after the National Security Advisory Board had concluded that the government should fund long-term research on 'countries that pose a security challenge to India — China and Pakistan' (Baru, 2017). According to Sanjaya Baru (n.d.), the ICS was supposed to be 'India's window to China'. However, the ICS had apparently not approved of the government's stance on certain issues, notably on the Belt and Road Initiative (Haidar & Bhattacherjee,). The Centre of Contemporary China Studies (CCCS) was set up as an internal think tank working on China

---

[19] According to the official FCRA website, 20,673 organisations are on the Registration Cancelled List. See https://fcraonline.nic.in/fc8_cancel_query.aspx.

[20] In 2019, the Union minister of state for Home Affairs, Nityanand Rai, told the Lok Sabha that the government had in the precedent five years deregistered more than 14,800 NGOs. Around 4,800 licences were cancelled in 2017 alone (Bhagwati et al., 2019; *Business* Standard 2019).

[21] It came after a leaked Intelligence Bureau report accused 'foreign-funded' NGOs in 2014 of 'serving as tools for foreign policy interests of western governments' (*The Times of India*, 2014). Two years later, a senior home ministry officer argued that 'NGOs that are not serving larger national interest or indulg[e] in subversive activities should not be allowed foreign founding' (Jain 2016; see also Doshi 2016).

within the MEA that same year (Mitra, 2017). It was also reported that the grant to the ICS went to the Centre for China Analysis and Strategy, headed by Jayadeva Ranade, a specialist on China and former member of the National Security Advisory Board (Malhotra, 2017).

Amended FCRA regulations meant less funding was available for NGOs. According to Bain & Company, foreign contributions decreased by approximately 40% between 2014 and 2018 (Bhagwati et al., 2019). Yet in the case of foreign policy think tanks, Baru (2017) notes that well-known Indian companies liberally funded the Indian branches of Brookings and Carnegie. Organisations such as ORF have also benefited from such support. Its inflows in 2017–2018 amounted to approximately ₹35 crore (US$5.5 million), Urvashi Sarkar (2019) suggests. Between 2014 and 2019, it received approximately €540,000 in government funding—the largest governmental funding for a non-state think tank (MEA, 2020). Overall, however, funding from Indian companies to think tanks remains 'still very limited, hard to get and based on personal contacts more than professional criteria' (Baru, 2017). Government support is also limited. Despite newer and larger sources of funding to think tanks, long-term, substantial funding without strings attached is still scarce (ibid.; Katz, 2016). This funding issue affects negatively the development of expertise on security issues in India, which in turn contributes to hinder the development of India's foreign policy capacity (see Bajpai & Chong, 2019).

Conclusions

In 2015 the Indian journalist Prashant Jha noted the seemingly paradoxical combination of a centralised power under the Modi Government and a greater openness of the system to 'outside inputs and engagements' (Jha, 2015). As shown in this chapter, both the government's and the business sector's growing demand for expertise and organisational skills have provided a select number of foreign policy think tanks with access to more (often combined) private and governmental funding and more information than in the past. This, in turn, has enabled them to take up new research, outreach and advocacy roles in co-operation with the incumbent government, and to increase their visibility in the public sphere and internationally. Due to their expanding roles as event conveners and information disseminators, and due to their connections to the incumbent government, these think tanks have become important players to watch and engage with.

The rise of this select group of foreign policy think tanks in the 2000s and 2010s has led to a certain pluralisation of voices on international affairs and the consolidation of a limited pool of prominent organisations in India. There is, however, substantial variance within the Indian foreign policy think-tank sector in ideological leanings, research capacities and convening power of the organisations involved. Two distinct new groups have emerged: some organisations—like the IF and the VIF—are ideologically close to the government, while others—like ORF, Brookings and Carnegie—are closer to Indian businesses and their more liberal world views. Reflecting the prime minister's distinct style of diplomacy,[22] the Modi Government has shown a preference for these newer think tanks for its public diplomacy outreach over older state-controlled think tanks. Policymakers and other stakeholders need to be aware of the diversity in the changing landscape of foreign policy think tanks in India if they wish to engage in the most functional and effective way with these organisations.

At one level, the government's growing engagement with these organisations illustrates its desire to further India's image at both the regional and global levels and to develop the country's international clout. Think tanks like ORF have successfully become visible, are well inserted in global networks and are openly interested in shaping global governance debates. The new prominence of these think tanks reflects India's new and growing global stakes and the commensurate desire of the government and corporations to project India internationally. At the inauguration of Carnegie India in 2016, Foreign Secretary Jaishankar made it clear that the government understood this new engagement with think tanks through the prism of India's changing global status. He argued that

one aspect of transitioning to a leading power is to build rigorous and competitive think-tanks ... an aspiring power must assess new opportunities and challenges and put out its narrative. It must influence global thinking while being well-informed of how it is perceived by others.' (S. Jaishankar, 2016)

---

[22] See the chapter by Ian Hall in this volume.

The Modi Government thus also considers think tanks as narrative-builders and spinners that can help to buttress India's ambitions as a global power. There is, however, more. The rise of new-generation Indian foreign policy think tanks like the VIF and IF also exemplifies an ideological turn within the larger sphere of foreign policymaking, in which Hindu nationalist ideology has become more prominent. Their creation and emergence as important political players in New Delhi illustrate the government's desire to promote a Hindu nationalist agenda. By contributing to projecting and mainstreaming an official Hindu nationalist discourse, these organisations can be understood as part of a larger project of the BJP and the RSS to transform the intellectual space in New Delhi and to replace what they perceive as a dominant left-of-centre ideology with a right-wing nationalist ideology (Shukla & Pandey, 2019). They can be understood as part of a 'strategy to create a competitive Hindutva intellectual narrative' (Andersen & Damle, 2019, p. 71). The ideological role of these think tanks complements government attempts to rewrite the country's history and to transform Nehruvian institutions by replacing their leadership.[23] Overall, the rise of this particular kind of new-generation think tanks, which are both globally and Hindu nationalist in orientation, reflects and contributes to the Janus-faced nature of the emerging 'New India'.

References

Andersen, W., & Damle, S. D. (2019). *Messengers of hindu nationalism: How the RSS reshaped India*. Hurst and Company.
Anderson, E. (2015). 'Neo-Hindutva': The Asia House M. F. Husain campaign and the mainstreaming of Hindu nationalist rhetoric in Britain. *Contemporary South Asia, 23*(1), 45–66.
Anderson, E., & Longkumer, A. (2018). 'Neo-Hindutva': Evolving forms, spaces, and expressions of Hindu nationalism. *Contemporary South Asia, 26*(4), 371–377.
Bagchi, I. (2016a, January 17). 'Outside ideas' trickle in as think tanks set up base. *The Times of India*, https://timesofindia.indiatimes.com/india/Out

---

[23] For the cases of the Nehru Memorial Museum & Library and the Jawaharlal Nehru University see Sharma (2019).

side-ideas-trickle-in-as-think-tanks-set-up-base/articleshow/50609513.cms. Accessed 21 April 2020.

Bagchi, I. (2016b, August 2). MEA looks for ways to expand pool to meet crunch. *The Times of India.* https://timesofindia.indiatimes.com/india/ MEA-looks-for-ways-to-expand-cadre-pool-to-meet-crunch/articleshow/535 09625.cms. Accessed 12 February 2018.

Bajpai, K., & Chong, B. (2019). India's foreign policy capacity. *Policy Design and Practice, 2*(2), 137–162.

Baru, S. (2017). Funding the Indian think tank. *Civil Society Online.* https:// www.civilsocietyonline.com/column/delhi-darbar/funding-the-indian-think-tank. Accessed 21 April 2020.

Baru, S. (n.d.). An Indian view of the world. *Civil Society Online.* https://www. civilsocietyonline.com/column/delhi-darbar/an-indian-view-of-the-world. Accessed 3 March 2021.

Bhagwati, A., Sheth, A., Sanghavi, D., & Srinivasan, S. (2019). India's Philanthropy Report 2019. Bain & Company. https://www.bain.com/insights/ india-philanthropy-report-2019. Accessed 21 April 2020.

Bhatnagar, S. (forthcoming). *India's Pakistan policy: How think tanks are shaping foreign relations.* Routledge India.

Bhatnagar, S., & Chacko, P. (2019). Peacebuilding think tanks, Indian foreign policy and the Kashmir conflict. *Third World Quarterly, 40*(8), 1496–1515.

Business Standard. (2019, July 16). Over 14,800 foreign-funded NGOs deregistered in last 5 yrs: Govt. https://www.business-standard.com/article/pti-stories/over-14-800-foreign-funded-ngos-deregistered-in-last-5-yrs-govt-119 071600672_1.html. Accessed 22 April 2020.

Celestine, A. (2012, April 9). Why India's think-tank community fails in raising funds from Indian entrepreneurs. *The Economic Times.* https://eco nomictimes.indiatimes.com/news/company/corporate-trends/why-indias-think-tank-community-fails-in-raising-funds-from-indian-entrepreneurs/articl eshow/12572201.cms. Accessed 21 April 2020.

Chatterjee Miller, M. (2013). India's feeble foreign policy: A world-be-great power resists its own rise. *Foreign Affairs, 92*(3), 14–19.

Chaturvedi, S. (2017, November 4). Exclusive: Think-tank run by NSA Ajit Doval's son has conflict of interest writ large. *The Wire.* https://thewire. in/politics/exclusive-think-tank-run-nsa-ajit-dovals-son-conflict-interest-writ-large. Accessed 21 January 2018.

Doshi, V. (2016, November 24). India accused of muzzling NGOs by blocking foreign funding. *The Guardian.* https://www.theguardian.com/global-dev elopment/2016/nov/24/india-modi-government-accused-muzzling-ngos-by-blocking-foreign-funding. Accessed 22 April 2020.

Gogna, S. (2016, February 16). The rise of India's think tank diplomacy. *South Asian Voices.* https://southasianvoices.org/rise-indias-think-tank-diplomacy. Accessed 12 January 2018.

Gonzalez Hernando, M., Pautz, H., & Stone, D. (2018). Think tanks in 'hard times': The global financial crisis and economic advice. *Policy and Society, 37*(2), 125–139.

Goyal, N., & Srinivasan, S. (2013, May 21). Why think tanks struggle in India. *First Post.* https://www.firstpost.com/india/why-think-tanks-struggle-in-india-800929.html. Accessed 21 April 2020.

Haidar, S. (2015, June 29). MEA opens doors to IR experts as consultants. *The Hindu.* https://www.thehindu.com/news/external-affairs-ministry-opens-doors-to-international-relations-experts-as-consultants/article7367713.ece. Accessed 21 April 2020.

Haidar, S., & Bhattacherjee, K. (2017a, February 8). MEA cuts grants for think tank on China. *The Hindu.* http://www.thehindu.com/news/national/MEA-cuts-grants-for-think-tank-on-China/article17244004.ece. Accessed 10 November 2017.

Haidar, S., & Bhattacherjee, K. (2017b, March 13). MEA cuts funds to one more China think tank. *The Hindu.* http://www.thehindu.com/news/national/mea-cuts-funds-to-one-more-china-think-tank/article17453416.ece. Accessed 20 December 2017.

Hindu. (2012, September 19). The Hindu Centre for Politics and Public Policy. *The Hindu.* https://www.thehindu.com/news/national/the-hindu-centre-for-politics-and-public-policy/article3915518.ece. Accessed 22 April 2020.

India Foundation. (n.d.). About us. https://indiafoundation.in/about-us. Accessed 6 May 2020.

Jain, B. (2016, November 5). 'Anti-national acts': 25 NGOS lose foreign fund licences. *The Times of India.* https://timesofindia.indiatimes.com/india/Anti-national-acts-25-NGOs-lose-foreign-fund-licences/articleshow/552546 13.cms. Accessed 22 April 2020.

Jaishankar, S. (2016). Indian Foreign Secretary Subrahmanyam Jaishankar's Remarks. Carnegie India. https://carnegieindia.org/2016/04/06/indian-foreign-secretary-subrahmanyamjaishankar-s-remarks/iwq8. Accessed 22 April 2020.

Jha, P. (2015, August 16). India's most influential think-tanks. *Hindustan Times.* http://www.hindustantimes.com/india/india-s-most-influential-think-tanks/story-emb0db2lmqltL8pKeYuZiL.html. Accessed 10 November 2017.

Katz, A. (2016). The remarkable rise of India's think tanks. *Global Government Forum.* https://www.globalgovernmentforum.com/the-remark able-rise-of-indias-think-tanks. Accessed 3 March 2021.

Khan, R., & Köllner, P. (2018). Foreign policy think tanks in India: New Actors, Divergent Profiles. *GIGA Focus Asia*, 1/2018. Hamburg: GIGA. https://www.giga-hamburg.de/en/publication/foreign-policy-think-tanks-in-india-new-actors-divergent-profiles. Accessed 3 March 2021.

Köllner, P. (2011). Think tanks: Their development, global diversity and roles in international affairs. *GIGA Focus International Edition*, 6. GIGA. https://www.giga-hamburg.de/en/publication/think-tanks-their-dev elopment-global-diversity-and-roles-in-international-affairs. Accessed 3 March 2021.

Köllner, P. (2013). Think tanks: The quest to define and to rank them. *GIGA Focus International Edition*, 10. GIGA. https://www.giga-hamburg.de/ en/publication/think-tanks-the-quest-to-define-and-to-rank-them. Accessed 3 March 2021.

Köllner, P., Zhu, X., & Abb, P. (2018). Understanding the development of think tanks in Mainland China, Taiwan, and Japan. *Pacific Affairs, 91*(1), 5–26.

Kumar, R. (2015). The private sector. In D. M. Malone, C. R. Mohan, S. Raghavan (Eds.), *The Oxford Handbook of Indian Foreign Policy*, online version. Oxford University Press.

Ladi, S. (2011). Think tanks. In B. Badie, D. Berg-Schlosser, & L. Morlino (Eds.) *International Encyclopedia of Political Science*. SAGE Publications, http://sk.sagepub.com/reference/intlpoliticalscience/n604.xml. Accessed 23 January 2018.

Lok Sabha Secretariat. (2017). Standing Committee on International Affairs (2016–2017), sixteenth Lok Sabha, Ministry of External Affairs [Action Taken by the Government on the recommendations contained in the Eleventh Report (16th Lok Sabha) on Demands for Grants of the Ministry of External Affairs for the year 2016–2017] fourteenth report. Lok Sabha Secretariat.

Malhotra, J. (2017, March 1). The growing role of government-approved think tanks, *NDTV*. https://www.ndtv.com/opinion/think-tanks-controlled-by-foreign-ministry-are-supplanting-the-media-1664683. Accessed 15 November 2017.

Markey, D. (2009). Developing India's foreign policy 'Software.' *Asia Policy, 8*, 73–96.

Mathur, N., & Mathur, K. (2019 [2007]). Policy analysis in India: Research bases and discursive practices. In F. Fischer, G. J. Miller, M. S. Sidney (Eds.), *Handbook of Public Policy Analysis: Theory, Politics and Methods* (pp. 603–616). Routledge.

Mathur, K. (2013). *Public policy and politics in India: How institutions matter*. Oxford University Press.

Mattoo, A., & Medcalf, R. (2015). Think-tanks and universities. In D. M. Malone, C. R. Mohan, & S. Raghavan (Eds.), *The Handbook of Indian Foreign Policy* (pp. 271–284). Oxford University Press.

McGann, J. (2008–20). TTCSP global go to think tank index reports. University of Pennsylvania, reports 1–14, https://repository.upenn.edu/think_tanks. Accessed 2 February 2020.

MEA [Ministry of External Affairs, Government of India]. (2020). Annexure A to 'Answer [of] the Minister of State in the Ministry of External Affairs' [Shri V. Muraleedharan] in response to the Lok Sabha unstarred question No. 4045. https://www.mea.gov.in/Images/amb1/lu4045Ann.pdf. Accessed 2 May 2020.

Mitra, D. (2017, October 30). As Dokhlam Embers die down, MEA puts finishing touches to China-Centric Research Centre, *The Wire*. https://thewire.in/192497/mea-china-research-centre. Accessed 21 November 2017.

Mohan, A. (2015, June 22). Future BJP leadership trained at plush institute. *Business Standard*. https://www.business-standard.com/article/politics/future-bjp-leadership-trained-at-plush-institute-115062100957_1.html. Accessed 30 April 2020.

Mohan, C. R. (2016, January 26). Interview: India's newest think tank chief talks global leadership. Carnegie India. http://carnegieindia.org/2016/01/26/india-s-newest-think-tank-chief-talks-global-leadership-pub-62589. Accessed 15 January 2018.

Pautz, H. (2011). Revisiting the think-tank phenomenon. *Public Policy and Administration, 26*(4), 419–435.

PIB [Press Information Bureau, Government of India, Prime Minister's Office]. (2014). PM calls for enhancing the input of intellectual think-tanks in policy frameworks, http://pib.nic.in/newsite/PrintRelease.aspx?relid=105487. Accessed 13 February 2018.

Ravichander, A. (2018), Indian think tanks: A view on their journey. On Think Tanks. https://onthinktanks.org/series/indian-think-tanks-a-view-on-their-journey. Accessed 15 August 2019.

Saran, S. (2020). Note from the curator: President, Observer Research Foundation. In Observer Research Foundation, 'Raisina Dialogue — Conference booklet 2020: 21@20 Navigating the Alpha Century, January 14–16, 2020, (p. 13). https://www.orfonline.org/raisina-dialogue. Accessed 20 February 2020.

Saran, S., & Mohan, A. (2018). Helping build an emerging power narrative: Reforming global governance. In J. G. McGann (Ed.), *Think tanks and emerging power policy networks* (pp. 17–30). Palgrave Macmillan.

Sarkar, U. (2017, August 31) Carnegie endowment in India: Promoting US leadership with Indian corporate wealth. *The Wire*. https://thewire.in/business/carnegie-india-think-tank-role. Accessed 21 April 2018.

Sarkar, U. (2018, January 3). Brookings demystified: Overlapping networks and the business of influencing policy. *The Wire*. https://thewire.in/diplomacy/brookings-business-influencing-policy. Accessed 14 February 2018.

Sarkar, U. (2019, March 1). Readiness and reliance: The aims of observer research foundation. *The Caravan.* https://caravanmagazine.in/reportage/ the-aims-observer-research-foundation. Accessed 14 February 2018.

Sen, G. (2015, July 6). How workable will consultants be in the existing framework of the ministry of external affairs? *IDSA Comment.* https://idsa. in/idsacomments/HowWorkablewillConsultantsbeintheExistingFrameworko ftheMEA_GautamSen_060715. Accessed 13 February 2018.

Sharma, P. (2019, December 21). Might of the right: The intrinsic feature of the Modi govt has been the influence exerted by the RSS. *The Week.* https://www.theweek.in/theweek/current/2019/12/17/might-of-the-right.html. Accessed 22 April 2020.

Shukla, S., & Pandey, N. (2019, December 30). How the right is tackling left's intellectual hegemony in Delhi — one think-tank at a time. *The Print.* https://theprint.in/india/how-the-right-is-tackling-lefts-intellect ual-hegemony-in-delhi-one-think-tank-at-a-time/341760. Accessed 22 April 2020.

SPMRF [Dr. Syama Prasad Mookerjee Research Foundation]. (n.d.). Category: PM Modi's Vision. https://www.spmrf.org/category/pm-modis-vision. Accessed 6 May 2020.

Stone, D. (2004). Introduction: Think tanks, policy advice and governance. In A. Denham & D. Stone (Eds.), *Think tank traditions: Policy research and the politics of ideas* (pp. 1–18). Manchester University Press.

Stone, D. (2007). Recycling bins, garbage cans or think tanks? Three myths regarding policy analysis institutes. *Public Administration, 85*(2), 259–278.

Thakur, V., & Davis, A. E. (2017). A communal affair over international affairs: The arrival of IR in late colonial India. *South Asia: Journal of South Asian Studies, 40*(4), 689–705.

Times of India. (2014, June 12). Foreign-funded NGOs stalling development: IB report. *The Times of India.* https://timesofindia.indiatimes.com/india/ Foreign-funded-NGOs-stalling-development-IB-report/articleshow/364111 69.cms. Accessed 22 April 2020.

Tripathi, R. (2015, August 3). How National Security Advisor Ajit Doval's son Shaurya reinvented himself into a key policy player. *The Economic Times.* https://economictimes.indiatimes.com/news/politics-and-nation/how-nat ional-security-advisor-ajit-dovals-son-shaurya-reinvented-himself-into-a-key-policy-player/articleshow/48322773.cms. Accessed 2 November 2017.

United Nations. (2016, June 16). UN rights experts urge India to repeal law restricting NGO's access to crucial foreign funding. United Nations Human Rights Office of the High Commissioner. https://www.ohchr.org/EN/New sEvents/Pages/DisplayNews.aspx?NewsID=20112&LangID=E.a. Accessed 23 April 2020.

VIF [Vivekananda International Foundation]. (2017). SAMVAD-II: Dialogue for Peace, Harmony and Security — Global Initiative for Conflict Avoidance and Environmental Consciousness. https://www.vifindia.org/article/2017/september/28/samvad-ii-dialogue-for-peace-harmony-and-security. Accessed 7 May 2020.

Vivekanandan, B. (2010). A tribute to life and work of Professor M.S. Rajan. *International Studies, 47*(2–4), 99–111.

Building ASEAN Identity Through Regional Diplomacy

Elaine Tan

INTRODUCTION

When the historic Bangkok Declaration was signed on 8 August 1967, creating the Association of Southeast Asian Nations (ASEAN), the region was confronted with conflicts and the potential instability largely because of Cold War tensions. After 53 years of enlargement and development, ASEAN is viewed as one of the more successful regional organisations in the world. The ASEAN leaders launched the ASEAN Community in 2015 to underline ASEAN's centrality and its role as the driving force in addressing the evolving regional architecture in South East Asia. ASEAN centrality is about maintaining ASEAN's relevance and ASEAN's convening power to manage regional processes for dialogue (Chalermpalanupap, 2017). ASEAN centrality calls on ASEAN member states to prioritise ASEAN in fulfilling its regional commitments by remaining united, strengthening co-ordination and contributing as a cohesive group (Ong, 2007).

E. Tan (✉)
USAID ASEAN Policy Implementation, Jakarta, Indonesia
e-mail: etan@ibi-worldwide.com

© The Author(s), under exclusive license to Springer Nature Singapore Pte Ltd. 2022
R. Patman et al. (eds.), *From Asia-Pacific to Indo-Pacific*, Global Political Transitions, https://doi.org/10.1007/978-981-16-7007-7_11

235

The launch of the ASEAN Community was also a move towards ASEAN being forward-looking and people-centred, departing from the former ASEAN way of doing things, which was slow, status quo and state-centric (Hernandez, n.d). It was a progressive development in response to integration and community building needs as well as the growing levels of comfort, trust and political maturity among ASEAN member states over the years (Hoang, 2017). The development and the adoption of the ASEAN Charter at the 13th ASEAN Summit in November 2007 and its ratification paved the way for consultations with non-state actors and the use of Track II dialogues to include their peoples in community building (Hernandez, n.d).

The community building approach now takes a people-centred approach to strive for further integration and stronger cohesiveness among member states. As a regional organisation composed of small- to medium-sized states, ASEAN cultivates a strong voice in the world through its institutional regional identity. On the other hand, there is a perception that ASEAN co-operation is more about high politics and diplomacy than about the day-to-day issues that affect the 650 million people in South East Asia. Diplomacy appears to have little impact on ordinary people's lives (Thuzar, 2014). But ASEAN's efforts in diplomacy allow the region to reap the benefits of stability, economic success and improved living standards. Yet ordinary people often do not know about ASEAN's accomplishments that allow them to go about their business in tranquillity (Thuzar, 2015).

This chapter highlights ASEAN's relative success at the level of state decision-making in forging its institutional identity building through regional diplomacy efforts, and because of this progress, the priority task ahead is to get the ordinary people of ASEAN to rally behind the ASEAN community building process. Popular support is necessary for the further development of ASEAN over the next fifty years. Strengthening ASEAN identity allows its wider public to be more involved in its regional co-operation efforts in order that issues that affect daily life in South East Asia matter. It also discusses the role of the ASEAN Foundation in recent years to promote ASEAN awareness and identity by targeting youth in the region to connect and collaborate with one another.

DIVIDENDS OF PEACE

ASEAN was established to keep peace. Its community building process is anchored on peace and freedom, economic prosperity and better quality of life for its people. The ASEAN Community captures ASEAN's resilience and dynamism. It is a community of opportunities for all, consisting of three pillars—political security, economic and sociocultural—and its launch at the end of December 2015 was viewed as a historic milestone. It was an announcement of how far ASEAN had come and how well the ASEAN member states have achieved working together (ASEAN, 2015). It is a journey spanning more than five decades where the representatives of ASEAN member states came together in friendship and co-operation to pursue the dream of ASEAN's founding fathers to improve the lives of its peoples.

ASEAN has made tremendous strides in promoting peace and stability in the region. It adopted an outward-oriented development strategy. This has resulted in ASEAN's economies remaining robust despite uncertainties in the regional and global economies. The region's free trade agreement among ASEAN member states, the ASEAN Free Trade Area agreement (AFTA) was signed in 1992. AFTA eliminated tariffs to reduce the price of products manufactured within ASEAN. It gave rise to the goal of creating a single market and production base to attract foreign direct investment and expand intra-ASEAN trade and investment, and now AFTA is in place it is challenged by domestic acceptance and enforcement of regional commitments. ASEAN's external economic relations have met with greater success, as can been seen by several free trade agreements (FTAs) with countries throughout the world, including those with China and India (Thuzar, 2014).

According to a McKinsey Global Institute report, ASEAN comprises eight of the 18 developing economies that averaged at least 3.5% annual per capita GDP growth over 50 years, or 5% annual growth over 20 years (Das et al., 2018). ASEAN has doubled its share in the world's GDP from 3.3% in 1967 to 6.5% in 2018. Real GDP growth for 2018 stood at 52%, with forecasted growth of 4.9% for 2019, according to the Asian Development Bank (ASEAN, 2019a).

Preliminary ASEAN statistics also indicate that total merchandise trade in 2018 grew by an estimated 8.1% year-on-year to reach US$2.8 trillion, while foreign direct investment (FDI) inflows increased by 5.3% year-on-year to reach US$154.7 billion (ASEAN, 2019a) With a combined

GDP of US$3 trillion in 2018, ASEAN in that year was collectively the fifth-largest economy in the world, and the third-largest economy in Asia. ASEAN's combined population of 650 million people is the third largest in the world, representing 8.7% of the world's population in 2018. It has a growing middle class that offers opportunities for investment in the region. ASEAN has emerged as a preferred destination for investment, attracting US$154.7 billion of foreign direct investment net flows in 2018, which was a significant increase from US$21.8 billion in 2000 (ASEAN, n.d).

ASEAN has a young population. The youth of ASEAN, defined here as persons aged fifteen to 35, represent over 33% of ASEAN's population and are key stakeholders in its contribution to ASEAN's future. The 213 million youth who constitute the region's largest-ever cohort is expected to rise to a peak of 220 million in 2038. Except for Singapore and Thailand, the youth population in the rest of the ASEAN member states is between 25 and 30% of their respective total populations. This augurs well for the region as it is attractive as a market because of its growing consumer base (ASEAN, 2017a).

Another McKinsey report states that some 67 million households in ASEAN states are part of the 'consuming class', with incomes exceeding the level at which they can begin to make significant discretionary purchases. That number could almost double to 125 million households by 2025, making ASEAN a pivotal consumer market of the future. At the same time ASEAN cities are booming because of urbanisation. Today, 22% of ASEAN's population lives in cities of more than 200,000 inhabitants and these urban centres account for more than 54% of the region's GDP. An additional 54 million people are expected to move to cities by 2025. ASEAN consumers are increasingly moving online, with mobile penetration of 110% and internet penetration of 25% across the region. ASEAN member states make up the world's second-largest community of Facebook users, behind only the United States, but the adoption of social media varies in the different countries (HV et al., 2014).

With the formation of ASEAN, member states concentrated their efforts to improve the quality of life of ASEAN's peoples. Progress is reflected by the reduced proportion of people living on less than US$1.25 per day, from one in two to one in eight persons over the last two decades. (ASEAN, 2015). There was a reduction in maternal mortality per 100,000 live births from 286 in 1990 to 197 in 2015. The proportion of the population with improved sanitation facilities increased from

37% in 1990 to 78% in 2015. Examples of stability brought about by regional co-operation include an increase in the net enrolment ratio in primary education from 83% in 1990 to 96% in 2015 and an increase in the proportion of seats held by women in parliaments from 9% in 1995 to 18% in 2015 (ASEAN, 2017b).

Increasing a Sense of Belonging

When ASEAN celebrated its 50th anniversary in 2017, there was much praise for the institution, as highlighted by the World Economic Forum's regional focus on ASEAN in Phnom Penh in 2017 to Economic Research Institute for ASEAN and East Asia (ERIA)'s ASEAN@50 volume, *The ASEAN Journey: Reflections of ASEAN Leaders and Officials*, as well as Kishore Mahbubani and Jeffery Sng's *The ASEAN Miracle: A Catalyst for Peace*. It has helped keep the peace for the last fifty years in a diverse region comprising ethnically and culturally diverse people, and different religious and political systems. Its diplomatic platform regularly brought together major powers such as the United States, the European Union, China, India, Japan, Russia, and South and North Korea creating a conducive environment for them to talk to each other. ASEAN's rich experience of managing such stakeholders' interests and the 'ASEAN Plus' processes such as ASEAN Plus Three (the ten ASEAN countries, China, Japan and the Republic of Korea) and the East Asia Summit (ASEAN, China, Japan, the Republic of Korea, India, Australia and New Zealand) have mutually engaged these stakeholders in an orderly and rewarding manner. As a result, ASEAN has been recognised as playing a central role and has been acknowledged to be the 'the primary driver' of regional architecture development in East Asia. In the process, a nascent regional identity was being built among government officials because of a common purpose of promoting solidarity and co-operation on the regional stage (Ong, 2009).

ASEAN currently holds more than 1,000 meetings every year. The constant interaction and co-operation among government officials at these meetings can result in an 'invisible formal network' being developed that can lead to top-level community building (Mahbubani & Severino, 2014). Developing shared norms like dialogue, consultation and consensus, known as the 'ASEAN Way', into customised mechanisms has helped promote a strong sense of common identity. ASEAN's framework and community building have enriched the organisation's standing, notwithstanding the imperfections of the regional body. This in turn has enhanced the political and strategic position of each member state. This has elevated ASEAN's prestige and recognition, increasing a sense of belonging to a region (Ong, 2009).

When the ASEAN leaders adopted the ASEAN Concord II in October 2003 with the aim of establishing the ASEAN Community by 2020, it was upon the realisation that the closeness of geography and the 'ASEAN Way' were insufficient to forge closer regional integration. It was necessary to move from the loose 'association of regional countries' into a much closer 'ASEAN community of nations'. To build a strong ASEAN Community, a genuine sense of belonging to the region and shared destiny would be critical components to instil a sense of an ASEAN identity (Lee, 2018).

There was no mention of an ASEAN identity in the Bangkok Declaration and it was not until 30 years after its adoption that the 'promotion of ASEAN awareness' appeared in the 1997 Hanoi Plan of Action. Furthermore, the word 'identity' entered the ASEAN lexicon through the Bali Concord II in 2003, which laid the foundation for the ASEAN Community's formation by 2020, which was pushed forward to 2015 by the ASEAN Leaders in 2007 (Murti, 2016). Global events, starting with free trade areas being established in Europe and North America, the Asian financial crisis and the rise of China pushed ASEAN to adopt the Bali Concord II, seeking to establish an ASEAN Community by 2020. ASEAN had to remain relevant. ASEAN leaders recognised that integration and community building require some degree of similarities in the economic, political and sociocultural development of member states. There would be a need to include the interests and expectations of the peoples of ASEAN in its goals as well as in the shaping of its decisions (Hernandez, n.d.).

Paragraph 10 of the Bali Concord II stated that ASEAN shall continue to foster a community of caring societies and promote a common regional identity. It was a momentous step towards regional integration. Ever since Bali Concord II, it has been recognised that establishing a community requires a sense of common identity, which ASEAN has actively promoted ever since (Murti, 2016). ASEAN's motto of 'One Vision, One Identity, One Community' was adopted at the 11th ASEAN Summit in December 2005. The motto acknowledges that for the ASEAN Community to be real, fostering a sentiment of 'we-feeling' must be inculcated among the peoples of this region. This 'we-feeling' will inform regional efforts and facilitate better co-operation in the political, security, economic and sociocultural arenas (Lee, 2018).

ASEAN Identity as an Institutional Identity

Currently, the ASEAN identity is largely institutional. It finds expression in all the ASEAN meetings, summits, agreements and blueprints, and is also reflected by all the ASEAN institutions, programmes, initiatives and processes. The most prominent ASEAN institutions and processes are the ASEAN summits and the ASEAN Secretariat. They also include the numerous ASEAN committees and working groups, as well as the hundreds of meetings held every year. Over time, an ASEAN institutional identity has evolved and consolidated. As ASEAN grew, the organisation expanded its range of initiatives to include blueprints and action plans under the ASEAN Economic Community (AEC), the ASEAN Socio-Cultural Community (ASCC) and the ASEAN Political-Security Community (APSC). Hence, ASEAN's institutional identity, which was originally constructed to settle disputes and ensure peace in the region, enlarged in terms of organisational processes but was not as centralised or as bureaucratic as the European Union, which ASEAN is often compared to (ERIA, 2015).

The institutional identity of ASEAN that has become its top brand, the ASEAN Way, is synonymous with how ASEAN engages with both its members and its external partners (Chongkittavorn, 2019). It encompasses the shared principles guiding ASEAN, namely the culture of non-interference and non-intervention to resolve conflicts among the members of ASEAN. The ASEAN Way involves mutual consensus and more informal understandings and loose agreements instead of a more formal and legalistic manner of working, to increase co-operation among its members (Woon, 2016). This way of working has kept ASEAN together despite the diversity in the region from the perspective of socio-cultural, economic and political differences, along with mistrust between different members (Ebbighausen, 2017).

At the same time, the institutional identity of ASEAN includes having an ASEAN emblem, the ASEAN flag, the ASEAN anthem and an annual ASEAN Day. These existential identities were adopted to broaden the appeal of an ASEAN identity for everyday people, instead of the ASEAN identity being institutional and confined to the bureaucratic circles (Chongkittavorn, 2019). The institutional identity of ASEAN, which provides recognition for all, does not engender the 'we-feeling' among the peoples in the region. The perception is that ASEAN is an elitist organisation, where political leaders meet regularly, but their coming together does not affect the bulk of the 650 million people in the region. For ASEAN to matter to these people, they must feel a sense of participation in the various regional processes (Thuzar, 2014).

ASEAN Identity as a Communal Identity

The idea of ASEAN identity as a communal identity stems from the conviction of political leaders that the general population of the region must feel a shared sense of ASEAN belonging in order to support the further development of the organisation. That is, the concept of ASEAN identity has to move from a high-level institutional perspective towards a bottom-up sense of ASEAN commonality, interconnectedness, belonging, shared destiny and greater public engagement, together with a sense of wider ownership of ASEAN initiatives (ERIA, 2015).

Constructing a broader identity and community requires greater public participation and buy-in. It is about extending social relationships (Murti, 2016). The building of an ASEAN communal identity involves the deliberate promotion of initiatives, processes and sentiments of the 'we-feeling', the 'ours feeling' and the feeling that 'we are in this together'. Engendering a deep sense of a shared ASEAN identity and destiny require a more nuanced understanding of ASEAN's past to appreciate ASEAN's future. There is a need to deepen awareness of the interconnectedness among peoples within the region, facilitate people's participation and advance a sense of public ownership of the ASEAN Community (ERIA, 2015).

The quest for an ASEAN identity suffers from a gulf between the official ASEAN vision and a communal ASEAN perspective. The latter requires a conscious effort of engagement in a variety of areas, such as arts, education or tourism, that promote mutual understanding among peoples and create the 'we-feeling'. Developing a community ASEAN identity needs to be a bottom-up initiative rather than a top-down effort, and involves identity formation among peoples, not just states. ASEAN as a regional organisation will have to shed its elite-driven agenda and identity if more people are going to be involved in regional construction. This presents an especially important challenge for ASEAN (Acharya, 2017).

For a long time, ASEAN has been viewed as an elitist organisation largely controlled by diplomats and government officials that are responsible for much of the high-level interactions through governmental and bureaucratic channels. After all, ASEAN is, by definition, an intergovernmental organisation. Over the past decade, the ASEAN organisation has been trying to connect to the grassroots through consultation and engagement with many stakeholders, especially business and civil society, to get their views and feedback regarding making regional policy. However, many such consultations still focus more on form than substance, especially at the summit level (Hoang, 2017). The outreach to the wider public remains limited.

The creation of a communal ASEAN identity is getting ordinary people involved so that they feel they have a direct stake in the association. This is crucial to deepening and speeding up regional integration efforts. Nevertheless, a sense of ASEAN detachment from the general population was highlighted by the Malaysian Prime Minister Najib Razak during the 27th ASEAN Summit in Kuala Lumpur in November 2015. He was quoted as saying that 'many still cannot relate to ASEAN and its significance, they are still unable to appreciate ASEAN' (Lim, 2015). Similarly, Singapore's Prime Minister Lee Hsien Loong, during an interview at the summit, stressed the need for forging a shared ASEAN identity because

> one of the reasons ASEAN finds it difficult to make progress together is [that] there is not a very strong sense of ASEAN identity: it's really a Singaporean identity, a Malaysian identity or Indonesian identity. People don't think of themselves as being ASEAN, except when you have an ASEAN meeting and you have singsongs together and you see what the ideal is. But to go from that ideal to a reality, I think there is some distance yet. (Lim, 2015)

At the 27th ASEAN Summit, the leaders adopted the 'ASEAN 2025: Forging Ahead Together' document as the reference for the next stage of ASEAN community building efforts. The focus of the ASEAN community building in the next ten years will be, among others:

- Placing greater emphasis on the peoples of ASEAN and their well-being.
- Enhancing awareness of ASEAN and its vision of a politically cohesive, economically integrated and socially responsible community.

- Engaging all nationals of ASEAN member states through effective and innovative platforms to promote commitment and identification with ASEAN policies and regional interests.
- Ensuring fundamental freedoms, human rights and better lives for all ASEAN peoples.

The above goals are in principle shared and understood by ASEAN at the institutional and government level, but are limited at the grass-roots level. It remains to be seen whether the peoples of ASEAN know about them, really understand, and share what is being envisioned and captured in the ASEAN 2025 document. Expanding an ASEAN identity into a wider, communal identity is largely a matter of feeling, awareness and connection. ASEAN's history has largely been associated with government activities, which have changed the nature of relations between the ASEAN member states. In moving forward, ASEAN member states should use ASEAN instruments and frameworks by integrating and streamlining them into domestic policies, programmes, practices and modalities (Natalegawa, 2018). Doing so allows for a broad-based ASEAN identity to flourish, as citizens in the region can appreciate and understand ASEAN and how its developments affect their day-to-day lives.

An expanded ASEAN identity could facilitate recognition of the shared historical heritage and cultural traits which existed long before the establishment of ASEAN. It is about celebrating shared stories of the vast interconnected histories of the region instead of narrating the experiences of decolonisation of the many countries in the region. Hence, raising a broader understanding and awareness of ASEAN through greater information sharing and enhancing mutual understanding through people-to-people interaction can allow people to contribute to building ASEAN as a community (Tan, 2020).

ASEAN AWARENESS

Surveys on ASEAN awareness and identity have been conducted since 2007. They show that public awareness of ASEAN in member states appears to be getting stronger (Murti, 2016). Measuring to what extent ordinary people know about ASEAN and what it does to impact on the lives of ordinary people can be challenging. The latest survey is the Poll on ASEAN Awareness commissioned by the ASEAN Secretariat in 2018.

It revealed that 96% of over 4,400 respondents in the ten member states were aware of ASEAN, and 66% of the respondents believed that a shared identity is essential in creating a stronger region. Yet less than one-third claimed to have knowledge of the ASEAN Community and its three pillars. At the same time, 90% of the respondents identified themselves firstly by nationality (98%), then as an Asian (96%) and as an ASEAN citizen (94%) (Tan, 2020).

In 2016, ERIA developed a public opinion survey to ask over 2,000 respondents comprise students, labour, business, government officials, civil society, academia and others, a series of questions regarding the concerns, aspirations and expectations of ASEAN people for ASEAN. The result showed that all respondents were at least 'slightly familiar' with ASEAN, while three-fifths of them were 'moderately' to 'very' familiar with ASEAN. Like the 2018 survey, respondents in the 2016 examination of public opinion were mostly aware of ASEAN's economic pillar.

Interestingly in ERIA's survey, older respondents (those aged 50 or over) generally tended to be more familiar with ASEAN than younger respondents (those aged 15–30). Also, those respondents who were academics and government officials tended to be more aware of ASEAN than the other groups, especially students. In the focus group discussions (FGDs), a number of participants said they had learned about ASEAN first in their primary school, high school or university classes, while there were also a number who had learned about ASEAN only in 2015 from the news and media as the ASEAN member states prepared for the realisation of the AEC.

Besides these two recent surveys, two other known studies on ASEAN awareness targeted undergraduate students. These were conducted by the ISEAS-Yusof Ishak Institute in 2007 and 2014. The first survey, on 'Awareness and Attitudes towards ASEAN', was undertaken in ten universities in the main cities of ASEAN countries, from September to November 2007. The 2014 version aimed to update the findings of the 2007 survey. There was a strong trend in the commonality of responses and overall positive attitudes towards ASEAN throughout the region in both the 2007 and 2014 surveys. Positive attitudes towards ASEAN have remained generally consistent, while awareness and knowledge of ASEAN have shown some increase. Overall, the student survey participants displayed good knowledge of ASEAN, held positive attitudes towards ASEAN and considered themselves 'citizens of ASEAN' (over 80%) (ISEAS and ASEAN Foundation, n.d.).

Subsequent surveys following the two evaluations by the ISEAS-Yusof Ishak Institute indicated a growing awareness of ASEAN—perhaps because of all the news about the establishment of the AEC in 2015. In the ISEAS's 2014 survey of students, only 56% were aware of ASEAN—this jumped to 87% in ERIA's survey in 2016. However, comments during the FGDs made it clear that much of the participants' awareness was related to ASEAN's economic pillar. Indeed, several respondents stated that they believed the AEC and ASEAN were the same. Many respondents could not identify the other two pillars of ASEAN. Considering some of the key findings related to the challenges and aspirations for ASEAN (which are largely non-economic in nature), awareness limited only to ASEAN's economic pillar is an issue that should be addressed (ERIA, 2017a). The 2018 Poll on ASEAN Awareness survey by the ASEAN Secretariat supported this finding, where respondents often conflated the AEC with the ASEAN Community.

THE ASEAN FOUNDATION

ASEAN leaders have recognised that awareness of and contact among the populations of the ASEAN states was limited and, on the institution's 30th anniversary, established the ASEAN Foundation on 15 December 1997. The ASEAN Foundation was formed to try and deepen bonds for a cohesive ASEAN Community and strengthen the sense of an ASEAN identity. Now, 53 years on, ASEAN needs to intensify engagement with its peoples for them to feel the sense of a community through initiatives that revolve around their daily experiences. Since its inception in 1997, the ASEAN Foundation has managed initiatives in the ten ASEAN countries to realise its mandate. The range of projects and activities of the foundation includes training, workshops, scholarship grants, regional forums and meetings, interaction activities and exchanges, seminars and conferences, publicity and promotions. By involving various stakeholders in its efforts, the Foundation creates opportunities for ASEAN people from all walks of life to connect and bond over meaningful, shared experiences.

The ASEAN Foundation's programmes, such as ASEAN Data Science Explorers, the ASEAN Digital Innovation Programme, eMpowering Youths Across ASEAN, and ASEAN Foundation Model ASEAN Meeting, have targeted young people since they comprise 30% of ASEAN's population. The younger generation are the future of ASEAN and the ASEAN Foundation's efforts to strengthen and foster an ASEAN identity. The programmes of the ASEAN Foundation encompass leadership training, capacity-building workshops and interactive forums at the regional level. All these activities cover topics that concern younger people and contribute to addressing ASEAN priorities. These ASEAN Foundation programmes indicate the central objective is 'to promote a people-oriented ASEAN in which all sectors of society are encouraged to participate in, and benefit from, the process of ASEAN integration and community building' (Hoang & Ong, 2020, p. 4). It is hoped that such programmes will nurture future leaders who are familiar with ASEAN issues and who can identify themselves as citizens of ASEAN.

These programmes bring together young people so that they can forge stronger ties and closer relations among themselves. It expands and strengthens the connectivity among the youth of ASEAN, hence contributing to the 'we-feeling'. In a study initiated by C asean, the research team observed that most young people believe the most important factor for successful integration among ASEAN member states is networking. Hence, having the opportunity to meet peers from different countries is invaluable. Networking allows for the development of personal skills and interaction with people from different parts of the ASEAN region. Young people that network with their peers in the region gain cultural awareness as well as technological sophistication. Leveraging on business and technology, as well as art and culture, can influence youth's mindsets and attitudes towards ASEAN. Young people are positive about new business opportunities, curious about cultural differences, comfortable with technology, are open to the world outside their communities, and most importantly, look forward to deepening ASEAN integration (Leopairote et al., 2017).

The ASEAN Foundation, in general, has succeeded in promoting awareness of ASEAN through its different programme activities largely pitched at young people. This is reflected by the high amount of interest in participation in the organisation's activities. Data obtained from an independent evaluation of the ASEAN Foundation's programme in 2019 showed high and rising interest from participants, mostly millennials, towards its programme activities. As these programme activities select participation through a competitive process, interest in applying is high among youth in the region. This is reflected in the increasing number of young applicants over the years for some programme activities of the Foundation. This, to a certain extent, reflects the broader trend in society, especially regarding ASEAN awareness, which has also increased in recent years (Circle Indonesia, 2020).

An independent assessment of the ASEAN Foundation's programme activities in 2019 revealed that they allowed participants to acquire a better and broader awareness of ASEAN through understanding its history and the working relationship among the member states, linked with current socio-economic developments in ASEAN like poverty eradication, environment, migration and so on.

The 'we-feeling' is intensified through exhaustive interactions with participants recruited from the ten ASEAN member states over a course of a few days. The constant interaction, both formally through structured discussions and informally during breaks when mixing together with new friends, reinforced the communal ASEAN identity. In getting to know each other and forming new friends from other ASEAN member states and experiencing the different cultures from the interaction processes, participants can learn first-hand about the culture and customs of each respective member country. In this way, the participants learn about the ASEAN Community in a practical and direct way because of their interactions with their new friends (Circle Indonesia, 2020).

Besides the engagement between participants, some of the programme activities of the Foundation allow participants to engage with different stakeholders such as civil society partners, local institutions and local government bodies. Through interaction with them, the participants are introduced to different perspectives on the management of local governance in some ASEAN member states. That experience has gradually strengthened their awareness of the complexities of issues of governance and systems of government in a number of countries in South East Asia. Such activities have allowed participants to know more about what is happening on the ground, and to understand the diversity of people's lives in the ASEAN countries (Circle Indonesia, 2020). Consequently, the ASEAN Foundation has managed to play an active role in promoting public awareness of ASEAN through investment in learning, deepening connections and linkages, by building people-to-people ties among young people in the region.

The Feeling of ASEAN Citizenship

Developing a sense of ASEAN citizenship requires constant interaction that can lead to social trust (Gnanasagaran, 2018). The constant interface between diplomats and government officials allowed for an 'invisible formal network' to develop in the early days of ASEAN. With the evolution of the ASEAN Community, it becomes more critical to strengthen peoples' participation and their sense of involvement in ASEAN's activities. Interpersonal trust is strong in Asia where people and relationships matter. In the first 30 years of ASEAN's existence, there were solid connections and a strong collective memory of ASEAN among leaders from its member states. As ASEAN moves towards the future, a broader and stronger collective memory must be cultivated among the wider public (Chongkittavorn, 2015). ASEAN citizens must therefore be orientated to adopt the ASEAN Community as one of their primary identity anchors. Establishing an ASEAN Community is inadequate if the people of ASEAN do not feel a sense of identification with this community. They must feel part of it and accrue the benefits of the community building (Hoang & Ong, 2020).

The latest Poll on ASEAN Awareness revealed that across the region, 94% of the public identified themselves as ASEAN citizens at some level. This was an increase of 13 percentage points from the result of a previous study conducted by ERIA in 2017. According to the new research, two-fifths of citizens strongly affiliated themselves with ASEAN. In addition, the sense of belonging is also tied with a feeling of 'shared identity', with the economy being identified as the key factor creating a sense of belonging (ASEAN, 2019b).

The finding is underscored by an online poll that was conducted by Blackbox in Singapore in October 2017 in which 3,040 adult ASEAN citizens were surveyed across the ten ASEAN nations. The study revealed that nearly three in five (58%) of respondents believe that people born and raised in South East Asia have a lot in common, while 31% think they have at least a little in common. Furthermore, in the 2017 ERIA's ASEAN-wide survey where over 2,322 people were asked a series of questions regarding the concerns, aspirations and expectations of ASEAN people for ASEAN. More than three-quarters of all respondents felt from 'moderately' like to 'very much' like ASEAN citizens. Combined with those who indicated feeling somewhat like ASEAN citizens, a sense of ASEAN belonging was shared by virtually all the respondents. Much of this sense of ASEAN identity is shaped by geography. A full sense of ASEAN citizenship may call for ASEAN to be more deeply engaged and more aligned with the concerns and interests of the non-elites. Only 3% of the respondents said they did not feel like they were ASEAN citizens. However, in the Blackbox poll, less than half of the respondents (43%) said they define themselves as South East Asian first ahead of being Asian (51%). Despite the lower self-identification with being South East Asian, nearly three quarters (74%) rate the current state of relationships between ASEAN member states to be positive (Chongkittavorn et al., 2019).

Meanwhile, in a 2014 survey measuring attitudes towards ASEAN among the region's university students, over 80% considered themselves as 'citizens of ASEAN'. Furthermore, most of the respondents perceived ASEAN members as similar culturally but economically and politically different (Thuzar, 2014). The most effective way to inculcate the communal identity is to create opportunities for youth to interact. Greater interaction among the different nationalities of youth in the region certainly builds strong connections and through the sharing of knowledge can spark a robust exchange of ideas that can lead to greater collaboration to grow their countries and ASEAN as a region (Chongkittavorn, 2019).

These survey results can be viewed as the fruition of the ASEAN leaders' community-building aspirations, which started with the association's establishment in 1967 when, as former ASEAN Secretary-General Rodolfo Severino explained, 'Southeast Asia's peoples hardly knew one another, having been cut off and kept isolated from one another by the colonial powers' (Intal et al., 2017, p. 4). The sense of ASEAN belonging, shaped primarily by geographic and ethnic closeness, and facilitated by the ease of travel within the region, could blossom into a full sense of ASEAN citizenship. This can be achieved as ASEAN becomes less elitist, better connected with the average person, and more aligned with the concerns and interests of the ASEAN peoples (Intal et al., 2017).

The Poll on ASEAN Awareness in 2018 surveyed the general public's perspectives on their concerns regarding the ASEAN Community. Interestingly, the top five key regional issues that the general public were concerned about were the following: protection of human rights; combating transnational crime, terrorism and drug trafficking; promotion of peace and stability in the region; prevention of corruption, and promotion of good governance and poverty reduction. The results mirrored the ERIA survey where corruption, income disparity and social inequality are currently considered pressing challenges facing ASEAN. The pressing concerns are non-economic in nature. The implication is that people in ASEAN do not view ASEAN solely from an economic integration perspective, even though the public often equate the ASEAN Community with the economic pillar of ASEAN. This suggests that a key means of deepening the sense of ASEAN belonging, identity and citizenship—and, thus, a deep sense of the ASEAN community—is to address the common concerns of ASEAN people (Intal et al., 2017).

CONCLUSION

ASEAN has successfully cultivated a culture of dialogue and consultations among its member states, allowing them to exchange ideas and address differences. That is ASEAN's biggest achievement. By focusing on confidence-building and surmounting distrust and suspicion, the establishment of ASEAN has resulted in a region that has been largely peaceful for the last 53 years. ASEAN's diplomatic and economic standing have flourished, and ASEAN has often been referred to 'as the most successful regional organization after the European Union' (Mahbubani & Severino, 2014).

ASEAN's success in transforming the relationship among the countries in the region, along with the launch of the ASEAN Community, has led to increased calls for more bottom-up inputs from civil society and grassroots organisations to contribute and co-operate in the community building process. ASEAN citizens are becoming more demanding. Compared to the past, ASEAN leaders are now challenged to show the benefits of ASEAN integration. For ASEAN to thrive, the people have to be satisfied (Chongkittavorn, 2017). For ASEAN to gain wider traction among its people and for regional integration to be successful, it must not only deliver the material benefits but also create ownership and belonging. The ISEAS-Yusof Ishak Institute's ASEAN Studies Centre's State of Southeast Asia 2020 Survey Report revealed that ASEAN member states must do more to deliver tangible results to the citizens of ASEAN and be more proactive in dealing with regional challenges like the situation in Myanmar's Rakhine state. A large majority (79.4%) who were surveyed chose 'ASEAN's tangible benefits are not felt by the people' as their top concern about the regional grouping. Making ASEAN relevant to its people calls for internalising domestic support for regional commitments. ASEAN member states need to push for national implementation and compliance with regional commitments. This is challenging as there are structural constraints, as ASEAN agreements are ratified through national implementation for the benefit of each state's people. Delays in national implementation are the biggest blockage in delivering ASEAN's benefits (Hoang & Ong, 2020).

Increasing the presence of ASEAN in the lives of its citizens across the region would mean addressing regional goals for human development and security, environmental sustainability and a shared sense of community that resonates with national priorities and local needs as well (Thuzar, 2016). Encouraging a strong sense of collaboration, and deepening strong social ties and mutual support reinforces the sustainability of sociocultural integration through the promotion of an ASEAN identity. Sociocultural integration may lead to more problematic discourse regarding how ASEAN functions or the ASEAN Way (Yu, 2020). This is a delicate balance. Nevertheless, the State of Southeast Asia 2020 Survey Report highlights the preference for a more impactful and visible ASEAN for the people of ASEAN to put their support behind the ASEAN Community. Without buy-in and ownership, ASEAN could lose support for its substantive initiatives. This could lead to a decline in ASEAN's perceived influence in the region because of its inability to communicate its work to the public (Hoang & Ong, 2020).

Improved communication and co-ordination can bridge the challenges of implementation and delivery co-ordination in ASEAN. To inspire and move towards the next decade of ASEAN Community building, ASEAN identity building should be less about institutional forms and more about people seeing themselves as belonging to this region. This entails developing friendship to embrace and recognise diversity while realising the similarities that are shared in cultures and heritage of this region. As such, the ASEAN community can move towards truly embodying what it is to 'Think, Feel, and #BeASEAN'.

References

Acharya, A. (2017). The evolution and limitations of ASEAN identity. In A. Baviera, & L. Maramis (Eds.), *Building ASEAN community: Political–security and socio-cultural reflections* (pp. 25–38). ERIA.

ASEAN. (2015). ASEAN community. ASEAN Secretariat. https://asean.org/storage/2012/05/7.-Fact-Sheet-on-ASEAN-Community.pdf. Accessed 12 August 2020.

ASEAN (2017a). First ASEAN Youth Development Index (YDI). ASEAN Secretariat.

ASEAN. (2017b). ASEAN Statistical Report on the Millennium Development Goals. ASEAN Secretariat.

ASEAN. (2019a). Fact Sheet of ASEAN Community. ASEAN Secretariat. https://asean.org/storage/2012/05/39.-December-2019-Fact-Sheet-of-ASEAN-Community.pdf. Accessed 12 August 2020.

ASEAN. (2019b). Poll on ASEAN Awareness 2018 – PoAA Report. ASEAN Secretariat.

ASEAN. (n.d). Infographics on Socio-Demographics and Economics Indicators. https://www.aseanstats.org/infographics/socio-demographic-and-eco nomic. Accessed 12 August 2020.

Chalermpalanupap, T. (2017). The genesis of ASEAN centrality. *ASEAN Focus*, 5 (p. 12). ASEAN Studies Centre, ISEAS-Yusof Ishak Institute.

Chongkittavorn, K. (2015, January 19). ASEAN community without ASEAN identity. *The Nation*. https://humanrightsinasean.info/news/asean-commun ity-without-asean-identity/. Accessed 12 August 2020.

Chongkittavorn, K. (2017, August 7). Will ASEAN still be relevant in 50 years? *Myanmar Times*. https://www.mmtimes.com/opinion/27134-will-asean-still-be-relevant-in-50-years.html. Accessed 18 October 2020.

Chongkittavorn, K. (2019, November 28). ASEAN identity: Imagined or real? *Reporting ASEAN*. https://www.reportingasean.net/asean-identity-ima gined-real. Accessed 12 August 2020.

Chongkittavorn, K., Tan, E., Ruddy, L., & Abdulrahim, R. (2019). Leave no one behind. In F. Kimura, V. Anbumozhi, & H. Nishimura (Eds.), Transforming and Deepening the ASEAN Community (pp.163–174). ERIA.

Circle Indonesia. (2020). Impact Assessment Report of ASEAN Foundation Programme 2015–2019. ASEAN Foundation (unpublished).

Das, K., Diaan-Yi, L., Madgavkar, A., Russell, K., Seong, J., Sneader, K., Tonby, O., & Woetzel, J. (2018). Outperformers Maintaining ASEAN Countries' Exceptional Growth. Discussion Paper. McKinsey Global Institute, September 2018. https://www.mckinsey.com/~/media/McKinsey/Featured%20Insights/Asia%20Pacific/Outperformers%20Maintaining%20A SEAN%20countries%20exceptional%20growth/MGI-Outperformers-ASEAN-Discussion-paper.pdf. Accessed 14 August 2020.

Ebbighausen, R. (2017, August 7). The ASEAN way: Where is it leading? Deutsche Welle. https://www.dw.com/en/the-asean-way-where-is-it-leading/a-39998187. Accessed 12 October 2020.

ERIA [Economic Research Institute for ASEAN and East Asia]. (2015). Engendering a Deep Sense of ASEAN Identity and Density. In P. Jr. Intal, V. Anbumozhi, F. Zen, H. Nishimura, & R. Prassetya (Eds.), *Framing the*

ASEAN Socio-Cultural Community Post-2015 (pp. 209–231). ERIA Research Project Report 2014–01, ERIA.

Gnanasagaran, A. (2018, June 10). Developing an ASEAN citizenry. *The ASEAN Post*. https://theaseanpost.com/article/developing-asean-citizenry. Accessed 8 September 2020.

Hernandez, C. (n.d). Institutional building through an ASEAN charter. https://www.kas.de/c/document_library/get_file?uuid=c81cf9d9-b4d1-107b-6692-86b73e575ce8&groupId=252038. Accessed 21 September 2020.

Hoang, T. H. (2017). Five decades of ASEAN's evolution. *ASEAN Focus*, 5 (pp. 2–3). ASEAN Studies Centre, ISEAS-Yusof Ishak Institute.

Hoang, T. H., & Ong, G. (2020, March 12). Surveying ASEAN's horizons: The State of Southeast Asia's 2020 Key Takeaways. *Perspective*, 15. ISEAS-Yusof Ishak Institute. https://www.iseas.edu.sg/wp-content/uploads/2015/11/ISEAS_Perspective_2020_15.pdf. Accessed 14 August 2020.

HV, V., Thompson, F., & Tonby, O. (2014, May 1). Understanding ASEAN: Seven things you need to know. McKinsey & Company. https://www.mckinsey.com/industries/public-and-social-sector/our-insights/understanding-asean-seven-things-you-need-to-know. Accessed 12 August 2020.

Intal, P., Jr., Ruddy, L., Setyadi, E., Suhud, Y., & Hapsari, T. S. (2017). Integrative Chapter. In P. Jr. Intal, & L. Ruddy (Eds.), *Voices of ASEAN: What does ASEAN mean to ASEAN Peoples?* ERIA.

ISEAS and ASEAN Foundation. (n.d). An Update of ASEAN Awareness and Attitudes — A Ten Nation Survey Fact Sheet on the Preliminary Findings. https://www.iseas.edu.sg/wp-content/uploads/2015/04/FactSheet_ASEANAwarenessSurvey2015-revised.pdf. Accessed 12 August 2020.

Lee, J. J. (2018). Colonialism and ASEAN identity: Inherited 'mental barriers' hindering the formation of a collection ASEAN Identity. *Kyoto Review of Southeast Asia*. https://kyotoreview.org/trendsetters/colonialism-asean-identity. Accessed 14 August 2020.

Leopairote, K., Promyotin, M., & Giorgio, S. (2017). Leveraging on Business, Art/Culture, Technology, and Networking in Building ASEAN's Young Generation in an Integrated ASEAN. In A. Baviera & A. Maramis (Eds.), *Building ASEAN community: Political security and socio-cultural reflections* (pp. 194–207). ERIA.

Lim, Y. L. (2015, November 23). ASEAN summit: Forging shared ASEAN identity a top priority: PM Lee. *Straits Times*. https://www.straitstimes.com/asia/se-asia/asean-summit-forging-shared-asean-identity-a-top-priority-pm-lee. Accessed on 7 September 2020.

Mahbubani, K., & Severino, R. (2014). ASEAN: The way forward. Commentary, McKinsey & Company. https://www.mckinsey.com/industries/public-and-social-sector/our-insights/asean-the-way-forward. Accessed 14 August 2020.

Murti, G. L. (2016). ASEAN's 'One identity and one community': A slogan or a reality? *Yale Journal of International Affairs*. http://yalejournal.org/art icle_post/asean-one-identity-one-community. Accessed 12 August 2020.

Natalegawa, M. (2018, May 6). ASEAN must be more than convenor of meetings: Diplomat. Viet Nam News. https://vietnamnews.vn/world/427450/asean-must-be-more-than-convener-of-meetings-diplomat.html. Accessed 12 October 2020.

Ong, K. Y. (2007). Speech by Secretary-General of ASEAN at the Opening Ceremony of the Annual German Ambassadors' Conference 'ASEAN at the Heart of Dynamic Asia', 3 September 2007. https://asean.org/?static_post=speech-by-secretary-general-of-asean-h-e-ong-keng-yong-at-the-opening-cer emony-of-the-annual-german-ambassadors-conference-asean-at-the-heart-of-dynamic-asia-berlin-3-september-2007. Accessed 6 September 2020.

Ong, K. Y. (2009, 17 December). In defence of ASEAN. *The diplomat*. https://thediplomat.com/2009/12/in-defence-of-asean. Accessed 12 August 2020.

Tan, J. (2020, May). Celebrating ASEAN identity: Now and beyond. *The ASEAN*, 1, 26–27. https://asean.org/storage/2017/09/The-ASEAN-Mag azine-Issue-1-May-2020.pdf. Accessed 14 August 2020.

Thuzar, M. (2014, December). ASEAN integration: Translating vision into reality. *Kyoto Review of Southeast Asia*, 16. https://kyotoreview.org/yav/asean-integration-translating-a-vision-into-reality. Accessed 14 August 2020.

Thuzar, M. (2015, March 13). ASEAN community 2015: What's in for the region? *Perspectives*, 13. ISEAS-Yusof Ishak Institute. https://www.iseas. edu.sg/wp-content/uploads/pdfs/ISEAS_Perspective_2015_9.pdf. Accessed 7 September 2020.

Thuzar, M. (2016, September 3). To remain relevant, ASEAN needs a stronger nerve centre. Nikkei Asia. https://asia.nikkei.com/Economy/Moe-Thu zar-To-remain-relevant-ASEAN-needs-a-stronger-nerve-center. Accessed 18 October 2020.

Yu, T. (2020, June 5). What does a new magazine tell us about ASEAN's push for regional integration? *The Diplomat*. https://thediplomat.com/2020/06/what-does-a-new-magazine-tell-us-about-aseans-push-for-regional-integr ation. Accessed 18 October 2020.

Woon, S. (2016). ASEAN at the crossroads: An analysis of the ASEAN way and its approach in conflict resolution. Unpublished thesis, Hwa Chong Insti- tution. https://www.researchgate.net/publication/308515608_ASEAN_at_ the_Crossroads_An_Analysis_of_the_ASEAN_Way_and_its_Approach_in_Con flict_Resolution. Accessed 12 October 2020.

Confidence, Trust and Empathy: Threat Perception and the Prospects for Peace in Korea and the South China Sea

David A. Welch

Two of the most dangerous flashpoints in the world today are the Korean Peninsula and the South China Sea. In the former case, the crucial issue is whether North Korea should be permitted to have nuclear weapons and the missiles to deliver them, and, if so, under what restrictions. In the latter, the crucial issue is whether China should be permitted to exercise exclusive jurisdiction or control over one of the world's most important sea routes.

Framing these issues this way presumes that both North Korea and China represent serious strategic threats and that solving these problems peacefully represents a serious diplomatic challenge. How might we be confident that neither North Korea nor China will threaten others' vital interests? Can they be trusted to respect international agreements, or international law? In recent years, anxieties about these issues have preoccupied foreign and defence officials everywhere from Washington to Tokyo to Seoul to Manila to Hanoi to Canberra to Wellington, and to capitals of countries everywhere who value and seek to uphold what

D. A. Welch (✉)
University of Waterloo, Waterloo, ON, Canada
e-mail: dawelch@uwaterloo.ca

© The Author(s), under exclusive license to Springer Nature
Singapore Pte Ltd. 2022
R. Patman et al. (eds.), *From Asia-Pacific to Indo-Pacific*, Global Political
Transitions, https://doi.org/10.1007/978-981-16-7007-7_12

257

we have come, rather nostalgically, to call the 'rules-based international order' (Strating, 2019) or to promote what many are rather hopefully beginning to call a 'free and open Indo-Pacific' (Szechenyi & Hosoya, 2019). How serious are the North Korean and Chinese challenges? How can we know? Are we responding appropriately and constructively, or inappropriately and dangerously?

These are the questions I seek to address in this chapter. I will argue that the answers depend crucially upon psychological considerations rarely taken into account in the power-political style of analysis that dominates Asia-Pacific security discourse. I will also argue that the prescriptions that follow from that style of analysis may well themselves represent serious threats to regional peace and stability. Put another way: responding appropriately to North Korea's nuclear programme or China's 'aggressive behaviour' in the South China Sea requires first and foremost accurately diagnosing what drives North Korea and China, and that this, in turn, requires cultivating empathy. Empathy, once achieved, would, I believe, lead to a rapid de-escalation of tensions in the South China Sea, because China is not, in fact, engaged in the project of regional domination that most countries fear. It is less clear what empathy would achieve in the case of North Korea. Possibilities range from identifying currently unknown 'win-sets' (Putnam, 1988) to an even more dire estimation of the North Korean threat. But to make this case, I must begin with some crucial conceptual brush-clearing.

KEY CONCEPTS

'Confidence' and 'trust' are terms widely used not only in Asia-Pacific security discourse, but in international security discourse globally. They are not, however, particularly clearly defined or distinguished, in part because there are few isomorphic translations to other languages. Despite the imprecision of these terms, the purpose of building confidence or trust is relatively clear: to reduce tension and the dangers of accidental or inadvertent war arising primarily from misperception (Capie & Evans, 2002, pp. 88, 93, 246). Confidence-building measures (CBMs)—sometimes called confidence- and security-building measures (CSBMs)—include, for example, prior notification of military exercises; invitations to observe military manoeuvres; other forms of military-to-military contacts; co-operation on peripheral security matters of joint concern (e.g. combating drug trafficking or other forms of transnational crime); hotlines; and

other steps to increase transparency so as to enable actual or potential adversaries to see more easily that their intentions are defensive and
benign.

CBMs can be credited with significant historical achievements, perhaps
the most important of which was facilitating a peaceful end to the Cold
War. By clearing roadblocks to meaningful co-operation in arms control,
they provided opportunities for US and Soviet leaders and officials to get
to know each other better, to discover shared interests and concerns, to
overcome (or at least moderate) their mutual suspicions and to rethink
their conceptions of threat. They gave leaders a chance, in short, to
improve *empathy*.

'Empathy' is not a term commonly encountered in Asia-Pacific security discourse, unfortunately. In my view, empathy is a vital condition
for a stable peace. Before I attempt to justify this claim, however, I
must first clarify the relationships between confidence, trust and empathy.
I would like to suggest that it would be helpful to settle on conventional definitions of these terms that, when translated into the dominant
languages of the region, denote—and can reliably be known by others to
denote—exactly the same thing.

The necessity for linguistic landscaping arises as a result of the unfortunate fact that English has become the dominant language of global
communication. This is unfortunate because it is messy and unsystematic.
As a living language, English evolves over time, adding far more than it
sheds and embracing usage without much regard for formal constraints
(grammatical, syntactical, typographical and so on). The result is that
many commonly used words become overburdened with possible meanings, some of which are synonymous with other words' possible meanings,
and some of which are not. Among the oddities of the English language
is the fact that some words can mean both one thing and its opposite.
To 'sanction' behaviour, for example, can mean either to approve it or to
punish it.

Dominant English-language dictionaries define confidence as trust and
trust as confidence in at least one of the typically several definitions they
offer for each.[1] This both reflects and sanctions (in the sense of approves)
common usage—so it is no wonder that people readily use confidence and
trust interchangeably. But there are slight nuances in the ways dictionaries

---

[1] This is true, for example, of the Oxford English Dictionary, Merriam-Webster's, and
Collins.

typically define these terms, and these nuances open up a window for clear, conventional understandings that are more useful both analytically and prescriptively.

Confidence

If there is a standard reference for the meanings of English words, it is the *Oxford English Dictionary* (OED), whose first two definitions of 'confidence' are as follows:

1. The mental attitude of trusting in or relying on a person or thing; firm trust, reliance, faith.
2. The feeling sure or certain of a fact or issue; assurance, certitude; assured expectation.

For the moment, let us ignore the references to 'trust' and 'trusting' in the first definition, as I wish to distinguish these words from 'confidence' as far as possible. The first point to note is that both definitions refer to a subjective state of mind: confidence is an *attitude* or a *feeling*. There is some evidence to suggest that confidence is not a uniquely human characteristic—our closest animal relatives, at least, may also be capable of it (Beran et al., 2015)—but confidence is, in any case, a conscious judgement.

Appropriately, confidence admits of degree. 'I am somewhat confident that my team will win the championship next year' is less likely to provoke debate than 'I am very confident that my team will win the championship next year'. In contrast, anything less emphatic than 'I am very confident that the sun will rise tomorrow' is likely to raise eyebrows. In the latter case, we might well wonder why someone would use the word 'confident' instead of the word 'know'—which helpfully points towards the conclusion that 'confidence' is a word best reserved for cases where there is at least room in principle for reasonable doubt.

The earliest understandings of CBMs referred explicitly to confidence in a particular set of propositions. Prior notification of military exercises, exchanges of observers, increased military transparency and the like all served to alleviate anxieties that military exercises were a cover for a surprise attack and to reassure that they were intended to hone defensive rather than offensive skills. This sort of confidence could be expressed thus: 'I am confident that my adversary does not pose an immediate threat to my security. He does not, because he cannot — at least, not yet'.

Trust

The OED defines trust as 'confidence in or reliance on some quality or attribute of a person or thing, or the truth of a statement'. At first glance, this would not appear to be an especially helpful definition, because it does not differ dramatically from either of the two definitions of confidence that we discussed earlier. In fact, taken together these definitions are not merely unsatisfactory; they are circular. If confidence means trust and trust means confidence, then confidence means confidence and trust means trust. With dictionaries like that, who needs enemies?

Note, however, the reference to 'some quality or attribute of a person' (for the moment let us ignore the phrase 'or thing'). In interpersonal relationships, the word 'trust' usually arises with reference to promise-keeping, truth-telling, or acting out of concern for one another's well-being. I am unlikely to say, 'I trusted you!' unless (a) I expected you to do something of which I approve and you did not; (b) I expected you not to do something of which I disapprove and you did; or (c) my trust proved to be warranted and I wish to acknowledge your trustworthiness. A classic trust-building exercise widely used in organisational settings involves asking people to fall backward, blindly hoping that their colleagues will catch them, preventing certain pain and possible injury or death.[2] An unwillingness to fall backward is a clear behavioural indicator of a lack of trust.

Relationships with very high levels of trust are devoid of suspicion and are typically characterised by generalised reciprocity. Trust is an important and underappreciated concept in International Relations (Kydd 2005). While states are only persons in an abstract sense, decision-makers can and do routinely distinguish states they trust from states they do not trust. Interstate trust is highest in so-called security communities in which the threat or use of force plays no role in the management of disputes (Adler & Barnett, 1998).[3] The United States and Canada, for example,

---

[2] For an example, see Trust Fall Finale: Teambuilding and Leadership Development, https://www.youtube.com/watch?v=7z1tTp2WHeU. Accessed 26 April 2020.

[3] At present, security communities exist in and between Europe, North America, Australasia and Japan.

are members of a security community. It has been more than 80 years since the two countries updated plans for war with one another (Preston, 1977), and today neither country bothers to defend their border. The prospect of a United States–Canadian war at present seems downright laughable. Indeed, the box-office success of comedies such as *Canadian Bacon* (http://www.imdb.com/title/tt0109370) depends upon it.

Note that CBMs add nothing to a relationship characterised by high levels of trust. The absence of anxiety is not a function of *situational considerations* such as a technical incapacity to launch a surprise attack, but of *dispositional considerations*. In point of fact, the United States could, if it wanted, conquer Canada militarily in at most a week or two. But it is not so inclined. The two countries are not adversaries. It is precisely this difference in the nature of a relationship that explains (for example) why the United States is concerned and alarmed by the prospect of Iran acquiring nuclear weapons, but not at all concerned or alarmed by the fact that the United Kingdom or France already has them.

Technically, trust so understood is, in fact, a species of confidence. It, too, is a mindstate—an attitude or a feeling—reflecting a judgement of propositional truth-value. It can also be misplaced, though when this happens it triggers a distinctive, intense kind of hurt and disappointment. But though trust is a special kind of confidence, leveraging the potential utility of having two different words available to us requires that we be careful not to use them interchangeably. We should focus on how they differ, not on what they share. The key difference is that trust is an appropriate word to use when the ground of confidence lies in the character and disposition of parties and in the nature of their relationship. When one's subjective sense of security depends entirely upon situational constraints rather than dispositional considerations, trust is an unsuitable word.

Empathy

The OED definition of empathy is 'the power of projecting one's personality into (and so fully comprehending) the object of contemplation'. Notice that empathy is a *power*, or a *capacity*, not an attitude or a feeling. Right away we can see that empathy differs in kind from both confidence and trust.

While the OED definition is somewhat vague (exactly what does it mean to 'project one's personality into' an object of contemplation?), there are common metaphors that capture the idea extremely well—for example, putting oneself into another person's shoes, or seeing the world through another person's eyes. Importantly, the definition says nothing about sharing that perspective or agreeing with it. For this we have another word: sympathy.

Now, like most interesting concepts in English, empathy is defined in various ways by various dictionaries and often used by people very loosely. As a result, it is not always clear which of several possible meanings of a word one has in mind at any given time. Often people are not even aware that they are sliding back and forth between different meanings. Even smart people can fall prey to this tendency. A prominent psychologist at Yale University, for example, penned a widely read piece in *The New Yorker* that failed to distinguish empathy not only from sympathy but also from compassion and pity, rendering his argument incoherent (Bloom, 2013; Welch, 2013). The example nicely illustrates the importance of specifying exactly what sense of a word one has in mind when one uses it.

Constraining the definition of empathy to the capacity to put oneself in another's shoes is useful because it is precise. The importance of empathy to conflict management so conceived cannot be overstated. Without understanding how others see a problem—what they believe, what they fear, what they want, what they need, how they feel—one can neither sensibly identify outcomes they would consider acceptable, nor give sustained attention to exploring possible ways of reaching them. Former US Secretary of Defense Robert S. McNamara's primary conclusion from his own soul-searching at the end of his career about his role in world affairs was that empathy is crucially important, a point he made repeatedly in his own writings and in Errol Morris's Academy Award-winning documentary *The Fog of War* (Blight & Lang, 2005; McNamara, 1995; McNamara & Blight, 2001; McNamara et al., 1999).[4]

Of course, cultivating empathy is not a sure-fire recipe for peace. Sometimes knowing one's adversary's mind will serve only to dispel hope for

---

[4] Those who knew McNamara well know that he ultimately came to believe that the failure of US leaders to cultivate empathy with Vietnam in the 1960s resulted in the unnecessary deaths of tens of thousands of American soldiers and perhaps as many as three million Vietnamese. This realisation haunted him. The trailer for *The Fog of War* (https://www.youtube.com/watch?v=VgA98V1Ubk8), ends with McNamara both confessing a tragic lack of empathy while in office and demonstrating his capacity to acquire it later: 'We saw Vietnam as an element of the Cold War—not what [the Vietnamese] saw it as: a civil war. We were wrong'.

a peaceful solution to a dispute. A greater degree of empathy with Adolf Hitler in the 1930s would only have convinced European leaders of the inevitability of war, because war is what Hitler wanted (Bullock, 1971; Hill, 1968; Watt, 1989). But even in this (almost certainly rare) case, more empathy is better than less. The Second World War would have been shorter and less costly if European leaders had seen it coming sooner and had started to prepare accordingly.

CONFIDENCE, TRUST AND EMPATHY: CONNECTIONS, PATHWAYS, SEQUENCING

In the hope that I have made a good case for restricting the use of these three terms in Asia-Pacific security discourse to the meanings specified here, what are the logical and empirical connections between them? How might they be leveraged to the cause of peace?

It is clear that empathy is a necessary condition for trust—at least, for trust that is not misplaced. Judging someone well-disposed and reliable enough not to pose a threat requires imagining correctly that they see you in a positive light. Empathy is not, however, a sufficient condition for trust, as the Hitler example shows. Does the causal arrow point equally in the opposite direction? Perhaps ironically, the answer is no. Trust represents certainty that someone's well-meaning disposition will endure, and that certainty may blind you to signs of change. Most people are caught by surprise when they discover that their spouses or partners have been unfaithful. Trust tends to perpetuate trust, and an erosion of its foundations can go unnoticed as a result. Small wonder that 'trusting someone blindly' is never thought of as a good thing.

Empathy is neither a necessary nor a sufficient condition for confidence. One is likely to be utterly incapable of empathising with a violent criminal, but as long as he is locked away in a secure prison, one can have confidence that he is not a threat. Recall that as I am using the term here, confidence is a feeling of relative security that rests entirely on situational factors. On the other hand, confidence is a permissive condition for empathy. Cultivating empathy with someone is almost certainly easier when one is not preoccupied with fear that she will attack you at any moment. A generalised relaxation of tensions opens up spaces for creative interactions that may well lead to improved empathy. I say 'may well', because it is possible that it may not. Sometimes people are simply unfathomable no matter how many opportunities one has to interact with them.

I have already argued that trust is a special kind of confidence, so there is a clear logical connection between these two concepts. Is there also an empirical one? If we look at the history of security communities, we can see clearly that they evolve over time—in almost all cases (Australasia would appear to be the only exception) from previously hostile relationships. There is a natural (but not inevitable) progression from active hostility to confidence to trust. Andrew Kydd has argued — convincingly, in my view—that this progress is facilitated by a 'virtuous spiral' for which reciprocity is key (Kydd, 2005). But by the same token, breakdowns in reciprocity can interrupt, set back or destroy the progression altogether. It is interesting but not entirely surprising that some former Soviet bloc countries such as Poland and the Czech Republic integrated into the European security community relatively smoothly once the Berlin Wall fell; there were no major missteps or misunderstandings to disrupt the process. Russia, on the other hand, did not. The 'realist' explanation for this is quite simply that Russia is a great power, and great powers tend to be rivals unless they face a common threat. But this explanation is too abstract to be compelling, particularly in view of the fact that some analysts actively predicted Russia's smooth integration. A more persuasive explanation turns on the lack of empathy that prevented the final step from confidence to trust. At the end of the Cold War, the United States saw Russia as defeated and diminished, whereas Russia saw itself as America's equal. The many slights and disappointments Moscow felt from Washington undermined early progress towards a more positive relationship (Pouliot, 2010).

Just as a virtuous spiral can smooth the way for trust, the opposite vicious spiral can in principle undo it. At present there are no empirical examples of genuine security communities unravelling, but there are many historical cases of countries with generally peaceful and sometimes even friendly relations sliding into hostility and war. Sometimes, no doubt, the quality of the relationship in a vicious spiral simply reflects the true feelings of the parties, in which case empathy can shine a bright light on it but will not stop it. But my sense is that in far too many cases conflict arises not because the parties are actively hostile, but because they fail to understand that they are not. In these cases, empathy can help reverse a vicious spiral and increase the odds of long-term genuine trust. Put another way: in dangerous situations where conflicts of interest are more apparent than real, confidence-building and empathy-building are both needed to create space for trust.

CBMs are useful preliminary technical exercises to increase transparency and to establish norms and procedures intended simply to reduce fears of imminent or inadvertent conflict so that serious efforts to work towards trust by building empathy can begin. Empathy-building measures, such as Track 1.5 or Track II dialogues, may then reduce mutual misperceptions of threat (Jones, 2015). Trust-building measures, on this view, are an empty set. Trust develops organically as parties come to know each other better, as the fear or expectation of ill will and false dealing fades away (assuming no duplicity), and as they begin to develop the kind of relationship in which the threat or use of force to resolve disputes ultimately becomes unthinkable. This organic process cannot begin until the obstacles to trust are cleared, which requires building empathy. One might think of empathy, therefore, as the transmission belt connecting confidence to trust.

FROM THEORY TO PRACTICE: THREAT AND THREAT PERCEPTION IN KOREA AND THE SOUTH CHINA SEA

How do these concepts help us understand the challenge of threat perception and conflict management on the Korean Peninsula and in the South China Sea? In both cases, well-founded trust is in short supply at the moment. Confidence, such as it is, rests primarily upon deterrence and the concomitant hope that leaders in Pyongyang and Beijing understand that the costs of conflict would far outweigh any possible gain. To assess the robustness of deterrent-based confidence and the prospects of building genuine trust requires cultivating empathy, which is also in short supply.

North Korea

North Korea—formally, the Democratic People's Republic of Korea—is an authoritarian dictatorship with an all-powerful 'Supreme Leader', Kim Jong Un. The big question, quite simply, is whether Kim more closely resembles former Romanian dictator Nicolae Ceauşescu—a run-of-the-mill autocrat concerned primarily with maintaining his personal power, wealth and prestige—or Hitler, an opportunistic aggressor with a thirst for glory that could only be satisfied by grand historical achievements such as the conquest of Europe and the creation of a 'Thousand-Year Reich'.

Kim's father, Kim Jong Il clearly fell into the former category, famously contenting himself with personal pleasures (see, e.g.Greene, 2011; Collis, 2013). In contrast, Kim Jong Un's grandfather, Kim Il Sung, more closely resembled the latter, though his ambition appears to have been limited to unifying all of Korea under his personal rule (Weathersby, 1995).

It is easy to see the importance of empathy for diagnosing the real problem, if there is one, with North Korea possessing nuclear weapons and strategic ballistic missiles. If Kim is like his father, the international community can probably rest easy. North Korean nuclear weapons would serve in this context solely as insurance against the Kim regime suffering the fate (for example) of Iraq's Saddam Hussein, a fellow member of US President George W. Bush's infamous 'Axis of Evil'. But if Kim is like his grandfather—or wishes to surpass his grandfather in the North Korean pantheon—then, having achieved a certain level of nuclear capability, and having convinced himself of his ability to cow or neuter international opposition, he might well roll the dice and attempt to reunite the two Koreas by means of nuclear blackmail.

In one sense, the fact that North Korea has one-man rule should make it relatively easy to cultivate the requisite empathy. It is, after all, comparatively easy to reconstruct the wants, needs, fears, perceptions and beliefs of one man rather than a large decision-making group. But North Korea is famously secretive, and, compared to most world leaders, Kim is relatively mysterious. As far as we know, there are no good human intelligence sources anywhere near Kim and his inner circle. Everything we know about him comes either from statements or actions that are ambiguous or possibly deliberately deceptive, or from personal interactions with a relatively small number of people of dubious reliability, such as his high-school classmates in Switzerland, Chinese President Xi Jinping, US President Donald Trump and the former basketball star Dennis Rodman.

The bulk of the available evidence and testimony, low-grade though it may be, suggests that Kim is clever, confident, outgoing, affable, domineering, intolerant of dissent, acutely sensitive to slights and something of a bully. He is also capable of ruthless decision-making and action to quell real or imagined threats to his position—though whether this reflects dispositional or situational factors (specifically, regime dynamics) remains an open question (Immelman, 2018; Kuo, 2017). But personality traits tell us nothing about goals. Both status quo autocrats and megalomaniacs can be clever, confident, outgoing, affable, domineering, intolerant, sensitive, ruthless bullies. Most public commentary and analysis inclines towards the benign autocrat/'rational actor' view of Kim, but there are grounds to worry that this is incorrect. Kim came to power at an unusually young age, clearly groomed to rule, and by now has become accustomed to absolute power and fawning adoration. These can have real physiological consequences over time. Adoration and power trigger high levels of dopamine production, an addictive neurotransmitter closely associated with the pleasure reaction in the brain. In high doses and over an extended period of time, dopamine can lead to 'a sense of personal destiny, risk-taking, preoccupation with the cosmic or religion, and emotional detachment that can lead to ruthlessness, and an obsession with achieving goals and conquests' (Al-Rodhan, 2014). Dopamine-addled dictators typically lack empathy, think themselves infallible, and believe they are invincible, much as Hitler did when he ordered, then disastrously micromanaged, Germany's Russian campaign in the Second World War (Middleton, 1981). Quite possibly, Kim's dopamine addiction is in the process of convincing him that he has bested his international opposition and that at some point soon he will have the weapons he needs to succeed where his godlike grandfather failed.

If this is the case, President Trump will have played no small role in feeding Kim's delusions of grandeur. Although Trump took a hard line against North Korean nuclear and missile capability early in his administration, threatening to rain 'fire and fury' if Kim did not bend to his will and denuclearise (Baker & Choe, 2017), Kim easily managed to neuter Trump in personal encounters in Singapore, Hanoi and at the DMZ (Kheel, 2019; Stracqualursi, 2018). Trump 'fell in love' with Kim and subsequently took his eye off the ball (Manchester, 2018). Subsequently, Trump redirected the bulk of his ire towards Seoul, increasingly stridently demanding that South Korea pay more to host US forces on the Korean Peninsula (Starr & Atwood, 2020), potentially undermining the deterrence of North Korea.

If Trump is indeed responsible for fuelling Kim's ambitions, it will be in large part because of his own incapacity for empathy. In many respects, Trump's personality mirrors Kim's. He, too, is confident, outgoing, affable, domineering, intolerant of dissent, acutely sensitive to slights and something of a bully.[5] He also basks in adoration and craves attention—possibly even more than Kim does. Where he fares poorly in comparison is on the dimension of cleverness. Trump, unlike Kim, can be played. This combination of gullibility and lack of empathy has clearly led to a sense of misplaced trust.

The South China Sea

Informed analysts vary widely in their general characterisations of Chinese wants, needs, fears, perceptions and beliefs. At one end of the spectrum are what we might call 'China risers' who see Chinese leaders as confident, ambitious, obsessed with restoring China's historical greatness and determined to recreate a 'Middle Kingdom' order that would reduce neighbouring countries to tributaries or vassals (Danner & Martín, 2019; Jacques, 2009; Mearsheimer, 2010). At the other end are what we might call 'regime pessimists' who see Chinese leaders as vulnerable and panicked by threats to Communist Party rule (Chang, 2001; Pei, 2012, 2013). My own view accords more closely with the latter than the former. Elsewhere I have argued that China is approaching its limits to growth and would be unable to exercise hegemony even if it wanted to (Welch, 2020; see also Allan et al., 2018). Moreover, the regime faces an unprecedented legitimacy crisis. As China is no longer in any meaningful sense a 'communist' country—capitalism with Chinese characteristics long ago displaced Maoism—the legitimacy of Communist Party rule no longer rests on ideology and now instead rests on two increasingly shaky pillars: (1) high year-on-year economic growth rates that underwrite the regime's implicit deference-for-welfare-gains deal with the Chinese people; and (2) the ability of the regime to uphold and defend China's dignity, prestige, sovereignty and territorial integrity. Demographic, environmental, financial and other factors threaten the former; Hong Kong, Taiwan and to a lesser extent both Xinjiang and Tibet, acutely threaten the latter.[6]

Part of what makes such divergent interpretations of China possible is the fact that, while the regime takes great pains to present a public image

---

[5] Trump is also clearly at least as narcissistic as Kim, but whether he technically satisfies the diagnostic requirements of narcissistic personality disorder is a matter of debate (he exhibits the traits, but not the dysfunctions; see Frances 2017; Lee 2019).

[6] The fact that China spends vastly more on domestic than international security strongly suggests that the regime feels extremely vulnerable (Tan 2018).

of unity and confidence—and despite the fact that President Xi, like Kim Jong Un, is an unusually powerful autocrat—China is a large, complex state with active factional and bureaucratic rivalries bubbling just below the surface. Xi may be receptive to one ministry on one issue at one time, and another ministry on the same issue at another. This has certainly been the case with respect to the South China Sea, and, as we shall see, is largely responsible for the low level of international empathy on this particular issue.[7]

To understand Chinese policy in the South China Sea, it is necessary to recognise that for most of its long history the South China Sea was, in effect, a regional commons in which no polity of any kind claimed or exercised what we would today call 'sovereignty' or 'maritime jurisdiction' (Hayton, 2014). Only in the aftermath of the Second World War—in the process of decolonisation—did littoral states begin to stake sovereignty claims. The Republic of China's claims were the most extensive. In 1947, the Nationalist Government of Chiang Kai-shek published a map on which it delineated its claims by means of an 11-dash line encompassing all of the Spratly and Paracel Islands, Scarborough Shoal and Macclesfield Bank. When Mao Zedong's communist forces took over in mainland China, they adopted the Nationalist claim, though later dropped two of the lines. The infamous 'nine-dash line' has driven much of the anxiety about China's claims in the South China Sea since then, essentially because Beijing refused to specify whether it denoted territorial claims alone or maritime claims as well. Taiwan, in contrast, would eventually clarify that it considered the nine-dash line nothing more than a cartographic convenience delineating their territorial claims; but neighbouring countries feared—and Beijing refused to explicitly deny—that the People's Republic of China considered the entire South China Sea to be, in effect, a Chinese lake.

By means of textbooks, maps and official statements, the Chinese people have been led to believe—wrongly—that the South China Sea was indisputably China's and had been 'from time immemorial' (Hayton, 2018). Socialisation via education is, in fact, a common process occasionally used deliberately by political elites to bolster nationalist sentiment and cultivate domestic support for maritime or territorial claims (see, e.g. Escudé, 1992). In the case of China, it worked too well. By insisting

---

[7] A fuller exposition may be found in Raymond and Welch (in progress).

that China enjoyed sweeping rights in the South China Sea, the regime inadvertently staked its legitimacy, in part, on defending those rights. The problem was that they could neither justify nor defend expansive claims after having ratified the United Nations Convention on the Law of the Sea (UNCLOS) in 1996. UNCLOS swept aside all previous bases for maritime claims, replacing them with a single, systematic, codified body of positive international law. UNCLOS provided no basis for 'historic' or 'archipelagic' claims to the South China Sea as a whole and specified a regime of maritime entitlements that dramatically constrained what China—or any other country—could legally claim.

The year 2012 was a turning point in Chinese policy on the South China Sea. Until then, Beijing had pursued a policy of quiet intransigence while making a show of engaging in dialogue with competing claimants— a policy we might label 'obstructive engagement'—hoping that in the fullness of time opposition to its claims would wear down. It manifestly did not. In 2012, China suddenly shifted to a policy of assertive unilateralism that included issuing biometric passports featuring the nine-dash line ('China's passport move stokes South China Sea dispute', 2012), passing laws extending administrative jurisdiction over disputed features, seizing control of Scarborough Shoal from the Philippines (Bradsher, 2014), and embarking upon an ambitious land-reclamation programme designed to turn the seven low-grade territorial features China controlled in the Spratly Islands into substantial artificial islands with the infrastructure required to operate an intended Air Defence Identification Zone (ADIZ). Not long after, China began more rigorously enforcing its annual seasonal fishing ban in the South China Sea, and in 2014 dispatched its largest oil rig to waters off the Paracel Islands claimed also by Vietnam, triggering a violent reaction that saw confrontations at sea with Vietnamese vessels and anti-Chinese protests in Vietnam.

China's new policy of assertive unilateralism backfired badly. It fanned the flames of anti-China sentiment, cemented an image of China as an outlaw and aggressor, triggered balancing behaviour and, most significantly, led directly to Beijing's humiliating 2016 defeat in *Philippines v. China*, a case brought by Manila to the Permanent Court of Arbitration at The Hague under UNCLOS, in which the government of President Benigno Aquino asked an international tribunal to rule on a series of issues, including the legal status of the nine-dash line, the maritime entitlements that attached to Scarborough Shoal and various features in the Spratly Islands, and whether China had violated its international legal obligations by excluding Philippine fishing boats from Scarborough Shoal and destroying sensitive maritime ecosystems in the course of building artificial islands. The result was a clean sweep for Manila. On every major point, the tribunal ruled against Beijing (Permanent Court of Arbitration, 2016). When the dust settled, Beijing was left with no basis for its expansive maritime claims in the South China Sea, and, perhaps most embarrassingly, was found to have built an illegal artificial island in the Philippines' exclusive economic zone (EEZ) at Mischief Reef. Beijing officially pretended that the tribunal lacked jurisdiction and that the ruling was null and void—but, fascinatingly, suddenly changed tack, stealthily complying with much of the ruling (Hayton, 2017). China quietly dropped all official references to the nine-dash line, renewed Philippine access to Scarborough Shoal, stopped attempting to enforce fisheries jurisdiction more than 12 nautical miles (22 km) from features that it claimed, stopped reclaiming land, and shelved plans for a South China Sea ADIZ without having so much as landed a single military aircraft as a proof of concept on any of the three airstrips it had built on its artificial islands.[8] Perhaps most importantly, China desperately began trying to change the channel, avoiding whenever possible discussion of territorial sovereignty or maritime jurisdiction and attempting to engage rival claimants in negotiations on joint stewardship and the co-operative management and development of natural resources. Despite recent hand-wringing that China is continuing to militarise its artificial islands and continues to act aggressively in support of its unsupportable claims, China has, in fact, only completed pre-planned infrastructure bought and paid for years in advance, and has been extremely careful to not to stray offside the PCA ruling when attempting to elicit co-operative resource governance (Welch & Logendrarajah, 2019).

The explanation for this head-spinning series of events is largely bureaucratic.[9] In 2012, assertive nationalists—primarily in the People's

---

[8] In May 2018, China did land a bomber on Woody Island in the Paracels for the first time, where it also periodically deploys fighter jets; but China's artificial islands are all in the Spratlys, not the Paracels. See Asia Maritime Transparency Initiative (2018) and Dominguez and O'Connor (2019).

[9] What follows is based largely on conversations with knowledgeable Chinese foreign and defence officials who spoke with me only on deep background, given the sensitivity of the issues involved and the fact that disputes are ongoing.

Liberation Army and state security organs—managed to argue success-fully that the kid-glove approach internationalists in the foreign ministry had favoured was causing China to lose ground in its legitimate efforts to persuade other countries, and most notably the United States, to treat China with the respect, and give it the voice, that it deserved as a renascent great power. With the foreign ministry marginalised, actors in China who neither understood the relevant legal subtleties nor anticipated the costs of diplomatic blowback overreached, dramatically worsening what they had seen as an already intolerable situation. The loss to the Philippines at The Hague put the final nail in their coffin. In 2016, the internationalists in the foreign ministry who had anticipated this disaster all along were finally able once again to assert the value of their expertise and began winning the internal foreign policy debates. They understood the extent to which China benefited from international law in general and UNCLOS in particular, and they realised that China only stood to lose from having a reputation as an outlaw state.

But the regime could not afford to look to the domestic audience as though it had suffered a humiliating defeat. Stealthy compliance, there-fore, went hand in hand with public denunciation of the ruling. To this day, the Chinese people believe that their leaders have stood up to the Philippines and others in defence of China's 'legitimate' rights. Chinese citizens have not noticed Beijing's efforts to avoid being in technical violation of the arbitration ruling. But for the most part, neither has the international community. The dominant narrative both among Western officials and in the Western media continues to be that China is behaving aggressively and 'claims virtually the entire South China Sea' (see, e.g. 'US Envoy Decries Chinese "Intimidation" in South China Sea', 2019). In response, the United States and others have stepped up 'Freedom of Navigation Operations' (FONOPs) and various aerial and naval activities designed to challenge claims that China is delicately attempting to back away from, elevating the risk of inadvertent clashes that could potentially escalate to war. No one seems to appreciate the fact that China's artificial islands are nothing but enormously expensive white elephants—useless in peacetime without an ADIZ to operate, and extremely vulnerable early casualties in wartime—and that China's efforts to dissuade competing claimants from taking unilateral actions that would make it impossible for Beijing to maintain the domestic pretence of not having lost at The Hague—such as the deployment of the *Haiyang Dizhi 8* survey ship in

Vietnam's EEZ—are not 'sovereignty assertion' activities (Vu & Pearson, 2020) but technically legal signals of desperation by a cornered regime.[10] The inability of most outside observers to achieve empathy with China on South China Sea issues has a number of likely causes, one of which, surely, is the fact that China is doing its best not to be too obvious about acknowledging that it overreached and was caught. Again, the regime's priority is maintaining face with the domestic audience. This speaks clearly to its insecurities. But part of the explanation for the failure to achieve empathy must surely also be perfectly normal cognitive psychology. Schema theory tells us two crucial things about how we make sense of the world (Fiske, 1982; Kelley, 1972; Thorndyke & Hayes-Roth, 1979): first, we interpret new, ambiguous information in light of our pre-existing beliefs; second, we form beliefs easily, on the basis of relatively little information, but once we have formed them, we resist changing them. We have, as it were, a cognitive double standard. A classic illustration is Jane Austen's famous novel *Pride and Prejudice*, in which the heroine, Elizabeth Bennet, forms a negative opinion of Mr Darcy on the basis of a single brief encounter at the beginning of the novel, and only changes her mind about him at the very end, after a mountain of discrepant information. The international audience was already wary of China in 2012, and the relatively brief period of assertive unilateralism that followed only drove home everyone's worst fears about Chinese goals and intentions. Primed to interpret Chinese statements and actions through the lens of a now-entrenched 'aggressive China' narrative, most have simply failed to notice Beijing's back-pedalling and desperation to avoid the Scylla of being outed domestically as having failed to defend what everyone in China believes (incorrectly) to be China's sovereign rights, and the Charybdis of being seen internationally as an outlaw state that has no concern for a rules-based international order that benefits China at least as much as it does anyone else.

Conclusion

There is good news and bad news in my tale. With respect to China, the good news is that our lack of empathy indicates that we have underestimated the degree to which Beijing can be trusted to respect

---

[10] UNCLOS prohibits foreign vessels' geological surveys only in the territorial sea (Arts. 19, 21).

the current rules-based international order in general, and UNCLOS in particular. Beijing is not the traditional security threat that many fear it to be. China may well be a serious non-traditional threat to Western and other interests—most notably, by meddling in others' domestic affairs to promote pro-regime narratives, by penetrating critical infrastructure, by conducting cyber operations, by stealing intellectual property, and so on—but it is much more of a status quo power than most realise when it comes to old-school high politics. The regime has enough on its hands domestically; it cannot afford to take on the costs of being a revisionist or pariah in foreign affairs. The bad news is that our misdiagnosis of China poses risks of conflict in its own right (Welch, 2015). Obsessing unnecessarily about Chinese policy in the South China Sea also distracts us from the unconventional ways in which China does, in fact, threaten our interests and values.

With respect to North Korea, there is mostly just bad news. We have not yet achieved the level of empathy required to understand what drives Kim Jong Un or to enable us to anticipate the consequences of choices we make in dealing with both North and South Korea. In the absence of empathy, there are no grounds for trust. If Kim Jong Un is the run-of-the-mill autocrat that most analysts seem to believe, then the odds of avoiding a cataclysmic conflict on the Korean Peninsula are probably at least halfway decent. But if he harbours ambitions of conquest and glory, we are almost certainly inadvertently feeding the beast by failing to recognise them.

References

Adler, E., & Barnett, M. (1998). *Security communities*. Cambridge University Press.

Al-Rodhan, N. (2014). The neurochemistry of power has implications for political change. *The Conversation*. https://theconversation.com/the-neurochemistry-of-power-has-implications-for-political-change-23844. Accessed 23 April 2020.

Allan, B. B., Vucetic, S., & Hopf, T. (2018). The distribution of identity and the future of international order: China's hegemonic prospects. *International Organization, 72*(4), 839–869.

Asia Maritime Transparency Initiative. (2018). *China lands first bomber on South China Sea Island*. https://amti.csis.org/china-lands-first-bomber-south-china-sea-island. Accessed 23 April 2020.

Baker, P., & Choe, S.-H. (2017). Trump threatens 'fire and fury' against North Korea if it endangers U.S. *New York Times*. https://www.nytimes.com/2017/08/08/world/asia/north-korea-un-sanctions-nuclear-missile-united-nations.html. Accessed 23 April 2020.

Beran, M. J., Perdue, B. M., Futch, S. E., Smith, J. D., Evans, T. A., & Parrish, A. E. (2015). Go when you know: Chimpanzees' confidence movements reflect their responses in a computerized memory task. *Cognition, 142*, 236–246.

Blight, J. G., & Lang, J. M. (2005). *The fog of war: Lessons from the life of Robert S. McNamara*. Rowman & Littlefield.

Bloom, P. (2013). The baby in the well: The case against empathy. *The New Yorker*. https://www.newyorker.com/magazine/2013/05/20/the-baby-in-the-well. Accessed 23 April 2020.

Bradsher, K. (2014). Philippine leader sounds alarm on China. *The New York Times*. https://www.nytimes.com/2014/02/05/world/asia/philippine-leader-urges-international-help-in-resisting-chinas-sea-claims.html. Accessed 23 April 2020.

Bullock, A. (1971). *Hitler: A study in tyranny*. Harper & Row.

Capie, D. H., & Evans, P. M. (2002). *The Asia-Pacific security lexicon*. Singapore: Institute of Southeast Asian Studies.

Chang, G. G. (2001). *The coming collapse of China*. Random House.

China's passport move stokes South China Sea dispute. (2012). *Strategic Comments, 18*(10), v–vii.

Collis, H. (2013). Which politician was a brandy firm's biggest customer? Kim Jong-Il spent £700,000 a year on Hennessy. *Daily Mail*. https://www.dailymail.co.uk/news/article-2357393/Can-guess-bought-cognac-Kim-Jong-Il-revealed-Hennessy-s-biggest-customer-spending-700-000-year-brandy.html. Accessed 23 April 2020.

Danner, L. K., & Martín, F. E. (2019). China's hegemonic intentions and trajectory: Will it opt for benevolent, coercive, or Dutch-style hegemony? *Asia Pacific Policy Studies, 6*(2), 186–207.

Dominguez, G., & O'Connor, S. (2019). China deploys J-10 fighters to Woody Island, says report. *Jane's Defence Weekly*. https://www.janes.com/article/89458/china-deploys-j-10-fighters-to-woody-island-says-report. Accessed 23 April 2020.

Escudé, C. (1992). *Education, political culture, and foreign policy: The Case of Argentina*. Duke-University of North Carolina Program in Latin American Studies.

Fiske, S. T. (1982). Schema-triggered affect: Applications to social perception. In M. S. Clarke & S. T. Fiske (Eds.), *Affect and cognition: The 17th annual symposium on cognition* (pp. 55–78). Lawrence Erlbaum.

Frances, A. (2017). Misdiagnosing Donald Trump. *Journal of Mental Health, 26*(5), 394.

Greene, B. (2011). 5 strange things you didn't know about Kim Jong-Il. *U.S. News & World Report.* https://www.usnews.com/news/articles/2011/12/19/5-strange-things-you-didnt-know-about-kim-jong-il. Accessed 23 April 2020.

Hayton, B. (2014). *The South China Sea: The struggle for power in Asia.* Yale University Press.

Hayton, B. (2017). Denounce but comply: China's response to the South China Sea arbitration ruling. *Georgetown Journal of International Affairs, 18*(2), 104–111.

Hayton, B. (2018). The modern creation of China's 'historic rights' claim in the South China Sea. *Asian Affairs, 49*(3), 370–382.

Hill, L. (1968). Three crises, 1938–39. *Journal of Contemporary History, 3*(1), 113–144.

Immelman, A. (2018). *The personality profile of North Korean supreme leader Kim Jong Un* (Working Paper no. 2.0). Collegeville and St. Joseph, MN: St. John's University and the College of St. Benedict, Unit for the Study of Personality in Politics. https://digitalcommons.csbsju.edu/psychology_pubs/119/. Accessed 23 April 2020.

Jacques, M. (2009). *When China rules the world: The rise of the middle kingdom and the end of the western world.* Allen Lane.

Jones, P. L. (2015). *Track two diplomacy in theory and practice.* Stanford University Press.

Kelley, H. (1972). *Causal schemata and the attribution process.* General Learning Press.

Kheel, R. (2019). Trump: I 'trust' Kim's promise he won't resume nuclear, missile tests. *The Hill.* https://thehill.com/policy/defense/431961-trump-i-trust-kims-promise-he-wont-resume-nuclear-missile-tests. Accessed 23 April 2020.

Kuo, M. A. (2017). Kim Jong Un's political psychology profile: Insights from Ken Dekleva. *The Diplomat.* https://thediplomat.com/2017/10/kim-jong-uns-political-psychology-profile. Accessed 23 April 2020.

Kydd, A. H. (2005). *Trust and mistrust in international relations.* Princeton University Press.

Lee, B. X. (Ed.). (2019). *The dangerous case of Donald Trump: 37 psychiatrists and mental health experts assess a president.* Thomas Dunne Books.

Manchester, J. (2018). Trump's comments on falling in love with Kim Jong Un 'shocking and appalling,' says conservative writer. *The Hill.* https://thehill.com/hilltv/rising/409245-trumps-comments-on-falling-in-love-with-kim-jong-un-are-shocking-and-appalling. Accessed 23 April 2020.

McNamara, R. S. (1995). *In retrospect: The tragedy and lessons of Vietnam.* Times Books.

McNamara, R. S., & Blight, J. G. (2001). *Wilson's ghost: Reducing the risk of conflict, killing, and catastrophe in the 21st century.* PublicAffairs.

McNamara, R. S., Blight, J. G., & Brigham, R. (1999). *Argument without end: In search of answers to the Vietnam tragedy.* PublicAffairs.

Mearsheimer, J. J. (2010). The gathering storm: China's challenge to US power in Asia. *Chinese Journal of International Politics, 3*(4), 381–396.

Middleton, D. (1981, June 21). Hitler's Russian Blunder. *New York Times Magazine,* 309–318.

Pei, M. (2012). Is CCP rule fragile or resilient? *Journal of Democracy, 23*(1), 27–41.

Pei, M. (2013). Asia's real challenge: China's 'Potemkin' rise. *The Diplomat.* http://thediplomat.com/2013/05/asias-real-challenge-chinas-potemkin-rise. Accessed 23 April 2020.

Permanent Court of Arbitration. (2016). *Award, Philippines v. China (case no. 2013–19).* The Hague: Permanent Court of Arbitration. https://pcacases.com/web/sendAttach/2086. Accessed 23 April 2020.

Pouliot, V. (2010). *International security in practice: The politics of NATO–Russia diplomacy.* Cambridge University Press.

Preston, R. A. (1977). *The defence of the undefended border: Planning for war in North America, 1867–1939.* McGill–Queen's University Press.

Putnam, R. (1988). Diplomacy and domestic politics: The logic of two-level games. *International Organization, 42*(3), 428–460.

Raymond, M., & Welch, D. A. (in progress). *What's really going on in the South China Sea? explaining China's (largely unnoticed) stealthy compliance.*

Starr, B., & Atwood, K. (2020). Concern growing US and South Korea could fail to reach an agreement on troop cost-sharing. *CNN.* https://www.cnn.com/2020/02/20/politics/us-south-korea-troops-costs/index.html. Accessed 23 April 2020.

Stracqualursi, V. (2018). Trump says Kim 'trusts me, and I trust him'. *CNN.* https://www.cnn.com/2018/06/12/politics/trump-north-korea-kim-jong-un-trust/index.html. Accessed 23 April 2020.

Strating, R. (2019). Maritime disputes, sovereignty and the rules-based order in East Asia. *Australian Journal of Politics & History, 65*(3), 449–465.

Szechenyi, N., & Hosoya, Y. (2019). *Working Toward a Free and Open Indo-Pacific.* Carnegie Endowment for International Peace. https://carnegieendowment.org/files/ChinaRiskOpportunity-Open_Indo-Pacific.pdf. Accessed 23 April 2020.

Tan, C. K. (2018). China spending puts domestic security ahead of defense. *Nikkei Asian Review.* https://asia.nikkei.com/Spotlight/China-People-s-

Congress-2018/China-spending-puts-domestic-security-ahead-of-defense. Accessed 23 April 2020.

Thorndyke, P. W., & Hayes-Roth, B. (1979). The use of schemata in the acquisition and transfer of knowledge. *Cognitive Psychology, 11*(1), 82–105.

US Envoy Decries Chinese 'Intimidation' in South China Sea. (2019). *Al Jazeera.* https://www.aljazeera.com/news/2019/11/envoy-decries-chinese-intimidation-south-china-sea-191104050635259.html. Accessed 23 April 2020.

Vu, K., & Pearson, J. (2020). *Chinese survey ship returns to Vietnam's exclusive economic zone.* https://www.reuters.com/article/vietnam-china-southchinasea/chinese-survey-ship-returns-to-vietnams-exclusive-economic-zone-idU SL3N2C20YQ. Accessed 23 April 2020.

Watt, D. C. (1989). *How war came: The immediate origins of the Second World War, 1938–1939.* Pantheon Books.

Weathersby, K. (1995). Korea, 1949–50: To attack or not to attack? Stalin, Kim Il Sung, and the prelude to war. *Cold War International History Project Bulletin, 5,* 1–9.

Welch, D. A. (2013). *The case against the case against empathy.* http://davidwelch.ca/2013/the-case-against-the-case-against-empathy. Accessed 20 May 2013.

Welch, D. A. (2015). Can the United States and China avoid a Thucydides trap? *e-International Relations.* http://www.e-ir.info/2015/04/06/can-the-united-states-and-china-avoid-a-thucydides-trap. Accessed 23 April 2020.

Welch, D. A. (2020). China, the United States, and 'Thucydides's trap.' In H. Feng & K. He (Eds.), *China's challenges and international order transition: Beyond Thucydides's Trap* (pp. 47–70). University of Michigan Press.

Welch, D. A., & Logendrarajah, K. (2019). Is China still an outlaw in the South China Sea? *Open Canada.* https://www.opencanada.org/features/china-still-outlaw-south-china-sea/. Accessed 29 July 2019.

The End of the Golden Weather: New Zealand's Trade Policy During a Time of International Transition

Vangelis Vitalis

INTRODUCTION

The period 1995–2019 was the 'golden weather' for New Zealand trade policy. The establishment of the World Trade Organization (WTO); the legal enforceability of its disciplines from 1995[1]; and a reduction of global protectionism over this period for New Zealand exporters—facilitated in part by New Zealand's expanding network of free trade agreements (FTAs) which, with the Comprehensive and Progressive Agreement for Trans-Pacific Partnership (CPTPP) now in force, covers nearly 70% of New Zealand exports—has delivered significant benefits. These range

---

[1] Including, for the first time, enforceable rules and disciplines on agriculture, services and intellectual property.

The views contained in this paper are those of the author alone and do not necessarily represent those of the New Zealand Ministry of Foreign Affairs and Trade.

V. Vitalis (✉)
Ministry of Foreign Affairs and Trade, Lambton Quay, New Zealand
e-mail: Vangelis.Vitalis@mfat.govt.nz

© The Author(s), under exclusive license to Springer Nature Singapore Pte Ltd. 2022
R. Patman et al. (eds.), *From Asia-Pacific to Indo-Pacific*, Global Political Transitions, https://doi.org/10.1007/978-981-16-7007-7_13

from greater certainty, transparency and the enforceability of international trade rules through to improved and often preferential access to key markets for New Zealand goods, services and investment.

Unfortunately, the period since 2019 suggests that this 'golden weather' for New Zealand trade policy is now at an end. The coronavirus (COVID-19) pandemic has underlined the significance of the emerging challenge and the essential fragility of globalisation and international co-operation. In fact, it is far from clear how the new and still emerging external operating environment will evolve over the coming decade or how New Zealand can effectively respond to and mitigate this increased turbulence internationally.

The following briefly recalls why trade matters for New Zealand and situates the country's trade policy within international relations theory. This is followed by an overview of the domestic and international context and the identification of two specific reference points that have informed the development of New Zealand's trade policy strategy. That strategy consists of a six-part framework designed to (a) manage and mitigate as far as possible the risks to the New Zealand national interest from the possible fragmentation and disorder likely to characterise the evolution of the rules-based trading system; and (b) ensure that New Zealand retains a measure of agency over the changing nature of that system over time.

WHY TRADE MATTERS FOR NEW ZEALAND

The New Zealand export sector sustains more than half a million jobs. Put another way, one in every four New Zealanders in work depends on exports for their livelihood. Trade is also an important driver of productivity, employment and incomes. We know, for instance, that productivity per New Zealand worker is 36% greater if they are in a firm that is exporting, compared to one that is not (MFAT, 2017). It has also been established that employment grows 7–12% faster when New Zealand firms start exporting (Fabling & Sanderson, 2010). International research also tells us that exporting firms pay higher wages—up to 6% more than non-exporters (Bernard et al., 2012). In short, trade—underpinned by the rules and market access openings that facilitate this—matters for New Zealand's prosperity and well-being.

New Zealand also faces specific challenges as a small economy that is also a significant global agricultural exporter—nearly 98% of its agricultural production is exported. These products face the highest levels of global protection—tariffs often in excess of 100% and an average of 23% across the WTO membership—compared to less than 6% for exporters of manufactured goods. New Zealand's distance from markets matters too. Hervé Boulhol et al. (2008, pp. 7–8, 20–23) have observed that distance has a statistically significant (negative) effect on gross domestic product (GDP) per capita. While the impact may vary somewhat, it is far from trivial. In the case of New Zealand, distance from and access to markets may contribute negatively to GDP per capita by as much as 10%. Conversely, other small countries like Belgium, with a more favourable trading location at the heart of the European Union, may benefit through their location by up to 7% of GDP. Indeed, there is little evidence of the 'death of distance' (Berthelon & Freund, 2004) and for most industries— including a range of key New Zealand ones—the distance-related costs of exporting have remained broadly unchanged.

New Zealand Trade Policy and International Relations Theory

According to International Relations theory, particularly the realist and neorealist schools (Dunne et al., 2013) small states like New Zealand have significant constraints on their ability to act independently (Lebow, 2013, pp. 59–76). There is also scepticism about the extent to which larger states are prepared to allow the rules of multilateral institutions to constrain their actions. This especially applies when these rules might alter their security environment. There is also a perception that the institutions that implement and monitor these kinds of international rules will only survive so long as they satisfy the interests of large and powerful states (see for instance Waltz, 1979; Keohane, 1984). In a similar vein, rationalist approaches are pessimistic about the ability of small states to genuinely influence or shape events (Keohane, 1984).

New Zealand's trade policy contradicts these assumptions. John Leslie (2015, pp. 11–13), for instance, suggests that on balance the empirical evidence is less clear than the realists would have us believe. The World Trade Organization (WTO)—notwithstanding its current travails—the European Union (EU), the Association of Southeast Asian Nations (ASEAN), the East Asia Summit, the ASEAN dialogue with regional partners, the Organisation for Economic Co-operation and Development (OECD), Asia–Pacific Economic Cooperation (APEC) and even the Closer Economic Relations (CER) cluster of agreements between

Australia and New Zealand are all empirical demonstrations that pose a challenge to the realists. These show that small- and medium-sized states can contribute to structuring norms, behaviours and rules that are not solely dependent on support from a hegemon (Brady, 2019, pp. 2–10). Constructivist approaches to International Relations theory which emphasise the role of ideas, credibility, norm setting and influencing policy action may perhaps better explain the conduct of small state trade diplomacy (Wendt, 1992; Copeland, 2000). Looking ahead, the interesting question for International Relations theory will be how small states adapt to the current turbulence and the present difficulties posed by COVID-19 and whether the realist or constructivist approaches better explain the orientation of small state trade diplomacy.

THE END OF THE GOLDEN WEATHER FOR NEW ZEALAND TRADE POLICY

The catalyst for the end of the 'golden weather' has been the US–China 'trade war', but the shift has been under way for some time. The implications and spill-overs are global, with direct impacts on New Zealand. This has been deeply unsettling, and by 2019 it became clear that the three working assumptions that have underpinned New Zealand trade policy for nearly a quarter of a century no longer hold. And that situation has been exacerbated by the COVID-19 pandemic which has magnified these emerging challenges. The first of these assumptions was that enforceable multilateral trade rules would expand over time—an expectation supported by the launch of the Doha Development Round in 2001. The conclusion of the WTO Trade Facilitation Agreement in 2013 and the elimination of agricultural export subsidies at the Nairobi WTO Ministerial Conference in 2015—the latter a key priority for New Zealand since the late 1980s—have been significant multilateral outcomes that validated New Zealand's trade policy assumptions. Unfortunately, there have not been any others. Nevertheless, New Zealand continues to actively support and invest in the WTO. This is because, aside from its negotiating function, the WTO embodies the world's only legally enforceable set of trade rules and disciplines that bind all of the world's economies. It also remains central to any effort to eliminate some of the more significant global barriers to New Zealand exporters, i.e. in agriculture. The WTO is therefore still the first best option for developing and implementing international trade rules. Unfortunately, the enforceability of

WTO rules is in question. This hinged on a functioning Appellate Body (AB). With the blocking of the appointment of new AB members at the end of 2019, this body no longer has a quorum to hear appeals. New Zealand however has worked with other WTO members to support an interim mechanism to replace, albeit temporarily, the AB, at least among the participating members. To this end, the multi-party interim arrangement was announced on 29 March 2020 and formally notified to the WTO on 30 April 2020.[2]

The second working assumption has been that international markets would, over time, become increasingly open to New Zealand traders. The reverse is now happening—global protectionism is on the rise and the past two years have seen the sharpest increase in trade restrictive measures since the establishment of the WTO. In fact, the return to an era of tariff escalation is only part of the problem. Tariff increases are being supplemented by other trade restrictive measures, such as subsidies and a range of non-tariff measures designed to protect domestic industries. And the COVID-19 pandemic triggered a range of additional protectionist measures, including, for instance, new export requirements and restrictions on medical protection equipment.[3] Taken together, this is a troubling indication of a shift in global trade policy conditions. The numbers that underpin this change are significant. Analysis by Simon Evenett (2019) indicates that the 2018 spike in new protectionism was repeated in 2019, when it rose by 50%. What is particularly worrying is the increasing resort to trade-distorting subsidies and other non-tariff measures. To put this in context, a New Zealand Institute of Economic Research analysis suggested that in the Asia–Pacific alone, non-tariff measures on agricultural goods cost New Zealand exporters nearly NZ$6 billion a year (NZIER, 2016).

The third working assumption that underpinned New Zealand trade policy was that the domestic 'social licence' for trade would be sustained. Bipartisan political support for trade policy had been a given since before the Closer Economic Relations agreement was concluded with

---

[2] For more information about the Interim Mechanism, see the full WTO notification: https://trade.ec.europa.eu/doclib/docs/2020/april/tradoc_158731.pdf (Accessed 8 August 2020).

[3] On, for instance, EU legislation placing restrictions and specific additional requirements on the export of a range of medical equipment see: https://eur-lex.europa.eu/legal-content/EN/TXT/?uri=OJ:L:2020:077I:TOC (Accessed 8 August 2020).

Australia in 1989. Political bipartisanship characterised the approach taken by successive governments managing the 'shock' of London's decision to join the European Common Market. This bipartisan support also remained firm during successive General Agreement on Tariffs and Trade (GATT) negotiating rounds, the range of free trade agreements concluded with, inter alia, Singapore; Thailand; Pacific 4 (P4) partners (Brunei, Chile and Singapore); China; ASEAN and Australia (AANZFTA); Malaysia (MNZFTA); Korea (KNZFTA) and so on.

In 2016, however, political bipartisanship fractured when the Trans-Pacific Partnership Agreement (TPP) was brought to parliament. For the first time, the main opposition party did not support the ratification of a trade agreement. With the subsequent ratification of the CPTPP, bipartisanship appears to have been restored. The Trade for All Agenda established by the incoming government, and announced alongside the CPTPP signing ceremony together with Canada and Chile,[4] represented a deliberate attempt to refocus the trade agenda with a view to reinforcing and sustaining the social licence for trade policy.

THE GLOBAL TRADE POLICY CONTEXT—WE HAVE NOT BEEN HERE BEFORE

The former US Administration took its long-standing dissatisfaction with the WTO in particular, and global trade rules in general, to new levels. The implications are significant. For the first time since the GATT was established in 1947, New Zealand trade diplomacy is now necessarily less about expanding existing multilateral trade rules and rather more about preserving as much as it can of those rules and the WTO as an institution.

In addition, the long-standing revealed preference of the major Group of Seven (G7) economies for bilateralism has been compounded by their preparedness to also step outside of the existing rules-based system and act unilaterally. That situation is made more challenging by the impact of COVID-19 and the apparent willingness of these economies to adopt

---

[4] The statement is available at: https://www.mfat.govt.nz/assets/CPTPP/CPTPP-Joint-Declaration-Progressive-and-Inclusive-Trade-Final.pdf (Accessed 8 August 2020). It provided the basis for the work of the Trade for All Advisory Board.

protectionist measures and contemplate or conclude bilateral trade agreements that may breach WTO rules.[5] That these economies have been prepared to move in that direction is a troubling sign. It suggests that they may be making a judgement that the existing rules-based system may no longer meet their needs when confronted with the challenge posed by unorthodox trade policies or the kind of global public health crisis triggered by COVID-19.

While This is Happening, the Nature of Global Trade is Changing ...

The way global trade is conducted is undergoing a major shift towards digitisation. The reduction of transaction costs through this process has obvious appeal. Practical steps to give this effect range from 'paperless trading' through to digital 'single windows'. The impact of COVID-19 on global supply chains has accelerated this trend to digitisation. An emerging risk for New Zealand trade policy, however, is that the major technology companies—primarily in the G7 economies and China—will set the global norms for digital trading and eventually the attendant rules without necessarily paying too much attention to the needs and interests of smaller economies (and their smaller digital firms). Compounding the challenge New Zealand faces is that there is only a fragmented set of existing rules covering this fast-growing area of trade. CPTPP is one agreement that offers some, albeit incomplete, coverage.

New Zealand, alongside Chile and Singapore, has responded by launching and swiftly concluding and signing the Digital Economy Partnership Agreement (DEPA).[6] This matters because in a world where the major economies are stepping back from international trade rules, DEPA demonstrates that small economies can take the initiative to try and shape the emerging global architecture for digital trade. This is also a way for New Zealand to ensure to the greatest extent possible that any emerging rules and norms in digital trade reflect the interests of its small-

[5] This is a reference to GATT Article XXIV that specifies that regional trade agreements should cover 'substantially all trade'.

[6] This Agreement was (digitally) signed by all three partners on 12 June 2020. It is believed to be the first international trade treaty to be signed digitally. https://www.beehive.govt.nz/release/digital-trade-agreement-timely-response-covid-19 (Accessed 8 August 2020). More information about this agreement is available at https://www.mfat.govt.nz/en/trade/free-trade-agreements/free-trade-agreements-concluded-but-not-in-force/digital-economy-partnership-agreement (Accessed 8 August 2020).

and medium-sized companies. Moreover, and underlining the essential agility of small export-oriented nations, the three partners in DEPA have agreed in the context of COVID-19 to add a module to DEPA to address and enable co-operation between them in the digital provision of medical services.

... and so Are Public Expectations of Trade Agreements

Public scepticism in OECD countries about trade agreements has made the social licence for trade policy increasingly fragile. This scepticism has ranged from concerns about the erosion of sovereignty through to perceived negative effects on incomes, employment and sustainability. There is also very much an open question about the trade-related conclusions that the public both in New Zealand and beyond will draw from the experience of dealing with COVID-19. At the very least, the pandemic has revealed the essential weakness of the existing consensus regarding globalisation and open markets. Responding to these concerns—from which New Zealand has not been immune—in a practical but meaningful way will be crucial to sustaining public support for trade policy.

In fact, trade rules can make a difference and do make a meaningful contribution to the kinds of solutions needed for global challenges. In the context of COVID-19 for instance, a New Zealand–Singapore-led initiative launched on 21 March 2020—which within 12 hours included Chile—sought to keep supply and trade links open and remove any existing measures restricting trade in essential goods, especially COVID-19-related medical supplies. This initiative within days secured broader participation, with the announcement on 25 March 2020 that Brunei, Australia, Canada and others would join, with other economies continuing to join the statement over the following weeks, including, for instance, the United Arab Emirates, China and others.[7] Together with Australia, Canada, Korea and Singapore, New Zealand also launched a joint ministerial statement to facilitate the flow of goods and services, as

---

[7] The Joint Ministerial Statement (with updated participants) is available at: https://www.mfat.govt.nz/en/trade/covid-19-and-trade/joint-ministerial-statement-affirming-commitment-to-ensuring-supply-chain-connectivity-amidst-the-covid-19-situation-upd ated/ (Accessed 9 August 2020).

well as the essential movement of people.[8] More generally, and perhaps more 'traditionally', trade can positively address and support solutions to environmental challenges. An outcome from the WTO negotiations on fish subsidies, for instance, would help address collapsing global fish stocks. Most recently, the New Zealand-led initiative for an Agreement on Climate Change, Trade and Sustainability (ACCTS),[9] with its focus on reforming and eliminating fossil fuel subsidies, is the most ambitious attempt yet to show how trade rules can be used to mitigate climate change and make good on long-standing G7, G20, APEC and even United Nations Leaders' commitments in this area.

Filling the Trade Policy Leadership Vacuum

Given that the major economies appear unwilling and/or unable to lead multilateral trade policy, it is increasingly clear that *in the interim* New Zealand will need to be creative about how it can sustain global and regional trade policy engagement. The likely vector through which this can be advanced may necessarily be with other small and medium-sized economies—at least at the outset. Many of these already share New Zealand's concerns, are active in considering their implications, and can be expected to work together to support necessary processes and actions that may help shore up and protect as far as possible the existing rules-based trading system.

The response to the COVID-19 crisis is an example of this kind of creative trade diplomacy. Led initially by two, then three, small export-oriented economies (New Zealand, Singapore and Chile), the joint statement by their trade ministers in support of keeping trade and supply links garnered considerable cross-APEC support. The participation of G7 member Canada and G20 partner Australia added considerable heft to the initiative, which eventually also included China, other APEC economies, Uruguay and the United Arab Emirates. It was then given further impetus

---

[8] The statement is available here: https://www.mfat.govt.nz/en/media-and-resources/news/joint-ministerial-statement (Accessed 9 August 2020).

[9] Launched by the New Zealand Prime Minister Jacinda Ardern at the UN General Assembly together with Costa Rica, Fiji, Iceland, Norway and Switzerland. Negotiations will formally commence in 2021. More information is available at https://www.mfat.govt.nz/en/trade/free-trade-agreements/climate/agreement-on-climate-change-trade-and-sustainability-accts-negotiations (Accessed 9 August 2020).

through the launch of a new initiative by New Zealand and Singapore to eliminate barriers to the trade in COVID-19 goods (medicines, protective equipment and so on).[10] This was then circulated to the WTO membership to encourage broader adherence, with Singapore and New Zealand working together to encourage membership by other partners. Each of these initiatives followed an approach that New Zealand has pioneered called 'concerted open plurilateralism'.[11]

Concerts of small- and medium-sized countries will be useful, but they are insufficient by themselves as a long-term solution. It will be crucial therefore that when such groups of countries forge ahead with such trade policy entrepreneurship—a long-standing feature of New Zealand trade diplomacy (Hoadley, 2019, pp. 299–301)—they will also need to find bespoke ways to engage the major economies over time. This needs to be a central—indeed over-riding—feature of any forward strategy.

In sum, Panglossian hopes for a global trading system that would deliver a Kantian 'perpetual peace' have largely faded, a conclusion accelerated by the protectionist response to the COVID-19 crisis by many of the major economies. With the impact of COVID-19 bearing down on the trade policy architecture, there is a non-trivial risk of a return to a Hobbesian 'might makes right' world order. Recent moves by several of the major economies to work together in a non-inclusive format on certain trade issues underline a worrying direction of travel. The Melian Dialogue-type[12] implications are troubling.

[10] The press release announcing the launch of the initiative is available at https://www.beehive.govt.nz/release/covid-19-response-new-zealand-and-singapore-launch-initiative-ensure-free-flow-essential (Accessed 9 August 2020).

[11] See for instance, Minister Parker's speech 'Trade for All and the State of International Trade' available at https://www.beehive.govt.nz/speech/trade-all-and-state-international-trade (Accessed 24 August 2020).

[12] The Melian Dialogue refers to an exchange reported by Thucydides in his *History of the Peloponnesian War* between the major power of the era (Athens) and Sparta; during the Athenians' siege of the small neutral city state of Melos they chillingly declared 'the strong do what they can and the weak suffer what they must'. Following the 'dialogue' the state of Melos was extinguished.

Avoiding the 'Traps'[13]

Looking ahead to the kind of strategy needed to manage the growing global turbulence in trade policy, there are perhaps two reference points that can help illuminate the value of a creative and activist trade policy agenda for a small advanced economy like New Zealand. The first is the risk posed by what is known as 'Thucydides' Trap'. This phrase refers to the situation when a rising power is perceived to challenge an established power which then 'inevitably' escalates to war (whether kinetic or otherwise). The concept was elaborated by Harvard Professor Graham Allison (2017), drawing on the Athenian general Thucydides' seminal *History of the Peloponnesian War*, which analysed the epic struggle between the two most powerful Greek city states at the time—Athens, a rising power, and Sparta, the established one. The parallels with our current time have been remarked upon by China's President Xi Jinping, who reportedly said that '[w]e all need to work together to avoid the Thucydides trap — destructive tensions between an emerging power and established ones'.[14] What can small states like New Zealand do when confronted by this increasingly challenging geopolitical environment? In particular, what lessons can it draw from its own reading of the Peloponnesian War? A consideration of small states' interests through a 'Thucydidean prism' suggests there is value in understanding the experience and strategies of those smaller Greek city states that had to navigate their own turbulent times. Some were successful, while others such as Melos clearly were not. The policies pursued by the smaller Greek city states have some common characteristics, including their investment in and support for some 'global' norms and an 'international' architecture to maximise their own influence on the major powers, while also offering them some scope to defend and mitigate as far as possible risks against their interests.

The second reference point is the 'Kindleberger Trap'. This is the situation described by Charles Kindleberger, an architect of the Marshall

---

[13] The first exposition of these 'traps' for New Zealand trade policy is contained in a presentation to the parliamentary Foreign Affairs, Defence and Trade Select Committee available at https://www.parliament.nz/en/pb/sc/submissions-and-advice/document/52SCFD_ADV_78569_1971/ministry-of-foreign-affairs-defence-and-trade-ini tial (Accessed 14 March 2020).

[14] See https://www.scmp.com/comment/insight-opinion/article/1422780/china-needs-patience-achieve-peaceful-rise?page=all (Accessed 16 April 2020).

Plan. He argued that the disastrous decade of the 1930s was a consequence of the failure by the United States to take on the role of primary provider of key global public goods after it had replaced the United Kingdom as the leading global power. Global public goods include things like freedom of the high seas, financial stability and global trade rules. It has been suggested that this is the new 'trap' being confronted internationally, i.e. whether the major powers will support and invest in global public goods or create new ones to sustain the rules-based system (Nye, 2017). Against this risk, coalitions of smaller and medium-sized countries may need to step in to sustain these global public goods in the interim. CPTPP, the DEPA and ACCTS are good examples of coalitions of countries coming together on the basis of 'open plurilateralism' in a bid to support and sustain trade rules. Another recent example is the establishment of the multi-party interim mechanism to hear appeals in international trade disputes—of which New Zealand is also a founding member.

A FLEXIBLE SIX-PART FRAMEWORK
FOR TRADE POLICY IN TURBULENT TIMES

It is against this background that an elaborated framework for pursuing New Zealand's trade policy in a challenging external environment has been established. The New Zealand Minister for Trade and Export Growth, David Parker (Parker, 2019) outlined the framework as follows:

- *Defence of the 'rules-based system'.* This remains *the* priority. It will require a redoubling of current New Zealand efforts along with other small- and medium-sized economies to protect and sustain the existing system.
- *Embed New Zealand in the emerging economic architecture.* Implementing and expanding CPTPP; progressing the Pacific Alliance negotiations and concluding the RCEP negotiations. Intensifying the negotiations for an FTA with the EU and the United Kingdom.
- *Supporting regional and global public goods*—as a way to mitigate the risks of the 'Kindleberger Trap'. Examples of this—whether pre-existing or ones which New Zealand is helping to construct—include

the coalition supporting New Zealand's work on fossil fuel and fisheries subsidy reform (Friends of Fossil Fuel Subsidy Reform),[15] those working with New Zealand on the inclusive Trade for All agenda (on which more below),[16] the New Zealand-led Small Advanced Economies initiative, as well as the more traditional 'public goods' such as APEC, OECD and non-traditional trade policy forums like the Commonwealth.

- *Concerted open plurilateralism*—advancing this concept as an active deliberate and structured process of engagement through ACCTS and DEPA, and with CPTPP partners in particular, and to accelerate the consideration of new members as soon as possible. This concept is also a key organising construct for New Zealand's response to the COVID-19 pandemic.
- *Economic diplomacy*—to work with other New Zealand Government agencies onshore and offshore to help New Zealand exporters through the provision of bespoke advice and a range of practical web-based tools that help access new and existing markets. This function has been a particular focus for the COVID-19 response strategy.[17]
- *Implement the Trade for All agenda*—as a way of sustaining and reinforcing the social licence for trade.

The value of this framework is that it is adaptable and can respond to changing circumstances. Specifically, it provides for the ability to 'lean in' on particular elements and issues as needed and over time. In this way, it provides for the possibility of a recalibration of effort in the face of

[15] More information about this initiative is available at https://www.mfat.govt.nz/en/environment/clean-energy-and-fossil-fuels (Accessed 7 March 2020).

[16] See also https://www.beehive.govt.nz/release/nz%E2%80%99s-interests-advanced-international-trade-forums (Accessed 12 August 2020).

[17] An outline of the government's approach to the trade-led dimensions of the economic recovery from COVID-19 is provided at https://www.beehive.govt.nz/release/trade-can-help-economy-rebound-rebuild-and-recover. See also the Minister for Trade and Export Growth, David Parker, and senior officials' appearance before the parliamentary New Zealand Epidemic Response Committee available at https://www.parliament.nz/en/pb/sc/scl/epidemic-response/news-archive/watch-public-meetings-of-the-epidemic-response-committee (The minister's opening remarks commence at 0:42:30; with senior trade officials providing further detail from 1:19:30. Accessed 31 August 2020).

new and emerging challenges. This has been demonstrated in the context of the COVID-19 pandemic. In this case, particular emphasis has been placed on 'leaning in' on the economic diplomacy element of the framework—to help exporters recover and re-engage, as well as to invest in APEC as a public good that can help rebuild confidence to support the wider trade rules-based system.

Greater Emphasis on 'Concerted Open Plurilateralism'

Of particular interest will be the evolution of New Zealand's norm entrepreneurship in trade policy through concerted open plurilaterialism. The model for this is the evolution of the Singapore–New Zealand Closer Economic Partnership (CEP) agreement (2001) into the CPTPP agreement (2018) nearly twenty years later. The CEP with Singapore had been initiated in the context of the failure of the Seattle Ministerial Conference to launch a further WTO Round. It entered into force at the start of the year that launched the Doha round (2001). The symbolism is significant since both New Zealand and Singapore are committed multilateralists. The publicity around the agreement reinforced this point. It stressed that the conclusion of the CEP with Singapore did not change New Zealand's commitment to multilateralism as the preferred way to develop international trade rules, where 'all measures are consistent with trade liberalisation efforts pursued through the World Trade Organisation (WTO) and the Asia Pacific Economic Cooperation (APEC) process' (MFAT, 2014; see also Elms, 2009, pp. 4–5; Hoadley, 2019, p. 287).

With this agreement in place by early 2001, New Zealand together with Singapore actively worked to 'build out' the agreement, co-ordinating an approach that would use the CEP as the platform through which to support wider regional integration. New Zealand focused its efforts in two directions. The first was through the P4 Agreement with Chile and Brunei in 2004. The second was through the ASEAN–Australia–New Zealand FTA, concluded in 2009, a process during which Singapore's sustained support was critical. The first building block to evolve from the Singapore–New Zealand CEP therefore was the development of P4, which over time became the Trans-Pacific Partnership Agreement. The objective of P4 was less about the economic benefits to the existing partners, which were minimal (WTO, 2009), but rather on influencing and shaping the regional economic architecture, specifically by bringing the United States more directly into the region (Elms,

2009, pp. 6–9; National Business Review, 2008). New Zealand sought quite deliberately to shape the agreement to serve this end, emphasising, for instance the 'open accession' clause, which Deborah Elms calls a 'back-door' means of expanding the agreement to a larger coalition of states.

New Zealand, along with other P4 partners, marketed the agreement in Washington as a high-quality and comprehensive one, consistent with GATT Article XXIV and open regionalism, which the United States could use—should it so choose—to embed itself more directly in the Asia–Pacific. For New Zealand, there was an added incentive to secure US engagement. Unlike Chile and Singapore, New Zealand did not have an FTA with the United States and was increasingly concerned about the impact this was having on its commercial interests, not least against Australian competition in the US market. The efforts of the P4 partners were eventually successful. Negotiations to expand the agreement commenced in 2009, and this process morphed into the 12-member Trans-Pacific Partnership Agreement, which was concluded in December 2015 and signed in Auckland on 4 February 2016.[18] With the withdrawal of the United States from TPP in early 2017, New Zealand initiated, together with Singapore, Japan and Australia, a 'rescue mission' to establish a new agreement—CPTPP.[19] In practical terms, and as noted above, New Zealand has already used the concept of concerted open plurilaterals in support of both 'hard rules' and establishing or sustaining norms that support trade policy.

The principles which inform this concept of concerted open plurilateralism are that any such process will:

- respond to business needs and global priorities, including sustainable development
- deliver 'WTO-plus' rules and market access, or sustain or build on trade policy norms

---

[18] The members of the TPP are Brunei, Chile, New Zealand, Singapore (the P4); Australia, Canada, Japan, Malaysia, Mexico, Peru, United States and Vietnam. For more information about how the P4 morphed into the Trans-Pacific Partnership agreement, see http://www.mfat.govt.nz/Trade-and-Economic-Relations/2-Trade-Relationships-and-Agreements/Trans-Pacific/2-P4.php (Accessed 29 August 2020).

[19] More information about CPTPP is available at https://www.mfat.govt.nz/en/trade/free-trade-agreements/free-trade-agreements-in-force/cptpp (Accessed 29 August 2020).

- contain an open accession provision (i.e. any WTO member can join if they can meet the high standards of the agreement)
- involve the WTO Secretariat where possible and provide regularly briefings to WTO members on the process
- have a strategy to expand membership, including engaging the major economies in the initiative over time (to bring them in whenever possible)

CPTPP, DEPA and the recently launched negotiations for ACCTS are examples of the 'hard rules' strand of concerted open plurilateralism. COVID-19 triggered an expansion of the use of this model to help sustain existing trade policy norms (e.g. against protectionism and to keep trade links open). The expansion of the New Zealand–Singapore-led joint trade ministers' initiative to respond to the COVID-19 crisis (i.e. by establishing a ministerial-level commitment to keeping supply and trade links open) is one such example. As noted earlier, the initiative has grown to encompass an arrangement that eliminates tariffs and other restrictions on vital COVID-19-related products, building on the World Customs Organization's list of such products, in combination with groundbreaking work undertaken by Evenett (2020). This was then further developed with a New Zealand–Singapore-led initiative to evolve the norms-focused joint ministerial statement into 'hard' trade policy rules, i.e. to eliminate barriers (tariff and non-tariff) on COVID-19-related goods. Other examples of concerted open plurilaterals involving (if not led by) New Zealand include the current e-commerce negotiations involving nearly 80 WTO members.

Sustaining Global and Regional Public Goods to Shore up Institutions and the Rules

The fourth component of the New Zealand strategy is to ensure its active investment in 'public goods' that can help sustain trade norms and rules. New Zealand is the forthcoming host of APEC, so this regional body will be front and centre for its policymakers. Hosting APEC represents a unique and timely opportunity for New Zealand to show leadership that can advance and support APEC as an institution, including through the development of confidence-building measures for trade policy norms in a post-COVID-19 environment.

...while also Preserving the Social Licence for Trade Policy

The fifth element of New Zealand's six-point strategy is to ensure that the domestic 'social licence' for trade policy is sustained going forward. The Government's emphasis on the Trade for All agenda did not change as a result of COVID-19, though some points of emphasis may be adjusted somewhat over time. Work is already well under way across the five inter-related themes of this agenda, i.e. women, Maori, small- and medium-sized enterprises (SMEs), regional economic development and sustainability.[20]

The appointment of an Associate Minister for Trade and Export Growth (Nanaia Mahuta), with a particular focus on helping Maori exporters to succeed, is another practical example of seeking to ensure the benefits of trade are more inclusive. This was given concrete effect through the signing of an indigenous trade co-operation agreement between New Zealand and Australia—an expression of a shared interest in supporting indigenous exporter development.[21] A new collaborative partnership group—Te Taumata[22]—has also recently been established to work with, but be strictly independent from, the Ministry of Foreign Affairs and Trade (MFAT). The aim is to enhance the ability of Maori to have input into trade policy and improve negotiators' understanding of Maori priorities and interests in trade policy generally, and trade agreements in particular.

Finally, the internationalisation of the Trade for All agenda is well under way. This was formally launched in 2018 at the inaugural meeting of the ministerial-level Inclusive Trade Action Group[23] at the APEC meeting for Ministers Responsible for Trade in 2019. It is now expanding beyond CPTPP to meet as a caucus at the WTO and (again) in APEC.

---

[20] More information about the Trade for All Agenda is available at https://www.mfat.govt.nz/en/trade/nz-trade-policy/trade-for-all-agenda (Accessed 10 August 2020).

[21] Information about the New Zealand Australia Indigenous Cooperation Arrangement is available at https://www.beehive.govt.nz/release/australia-and-new-zealand-indigenous-arrrangement (Accessed 30 August 2020).

[22] For more information about Te Taumata see https://www.tetaumata.com (Accessed 29 August 2020).

[23] Including Chile and Canada. More information about this grouping is available at https://www.beehive.govt.nz/release/inclusive-trade-action-group-meets-port-moresby (Accessed 29 August 2020).

In the meantime, the review of CPTPP with regard to the Trade for All principles is a priority analytical commitment.

A Sharpened Economic Diplomacy Focus is a Key Part of the COVID-19 Trade Recovery Strategy

The economic diplomacy programme at MFAT has emerged as a central component of New Zealand's trade recovery strategy.[24] In practical terms, New Zealand's embassy network has been refocused to work in a more structured and co-ordinated way with other agencies offshore, particularly New Zealand Trade and Enterprise (NZTE), the Ministry for Primary Industries (MPI), the Customs Service and other government agencies to support New Zealand traders. In addition, the MFAT offshore network has been tasked to focus on delivering insights and advice to policy-makers in support of the domestic economic agenda, as well as to business (including, for instance, the provision of market information). Practical tools for exporters have also been updated/expanded, including taking account of COVID-19 needs, so that traders can make well-informed decisions and ensure the maximum uptake of new and existing trade agreements. This has included the non-tariff barrier portal through which the ministry and other agencies can better focus and help business over-come international barriers; an expanded tariff finder tool (providing detailed information on FTA tariff preferences for New Zealand firms)[25]; and the expected introduction of a services finder tool in 2021 (as with the tariff finder, this tool will help New Zealand service suppliers find where specific advantages exist for them among our FTA partners—in the case of services, this will be a world first).

...and Australia Remains the Indispensable Partner

Canberra remains central to New Zealand's efforts on trade policy in general, including at the WTO, but also in CPTPP, RCEP, PACER Plus and elsewhere. COVID-19 has served to reinforce the close trade policy

---

[24] New Zealand's Covid-19 trade recovery strategy is outlined at https://www.mfat.govt.nz/en/trade/trade-recovery-strategy (Accessed 31 August 2020).

[25] More information on both the trade barrier tool and the tariff finder is available at https://www.mfat.govt.nz/en/trade/how-we-help-exporters/services-for-exporters/barriers-to-trade (Accessed 30 August 2020).

relationship between the two countries, not least the depth and breadth of engagement. This represents a foundational element in the trade recovery of both countries from the pandemic. In particular, the joint announcement by the prime ministers of New Zealand and Australia in early May 2020 regarding the development of a COVID-safe travel zone underlines the direction of engagement in the trans-Tasman context.[26]

There will be differences of views between Canberra and Wellington on issues, e.g. on Brexit-related matters (tariff rate quotas, etc.), but in general, close collaboration remains a guiding principle for Wellington in this area. There is also room to expand the Single Economic Market (SEM) process and do interesting things bilaterally, including in the indigenous trade space, as well as potentially advancing a 'light touch' mediation mechanism for trans-Tasman SME traders. The opportunity with Australia is not only the deepening of the SEM relationship, but also the extent to which innovative approaches trialled successfully with New Zealand might then be taken to the wider Asia–Pacific/ASEAN region, including Singapore—a close partner for both countries, as the COVID-19 response underlined, with Singapore a member of a range of joint initiatives involving both Canberra and Wellington.

Conclusions

The period ahead is shaping up to be a particularly challenging one for a small, distant and trade-dependent country like New Zealand. There is now an existential threat to the existing trade policy order, not least as a consequence of the COVID-19 pandemic. These challenges require a tight focus by New Zealand on its six-part trade policy framework for managing the turbulence ahead. The recently launched COVID-19 trade recovery programme, with its emphasis on retooling support for exporters, reinvigorating New Zealand's trade architecture, and refreshing the country's wider relationships is an example of the tactical short- to medium-term implementation of the wider strategy. What is clear is that the period ahead requires new and invigorated forms of trade policy entrepreneurship which can secure New Zealand's ability to respond to

---

[26] More information about the joint announcement is available at https://www.bee hive.govt.nz/release/prime-ministers-jacinda-ardern-and-scott-morrison-announce-plans-trans-tasman-covid-safe (Accessed 30 August 2020).

changing circumstances. Concerted open plurilateralism is one example of this trade policy entrepreneurship, with DEPA and ACCTS practical recent manifestations of this, alongside the various plurilateral structures and initiatives New Zealand has advanced regionally and internationally to address the challenge of the COVID-19 pandemic. In addition, the ability to 'lean in' through this six-part framework, for instance to increase the investment in public goods, including when New Zealand hosts APEC, is another example of the framework's resilience, adaptability and continued salience in increasingly challenging times.

In practical terms, an intensified emphasis on advancing concerted open plurilateralism, with small- and medium-sized economies in particular, will be a way of protecting and preserving as much as possible of the existing (trade) rules-based system. It will also help to sustain New Zealand's continued relevance. But this can only be an interim solution. Over the medium term and as the impact of COVID-19 becomes clearer, New Zealand and others will need to work to ensure that the major economies are re-engaged on trade policy. Central to the success of concerted open plurilateralism therefore is finding ways to attract the major economies to return to and engage on regional and global norms and rules over time. Hosting APEC needs to be seen by New Zealand therefore as an important element in that broader strategy.

And finally, as New Zealand trade policy navigates past the end of the 'golden weather' and the COVID-19 pandemic, it will need to be alert to continuing challenges and turbulence. One way to frame New Zealand's approach is through the application of Aristotelian concepts of knowledge. This distinguishes between three types of knowledge, *episteme* (theoretical knowledge); *techne* (technical knowledge) and *phronesis* (practical wisdom). For Aristotle, these three forms of knowledge were at the heart of *eudaimonia*—the state of ethical and political well-being. New Zealand has traditionally been able to deploy all three of these forms of knowledge in support of its trade policy, but going forward, it will be the application of *phronesis* in particular that may best help it manage the challenging times ahead.

REFERENCES

Allison, G. (2017). *Destined for war: America, China and the Thucydides Trap.* Houghton Mifflin Harcourt.

Bernard, A. B., Jensen, J. B., Redding, S. J., & Schott, P. K. (2012). The Empirics of firm heterogeneity and international trade. *Annual Review of Economics, 4,* 283–313.

Berthelon, M., & Freund, C. (2004). *On the conservation of distance in international trade* (World Bank Research Working Paper 3293). Washington: The World Bank.

Boulhol H., de Serres, A., Molnar, M. (2008). The Contribution of Economic Geography to GDP Per Capita. OECD Economics Department Working Paper Number 602. Paris: Organisation for Economic Cooperation and Development.

Brady, A.-M. (Ed.). (2019). *Small States and the changing Global order: New Zealand faces the future.* Springer.

Copeland, D. C. (2000). The constructivist challenge to structural realism: A review essay. *International Security, 25*(2), 187–212.

Dunne, T., Kurki, M., & Smith, S. (Eds.). (2013). *International relations theories: Discipline and diversity* (3rd ed.). Oxford University Press.

Elms, D. (2009). *From the P4 to the TPP: Explaining expansion interests in the Asia–Pacific.* Paper prepared for the Asia-Pacific Trade Economists' Conference. Bangkok, 2–3 November.

Evenett, S. (2019, October 17). *The emerging global trade disorder.* Presentation to IMF, Washington.

Evenett, S. (2020, March 23). Tackling Covid19 together: The trade policy dimension. *Global Trade Alert.* https://www.globaltradealert.org/report s/51. Accessed 27 March 2020.

Fabling, R., & Sanderson, L. (2010). *Exporting and performance: Market entry, expansion and destination characteristics.* Reserve Bank of New Zealand Discussion Paper 2010/17. Wellington: Reserve Bank of New Zealand.

Hoadley, S. (2019). New Zealand's trade policy. In A.-M. Brady (Ed.), *Small states and the changing global order: New Zealand faces the future* (pp. 287–305). Springer.

Keohane, R. O. (1984). *After hegemony: Cooperation and discord in the world political economy.* Princeton University Press.

Lebow, R. N. (2013). Classical Realism. In T. Dunne, M. Kurki, & S. Smith (Eds.), *International relations theories: Discipline and diversity* (pp. 59–76). Oxford University Press.

Leslie, J. (2015). *New Zealand trade strategy and evolving Asia–Pacific regional economic architecture.* Asia New Zealand Foundation.

MFAT [New Zealand Ministry of Foreign Affairs and Trade]. (2014). *Agreement between New Zealand and Singapore on a closer economic partnership.* MFAT.

MFAT [New Zealand Ministry of Foreign Affairs and Trade]. (2017). *Estimating New Zealand's tradable and non-tradable sectors using Input–Output Tables.* Paper presented at the New Zealand Association of Economists' Conference, 12–14 July 2017.

National Business Review. (2008, September 23). Goff welcomes US FTA negotiations. *National Business Review.*

Nye. J. S. (2017, January 9). *The kindleberger trap.* Project Syndicate. https:// www.project-syndicate.org/commentary/trump-china-kindleberger-trap-by-joseph-s--nye-2017-01. Accessed 3 March 2021.

NZIER [New Zealand Institute for Economic Research]. (2016, November). *Quantifying the costs of non-tariff measures in the Asia-Pacific region* (Working paper 2016/4). Wellington: NZIER.

Parker, D. (2019, June 29). *The future of the WTO and trade structures.* Speech to the Otago Foreign Policy School. https://www.beehive.govt.nz/speech/ future-wto-and-trade-structures. Accessed 3 March 2021.

Waltz, K. N. (1979). *Theory of international politics.* Addison Wesley.

Wendt, A. (1992). Anarchy is what states make of it: The social construction of power politics. *International Organization, 46*(2), 391–425.

World Trade Organization. (2009). *Trade policy review report by New Zealand.* WTO.

Democracy Under Strain in the Philippines: The Populist Politics and Diplomacy of President Rodrigo Duterte

Aurora Javate de Dios

INTRODUCTION

For decades the Philippines has been hailed as one of the most enduring liberal democracies in Asia, with regular elections, a bureaucracy governed by civil service rules, a working parliament and a reasonably independent judiciary. This relative political stability was disrupted when in 1972 Ferdinand Marcos declared martial law, abolished democratic institutions and consolidated his monopoly of power, which lasted for 13 years. These years were marked by the most brutal record of human rights violations, such as murder, torture and the unjust detention of political prisoners (De Dios et al., 1988). The EDSA People Power uprising which overthrew the Marcos dictatorship in 1986 was a milestone in Philippine history, Filipinos overthrowing a dictatorship in a bloodless uprising (Official Gazette, n.d.).

The election of Rodrigo Duterte to the presidency in 2016 was unexpected and, to many, represented a disruption of the democratic reforms

A. Javate de Dios (✉)
Miriam College, Quezon, Philippines
e-mail: adedios@mc.edu.ph

that previous administrations had tried to institutionalise. This chapter will, firstly, consider whether Duterte, despite promises of change, has a coherent economic and political agenda, and basically continued the neoliberal economic policies and corrupt practices of previous governments. Secondly, Duterte has maintained the trappings of democratic institutions such as elections, Congress, the judiciary, media and civil society while systematically undermining them through threats, co-optation and vilification. Thirdly, by weaponising the law against those challenging his draconian policies, Duterte is simply replicating Marcosian methods of control, thereby firmly establishing his populist authoritarian regime. What distinguishes Duterte is his methodology as a 'fascist original' (Bello, 2017, p. 2). 'He begins with impunity on a massive scale — that is, the extrajudicial killings of thousands of alleged drug users and pushers — and leaves the violations of civil liberties and the grab for absolute power as mopping up operations in a political landscape devoid of significant organized opposition' (Bello, 2017, p. 3). Lastly, by strategically changing the course of the country's foreign policy, Duterte has subverted the country's diplomatic gains in human rights and risks endangering, rather than protecting, the sovereignty of the country by giving up the Philippines' victory in the arbitral ruling in The Hague and allowing China's intrusion into Philippine territorial waters.

AUTHORITARIAN POPULISM ON THE RISE

Populism has been conceptualised as a discourse, a strategy and a political style centred around the nodal points 'the people' and 'the elite', in which 'the people' and 'the elite' are constructed as antagonistic opposites. Populists claim to represent 'the people' against an illegitimate 'elite', and identify the political demands of the former as the *volonté générale* (general will) of 'the people' (De Cleen, 2017, pp. 347–354). They behave as if they and they alone can speak in the name of the real people, or the 'silent majority'. Kurt Weyland (2013) understands populism as a political strategy through which a personalistic leader seeks to exercise government power based on direct, unmediated, uninstitutionalised support from large numbers of mostly unorganised followers. Furthermore, personalistic leadership 'allows the leader great latitude for opportunistic calculations and maneuverings [and] gives populism the striking unpredictability, shiftiness, and disorganization in the exercise of government power and in public policy-making' (Weyland 2018, p. 60).

Viewed from a global and regional perspective, Duterte's 'populist revolt against elite democracy' follows the populist wave across Asia and the world. In Southeast Asia, Myanmar and Cambodia for instance have long been under dictatorships and military regimes known for their repressive policies against opposition leaders and the media. Despite the election of Aung San Suu Kyi in 2015, Myanmar's transitional democracy was still subjected to the influence of the country's powerful military. Among other things, Ms Suu Kyi's government was accused of complicity in human rights violations against the opposition and the Rohingya people before falling victim to a military coup in early February 2021. In Thailand, after some years of political turmoil involving Prime Minister Thaksin Shinawatra, a repressive military took over and are now fully entrenched as the duly elected government. Indonesia had its long record of military rule under Suharto (1967–1998) marked by arrests, killings and the bloody repression of the leaders of the Indonesian Communist Party and other opposition leaders. In 2014, a former General, Prabowo Subianto, who has a record of violence, including kidnapping and the disappearance of student activists, the rape of Chinese women and the burning of numerous buildings owned by the Chinese in 1997, nearly won the presidency from Joko Widodo. He remains a serious contender for the Indonesian presidency.

Making Sense of Duterte's Populism

Though there seem to be commonalities and similarities in populism around the world, it needs to be understood in its national context and specificities. Populism is deeply rooted in the historical and cultural milieu of Philippine politics. Past presidents also claimed to speak on behalf of the people to get the voters' support by portraying themselves as someone coming from humble beginnings, or one who identified and understood the problems of the masses. The fascination with and hope for a populist leader who would deliver the people from poverty and hopelessness has been a recurring theme in the political history of a country where class inequalities have been entrenched: more than 26 million Filipinos remain poor, and 12 million were living in extreme poverty in 2015 (Yap, 2015).

Before Duterte, there was Joseph Estrada, another populist candidate who became president from 2001 but was deposed in 2003 due to corruption charges. In many ways, Estrada's rise as a populist president paved the way for Duterte's ascent to the presidency. Both came from well-to-do families but chose to present themselves as 'rogue' leaders and benevolent champions of ordinary Filipinos while serving as mayors in their respective cities. They both presented themselves as 'outsiders' not in the least concerned with the formalities and niceties of elite behaviour. Though educated at an elite school, Estrada's performative populism highlighted his 'carabao English' that he had popularised in his action movies, as his way of associating himself with the uneducated masses while mocking the English-speaking elite of the country. Duterte, who is a lawyer, uses irreverent, curse-laden and misogynist street language that not only sets him apart from the language of the elite but also identifies him with ordinary Filipinos. More importantly, Duterte reflects the 'culturally dominant features that characterise the collective mind and that are deeply ingrained in the psyche of most Filipinos. These features include machismo, sexism, violence, the desire for social order and the need to discipline the citizenry' (Juego, 2017, p. 135).

From Aquino's Daang Matuwid (Straight Path) to Duterte's Strongman Rule

Despite the impressive achievements of President Benigno Aquino III from 2010 to 2016, including high GDP growth rates of up to 6.9%, the passage of progressive laws and the prosecution of high government officials for corruption, he was hounded by several corruption scandals and missteps that weakened his influence and the support of the people. Inefficient public services, poor infrastructure development and a slow response to the tragic Typhoon Haiyan disaster in 2013, capped by a bungled military operation in 2015 that killed 44 Special Forces soldiers, are some of the glaring failures of the Aquino Government (Thompson, 2019).

An Asian Development Bank (2009) study showed that economic growth rates did not translate into a reduction in poverty levels, and inequality has remained high. Many Filipino households were vulnerable to shocks and risks due to unemployment, natural disasters and, in some cases, conflict. Though the country had all the trappings of a working democracy, it was essentially a democracy in form and feudal in substance, or what Benedict Anderson (1988) refers to as 'cacique democracy'. Without any serious structural redistribution of wealth, the reality on the ground was that wealth continues to be concentrated in the hands of the few families that monopolised economic and political power in the country.

Why did Duterte, an outsider win? First, he is the first president to come from Mindanao, a historically marginalised and neglected region in the Philippines where Muslim rebellion has persisted for centuries. Many aggrieved Mindanaoans saw in Duterte their first shot at national leadership. Secondly, during the campaign, Duterte's curse-laden speeches focused on a crisis narrative blaming the past administration, the elites, corrupt politicians and drug syndicates for causing widespread suffering and the poverty of the people. He promised to eliminate the drug problem in six months, reduce crime, promote economic growth, develop infrastructure rapidly, end the war in Mindanao and bring about peace with the communists. A third and crucial factor in the election of Duterte was the aggressive and unprecedented use of social media to spread disinformation against his competitors. Duterte's campaign paid US$200,000 (₱19 million) to hire trolls who opened up spaces where 'communities of discontent can express unheard of sentiments' (Ong & Cabañes, 2018, p. 61). By using fake news on a massive scale, these operators were able to spread disinformation, and to silence and threaten people with dissenting opinions and perspectives, while extolling the virtues of Duterte. Lastly, Duterte's strongman image was buttressed by his infamous record in Davao as a no-nonsense mayor responsible for restoring peace and order in that city. For the residents it did not matter that Duterte achieved this by deploying the so-called Davao Death Squad, which was responsible for killing numerous drug addicts, criminals and even some opposition leaders.

Implementing the Davao Model: War on Drugs

To fulfil his promise, Duterte's first directive after becoming president was to initiate the 'war on drugs', notoriously called Operation Tokhang.[1] Led by his loyal police chief, General Ronald 'Bato' dela Rosa, this campaign unleashed the bloodiest police campaign ever in the history of the country against suspected drug dealers and drug users in metropolitan Manila and other major urban areas nationwide. The widespread killings

---

[1] *Tokhang* is a portmanteau of two Visayan words, *katok* (knock) and *hangyo* (plead). Operation Tokhang was used by police to flush out drug suspects by knocking from door to door in urban communities.

shocked the nation and sowed fear, mainly among the poorest in urban communities. Massive public outrage did not stop the Philippine National Police, which was given licence by Duterte to proceed in their campaign. Dead bodies wrapped in duct tape were dumped in dark alleys, dumpsites and under bridges with cardboard signs strapped around the bodies that said 'I am a drug addict/pusher. Do not imitate me' (Evangelista, 2018). Although the police acknowledged only 5,526 killed in their operations from July 2016 to June 2019, independent sources such as ABS–CBN, Inquirer, Rappler and Reuters give much higher estimates. Local and international human rights groups such as I Defend Rights, Human Rights Watch and Amnesty International called for the immediate investigation of the killings of an estimated 27,000 victims. The majority of the victims were men, but some were also women and children from urban poor areas of Caloocan, Malabon, Navotas, Valenzuela and Bulacan, and living in congested urban shanties, leading observers to conclude that the war on drugs is actually a 'war against the poor' (Philippine Human Rights Information Center, 2019).

Some Political Continuities: More of the Same

Despite his attacks on the previous administration, Duterte did not present any new vision of a transformative governance agenda, nor did he promise to implement revolutionary redistribution programmes for the poor. His economic policies never really challenged the neoliberal capitalist economic policies of the previous administrations, but made some token concessions to the workers and marginalised sectors. 'Dutertenomics' is the term used for the government's Philippine Development Plan for 2017–2022, which was aimed at reducing poverty, fostering economic growth and improving the infrastructure of the country through the 'Build, Build, Build!' programme. Other features of the plan include free college education; universal health care; rice tariffication; expanded value added tax and expanded conditional cash transfer (National Economic and Development Authority, 2017). Some of these measures, such as the free education and universal health care laws, were actually introduced by opposition leaders in the Senate.

Patronage Politics

In the Philippines, elections are exercises where intense elite competition is played out, often characterised by vote buying, the tampering of voter registration and electoral returns, pay-offs of election officials, and other fraudulent practices (Rivera, 2016, pp. 45–50). Politics is often centred on personalities rather than firm political ideologies or platforms, and 'turncoatism' or party switching, where politicians routinely switch party affiliations to whoever wins the election, is still the order of the day. It is no wonder therefore that as soon as Duterte won, most newly elected officials in the Congress and Senate lost no time in joining the so-called Super Majority consisting of pro-Duterte political parties so as not to be left out in the allocation of budgets and the distribution of political favours and largesse. This has enabled Duterte to directly control both the Congress and Senate in order to pass the legislation he needs. Facing just a handful of opposition legislators, the Duterte Government easily passed several controversial measures such as martial law in Mindanao, the grant of emergency powers to the president during the COVID-19 pandemic, and the recent draconian Anti-Terrorism Act which defines 'terrorism' broadly and allows the warrantless arrest and detention of suspected 'terrorists' for up to 24 days (Human Rights Watch, 2020).

Duterte created his own set of cronies, members of the cabinet and heads of key government agencies drawn from among his friends from Davao; classmates from schools where he studied; recycled politicians from the Marcos, Estrada and Arroyo camps, or *trapos* (a pejorative term for corrupt traditional politicians) who were alienated by the previous administration of Aquino; and social media manipulators, later dubbed Diehard Duterte Supporters (DDS). As is the practice in Philippine politics, plum appointments in the bureaucracy and in government corporations were given to known Duterte loyalists, some of whom lacked civil service eligibility.

In just over three years, business friends of Duterte have been mopping up company after company with the use of 'behest loans' from the government, to the dismay of other businesses. At the same time, Duterte has not hesitated to publicly shame, accuse and threaten companies, especially media companies, whom he perceives as opposing his policies. This practice is reminiscent of President Donald Trump's penchant for accusing media networks such as CNN of bias and 'fake news'. Among those on the receiving end of Duterte's threats were the Rufino-Prietos (owners of *Inquirer* newspaper), the Ayalas and Pangilinans (owners of the biggest water concessions and telecommunications companies) and the Lopezes (owners of Meralco, the biggest electricity company, and the broadcasting network ABS–CBN).

REHABILITATION OF THE MARCOSES

Duterte openly expressed his unabashed admiration for former President Marcos and his authoritarian leadership by allowing his reburial in the Heroes' Cemetery with full military honours despite massive protests by martial law victims, students and the opposition. Duterte has also openly endorsed the candidacy of 'Imee' Marcos as a senator and Ferdinand 'Bongbong' Marcos as Vice President. While such trends have encountered political pushback in the Philippines, Duterte has resorted to 'lawfare', which has been the main weapon used by his administration to suppress dissent, and is clearly a legacy of martial law (Nonato, 2020). Over the last three years, Duterte has effectively utilised his arsenal of repression to include guns, narco lists, trolls and the law—the most powerful weapon that the government is wielding to harass, silence, prosecute and arrest his perceived enemies. Having already demonised drug addicts as enemies of the state, Duterte regularly uses his presidential pulpit to relentlessly and publicly attack critics such as journalists, politicians and some businesspeople for alleged wrongdoing. Aided by an aggressive, often toxic, social media campaign against identified critics, such accusations are amplified to create a viral effect that often leads to the dismissal, arrest or prosecution of identified 'enemies of the people'.

POLITICISING THE MILITARY
AND MILITARISING THE BUREAUCRACY

Autocratic leaders like Duterte more often than not realise that the key to security in office, as well as minimising the risk of a coup, is to secure the support of the military. Duterte often expressed his preference for military officers because they are more disciplined and efficient, and obey the orders of the commander-in-chief without question. He has courted the military by visiting their camps numerous times, raising their salaries and providing perks such as trips abroad, as well as appointing them to government posts. In a bizarre and misogynist remark, he told military combat troops fighting the Maute and Abu Sayyaf terrorist groups in

Marawi they could rape up to three women each and he would back them up. By 15 July 2019, ten former military men had been appointed to the cabinet or were cabinet-level officials. In addition, he also appointed 31 ex-military/police officials to government posts, in Social Welfare and Development, Local Government, Environment, Housing and Customs, among others (Gita, 2019). In total disregard of the constitution, Duterte openly articulates his preference for a military junta to succeed him rather than the duly elected Vice President Leni Robredo. His response to the COVID-19 pandemic was haphazard, unplanned and highly militarised. Given his approach to the management and implementation of measures against the pandemic, Duterte's strategy has been mainly punitive. With direct orders from the president 'to shoot and kill' violators of quarantine rules (Thompson, 2020), thousands of poor people have been arrested and detained for weeks for breaking curfew and quarantine restrictions.

Strategic Shifts in the Philippines' Foreign Policy

Duterte has made two unprecedented foreign policy decisions that have drastically subverted the direction of the country's external relations. One is his total disregard for the Philippines' traditional support for the United Nations (UN) and the country's adherence to the universality of human rights. The second is the Philippines' departure from the United States' Asia-Pacific security umbrella and its policy of appeasement towards China. How has Duterte's populist style affected Philippine foreign policy?

The populist leader is often portrayed as the only true representative of the people, who embody the 'popular will'. As such, decision-making, even in foreign policy, is characterised by centralisation and personalisation. In the case of Duterte, the international arena became a domain for his populist performance, effectively sidelining bureaucrats in matters of foreign policy (Destradi & Plagemann, 2019). As Sheila Coronel (2019) notes,

> Duterte is not an ideologue. His rants against imperialist elites in Manila and the United States and his overtures to China and Russia are driven not by ideology but by emotion. They are salve for wounded pride. They are also political gamesmanship: whether in foreign policy or domestic affairs, Duterte likes to play off rivals against one another. Duterte's politics are defined by his gut, his experience, and his friends. He *didn't* promise

Filipinos a statesman. He offered them Duterte, Punisher of Criminals, Avenger of Filipinos' Wounded Pride, a man who would also build roads, fix traffic, and get things moving in their gridlocked democracy. (emphasis added)

Duterte is at his performative best when he invokes the interest of the people/nation by saying that 'human rights cannot be used as a shield or an excuse to destroy the nation' in response to his critics against his war on drugs (Curato, 2017, p. 10). For this reason, Duterte takes criticisms of his war on drugs personally and responds with foul language to insult and threaten UN officials such as Agnes Callamard, Special Rapporteur on Extrajudicial Killings, the former UN High Commissioner for Human Rights Zeid Ra'ad Al Hussein, and the Human Rights Council and other international organisations such as the European Union and Human Rights Watch (UN News, 2018). In retaliation for the scheduled preliminary investigation of extrajudicial killings by the International Criminal Court, Duterte announced the formal withdrawal of the Philippines from the court on 19 March 2018. When the UN Human Rights Council's members voted to call on the High Commissioner Michelle Bachelet to prepare a comprehensive report on the alleged extrajudicial killings in the Philippines, Duterte responded by rejecting the official development assistance of those European Union (EU) countries who voted for the resolution.[2]

Philippine Relations with China Under Arroyo and Aquino

During the term of President Arroyo (2001–2010), the government earnestly pursued economic negotiations with China, which resulted in 38 economic agreements. However, two large projects, the NBN–ZTE and the Northrail project, were exposed by the media as being mired in corruption involving Arroyo's allies. In contrast to Arroyo's policy of friendly bilateral relations with China, President Aquino adopted a balancing strategy in an effort to deter its aggressive maritime claims which threatened the Philippines' territorial waters. A series of irritants,

---

[2] The Human Rights Council went ahead and produced a report on the human rights situation in the Philippines which was released in May 2020 despite the intense campaign of the Department of Foreign Affairs to defeat the resolution filed by Iceland.

including Chinese incursions and harassment of fisherfolk and Philippine survey ships in the Spratly Islands, the Kalayaan group of islands and the Exclusive Economic Zone of the Philippines, prompted President Aquino to file diplomatic protests, which were dismissed by China. After two months of tense stand-off in the Scarborough Shoal, China now maintains a permanent surveillance after reneging on a promise to withdraw.

In response, President Aquino took a series of military and diplomatic initiatives to try to buttress the Philippines' position against China (Heydarian, 2018). First, he sought to strengthen US bilateral defence presence in the region by signing the Framework Agreement on Increased Rotational Presence and the Agreement on Enhanced Defense Cooperation, the latter considered an updating of the 1951 Mutual Defense Treaty with the United States. Secondly, to improve and modernise the Philippines' naval and military forces, the Aquino Government also entered into various defence-related agreements with the Japan such as the 2015 'Strategic Partnership for Advancing the Shared Principles and Goals of Peace, Security and Growth in the Region and Beyond'. This declaration provided for the transfer of defence technology to the Philippines in return for the country allowing the Self-Defense Forces of Japan access to Philippine bases on a limited and rotational basis (De Castro, 2016). Thirdly, on 5 September 2012, President Aquino issued Administrative Order 29, which renamed the maritime areas west of the Philippines as the West Philippine Sea, which includes the Kalayaan island group and the Bajo de Masinloc or Panatag Shoal, internationally known as Scarborough Shoal. These maritime areas are critical to the Philippines for strategic, security and economic reasons.

Realising that China will not slow down in its campaign to promote its 'nine-dash' claim to the entire South China Sea, the Philippines filed an arbitration case against China in the International Court of Justice in The Hague on January 2013 to determine and clarify its claims under the UN Convention on the Law of the Sea. On 12 July 2016, the Permanent Court of Arbitration (PCA) in The Hague, ruled in favour of the Philippines in 14 out of its 15 submissions. It found that China has no historic rights to resources within the so-called 'nine-dash line', a demarcation line which was used by the Republic of China for the first time on an official map in 1947 and later by the People's Republic of China. The tribunal concluded that to the extent China had historic rights to resources in the waters of the South China Sea, such rights were extinguished to the extent they were incompatible with the exclusive economic zones provided for in the [Law of the Sea] Convention. The Tribunal also noted that, although there is evidence that Chinese navigators and fishermen, as well as those of other States, had historically made use of the *islands* in the South China Sea, there was no evidence that China had historically exercised exclusive control over the *waters* or their resources. The Tribunal concluded that there was no legal basis for China to claim historic rights to resources within the sea areas falling within the 'nine-dash line'. (Permanent Court of Arbitration, 2016, p. 473)

The second important ruling of the Court was that China had inter-fered with traditional Philippine fishing rights at Scarborough Shoal, and had no rights to an economic zone within 200 miles of Mischief Reef or the Second Thomas Shoal. China had violated the Philippines' sovereign rights in its exclusive economic zone by (a) interfering with Philippine fishing and petroleum exploration, (b) constructing artificial islands and (c) failing to prevent Chinese fishermen from fishing in the zone. The tribunal also held that fishermen from the Philippines (like those from China) had traditional fishing rights at Scarborough Shoal and that China had interfered with these rights in restricting access. The tribunal further found that Chinese law enforcement vessels had unlawfully created a serious risk of collision when they physically obstructed Philippine vessels. A third ruling has to do with the occupation and building of bases encroaching on Philippine maritime territory:

China's occupation of and construction activities on Mischief Reef (a) violate the provisions of the Convention [on the Law of the Sea] concerning artificial islands, installations and structures; (b) violate China's duties to protect and preserve the marine environment under the Conven-tion; and (c) constitute unlawful acts of attempted appropriation in violation of the Convention. (Permanent Court of Arbitration, 2016, p. 476)

The decisions of the PCA were a historic legal victory and milestone for the Philippines with regard to international law. Although China did not participate in the proceedings and chose to ignore and oppose the decision, it was, for all intents and purposes, an embarrassing legal defeat for China. Filipinos worldwide took to social media to celebrate the ruling of the PCA with the hashtag #chexit, referring to China's anticipated exit from the disputed areas in the South China Sea. Supreme Court Justice Antonio Carpio, one of the proponents of the Philippine position, stated that

> the ruling also re-affirms UNCLOS [the UN Convention on the Law of the Sea of 1982] as the Constitution for the oceans of our planet, a treaty ratified by 167 States, including China and the Philippines ... The ruling applies the fundamental law of the sea principle that 'land dominates the sea,' that is, any claim to maritime zones must emanate from land and can extend only to the limits prescribed under UNCLOS.' (Malig, 2016)

President Aquino, quoted in Dizon (2016), said:

> Instead of viewing this decision as a victory of one party over another, the best way to look at this judgment is that it is a victory for all. I say this because the clarity rendered now establishes better conditions that enable countries to engage each other, bearing in mind their duties and rights within a context that espouses equality and amity.

From Aquino's Balancing Act to Duterte's Rapprochement with China

Instead of celebrating the legal victory of the Philippines in The Hague, however, the Duterte Government received the news with sober and muted acceptance, even cautioning the people not to celebrate so as not to antagonise China. It soon became clear that Duterte was going to set aside the PCA ruling before initiating bilateral talks with China. He justified this position by saying that the arbitral ruling is just a piece of paper that is not enforceable in any way. From his perspective, the Philippines is in no position to assert itself lest it risk going to war with China, a conflict which the Philippines could never win. Duterte views China as a rising economic and political power who can provide the much-needed economic assistance for his ambitious economic programmes, especially the 'Build, Build, Build!' project, and make the Philippines part of the Belt and Road Initiative, which already includes many ASEAN countries.

The other reason for this pivot to China was Duterte's abhorrence of the intensifying criticisms by the United States, EU and UN of his war on drugs policy. China on the other hand supports his war on drugs unconditionally and expressed its support by providing funding for the building of drug rehabilitation centres (*Straits Times*, 2020). In a speech in Tokyo, Duterte also announced that he was willing to revoke the EDCA of 2014 that bolstered the 1999 Visiting Forces Agreement (VFA) with the United States (Paddock, 2016). Duterte's foreign policy performance and his choosing the moment to unleash a dramatic policy shift has become part of his political style. During the ASEAN and East Asia Summit meeting held in Laos in September 2016, Duterte unleashed a tirade against the United States, denouncing its historical atrocities in Mindanao and its hypocrisy in accusing Third World countries such as the Philippines of human rights violations. Philippine foreign affairs officials were kept in the dark before the event, which caused the cancellation of a scheduled bilateral meeting between Presidents Duterte and Barack Obama. In a series of moves, Duterte announced on 12 September 2016 the end of the US Special Forces' presence in Mindanao and the end of the joint patrol by the Philippines and US Navies in the Philippines' Exclusive Economic Zone. Finally, miffed by the US refusal to grant a visa to Senator 'Bato' dela Rosa, a former police chief and close supporter, Duterte threatened the termination of the VFA (Lema et al., 2020).

On his first official visit to China in 2016, Duterte was received with great enthusiasm. He did not disappoint when he said: 'In this venue, your honors … I announce my separation from the United States' (Blanchard, 2016). By setting aside the International Court of Justice's decision on the South China Sea and appeasing China, Duterte radically reversed the direction of the Philippine foreign policy. In so doing, he was sending the message that the United States was no longer the principal economic and political power in the Asia-Pacific region and that the Philippines was ending its dependence on the US military and security umbrella. In return, China promised a package of loans, grants and investments to the Philippines amounting to US$24 billion. In March 2017 the Philippines and China signed a six-year economic agreement to finance 15 big-ticket projects, including the Chico River Pump Irrigation project, the Kaliwa Low Dam and the South Line of the North–South Railway (Padin, 2018). More importantly, China expressed support for Duterte's war on drugs.

DUTERTE'S GAMBLE: COSTS AND BENEFITS
OF APPEASEMENT POLICY TOWARDS CHINA

The 'pivot to China' policy was supposed to generate economic benefits for the Philippines, and appease China so it would refrain from further aggressive actions against the Philippines and Filipino fisherfolk, in particular, and to help maintain peace in the South China Sea. Duterte was more than generous in reciprocating China's support. As Chair of ASEAN in 2017, he did not raise the Philippines' legal victory in The Hague ruling on the South China Sea or the critical issues of China's territorial disputes with several ASEAN countries that affected Malaysia, Vietnam, Indonesia and the Philippines, saying that the issue of maritime disputes in the South China Sea was better left untouched. By not mentioning the Hague ruling in an international forum, Duterte effectively nullified the earlier attempts by Presidents Ramos and Aquino to rally ASEAN in pushing for a Code of Conduct against China's expansionist moves in the South China Sea.

In addition, Duterte has scaled back joint military exercises with the United States and barred US warships from using Filipino bases to conduct Freedom of Navigation Operations in the South China Sea. As Renato Cruz de Castro observes, Duterte considers the presence of US troops in the Philippines a 'fuse that can ignite a major conflict in East Asia' rather than as a stabilising factor in the region (De Castro, 2020). Having threatened the United States with the abrogation of defence agreements with the Philippines since 2016, Duterte renewed his threats to terminate the VFA following the US Senate's adoption of a resolution that seeks Global Magnitsky Act sanctions against Philippine officials involved in extrajudicial killings and the detention of Senator de Lima (Tomacruz, 2020).

The Chinese are now the second-largest source of tourists for the Philippines, registering about 645,000 arrivals in the first eight months of 2018, behind only the South Koreans. According to the Department of Tourism, close to 1.5 million Chinese tourists visited the Philippines in the first ten months of 2019. About 300 daily flights shuttle between the Philippines and various Chinese cities every week (Shi, 2019). Philippines–China trade has also grown from US$11.3 billion in the first half of 2017 to US$14.1 billion in 2018. However, these trade inflows increased the trade deficit of the Philippines by 42% during the same period. The Philippines–China economic agreement has largely focussed on the financing of the government's ambitious 'Build, Build, Build!' infrastructure programme (Mendoza et al., 2018, p. 5). Chinese businessmen have been investing in real estate and online gaming, which is illegal in China itself. Despite reports of criminal activities by Chinese syndicates in the offshore gaming or 'POGO' business, the Philippines Government has welcomed them as they bring in substantial gambling revenues, estimated at US$4.1 billion since 2016 (*Manila Bulletin*, 2020). The big-ticket infrastructure projects to be funded by China, such as the Subic-Clark and trans-Mindanao railways, were eventually either shelved or discontinued altogether. The Chico River Pump Irrigation and Kaliwa Low Dam projects on the other hand have been delayed due to ecological concerns from environmental and indigenous groups. In order to fast-track some of the projects, the Duterte administration awarded the US$10 billion Sangley Point International Airport project in Cavite to a joint consortium of China Communications Construction and its local partner under the Chinese-Filipino tycoon Lucio Tan (Heydarian, 2020).

More Aggressive Chinese Naval Intrusions

Friendlier relations with China did not restrain China's aggressive moves in the South China Sea despite previous agreements of non-interference in Philippine waters. A series of alarming incursions have been observed by the Philippines Department of National Defense. China Coast Guard vessels have been guarding the Scarborough Shoal since 2012, often forcibly preventing Filipinos from fishing in the inner lagoon. At least two wooden vessels with Chinese flags were spotted harvesting giant clams from the shoal, despite a fishing ban. China Coast Guard ships have also been observed circling Ayungin Shoal (a.k.a. Second Thomas Shoal) in the Kalayaan Island group, which is part of the Spratlys within the Exclusive Economic Zone of the Philippines. The most serious of these incidents have been the ramming by the Chinese fishing vessel *Yuemaobinyu 42,212* of the Philippine fishing boat *Gem-Ver* in 2019 as it was anchored near Recto (or Reed) Bank in the West Philippine Sea, causing it to sink with 22 people on board. Instead of helping the Filipino fishermen to safety, they were left to die, though they were rescued by a Vietnamese fishing boat. On 17 February 2019, the Philippine Navy vessel BRP *Conrado Yap*, patrolling the Malampaya natural gas facility off Palawan, warned the Chinese corvette CNS *Liupanshui* (514) that they were trespassing in Philippine waters and that they should turn back. The

Chinese intruders shouted back that the area is part of China and aimed their guns at the BRP *Conrado Yap* (Tomacruz & Gotinga, 2019). Faced with these incursions, the Department of Foreign Affairs and the Defense Department could only issue diplomatic protests, which China seemingly ignored. During the COVID-19 pandemic, China has not stopped its aggressive moves against the claimant countries, including Malaysia, Vietnam, Indonesia and the Philippines.

In reaction to reported Chinese plans to enforce an Air Defence Identification Zone over the South China Sea, including Paracel and Spratly Islands, two US aircraft carriers, USS *Theodore Roosevelt* and *Nimitz*, and their strike groups recently began co-ordinated operations in international waters. These patrols, called 'Freedom of Navigation Operations' or FONOPs, are also the United States' way of maintaining dominance in the region faced with an increasingly aggressive China. Malaysia, Indonesia and the G7 have called on China to respect the UNCLOS and the Hague PCA ruling, in view of the current tensions in the South China Sea. During the ASEAN leaders' meeting on 26 June 2020, under the chairmanship of Vietnam, ASEAN issued a more assertive statement, calling on all parties to use the UNCLOS as the basis of sovereign rights and entitlements in the South China Sea (Associated Press, 2020). Duterte has now suspended the termination of the VFA, which would have lapsed in August 2020.

Towards a Perilous Future: Long-Term Implications of Duterte's Policies

Unlike dictatorships of the past which generally seized power through military coups, the success of modern authoritarian regimes such as Duterte's rely on the traditional channels of democracy: elections. Having secured convincing electoral mandates, authoritarian leaders use methods of control that are 'legal' and legitimised by legislative fiat and sanctioned by the courts. Arch Puddington (2017, p. 1) notes:

> Central to the modern authoritarian strategy is the capture of institutions that undergird political pluralism. The goal is to dominate not only the executive and legislative branches, but also the media, the judiciary, civil society, the commanding heights of the economy, and the security forces.

Because there is no single moment that signals a crossing of the line, such as the suspension of the constitution or the declaration of martial law, the erosion of democracy is almost imperceptible, like a 'thousand cuts' (Levitsky & Ziblatt, 2018, pp. 113–118). This chapter has shown that instead of the changes that Duterte promised during the 2016 election campaign, his first three years witnessed a reversion to a populist authoritarian past reminiscent of the Marcos years. Employing a performative populist style, Duterte effectively painted a picture of a nation in crisis from the threat of drugs which he alone was able to stop decisively. The use of gutter and sexist language in his speeches established a rapport with ordinary people who saw in his bad manners evidence of his authenticity. While criticising the inefficiencies, corruption and weaknesses of liberal democracy under previous elite rule, Duterte showed his decisiveness in waging a war on drugs which killed thousands. In consolidating his authoritarian rule, Duterte's methods simply resurrected many of the Marcosian policies of weaponising the law—and today also the social media—against perceived political enemies, politicising the bureaucracy and militarising aspects of civilian life. Stopping short of declaring martial law nationwide, as Marcos did, Duterte simply corrupted existing democratic institutions and suppressed civil liberties.

Decades of strengthening the Philippines' adherence to the UN and to the principles of international law and human rights have been discarded, and criticisms of extrajudicial killings have been dismissed as interference in the internal affairs of a sovereign country. In effect, the Philippines aligned itself with the most notorious 'rogue' states that defy international norms and standards. Duterte's appeasement policy and political alignment with China have significantly reconfigured the political and military security landscape in the Asia-Pacific region and emboldened China even more to intensify its intrusions into the territorial waters of the Philippines and other ASEAN countries. Duterte has not offered a coherent sociopolitical agenda or ideology, just a vague promise of change and simple solutions to complex problems. Kill the drug addicts to eliminate the drug problem; eliminate corruption of public officials by firing them on the spot; exterminate the communists; arrest or shoot to kill those who defy government orders to stay at home during the COVID-19 pandemic—these are some of his 'quick-fix' solutions to long-term social ills.

The temptation for Duterte to consolidate power because of his high popularity ratings and the capture of democratic institutions is almost inexorable. All that needs to happen now is a shift to a federal form of government to ensure his indefinite stay in power, the way Xi Jinping and Vladimir Putin have secured their lifetime rule. But Duterte, just like other Philippine presidents before him, cannot escape accountability for his crimes. Just as the previous Marcos martial law regime was undermined by its own weaknesses, this populist authoritarian regime will be evaluated on the strength and weaknesses of its own set of promises. Is the Philippines a drug-free country now? Has economic growth improved the lives of the poorest of the poor? Is corruption and cronyism gone and is the Philippines safer now, internally and externally?

After three years of brazen attacks on press freedom, freedom of assembly and human rights, a visible people's resistance movement with the increasing involvement of young people has begun to emerge. This post-EDSA generation has enjoyed a certain level of freedom, are not docile and are unafraid to assert their rights. The lesson of the Marcos martial law regime should serve as a reminder that governance by violence, intimidation and repression has its limits, and in the end those in power must realise that no shackle is strong enough to control people who are ready to fight for their freedoms and rights.

REFERENCES

Anderson, B. (1988). Cacique democracy in the Philippines: Origins, and dreams. *New Left Review, 169*, 3–33.

Asian Development Bank. (2009). *Poverty in the Philippines: Causes, constraints and opportunities*. Asian Development Bank.

Associated Press. (2020, June 26). ASEAN leaders cite 1982 UN treaty in South China Sea dispute. *The Guardian*. https://www.theguardian.com/world/2020/jun/27/asean-leaders-cite-1982-un-treaty-in-south-china-sea-dispute. Accessed 27 June 2020.

Bello, W. (2017, February 6). Rodrigo Duterte: A fascist original. *Foreign policy in focus*. https://fpif.org/rodrigo-duterte-fascist-original. Accessed 7 August 2020.

Blanchard, B. (2016, October 20). *Duterte aligns Philippines with China, says U.S. has lost*. Reuters. https://www.reuters.com/article/us-china-phi lippines/duterte-aligns-philippines-with-china-says-u-s-has-lost-idUSKCN12 K0AS. Accessed 27 June 2020.

Coronel, S. (2019, September/October). The Vigilante President: How Duterte's Brutal populism conquered the Philippines. *Foreign Affairs.* https://www.foreignaffairs.com/articles/philippines/2019-08-12/vigilante-president. Accessed 6 August 2020.

Curato, N. (2017). Flirting with authoritarian fantasies? Rodrigo Duterte and the new terms of Philippine populism. *Journal of Contemporary Asia, 47*(1), 142–153.

De Castro, R. (2016, March 15). *The Philippines and Japan sign new defense agreement.* Asia Maritime Transparency Initiative. Washington: Centre for Strategic and International Studies. https://amti.csis.org/the-philippines-and-japan-sign-new-defense-agreement/. Accessed 20 June 2020.

De Castro, R. (2020, May 11). The death of EDCA and Philippine–U.S. Security Relations. *Perspective,* No. 42. Singapore: ISEAS Yusof Ishak Institute. https://www.iseas.edu.sg/wp-content/uploads/2020/03/ISEAS_Perspective_2020_42.pdf. Accessed 7 August 2020.

De Cleen, B. (2017). Populism and nationalism. In C. Rovira Kaltwasser, P. Taggart, P. Ochoa Espejo & P. Ostiguy (Eds.), *The Oxford handbook of populism* (pp. 342–362). Oxford University Press.

De Dios, A. J., Daroy, P. N., & Kalaw-Tirol, L. (Eds.). (1988). *Dictatorship and revolution: The roots of people's power.* Conspectus Foundation.

Destradi, S., & Plagemann, J. (2019). Populism and international relations: (Un)predictability, personalization and the reinforcement of existing trends in world politics. *Review of International Studies, 45*(5), 711–730.

Dizon, N. (2016, July 13). Aquino on arbitral court ruling: 'A victory for all'. *Inquirer.net.* https://globalnation.inquirer.net/141043/aquino-on-arbitral-court-ruling-a-victory-for-all#ixzz6QU94G8Gs. Accessed 26 June 2020.

Evangelista, P. (2018). Murder in Manila. A Seven Part Series. *Rappler Investigative Report.* https://www.rappler.com/newsbreak/investigative/tondo-vigilante-gang-war-on-drugs-series-part-one. Accessed 19 June 2020.

Gita, R. (2019, July 20). *Special report: A militarized government. Duterte watch part I.* Sunstar. https://www.sunstar.com.ph/article/1815070. Accessed 25 March 2020.

Heydarian, R. (2018, June 23). *How the Scarborough Shoal came back to haunt China-Philippines relations.* Rappler. https://www.scmp.com/news/china/diplomacy-defence/article/2151923/how-scarborough-shoal-came-back-haunt-china-philippines. Accessed 23 June 2020.

Heydarian, R. (2020, January 18). Scepticism rises in Philippines about Chinese projects and Duterte's support of them. *South China Morning Post.* https://www.scmp.com/news/china/diplomacy/article/3046666/scepticism-rises-philippines-about-chinese-projects-and. Accessed 27 June 2020.

Human Rights Watch. (2020, June 5). *Philippines: New anti terrorism act endangers rights.* Human Rights Watch. https://www.hrw.org/news/2020/

06/05/philippines-new-anti-terrorism-act-endangers-rights. Accessed 20 June 2020.

Juego, B. (2017). The Philippines 2017: Duterte-led authoritarian populism and its liberal-democratic roots. *Asia Maior*, 28. www.asiamaior.org/the-journal/10-asia-maior-vol-xxviii-2017/the-philippines-2017-duterte-led-aut horitarian-populism-and-its-liberal-democratic-roots.html. Accessed 24 July 2020.

Lema, K., Petty, M., & Stewart, P. (2020, February 11). *Duterte terminates Philippines troop pact, U.S. calls move 'unfortunate'*. Reuters. https://www.reuters.com/article/us-philippines-usa-defence/duterte-terminates-philip pines-troop-pact-us-calls-move-unfortunate-idUSKBN2050E9. Accessed 30 June 2020.

Levitsky, S., & Ziblatt, D. (2018). *How democracies die*. Penguin Random House.

Malig, J. (2016, July 12). Carpio: Hague ruling reaffirms rule of law. *ABS-CBN News*. https://news.abs-cbn.com/news/07/12/16/carpio-hague-ruling-reaffirms-rule-of-law. Accessed 26 June 2020.

Mendoza, R. U., Banaag, M., Cruz, J. P., & Uy, I. K. (2018). The Philippines' China pivot: Yield and risks (ASOG Working Paper 18–009). Ateneo School of Government Working Paper Series. Quezon City: Ateneo de Manila University.

National Economic and Development Authority. (2017). Philippine development plan, 2017–2022. Abridged Version. Pasig City: NEDA. http://www.neda.gov.ph/wp-content/uploads/2017/12/Abridged-PDP-2017-2022_Final.pdf. Accessed 12 June 2020.

Nonato, V. (2020, February 20). 'Lawfare': When legal processes are used to crack down on dissent. *One News*. https://www.onenews.ph/lawfare-when-legal-processes-are-used-to-crack-down-on-dissent. Accessed 25 March 2020.

Official Gazette. (n.d.). *EDSA 30: A history of the Philippine political protest*. https://www.officialgazette.gov.ph/edsa/the-ph-protest/. Accessed 5 May 2020.

Ong, J., & Cabañes, J. V. (2018). *Architects of networked disinformation: Behind the scenes of troll accounts and fake news production in the Philippines*. Communication Department Faculty Publication, University of Massachusetts Amherst. https://doi.org/10.7275/2cq4-5396. Accessed 25 March 2020.

Paddock R. (2016, October 26). Rodrigo Duterte, pushing split with U.S., counters Philippines' Deep Ties. *The New York Times*. https://www.nytimes.com/2016/10/27/world/asia/philippines-duterte-united-states-alliance.html. Accessed 27 June 2020.

Padin, M. G. (2018, November 1). Philippines to sign 2 big-ticket infrastructure project[s] with China. *PhilStar Global*. https://www.philstar.com/business/

2018/11/01/1864805/philippines-sign-2-big-ticket-infrastructure-project-china. Accessed 1 July 2020.

Permanent Court of Arbitration. (2016). PCA Case N° 2013–19. In the matter of the South China Sea Arbitration before an Arbitral tribunal constituted under Annex VII to the 1982 United Nations convention on the law of the Sea between the Republic of the Philippines and the People's Republic of China (12 July 2016). https://assets.documentcloud.org/documents/299 0927/PCA-Case-No-2013-19-The-South-China-Sea.pdf. Accessed 25 June 2020.

Philippine Human Rights Information Center. (2019). *The killing state: The unrelenting war against human rights in the Philippines.* https://www.philri ghts.org/the-killing-state-the-unrelenting-war-against-human-rights. Accessed 19 June 2020.

Manila Bulletin. (2020, May 3). *PAGCOR: A primer on the truth about POGO.* https://mb.com.ph/2020/05/03/pagcor-a-primer-on-the-truth-about-pogo. Accessed 26 June 2020.

Puddington, A. (2017). *Breaking down democracy: Goals, strategies, and methods of modern authoritarians.* New York: Freedom House. https://freedomho use.org/sites/default/files/June2017_FH_Report_Breaking_Down_Demo cracy.pdf. Accessed 26 June 2020.

Rivera, T. C. (2016). Rethinking democratization in the Philippines: Elections, political families and parties. In F. B. Miranda & T. C. Rivera (Eds.), *Chasing the wind: Assessing Philippine democracy* (2nd ed., pp. 43–74). Commission on Human Rights and UNDP.

Shi, Y. (2019, December 20). *Philippines expects to attract 4 mln Chinese tourists annually by end of 2022.* Xinhua. http://www.xinhuanet.com/english/2019-12/20/c_138646442.htm. Accessed 24 July 2020.

Straits Times. (2020, October 14). China expresses support for Duterte's war against drug crime. https://www.straitstimes.com/asia/east-asia/china-exp resses-support-for-dutertes-war-against-drug-crime. Accessed 27 June 2020.

Thompson, M. (2019). The rise of illiberal democracy. In I. Deinla & B. Dressel (Eds.), *From Aquino II to Duterte (2010–2018)* (pp. 39–61). ISEAS Yusof Ishak Institute.

Thompson, M. (2020, May 6). Duterte's 'shoot-them-all' approach to Covid-19 threatens his legacy as poor suffer in the Philippines. *South China Morning Post.* https://www.scmp.com/print/week-asia/opinion/article/3083119/dutertes-shoot-them-all-approach-covid-19-threatens-his-legacy. Accessed 11 June 2020.

Tomacruz, S. (2020, June 2). Timeline Duterte's threats to terminate the visiting forces agreement. *Rappler.* https://www.rappler.com/newsbreak/iq/251 558-timeline-duterte-threats-terminate-visiting-forces-agreement. Accessed 23 June 2020.

Tomacruz, S., & Gotinga, J. (2019, August 22). List: China's incursions in Philippine waters. *Rappler*. https://www.rappler.com/newsbreak/iq/238 236-list-china incursions-philippine-waters. Accessed 27 June 2020.

UN News. (2018, March 9). *UN rights chief denounces 'unacceptable' charges of terrorism by Philippine's Duterte against UN Expert*. https://news.un.org/en/story/2018/03/1004622. Accessed 30 June 2020.

Weyland, K. (2013). The Threat from the Populist Left. *Journal of Democracy, 24*(3), 18–32. https://www.journalofdemocracy.org/wp-content/upl oads/2013/07/Weyland-24-3.pdf. Accessed 26 June 2020.

Weyland, K. (2018). Populism: A political strategic approach. In C. Rovira Kaltwasser, P. Taggart, P. Ochoa Espejo & P. Ostiguy (Eds.), *The Oxford handbook of populism* (pp. 48–72). Oxford University Press.

Yap, D. J. (2015, March 18). 12 million Filipinos living in extreme poverty. *Inquirer.net*. https://newsinfo.inquirer.net/775062/12m-filipinos-living-in-extreme-poverty. Accessed 26 June 2020.

INDEX